Ancient Rhetorics
for Contemporary Students

SECOND EDITION

ANCIENT RHETORICS FOR CONTEMPORARY STUDENTS

SHARON CROWLEY

The Pennsylvania State University

DEBRA HAWHEE

The Pennsylvania State University

Allyn and Bacon
Boston
London
Toronto
Sydney
Tokyo
Singapore

Vice President: Eben W. Ludlow
Series Editorial Assistant: Linda M. D'Angelo
Executive Marketing Manager: Lisa Kimball
Production Editor: Christopher H. Rawlings
Text Design: Carol Somberg/Omegatype Typography, Inc.
Editorial–Production Service: Omegatype Typography, Inc.
Composition and Prepress Buyer: Linda Cox
Manufacturing Buyer: Suzanne Lareau
Cover Administrator: Jenny Hart
Electronic Composition: Omegatype Typography, Inc.

Copyright © 1999 by Allyn & Bacon
A Viacom Company
160 Gould Street
Needham Heights, MA 02494

Internet: www.abacon.com

Previous edition, copyright © 1994 by Macmillan College Publishing Company, Inc.

Library of Congress Cataloging-in-Publication Data
Crowley, Sharon
    Ancient rhetorics for contemporary students / Sharon Crowley,
  Debra Hawhee. — 2nd ed.
      p.   cm.
    Includes bibliographical references and index.
    ISBN 0-205-26903-6
    1. English language—Rhetoric.   2. Rhetoric, Ancient.   I. Hawhee,
  Debra.   II. Title.
  PE1408.C725   1999
  808'.042—dc21   98-5535
                                                                   CIP

Printed in the United States of America
10 9 8 7 6 5 4 3 2 1   03 02 01 00 99 98

CONTENTS

PART ONE: INVENTION

CHAPTER 3

CHAPTER 4

CHAPTER 5

CHAPTER 6

Ethical Proof   *105*

CHAPTER 7

Pathetic Proof   *146*

CHAPTER 8

Reasoning in Rhetoric   *162*

CHAPTER 9

Extrinsic Proofs   *183*

PART TWO: ARRANGEMENT

CHAPTER 10

Arrangement   *198*

CHAPTER 11

The Formal Topics   *214*

PART THREE: STYLE, MEMORY, AND DELIVERY

CHAPTER 12

Style   *229*

CHAPTER 13

Memory   *264*

CHAPTER 14

Delivery   *275*

CHAPTER 15

CHAPTER 16

Preface

Ancient Rhetorics for Contemporary Students reclaims both the theory of knowledge and the argumentative strategies built into ancient rhetorics. While writing it, we adopted three ancient premises about composing: first, that nobody thinks or writes within a cultural vacuum; second, that disagreement is endemic to the human situation; and third, that the human desire to compose stems from the human desire to affect the course of events. Ancient rhetoricians invented and taught an art that was situational rather than conventional, that was immersed in the daily traffic of human events and in communal discourse about them. In this it differed markedly from modern school rhetoric, which presents composers with an abstract set of pseudo-scientific rules that dictate what a finished discourse ought to look like. Where ancient rhetorics began with rhetorical situations, modern discourse theory begins with forms or genres. We think that the modern approach to composing is impoverished in comparison to the rich fund of theories and strategies that can be found in ancient rhetorics.

We hope that this book will show writers and speakers that their rhetorical practice and their ethical obligations are always communal. The need to compose arises from composers' desire to insert their voices into the differences of opinion that occur within the discourse of a community. When they are read or heard, compositions enter into that discourse, either to maintain and reinforce it or to disrupt it. Compositions written in college are as communal as any other writing. Teachers and peers read student writing, and this writing becomes part of classroom discourse.

Compositions also reflect the commonplaces given to rhetors through communal discourse. Commonplaces are always in flux, always controversial, because human beings disagree with one another. Audiences never receive a rhetor's discourse neutrally or objectively. The reception accorded any discourse depends as much on the rhetor's relation to the community and her relation to the issue discussed as it depends on the content of her discourse. Modern rhetorics, particularly the version taught in college, pretend that this is not the case, that compositions on any topic can be made available to any educated reader who can consume them without prejudice. Ancient rhetoricians, on the other hand, taught their students how to analyze the contexts for which they composed and how to adapt their composing processes to fit these contexts as closely as possible. They never assumed that a given discursive situation could be adequately met by employing generic formulas.

Because we have adopted the ancient assumption that rhetoric cannot be fruitfully studied and practiced apart from the issues that engage the communities it serves, this book introduces its readers to some contested topics in contemporary political and ethical discourse. Its examples are drawn from popular and academic writing about controversial issues. We realize that to engage students in a discussion of values is a departure from traditional approaches to composition instruction. However, we feel that rhetoric cannot be taught without addressing the issues that vitally concern the people who use it. We are aware as well that some of our examples will soon become dated. However, it should not be difficult for teachers and students to supply their own contemporary examples in places where the immediate relevance of those provided is no longer apparent.

The book also includes some features of ancient rhetorics that have not received much attention in modern redactions. For example, it contains a thorough treatment of ancient discussions about figures of thought. There are chapters that show how to compose proofs from character and appeals to the emotions, which, so far as we know, are not treated at length in any other contemporary textbook, even though both are commonly practiced in contemporary political and commercial rhetorics.

Over half of this book (nine chapters) is devoted to invention. This proportion reflects the lavish attention given to invention by ancient rhetoricians. Of the three books in Aristotle's *Rhetoric,* two are devoted to invention; the third treats delivery, style, and arrangement. Of twelve books in Quintilian's *Institutes of Oratory,* five are devoted to invention, two are devoted to style; delivery and memory get a chapter each, and the rest of the work concerns the proper education of an orator. Cicero's *On Invention,* obviously, treats nothing else. These proportions testify to the importance of the first canon in ancient rhetorics. We represent that importance here because all the means of invention defined by ancient rhetoricians are still in use in public discourse.

In ancient rhetorics, a person who was inventing arguments might or might not make use of writing, depending upon the quality of his memory. It is likely that ancient rhetors composed arguments aloud and stored them in memory. The only ancient revision practices that are similar to literate revision occurred when students were working with the elementary exercises called *progymnasmata.* They copied passages onto wax tablets, working either from memory or from a text. They then tried out variations in writing. No doubt they memorized the variations that won the most approval.

However, literate revision practices can be built into the ancient system. Students can compose trial arguments as they work their way through this book, and they can revise their work as they master new rhetorical strategies. In other words, the ancient schemes of invention can all be worked out in writing, and so anyone can produce a great deal of writing while using this book. It is organized just as the ancients organized their rhetorical instruction, following the order of the canons of rhetoric: invention, arrangement, style, memory, and delivery. Even though its organization dimly reflects modern descriptions of the composing process—which is often characterized as moving through prewriting, writing, revision, and editing—people who use this book will soon discover that the linear economy of the modern composing process is far too simple to accommodate ancient notions of composition. Ancient teachers emphasized copiousness, or the art of having more to say or write than a rhetor needs for a single occasion. Ancient composing processes did not aim toward the production of a finished product; rather, they equipped rhetors with arguments and materials that would be readily available whenever they needed to compose for a given occasion.

The final chapters introduce students to the composing exercises used by students in ancient times. Even though these exercises appear at the back of this book, we recommend that teachers exploit them from the beginning, using them along with the work in invention. We explain each exercise, supply classical and modern examples, and make composing suggestions for each. There are plenty of examples and suggested exercises in the rest of the text, as well, and if readers follow ancient instructions for preparing and composing arguments, they will generate a lot of writing.

The exercises that appear at the conclusions of several chapters are generative: they ask students to employ what they have learned in their own reading and writing. There are no drills or canned exercises; that is, students are never asked to analyze or comment on prose written by other people. The book's most important pedagogical feature, we think, is that it provides students with motives for composing.

Obviously, this book differs from the general run of composition textbooks: it ignores all sorts of traditional and contemporary lore about composing, such as thesis statements and topic sentences or freewriting and brainstorming. There is no talk about the so-called "modes of discourse" or about writing the research paper, since these are nineteenth-century additions to the lore of school rhetoric. Indeed, the book abandons altogether the modern notion that composition is a formalist, rule-bound task. We think that this attitude toward composing is arhetorical and counterproductive for students and teachers alike, since it abstracts the act of composing from real human interaction. We also think that ancient attitudes about composing are preferable to the rule-governed, text-centered tradition of writing instruction that American composition teachers inherited from eighteenth- and nineteenth-century rhetorical theory.

A word about terminology: throughout the book, we use the term "modern" to indicate a specific set of beliefs about composition and composing. The term "modern" is not typically used in a generic sense meaning "the present." For that use we employ the term "contemporary." But the distinction between modern and contemporary becomes difficult to maintain, since modern ideas still persist in contemporary teaching practices. As a result, the terms we use become slippery because different oppositions are at work: ancient versus modern, modern and contemporary, modern versus postmodern. Since we use the term "modern" somewhat disparagingly, we want to be clear that we are not talking about contemporary students or teachers. Rather, we are referring to the habits of mind that still inform ways of thinking about composing. We write in a postmodern era, an era that embraces change and hence demands flexible communication strategies. Most of today's students and many teachers, raised in a complex and stimulating technological and ideological age, hold postmodern attitudes toward composing and composition. We believe ancient rhetorics, which are of course pre-modern, offer an interesting starting point from which postmodern rhetors might think discourse anew.

This book also differs in some respects from the few contemporary textbooks about ancient rhetorics that are currently available. It does not treat all the rhetorics produced during antiquity as a monolithic theory of discourse. Nor does it assume that the principles and techniques isolated by ancient rhetoricians can be usefully transferred to contemporary situations without qualification. Throughout the book we attempt to alert readers to the fact that cultures widely separated in time and space differ from one another, even though the cultures under study are regarded as the sources of what we now call western civilization. In the first chapter, we address some important differences between modern and ancient thought about knowledge and its production. We updated or abandoned altogether the features of ancient rhetorics that are simply too foreign to be of use. For example, we altered translations to mitigate ancient sexism (as well as that of modern translators). Where that was not possible, we point out the sexism.

Throughout, we followed ancient practice in assuming that everyone who wishes to speak or write possesses something to write or speak about, insofar as he or she participates in the common discourse of the communities to which he or she belongs. As a result, this book never asks students to write personal essays or to generate expressive discourse. We do not accept the modern assumption that writing should begin with personal expression and move outward into expository and persuasive modes. To the contrary, we agree with the ancients that there are no purely personal opinions; there is only communal discourse.

We hope that this book will interest its readers in further study of ancient rhetorics themselves. The major works of several ancient rhetoricians—Aristotle, Cicero, and Quintilian—are now available in relatively inexpensive paperback editions. A few anthologies are also available that include portions of their work, along with related ancient treatises on literary composition and elementary exercises. Accompanied by readings in ancient texts, this book might profitably be used in humanities or critical thinking classes as an introduction to ancient ways of knowing and thinking. Of course, it should also prove useful in undergraduate and graduate courses designed to introduce students to ancient rhetorics. In our experience, contemporary students find ancient texts difficult to read unless they are exposed to historical contextualization and commentary. This book attempts to fill that need.

We included a glossary that defines ancient or technical terms and supplies pronunciation guides for a few terms that have no ready equivalent in English. The two appendices contain overviews of the history of ancient rhetorics: Appendix A is a broad chronological outline, while Appendix B is a more detailed outline of major developments in ancient rhetorics themselves. The bibliography lists the modern sources of our quotations of ancient texts and supplies some suggestions for further reading in ancient rhetorics.

ACKNOWLEDGMENTS

Sharon thanks Deb, of course. She is (still) indebted to Doug Day and Eben Ludlow of Allyn and Bacon for encouraging her to write and rewrite this book. Thanks as well to Van Hillard, Rosa Eberly, Blake Scott, and Kakie Urch for telling us how it teaches. As always, Edward P. J. Corbett's *Classical Rhetoric for Modern Students* is paid the homage of my imitation by this book.

Debbie thanks Sharon for sharing her work, her wisdom, and her cats. She is grateful to be a part of such a supportive network of scholars—thanks especially to the Penn State faculty for their encouragement; to John Muckel-bauer for his incisive and relentless critiques; Kakie Urch for her insights on delivery; Blake Scott for the four-mile invention jogs; and Andy Alexander and Julie Vedder for sharing their personal archives.

We both would like to thank all the people who wrote reviews of the manuscript: Linda Bensel-Meyers, University of Tennessee; Michael Carter, North Carolina State University; Rosa Eberly, University of Texas at Austin; Kay Halasek, Ohio State University; Kristine Hansen, Brigham Young University; Van E. Hillard, Duke University; and Walter H. Kokernot, Texas A&M University.

ANCIENT RHETORICS: THEIR DIFFERENCES, AND THE DIFFERENCES THEY MAKE

For us moderns, rhetoric means artificiality, insincerity, decadence. Perhaps this is simply because we do not understand it and have become barbarians ourselves.

—H. I. Marrou

WHEN AMERICANS HEAR the word **rhetoric,** they tend to think of politicians' attempts to deceive them. Rhetoric is now thought of as empty words, or as fancy language used to distort the truth or to tell lies. Television newspeople often say something like "There was more rhetoric from the White House today" and editorialists write that politicians need to "stop using rhetoric and do something." Many people blame rhetoric for our apparent inability to communicate and to get things done.

But that isn't the way **rhetoricians** defined their art in ancient Athens and Rome. In ancient times, people used rhetoric to make decisions, resolve disputes, and to mediate public discussion of important issues. An ancient teacher of rhetoric named Aristotle defined rhetoric as the power of finding the available arguments suited to a given situation. For teachers like Aristotle or practitioners like the Roman statesman Cicero, rhetoric helped people to choose the best course of action when they disagreed about important political, religious, or social issues. In fact, the study of rhetoric was equivalent to the study of citizenship. Under the best ancient teachers, Greek and Roman students wrote themes and speeches about moral and political questions that daily confronted their communities.

Ancient teachers of rhetoric thought that disagreement among human be-ings was inevitable, since individuals perceive the world differently from one another. They also assumed that since people communicate their perceptions through language—which is an entirely different medium than thoughts or perceptions—there was no guarantee that any person's perceptions would be accurately conveyed to others. Even more important, the ancient teachers knew that people differ in their opinions about how the world works, so that it was often hard to tell whose opinion was the best. They invented rhetoric so that they would have means of judging whose opinion was most accurate, useful, or valuable.

If people didn't disagree, rhetoric wouldn't be necessary. But they do, and it is. A twentieth-century rhetorician named Kenneth Burke remarked that "we need never deny the presence of strife, enmity, [or] faction as a characteristic motive of rhetorical expression" (1962, 20). But the fact that rhetoric originates in disagreement is ultimately a good thing, since its use allows people to make important choices without resorting to less peaceful means of persuasion such as coercion or violence. People who have talked their way out of any potentially violent confrontation know how useful rhetoric can be. On a larger scale, the usefulness of rhetoric is even more apparent. If, for some reason, the people who negotiate treaties were to stop using rhetoric to resolve their disagreements about limits on the use of nuclear weapons, there might not be a future to de-liberate about. That's why we should be glad when we read or hear that our diplomats and their diplomats are disagreeing about the allowable number of warheads per country or the number of inspections of nuclear stockpiles per year. At least they're talking to each other. As Burke observed, wars are the re-sult of an agreement to disagree. But before people of good will agree to dis-agree, they try out hundreds of ways of reaching agreement. The possibility that one set of participants will resort to coercion or violence is always a threat, of course; but in the context of impending war, the threat of war can itself operate as a rhetorical strategy that keeps people of good will talking to each other.

Given that argument can deter violence and coercion, we are disturbed by the contemporary tendency to see disagreement as somehow impolite or even undesirable. In 1995, the Congress and President of the United States illustrated what can happen when those who disagree over policy refuse to argue their way through that disagreement. The federal government was briefly shut down because Congress and the President could not agree on a budget. Government workers went without pay, national parks were closed, maintenance on build-ings and roads was halted—all because political leaders stopped arguing about the issues that divided them.

It seems to us that Americans do not value disagreement as highly as an-cient rhetoricians did. Our culture does not look at disagreement as a way of un-covering alternative courses of action. Americans often refuse to debate each other about important matters like religion or politics, retreating into silence if someone brings either subject up in public discourse. In fact, if someone dis-agrees publicly with someone else about politics or religion, Americans some-times take that as a breach of good manners. This is so because we tend to link people's opinions to their identities. Americans assume that people's opinions result from their personal experiences, and hence that those opinions are some-how "theirs"—that they alone "own" them. Hence, **rhetors** are often reluctant to engage in arguments about religion or politics or any other sensitive issue, fear-ing that listeners might take their views as personal attacks rather than as an in-vitation to discuss differences.

This intellectual habit, which assumes that religious and political choices are thoroughly tied up with a person's identity, makes it seem as though people never change their minds about things like religion and politics. But as we all know, people do change their minds about these matters; people convert from one religious faith to another, and they sometimes change their political affilia-tion from year to year, perhaps voting across party lines in one election and vot-ing a party line in the next.

The authors of this book are concerned that if Americans continue to ignore the reality that people quite naturally disagree with one another, or if we pre-tend to ignore it in the interests of preserving etiquette, we risk undermining the principles on which our democratic community is based. People who are afraid of airing their differences tend to keep silent when those with whom they dis-agree are speaking; people who are afraid of airing their differences tend to as-sociate only with those who agree with them. In such a balkanized public sphere, both our commonalities and our differences go unexamined. In a democracy, people must call the opinions of others into question, must bring them into the light for examination and negotiation. In communities where cit-izens are not coerced, important decisions must be made by means of public dis-course. Otherwise, decisions are made for bad reasons, or for no reason at all.

Sometimes, of course, there are good reasons for remaining silent. Power is distributed unequally in our culture, and power inequities may force wise peo-ple to resort to silence on some occasions. We believe that in contemporary American culture men have more power than women, white people have more power than people of color, and people who enjoy high socioeconomic status have more power than those who have fewer resources and less access to others in power (and yes, we are aware that there are exceptions to all of these gener-alizations). We do not believe, though, that these inequities are a natural or nec-essary state of things. We do believe that rhetoric is among the best ways available to us for rectifying power inequities among citizens.

ANCIENT ATTITUDES TOWARD RHETORIC

The people who taught and practiced rhetoric in Athens and Rome during an-cient times would have found contemporary unwillingness to engage in public disagreement very strange indeed. Their way of using disagreement to reach so-lutions was taught to students in Western schools for over two thousand years, and is still available to us in translations of their textbooks, speeches, lecture notes, and treatises on rhetoric. Within limits, their way of looking at disagree-ment can still be useful to us. The students who worked with ancient teachers of rhetoric were members of privileged classes for the most part, since Athens and Rome both maintained socioeconomic systems that were manifestly unjust to many of the people who lived and worked within them. The same charge can be leveled at our own system, of course. Today the United States is home not only to its native peoples but to people from all over the world. Its non-native citizens arrived here under vastly different circumstances, ranging from colonization to immigration to enslavement, and their lives have been shaped by these circumstances, as well as by their gender and class affiliation. Not all—perhaps not even a majority—have enjoyed the equal opportunities that are promised by the Constitution. But unfair social and economic realities only underscore the need for principled public discussion among concerned citizens.

The aim of ancient rhetorics was to distribute the power that resides in language among all of its students. This power is available to anyone who is willing to study the principles of rhetoric. People who know about rhetoric know how to persuade others to consider their point of view without resorting to coercion or violence. For the purposes of this book, we have assumed that people prefer to seek verbal resolution of differences rather than the use of force. Rhetoric is of no use when people determine to use coercion or violence to gain the ends they seek.

A knowledge of rhetoric also allows people to discern when rhetors are making bad arguments or are asking them to make inappropriate choices. Since rhetoric confers the gift of greater mastery over language, it can also teach those who study it to evaluate anyone's rhetoric; thus the critical capacity conferred by rhetoric can free its students from the manipulative rhetoric of others. When knowledge about rhetoric is available only to a few people, the power inherent in persuasive discourse is disproportionately shared. Unfortunately, throughout history rhetorical knowledge has usually been shared only among those who can exert economic, social, or political power as well. But ordinary citizens can learn to deploy rhetorical power, and if they have the chance and the courage to deploy it skillfully and often, it's possible that they may change other aspects of our society as well.

In this book, then, we aim to help our readers become more skilled speakers and writers. But we also aim to help them become better citizens.

SOME DIFFERENCES BETWEEN MODERN AND ANCIENT RHETORICS

The great age of ancient rhetorics dictates that there will be differences between them and modern thinking about rhetoric. One such difference is that ancient rhetoricians did not value factual proof very highly, while **facts** and **testimony** are virtually the only proofs discussed in modern rhetorical theory (see the chapter on **extrinsic proofs**). Ancient teachers preferred to use arguments that they generated from language itself and from community beliefs. They invented and named many such arguments, among them **commonplaces, examples, conjectures, maxims,** and **enthymemes** (see the chapters on stasis, commonplaces, and on rhetorical reasoning).

Another difference is that ancient rhetoricians valued opinions as a source of knowledge, while in modern thought opinions are often dismissed as unimportant. But ancient rhetoricians thought of opinions as something that were held not by individuals but by entire communities. This difference has to do with another assumption that they made, which was that a person's character (and hence opinions) were constructions made by the community in which she lived. And since the ancients believed that communities were the source and reason for rhetoric, opinions were for them the very stuff of argument.

A third difference between ancient and modern rhetorics is that ancient rhetoricians always situated their teaching in place and time. Their insistence that local and temporal conditions influenced the act of composition marks a fairly distinct contrast with modern rhetoric's conventional treatment of rhetorical occasions as if they were all alike. For example, modern rhetoric textbooks insist that every essay display a thesis. Ancient teachers, on the other hand, were not so sure that every discourse has a thesis to display. For example, people sometimes write or speak in order to determine what alternatives are available in a given situation. In this case they are not ready to advance a thesis. And if a rhetor has a hostile audience, after all, it might be better (and safer) not to mention a thesis at all, or at least to place it near the end of the discourse (see the chapter on arrangement).

A last difference between ancient and modern rhetorics has to do with ancient teachers' attitudes toward language. Modern rhetoricians tend to think that its role is limited to the communication of facts. Ancient rhetoricians, on the other hand, taught their students that language does many things. Marcus Tullius Cicero, who was an extremely skilled and influential speaker in the days of the Roman Republic, asserted that the ends of language use are to instruct, to delight, and to move. But the point of instructing or delighting audiences is, finally, to move them to accept or reject some thought or action.

Just the Facts, Please

From an ancient perspective, one of the most troublesome of modern assumptions about the nature of argument goes like this: if the facts are on your side, you can't be wrong, and you can't be refuted. Facts are statements that somebody has substantiated through experience or proved through research. Or they are events that really happened, events that somebody will attest to as factual. Facts have a "you were there" quality—if the arguer doesn't have personal knowledge of the facts, she or he is pretty sure that some expert on the subject does know them, and that they can be looked up in a book. Here are some examples of factual statements:

Water freezes at 32 degrees Fahrenheit.

The moon orbits the earth.

Timothy McVeigh was convicted of blowing up the Alfred P. Murrah Federal Building in Oklahoma City, Oklahoma, on April 19, 1995.

These are facts because they can be verified through experience or by means of testimony. Individuals can test the accuracy of the first statement for themselves, and all three statements can be confirmed by checking relevant and reliable sources.

No doubt the importance given to facts derives from the modern faith in empirical proofs, those that are available to the senses: vision, smell, taste, touch, and hearing. During the nineteenth century, rhetoricians came to prefer empirical proofs to all the other kinds outlined in ancient rhetoric. After 1850, American rhetoric textbooks began to reduce the many kinds of evidence discriminated by ancient rhetoricians to just two: empirical evidence and testimony. Both of these kinds of evidence have the "you are there" quality: empirical evidence derives from someone's actual sensory contact with the relevant evidence; testimony involves somebody's reporting their acquaintance with the facts of the case. During the twentieth century, rhetoric textbooks enlarged testimony to include accounts by persons recognized as experts or authorities in specialized fields of study. The modern reverence for facts and testimonies explains why students are often asked to write research papers in school—their teachers want to be sure they know how to assemble empirical evidence and expert testimony into a coherent piece of writing.

There are some problems with the modern reliance on empirical evidence. For one thing, it ignores the possibility that the evidence provided by the senses is neither reliable nor conclusive. People are selective about what they perceive, and they continually reconstruct their memories of those perceptions, as well. Moreover, people don't always agree about their sensory perceptions. An ancient rhetorician named Protagoras pointed out that a blowing wind could feel cold to one person and hot to another, and that honey tasted bitter to some people although it tastes sweet to most.

Perceptions, and thus testimony about them, can also be influenced by an observer's perspective. The National Football League used to resort to the instant replay, where the referees watched video tapes of a controversial play taken from several different angles in order to decide what penalties to assess. Even though professional referees are trained observers of the game, sometimes they simply cannot see whether a defensive player used his arms illegally, or whether a receiver managed to keep his feet within bounds as he caught the ball. Sometimes this lack of perspective extended to the television cameras, as well. In other words, instant replay was little better at resolving disagreements about violations than were the referees. The NFL has now abandoned instant replay, but periodic calls are made for its return.

This example highlights the even more interesting observation that the facts of the physical world don't mean much to anybody unless they are involved in some larger **network of interpretation.** In football, the relevant network of interpretation is the rules of the game. Without these rules, the exact placement of a player's arm or the exact point at which his feet touched the ground lose their relevance. (Sometimes football players suddenly switch to a network of interpretation that allows them to read an arm in the face as an act of aggression. When this happens, referees have to stop the game until its more usual network of interpretation can be restored.)

Here's another example that demonstrates that facts are not very interesting or persuasive unless they are interpreted within a network of interpretation:

geologists point to the fossil record as evidence which supports the theory of evolution. They point to boxes and crates of mute, stony facts—fossilized plants and animals—as evidence that species have evolved over time. But the fossil record itself, as well as the historical relationships that geologists have established among fossils from all over the world, is a network of interpretation. That is, geologists have read a series of natural objects in such a way as to construe them as evidence for a huge natural process that nobody could actually have witnessed. If you want to object that a fossil is a fact, please do. You are quite right. Our point is that it is not a very useful (or interesting) fact apart from its interpretation as a fossil, rather than a rock, and its location within in the network of interpretation called evolutionary theory. Using another network of interpretation, we can read the fossil as a bookend or a doorstop.

Ancient philosophers understood the usefulness of empirical facts quite differently. Early Greek thinkers were skeptical about the status of phenomena, the name they gave to the facts of the physical world—stuff like trees, fossils, rocks, honey, cold winds, and the like. They argued about whether such things existed at all, or whether they existed only when perceived by the human senses. Most agreed that human perception of the facts of the physical world necessarily involved some distortion, since human thoughts and perceptions and language are obviously not the same things as physical objects like rocks.

Perhaps because of their skepticism about the nature of facts, ancient teachers of rhetoric were equally skeptical about the persuasive potential of facts. Aristotle wrote that facts and testimony were not truly within the art of rhetoric; they were *atechnoi*—"without art or skill"—and hence extrinsic to rhetoric. In Aristotle's Greek, a *techne* (art) was any set of productive principles or practices. Extrinsic proofs were not developed through a rhetor's use of the principles of rhetoric, but were found in existing circumstances. Aristotle defined an extrinsic proof as "all such as are not supplied by our own efforts, but existed beforehand" (*Rhetoric* I ii, 1356a). Such proofs are extrinsic to rhetoric, then, because no art is required to invent them. A rhetor only has to choose the relevant facts or testimony and present them to an audience.

Because facts are relatively mute in the absence of a relevant network of interpretation, rhetors seldom argue from a simple list of facts.[1] Today, practicing rhetoricians invent and use a wide variety of nonfactual arguments with great effectiveness. Take a trivial illustration: many detergent advertisements are arguments from *example.* Advertisers show a smiling woman folding a pile of sparkling clean clothes which she has washed with their product. They assume that the vividly presented example will make people reason as follows: "Well, that woman used 'Burble' and look at how clean her clothes are. If I use 'Burble,' my clothes will be clean, and I'll be happy too." The advertisers hope that viewers will generalize from the fictional example to their own lives, and draw the conclusion that they should buy the detergent. There are no facts in this argument, and yet it is apparently persuasive, since detergents continue to be advertised in this way.

Rhetors who rely only upon facts and testimony, then, place very serious limits on their persuasive potential, since many other kinds of rhetorical argument are employed daily in the media and in ordinary conversation. These arguments are invented or discovered by rhetors, using the art of rhetoric. Aristotle described invented arguments as *entechnoi*—"embodied in the art" of rhetoric. This class of proofs is **intrinsic** to rhetoric, since they are generated from its principles.

In rhetoric, intrinsic proofs are found or discovered by rhetors. **Invention** is the division of rhetoric that investigates the possible means by which proofs can be discovered; it supplies speakers and writers with sets of instructions which help them to find and compose proofs that are appropriate for any rhetorical situation. The word *invenire* means "to find" or "to come upon" in Latin. The Greek equivalent, *heuriskein*, also means "to find out" or "discover." Variants of both words persist in English. For instance, the proclamation "eureka!" means "I have found it!" The Greek word has also given us "heuristic," which means "an aid to discovery."

A **proposition** (Latin *proponere*, "to put forth") is any arguable statement put forward for discussion by a rhetor. A **proof** is any statement or statements used to persuade an audience to accept a proposition. Proofs are bits of language that are supposed to be persuasive. Ancient rhetoricians developed and catalogued a wide range of intrinsic rhetorical proofs, most of which relied on the rhetor's knowledge of a community's history and beliefs. The Older Sophists contributed the notions of commonplaces and **probabilities.** Aristotle contributed enthymemes, examples, **signs,** and maxims, and Hermagoras of Temnos is credited with the invention of **stasis theory** (for more information about these ancient rhetoricians, see the last chapter and the appendices of this book).

Aristotle discriminated among three kinds of intrinsic rhetorical proofs: *ethos, pathos,* and *logos.* These kinds of proofs translate into English as ethical, pathetic, and logical proofs. Ethical proofs depend on the rhetor's **character;** pathetic proofs appeal to the emotions of the audience; and logical proofs derive from arguments that reside in the issue itself. Our words "logic" and "logical" are derived from the Greek *logos*, which meant "voice" or "speech," to early Greek rhetoricians. Later, *logos* also became associated with reason.

Here is a hypothetical example of an argument in which a rhetor uses both intrinsic and extrinsic proofs. An astronomer appears before the city council of Ourtown to argue that the city should consider passing a "dark sky" ordinance which would reduce the amount of light emitted into the night sky by streetlights and billboards. Current light levels from these sources interfere with astronomers' ability to observe the night sky through their telescopes, mounted on a hill in the center of Ourtown. The astronomer's association with science gives her a strong ethical appeal, since scientists are generally respected in our culture. She can also make an emotional appeal by reminding her audience that human-made lighting interferes with the ordinary person's ability to see the moon and stars clearly, thus decreasing their enjoyment of the night sky. In addition, there are a good many logical proofs available to her in the issue itself. She can reason from **cause to effect:** "city lighting causes so much interference with telescopes and other instruments that the quality of observational work being carried out at the nearby observatory is diminished." Or she can reason from **parallel case:** "a dark sky ordinance was enacted in Othertown and the quality of astronomical observations has improved enormously there. The same thing will happen in Ourtown if we install a dark-sky ordinance here." In this argument the astronomer relied on only one fact: that current light levels from the city interfered with her ability to make astronomical observations. Interested citizens could contest even this statement (which the ancients would have called a conjecture), since it was produced by the astronomer and obviously serves her interests.

Ancient students of rhetoric practiced inventing a wide variety of intrinsic proofs while they were in school. By the time they finished their education, strategies of invention were second nature to them, so that whenever they were called on to construct a speech or to compose a piece of written discourse, they could conduct a mental review of the inventional processes. This review helped them to determine which proofs would be useful in arguing about whatever issue confronted them. The means of inventing rhetorical proofs can still provide rhetors with an intellectual arsenal from which they can draw whenever they need to compose. Anyone who becomes familiar with all of the strategies should never be at a loss for words.

That's Just Your Opinion

There is another category in popular notions about argument that deserves our attention. This is the category called "opinion." People can put a stop to conversation simply by saying: "Well, that's just your opinion." When someone does this, she or he implies that opinions aren't very important. They aren't facts, after all, and furthermore, opinions belong to individuals while facts belong to everybody. Another implication is this: because opinions are intimately tied up with an individual's thought and personality, there's not much hope of changing them without changing the person's identity. To put this another way, the implication of "Well, that's your opinion" is that Jane Doe's opinion about, say, abortion, is all tied up with who she is. If she thinks that abortion is murder, well, that's her opinion and there's not much we can do about changing her mind.

The belief that opinions belong to individuals may explain why Americans seem reluctant to challenge one another's opinions. To challenge a person's opinion is to denigrate that person's character, to imply that if he or she holds an unexamined or stupid or silly opinion, he or she is an unthinking or stupid or silly person. Ancient teachers of rhetoric would find fault with this on three grounds. First, they would object that there is no such thing as "just your opinion." Second, they would object to the implication that opinions aren't important. Third, they would argue that opinions can be changed. The point of rhetoric, after all, is to change opinions.

Ancient rhetoricians taught their students that opinions are shared by many members of a community. The Greek word for common or popular opinion was *doxa*, which is the root of English words like "orthodoxy" ("straight opinion") and "paradox" ("opinions alongside one another"). Opinions develop because people live in communities. A person living alone on an island needs a great many skills and physical resources, but has no need for political, moral, or social opinions until he or she meets up with another person or encounters animals since politics, morality, and sociality depend upon our relations with sentient (thinking) beings. (Today, some rhetors include animals and even plants in the category of sentient beings.) Equipped with the notion of shared opinion, we can see that Jane's opinion about abortion is probably not just hers. Rather, she shares it with a good many other people—her parents, most likely, perhaps some other family members, the members of her church, and some of her friends. But she also shares her opinion with thousands of people whom she has never met—with everyone who believes, as she does, that abortion is murder. Given the current popularity of this particular belief, it is hard to say that Jane's opinion is "just hers."

If we locate opinions outside individuals and within communities, they assume more importance. If a significant number of individuals within a community share an opinion about abortion, it becomes difficult to dismiss that opinion as unimportant, no matter how much we like or detest it. Nor can we continue to see opinions as unchangeable. If Jane got her opinion about abortion from somebody she knows or something she read, she can modify her opinion when she hears a different opinion from somebody else. Communication researchers have discovered that people generally adopt the opinions of people they know and respect. Our opinions are likely to change when we lose respect for the people who hold them, or when we meet new people whom we like and respect and who have different opinions.

The modern association of facts with scientific investigation, and opinion with everything else, draws on a set of beliefs that was invented during the seventeenth century in Europe. Science was associated with empirical proofs and rational problem solving, while non-scientific methods of reasoning came to be considered irrational or emotional. It was also during this period that the modern notion of the individual emerged, and the popularity of this notion convinced us that each person was an intellectual island whose unique experiences rendered his or her opinions as singular. The modern distinction between reason and other means of investigation keeps us from realizing how many of our beliefs are based in our emotional responses to our environments. Indeed, our acceptance of our most important beliefs—religious, moral, and political— probably have as much to do with our desires and interests as they have to do with rational argument. The reason/emotion distinction also keeps us from realizing how often we are swayed by appeals to our emotions, or, how difficult it is to distinguish between a purely rational appeal and a purely emotional one. And the notion of the unique individual makes it difficult for us to see how many of our opinions are derived from the beliefs that we share with other members of our communities.

We believe that rhetorical reasoning, which is used in politics, journalism, religious argument, literature, philosophy, history, and law, to name just a few of its arenas, is fully as legitimate as that used in science. And even though it uses appeals to community opinion and to emotions, if it is done responsibly, rhetorical reasoning is as valid as the reasoning used in science. In fact, scientific reasoning is itself rhetorical when its propositions are drawn from beliefs held by the community of trained scientists.

On Ideology and the Commonplaces

We suggested earlier that networks of interpretation—the way people interpret and use the facts—have persuasive potential, while facts by themselves do not. Postmodern rhetoricians use the term **ideology** to name networks of interpretation, and that is the term we use for such networks in the rest of this book.

An ideology is a coherent set of beliefs that people use to understand events and the behavior of other people; they are also used to predict events and behaviors. Ideologies exist in language. They are sets of statements that tell us how to understand ourselves and others, and how to understand nature and our relation to it as well. Furthermore, ideologies help us to assign value to what we know—they tell us what is thought to be true, or right, or good, or beautiful in a community.

Each of us is immersed in the ideologies that circulate in our communities once we begin to understand and use language. Hence ideologies actually produce "selves"; the picture you have of yourself has been formed by your experiences, to be sure, but it has also been constructed by the beliefs that circulate among your family, friends, the media, and other communities that you inhabit. You may think of yourself as a Christian, or a Jew, or a New Ager, or an atheist. In each case, you adopt a set of beliefs about the way the world works from some relevant community (in the last case, you may have reacted against an ideology or ideologies). Even though identities are shaped by ideologies, they are never stable because we can question or reject ideological belief. As we have suggested, people do this all the time: they undergo religious conversion; they adopt a political stance; they decide that UFO's do not exist; they take up exercise because they have become convinced it is good for them. Often, it is rhetoric that has brought about this ideological change. Ideology is the stuff with which rhetors work.

We mean no disrespect when we say that religious beliefs and political leanings are ideological. Quite the contrary: human beings need ideologies in order to make sense of their experiences in the world. Powerful ideologies such as religions and political beliefs help people to understand who they are and what their relation is to the world and to other beings.

Ideologies are made up of the statements that ancient rhetoricians called commonplaces. The distinguishing characteristic of a commonplace is that it is commonly believed by members of a community. These beliefs are "common" not because they are cheap or trivial but because they are shared by many people. Commonplaces need not be true or accurate (although they may be true, and they are certainly thought to be so within the communities that hold them). Some commonplaces are so thoroughly embedded in a community's assumptions about how the world works that their accuracy goes unexamined. Here are some examples of commonplaces that circulate in American discourse:

- Anyone can become President of the United States.
- All men are created equal.
- Everyone has a right to free speech because speech is protected by the Constitution.

Outside of the communities that subscribe to them, commonplaces may be controversial. If you disagreed with us when we asserted earlier on that "men have more power than women," your disagreement should alert you to the presence of a commonplace that is accepted in some community to which we belong but not in the communities with which you identify. In a case like this, the commonplace is contested. Contested commonplaces are called **issues** in rhetoric, and it is the point of rhetoric to help people examine and perhaps to achieve agreement about issues.

Most people probably subscribe to commonplaces drawn from many and diverse ideologies at any given time. It is also the case that our ideological beliefs may contradict one another, since they are only partially conscious. For instance, Jane's religious beliefs may teach her that abortion is murder, but this belief may contradict her liberal politics which teach her that women have the right to determine whether or not they wish to carry a pregnancy to term. Thus Jane's ideology potentially contains a contradiction. Ideology is seldom consistent with itself. In fact, it may be full of contradictions, and it may (and often does) contradict empirical evidence as well. For example, the commonplace which affirms that "Anyone can become President of the United States" overlooks the reality that all presidents to date have been white men. Americans maintain this commonplace because it is for some reason important to them to do so.

Rhetorical Situations

Ancient rhetoricians defined knowledge as the collected wisdom of those who know. In ancient thought, knowledge was not supposed to exist outside of knowers. Teaching and learning began with what people already knew. People talked or questioned each other, and worked toward new discoveries by testing them against what was already known (Aristotle, *Posterior Analytics* I, i). Ancient rhetoricians assumed that anyone who wanted to compose a discourse had a reason for doing so that grew out of his life in a community. Young people studied rhetoric precisely because they wanted to be involved in decisions that affected the lives of their family, friends, and neighbors. Students of ancient rhetoric did engage in a good deal of practice with artificial **rhetorical situations** taken from history or literature or law (the rhetorical exercises were called **progymnasmata** and **declamation**). However, this practice was aimed at teaching them something about the community they would later serve, as well as about rhetoric. In other words, they did not study rhetoric only to learn its rules. Instead, their study was preparation for a life of active citizenship.

A rhetorical situation is made up of several elements: the issue for discussion, the audience for the discussion and their relationship to the issue, as well as the rhetor, her or his reputation, and her or his relation to the issue. Rhetors must also consider the time and the place in which the issue merits attention (see chapter 2).

Ancient rhetoricians defined issues as matters about which there was some disagreement or dispute. In other words, nothing can become an issue unless someone disagrees with someone else about its truth or falsity or applicability or worth. Issues do not exist in isolation from the people who speak or write about them. Because of its emphasis on situatedness, on location in space and time, and on the contexts that determine composition, ancient rhetorical theory differs greatly from many modern rhetorical theories which assume that all rhetors and all audiences can read and write from a neutral point of view. The notion of objectivity would have greatly puzzled ancient rhetors and teachers of rhetoric.

Quintilian underscored the importance of rhetorical situations to composing when he suggested that students should consider

> what there is to say; before whom, in whose defence, against whom, at what time and place, under what circumstances; what is the popular opinion on the subject; and what the prepossessions of the judge are likely to be; and finally of what we should express our deprecation or desire. (IV 1, 52–53)

Rhetors who are at a loss for something to say or write can begin by thinking about the communities of which they are a part: their families, relatives, and friends; their street, barrio, town, city, or reservation; their school, college or university; groups they belong to; their country or nation, and even the world, these days. What issues are currently being debated in those communities? With which members of those communities do they disagree? On what issues? How do they feel about those issues? Are there policies they would advocate or reject? How will the community respond to their propositions? Answers to these questions usually provide plenty of stuff to write or talk about.

To become adept at invention is not easy. Invention requires systematic thought, practice, and, above all, thoroughness. But careful attention to the ancient strategies for discovering proofs will amply repay anyone who undertakes their study and use. Hermogenes of Tarsus wrote that "Nothing good can be produced easily, and I should be surprised if there were anything better for humankind, since we are logical animals, than fine and noble *logoi* and every kind of them" (*On Style* I, 214). In other words, to invent proofs is essentially human. But invention also has a less lofty, more practical aim: rhetors who practice the ancient means of invention will soon find themselves supplied with more proofs than they can possibly use.

LANGUAGE AS POWER

Many modern rhetoric textbooks assert that language is a reliable reflection of thought. Their authors assume that the main point of using language is to represent thought because they live in an age which is still influenced by notions about language developed during the seventeenth century. In 1690, John Locke announced to the Western world that words represent thoughts, and that the function of words was to convey the thinking of one person to another as clearly as possible. The assumption that language is transparent, that it lets meaning shine through it, is part of what is called a **representative theory of language.** The theory has this name because it assumes that language *re-presents* meaning, that it hands meaning over to listeners or readers, clear and intact.

Ancient rhetoricians were not so sure that words represented thoughts. As a consequence, they had great respect for the power of language. Archaic Greeks thought that the distinguishing characteristic of human beings—what made them different from animals—was their possession of *logos,* or speech. In archaic Greek thought, a person's *logos* was her name, her history, everything that could be said about her. Another word for *logos* was *kleos,* "fame" or "call." Thus, to be *en logoi* was to be taken into account, to have accounts told about one, to be on the community's roster of persons who could be spoken, sung, or written about. Any person's identity consisted in what was said about her or him. Someone's name, or tales told about her or him, defined the space in which she or he lived out her or his life.

In keeping with the archaic Greek emphasis on language as the source of knowledge, an ancient teacher called Protagoras taught that "Humans are the measure of all things." By this he apparently meant that anything which exists does so by virtue of its being known or discussed by human beings. Because knowledge originates with human knowers, and not from somewhere outside of them, there is no absolute truth that exists separately from human knowledge. Moreover, contradictory truths will appear, since everyone's knowledge differs slightly from everyone else's, depending on their perspective and their language. Thus Protagoras taught that at least two opposing and contradictory *logoi* (statements or accounts) exist in every experience. He called these oppositions *dissoi logoi.*

Another teacher, named Gorgias, apparently adopted Protagoras' skepticism about the relationship of language to truth or to some absolute reality. In his treatise on the nonexistent, Gorgias wrote: "For that by which we reveal is *logos,* but *logos* is not substances and existing things. Therefore we do not reveal existing things to our neighbors, but *logos,* which is something other than substances" (Sprague 1972, 84). In other words, language is not things, and language does not communicate things or thoughts or anything else. Language is not the same thing as honey or fossils or cold winds; nor is it the same as thoughts or feelings or perceptions. It is a different medium altogether. What language communicates is itself—words, syntax, metaphors, puns, and all that other wonderful stuff. Philosophers are mistaken when they argue that justice or reality exist; they have been misled into thinking that justice or reality are the same for everyone by the seeming unity and generality of the words "justice" and "reality."

Ancient rhetoricians were aware that language is a powerful force for moving people to action. Gorgias went so far as to say that language could work on a person's spirit as powerfully as drugs worked on the body. He taught his students that language could bewitch people, could jolt them out of their everyday awareness into a new awareness from which they could see things differently. Hence its persuasive force. As he said, language can "stop fear and banish grief and create joy and nurture pity" ("Encomium to Helen," 8). If you doubt this, think about the last time you read a book that moved you to tears, or saw a commercial that induced you to buy something, or heard a sermon that scared you into changing your behavior.

The ancient rhetorician named Isocrates argued that language was the ground of community, since it enabled people to live together and to create cultures ("Nicocles," 5–9). Communication was the mutual exchange of convictions, and communities could be defined as groups of human beings who operate with a system of roughly similar convictions. For Isocrates, language was the *hegemoon* (prince, guide) of all thought and action. He pointed out that language makes it possible for people to conceive of differences and to make distinctions such as man/woman or good/bad. It also allows people to conceive of abstractions such as justice or reality.

The Greek notion of *logos* was later translated into Latin as *ratio* (reason), and in Western thought the powers that were once attributed to language became associated with thinking rather than with talking or writing. Cicero blamed the philosophers for this shift:

> [Socrates] separated the science of wise thinking from that of elegant speaking, though in reality they are closely linked together. . . . This is the source from which has sprung the undoubtedly absurd and unprofitable and reprehensible severance between the tongue and the brain, leading to our having one set of professors to teach us to think and another to teach us to speak. (*De Oratore* III xvi, 60)

The notion that thought can be separated from language began with the philosopher Socrates, who was the teacher of Plato, who was in turn the teacher of Aristotle.

In one of his treatises on logic, Aristotle wrote that "spoken words are the symbols of mental experience and written words are the symbols of spoken words" (*On Interpretation,* 16a). This passage made two important assumptions: that mental experiences are independent of language, and that the role of language is to symbolize or represent mental experiences. The passage also suggested that written words are representations of spoken words, as though speech is somehow closer to thinking than writing. In the *Rhetoric,* Aristotle wrote that style and delivery—the rhetorical canons having to do with expression— were secondary to the substance of an argument (1404a). Even though it was necessary to study style and delivery because these forms of expression were persuasive, according to Aristotle the first prerequisite of style was clarity, which implied that whatever thoughts were being expressed should be immediately apparent to readers (1404b).

Here Aristotle expressed his subscription to a representative theory of language. The notion that a style can be clear, that language allows meaning to shine through it without distortion, makes sense only if language is thought to re-present something else. Naturally enough, philosophers are less interested in the rhetorical effects produced by language than they are in using language to say what they mean, as clearly and exactly as possible. That's why they prefer to argue that language somehow represents thought or reality. However, this argument presents a problem to rhetoricians, since the representative theory of language implies that some piece of language can be found that will clearly express any thought. So, if a piece of language is not clear to an audience, anyone who subscribes to this model of language must blame its author, who either had unclear thoughts or was unable to express them clearly. The only other possible explanation for misunderstanding is that the audience has not read the language carefully enough or is for some reason unprepared to understand it.

Aristotle also assumed that composers can control the effects of language—that they can make language do what they want it to do, can make readers read in the way they intended. Furthermore, Aristotle's attitude about clarity seriously underestimated the power of language. People who assume that it is "the thought that counts" must also assume that language is the servant of thought, and hence that language is of secondary or even negligible importance in the composing process. This attitude sometimes causes teachers to blame unintelligible compositions on a student's faulty thinking, when the difficulty might be that the student's language had more and different effects than intended.

Ancient teachers never assumed that there is only one way to read or interpret a discourse. Audiences inevitably bring their ideologies, their linguistic abilities, and their understandings of local rhetorical contexts to any reading they do. Contexts such as readers' or listeners' experiences and education or even the time of day inevitably influence their interpretation of any discourse. This is particularly true of written discourse, which, to ancient ways of thinking, was set adrift by authors into the community where people could and would read it in as many ways as there were readers (Plato, *Phaedrus*, 275). Today, however, people sometimes think that texts can have a single meaning (the right one), and that people who don't read in this way are somehow poor readers. This attitude is reinforced by the modern assumption that the sole purpose of reading is to glean information from a text, and it is repeated in school when students are expected to take tests or answer a set of questions about their reading in order to prove that they comprehended the assignment.

But people do many things when they read a text for the first time, and determining what it says is only one of these things. When you read any text, especially a difficult one, you simply can't find out what it says once and for all on your first trip through it. You can't consume written words the way you consume a cheeseburger and fries. When written words are banged up against one another, they tend to set off sparks and combinations of meanings that their writers never anticipated. Unfortunately, writers ordinarily are not present to tell readers what they intended to communicate.

Sometimes unintended meanings happen because written letters and punctuation marks are ambiguous. There are only twenty-six letters in the English alphabet, after all, and just a few marks of punctuation in the writing system. So most of these letters and marks must be able to carry several meanings. For example, quotation marks can signify quoted material:

"Get lost," he said.

But they can also be used for emphasis:

We don't "cash" checks.

Or they can be used to set off a term the use of which a writer wants to question:

To call Bill Clinton a "liberal" is to strain credulity.

The meanings of words differ, too, from person to person and from context to context. Indeed, the meanings of words are affected by the contexts in which they appear. In current political discourse, for example, the phrase "family values" means very different things to the people who use it, depending on whether they subscribe to conservative or liberal or some other ideology. Because people are different from one another, they have different responses to the same discourse.

When we listen to someone speaking, we have several contextual advantages that readers do not have. If we misunderstand a speaker, we can ask her or him to repeat herself, or to slow down. But our chances of misunderstanding spoken language are also decreased by the fact that we can see, hear, and interact with the person who is speaking. Thus we can support our interpretation of the meanings of words with our interpretations of facial and bodily gestures and the loudness and pitch of voice. Too, we are usually acquainted with people who speak to us, while often we do not know writers personally. And even if we don't know speakers well, we do understand our relationships to them. If a speaker is my mother, rather than my teacher or boss or aerobics instructor, I can rapidly narrow down the range of possible meanings she might convey when she commands me to "Shape up!" All of these kinds of contexts—physical and social—help us to interpret a speaker's meaning.

But these contexts are not available in any writing that is composed for an audience of people who are not known to the writer. So writers have to guess about the contexts that readers will bring to their reading. Usually those contexts will be very different from the writer's, especially in the case of a book, like this one, that introduces readers to a new field of discourse. Our experience as teachers has taught us that our familiarity with rhetoric and its terminology often causes us to take some of its fundamental points for granted. When we do this in a classroom, students can ask questions until they are satisfied that they understand. But readers cannot do this. So, even though we have tried very hard to make the contexts of ancient rhetorics clear in this book, people are bound to understand our text differently from each other and perhaps differently from what we tried to convey. Ancient rhetorics were invented by cultures that have long since disappeared, and that is one potential source of differential understanding in this particular text. But writers always fail to match their contexts with those of readers, and this kind of differential understanding is universal. It arises simply because writers can only imagine readers—who they are, what they know.

To put all of this another way: writers always fail to put themselves precisely in their readers' shoes. This potential for differential understanding is not a curse, as modern rhetorical theory would have it. Rather, it is what allows knowledge to grow and change. The ancients understood this, and that's why they celebrated copiousness—many arguments, many understandings.

Because ancient rhetoricians believed that language was a powerful force for persuasion, they urged their students to develop *copia* in all parts of their art. *Copia* can be loosely translated from Latin to mean an abundant and ready supply of language—something appropriate to say or write whenever the occasion arises. Ancient teaching about rhetoric is everywhere infused with the notions of expansiveness, amplification, abundance. Ancient teachers gave their students more advice about invention, arrangement, style, memory, and delivery than they could ever use. They did so because they knew that practice in these rhetorical arts alerted rhetors to the multitude of communicative and persuasive possibilities that exist in language.

Modern intellectual style, on the other hand, tends toward economy (from Greek *oikonomia,* a manager of a household or state, from *oikos,* house). Economy in any endeavor is characterized by restrained or efficient use of available materials and techniques. Of course, the modern preference for economy in composition is connected to modern insistence that clarity is the only important characteristic of style. People who bring modern attitudes about clarity and economy to the study of ancient rhetorics may be bewildered (and sometimes frustrated) by the profuseness of ancient advice about everything from invention to delivery.

They also miss an important aspect of ancient instruction: that messing around with language is fun. Composition need not be undertaken with the deadly seriousness that moderns bring to it. Moderns want to get it right the first time and forget about it. Ancient peoples, on the other hand, fooled around with language all the time. The Greeks sponsored poetry contests and gave prizes for the most daring or entertaining elaborations on a well-known theme. Romans who lived during the first centuries CE held rhetorical contests called declamations, the object of which was to compose a complicated and innovative discourse about some hackneyed situation involving pirates or outraged fathers. The winner was the person who could compose the most unusual arguments or who could devise the most elaborate amplifications and ornamentations for the old theme.

As you work through the chapters in this book, we hope you will compose a lot of discourse in response to the examples and exercises. You won't be able to use everything you compose in finished pieces of writing. Some exercises are just for practice, while others help you increase your understanding of the rhetorical principles you are studying. If this seems like wasted time and effort, remember that everything you compose increases your copiousness—your handy supply of arguments, available for use on any occasion.

EXERCISES

1. Look around you and listen. Where do you find people practicing rhetoric? Watch television and read popular newspapers or magazines. Jot down one or two of the rhetorical arguments you hear or see people making. Politicians are good sources, but so are journalists and parents and attorneys and clergy and teachers. Do such people try to support their arguments with facts? Or do they use other means of convincing people to accept their arguments?

2. Think about a time when you tried to convince someone to change his or her mind. How did you go about it? Were you successful? Now think about

a time when someone tried to get you to change your mind. What arguments did the person use? Was he or she successful?

3. Try to answer this question: What counts as persuasion in your community? Here are some questions to start from: Think of a time when you changed your mind about something. How did it happen? Did somebody talk you into it, or did events cause you to change the way you think? How do the people you know go about changing their minds? How does religious conversion happen, for example? What convinces people to stop smoking? How do people get to be racists, or become convinced they ought to stop being racist? How does a president convince a people that they ought to support a war? Make a list of arguments that seem convincing in these sorts of cases.

4. What positions do you take on issues that are currently contested in your communities? This exercise should help you to articulate what you think about such issues.

   a. Start with this question: what are the hotly contested issues in the communities you live in (the street, the barrio, your home town, the university you work in, the reservation, the state, the nation?) Make a list of these issues. (If you don't know what these issues are, ask someone—a parent, teacher, or friend—or read the editorial and front pages of a daily newspaper, watch the local and national news on television, or access news sources on the internet.)

   b. Pick two or three issues and write out your positions on them. Write as fast as you can without stopping or worrying about grammar and spelling. Use a word processor if you have access to one and are a fast typist, or write by hand if that is more comfortable for you. At this point you are composing material for your use only—so don't worry about neatness or completeness or correctness; write to discover what you think about these issues. Write for as long as you want to, but write about each issue for at least fifteen minutes without stopping.

   c. These writings should give you a clearer view of what you think about a few urgent issues. Let them sit for awhile—an hour is good but a couple of days is better. Then read them again. Now, rewrite your thoughts on one or two issues; select issues that you can comfortably discuss with other people.

   d. Give what you've written to someone you trust; ask him or her to tell you what else they want to know about what you think. Listen carefully, and take notes on the reader's suggestions. Don't talk or ask questions until the reader finishes talking. Then discuss your views on the issue further, if your reader is willing to do so.

   e. If your reader said anything that modifies your views, revise your writing to take his or her responses into account.

   f. Keep these writings, as well as your original list of issues. You can repeat this exercise whenever you wish to write about an issue or when you are asked to write for a class.

5. Begin recording in a journal or notebook the arguments that you commonly hear or read. (See the chapter on imitation for more information on how to keep a commonplace book.)

NOTE

1. It is true that the recital of the facts connected with an argument reinforces a rhetor's ethos, or persuasive character. If a writer or speaker demonstrates that she knows the facts of a case, her listeners or readers will increase their respect for her and her argument (see chapter 7).

WORK CITED

Burke, Kenneth. *The Rhetoric of Motives.* Berkeley: California UP, 1969.

A History of
Ancient Rhetorics

When anyone elects to speak or write discourses which are worthy of praise and honor, it is not conceivable that such a person will support causes which are unjust or petty or devoted to private quarrels, and not rather those which are great and honorable, devoted to the welfare of humanity and the common good. It follows, then, that the power to speak well and think right will reward the person who approaches the art of discourse with love of wisdom and love of honor.

—Isocrates,
Antidosis, 276–278

SOMETHING QUITE REMARKABLE happened in the small Greek city of Athens during the sixth, fifth, and fourth centuries BCE. During this period, the citizens of that community evolved a form of government they called *demokratia* (demos [people], and *kratos* [political power]). Any Athenian who was defined as a citizen played a direct role in making important decisions that affected the entire community: whether to go to war, to send ambassadors to neighboring countries, to raise or lower taxes, to build bridges or walls, to convict or acquit people accused of crimes against the state or other citizens.

In the Athenian political system, citizenship was determined by birthright, and thus citizenship was awarded to any adult male who could establish his Athenian heritage, whether he was wealthy or not, aristocratic or not. These were very inclusive requirements for the time, even though they excluded the bulk of the population, who were women, foreign-born men, or slaves. Because of this, classical Athens can hardly be said to have been a democracy in our more inclusive terms, although we remind readers that for almost half of its history, the United States limited suffrage to white males. Nor was Athens a representative democracy, as ours is said to be, since the few hundred people who were defined as Athenian citizens participated directly in making political and judicial decisions rather than acting through elected representatives. (Athenians scorned elections on the ground that they could too easily be rigged.)

The citizens met in the Assembly to make political decisions, and acted as jurors at trials. Athenian men apparently took their civic responsibilities seriously. Despite the difficulties entailed in meeting this responsibility—leaving work undone for several days, travel to the city from outlying farms—as many as five hundred or more citizens could be expected to attend and vote in the Assembly when it was in session.

Sometime during the fifth century BCE, all citizens earned the right to speak in the Assembly. This right was called *isegoria* ("equality in the agora" or assembly place). Most likely, very few citizens exercised their right to speak. When five hundred Athenians met to deliberate on important issues, not everyone could speak at once, nor was everyone sufficiently informed about the issue at hand to speak effectively. The task of filling in the details and of arguing for a course of action fell to persons who were trained in speaking, who had sufficient education to understand the issues, and who had the leisure to study the issues at hand. These were the professional *rhetores*. In the fifth century BCE, the term "rhetor" referred to someone who introduced a resolution into the Assembly, but by the fourth century BCE the term meant something like "an expert on politics." Later it came to mean "one skilled in public speaking" as well. In this book, we refer to people who practice rhetoric as rhetors. We refer to people who teach it or theorize about it as rhetoricians.

EARLY RHETORS, RHETORICIANS, AND TEACHERS

Ancient sources do not agree about who invented rhetorical theory. Some credit its invention to Empedocles, a sixth-century philosopher, poet, and magician. Others say that two Sicilian rhetoricians, Corax and Tisias, turned rhetoric into a teachable art, and some say as well that one or both of them wrote a handbook of rhetoric. There is a wonderful legend about these two fellows. According to this story, Corax was the teacher of Tisias. Tisias refused to pay for his rhetoric lessons until he won his first case. After a year had passed, Tisias had still not paid for his lessons, and Corax took Tisias to court. Corax argued that if he won his suit, Tisias would have to pay for the lessons since the court decreed it. If Corax lost, that would prove the worth of his lessons because Tisias had become a skilled enough advocate to win a suit. So, by Corax's logic, Tisias would have to pay no matter whether he won or lost. But Tisias argued that if the court decreed in his favor, he would not have to pay up, and if he lost, he would not have to pay either, since his inability to convince the court would prove that Corax' lessons were worthless. They were both kicked out of court, the story goes, and the judge said of them: "a bad egg from a bad crow" (*korax*).

During the fifth and fourth centuries BCE, many Greek orators achieved such fame that their speeches were written down and passed on to us. Among the more famous were Pericles and Demosthenes, whose careers exemplify the close connection of oratory to politics in ancient Athens. Pericles is usually credited with the establishment of democracy in that city: he began the practice of paying people to perform public service, and he may have opened an important office to poorer citizens. His democratic ideal, wherein citizens rendered free and intelligent obedience to a fair system of laws, is represented in the funeral oration attributed to him in Thucydides' history of the Peloponnesian War. Demosthenes was also intimately involved in the affairs of the city, although the major work of his career concerned Athens' uneasy relations with the Macedonian king Philip and his son, Alexander the Great. Demosthenes wrote and delivered many speeches against Philip in an attempt to alert Athenians to the king's acquisitive aims. He was widely regarded during antiquity as the greatest of the Greek orators, and his "On the Crown," a vindication of his political life, is still read as an outstanding example of the persuasive power of rhetoric.

THE OLDER SOPHISTS

Rhetoric was so obviously useful in the new Athenian democracy that teachers and practitioners of rhetoric flocked to Athens from other cities. Among these was a group now called the Older **Sophists**. *Sophos* meant "wise one" or "teacher" in ancient Greek (hence our word "philosopher," meaning "lover of wisdom" and our ironic "sophomore"). The most famous of the Older Sophists were Gorgias and Protagoras, but other people have also earned this title from historians: Hippias, Prodicus, Antiphon, and Thrasymachus.

Unfortunately, we must reconstruct what the Older Sophists taught from secondary sources. We possess only two speeches and some fragments of other works attributed to Gorgias. None of these were written down by him but were recorded later by scribes or scholars called doxographers (a "writer of opinion"; rendered more liberally, doxographers are recorders of important traditions). We have only a few recorded sayings and fragments from Protagoras. Unflattering portraits of both rhetors appear in Plato's *Dialogues* named after them. Plato was an Athenian aristocrat, an enemy of democracy, and a bit of a xenophobe (someone who fears foreign influences). He opposed rhetoric on the ground that rhetoricians did not search for truth, but aimed instead to persuade people to belief. Despite Plato's reservations about them, the Older Sophists prospered in Athens, attracting many students to their instruction.

Plato described a visit to Athens by Protagoras as follows:

> When we were inside [the house of Callias], we came upon Protagoras walking in the portico, and walking with him in a long line were, on one side Callias, son of Hipponicus; his stepbrother Paralus, the son of Pericles; and Charmides, son of Glaucon; and on the other side Pericles' other son, Xanthippus; Philippides, son of Philomelus; and Antimoerus of Mende, the most eminent of Protagoras' pupils, who is studying professionally, to become a Sophist. Those who followed behind listening to their conversation seemed to be for the most part foreigners—Protagoras draws them from every city that he passes through, charming them with his voice like Orpheus, and they follow spellbound—but there were some Athenians in the band as well. As I looked at the party I was delighted to notice what special care they took never to get in front or to be in Protagoras' way. When he and those with him turned round, the listeners divided this way and that in perfect order, and executing a circular movement took their places each time in the rear. It was beautiful. (*Protagoras*, 315a–b)

Protagoras' host, Callias, was a very rich man, and the young men listed here came from the best families in Athens at the time. Plato's account showed just a little contempt for the fashionableness of Protagoras' teaching and the obvious hero-worship of the young men.

The Older Sophists taught by example rather than precept. That is, they prepared and delivered specimen speeches for their students to imitate. Some may have prepared lists of sample arguments, later called commonplaces, that could be inserted into any speech for which they were appropriate. These collections of commonplaces, if they existed, would have been called arts (*technai*) of rhetoric. Certainly imitators and students of the Older Sophists did compose and collect lists of commonplaces, since several of these collections were available in Athens by the fourth century BCE.

The Older Sophists were skeptical that anyone could easily discover truth. Rather than philosophizing, they turned their attention to politics and ethics, teaching their students that vigorous rhetorical practice was essential to a stable, healthy community. Thoroughly pragmatic, they believed that people had to adjust their notions of what is good, useful, and true to the circumstances in which particular communities found themselves. Gorgias argued that rhetors had to take their immediate surroundings into account when they attempted to persuade people to a course of action, and so they could not worry about whether their message was true for all people at all times. This does not mean that the Older Sophists' teaching was unprincipled; in fact, a case could be made that their care for finding solutions to immediate problems rendered their practice more ethical than that of the philosophers who looked for some universal and timeless good.

PHILOSOPHERS ON RHETORIC

Plato was the first in a long line of Western philosophers to condemn the Older Sophists' insistence on immersion in the moment. Because of this, the rhetorical practice associated with their epistemology, called **sophistry,** now has a pejorative connotation that is entirely unfair to them and their work. Even though Plato was thoroughly opposed to sophistry, he appears to have understood the importance of rhetoric. In his dialogue named *Phaedrus*, he developed a philosophical rhetoric that could supposedly be used to find truth. This Platonic rhetoric involved studying the souls of human beings and learning how to properly define and divide an issue into its constituent parts. However, it was Plato's most famous student—Aristotle—who developed a fully theorized account of rhetoric.

During the fourth century BCE, Aristotle collected the rhetorical handbooks that were then available and assembled them into a collection called the *Synagoge Techne*. This research apparently convinced him that the current state of rhetorical theory was unacceptable. Since he was interested in theorizing about practice, Aristotle tried to discover general rules for rhetoric that would work in any given situation. While the Older Sophists taught by example, he preferred to develop principles that could be passed on to future students. Presumably, the text we now call the *Rhetoric* represents his lecture notes. In the famous opening of that work, Aristotle wrote:

> Rhetoric is an antistrophe to dialectic; for both are concerned with such things as are, to a certain extent, within the knowledge of all people and belong to no separately defined science. A result is that all people, in some way, share in both; for all, to some extent try both to test and maintain an argument and to defend themselves and attack. Now among the general public, some do these things randomly and others through an ability acquired by habit, but since both ways are possible, it is clear that it would also be possible to do the same by [following] a path; for it is possible to observe the cause why some succeed by habit and others accidentally, and all would at once agree that such observation is the activity of an art. (I i, 1354a)

Aristotle infers that all people learn how to argue in the course of their daily affairs. However, picking up the knack of arguing through experience may not be as helpful as studying the principles of argument, which Aristotle claims to have discovered by studying the practices of successful rhetors.

The *Rhetoric* is the earliest extant example of a complete theory, or art, of rhetoric. Aristotle's major contribution to rhetoric was his systematic and thorough treatment of invention—the art of finding the available arguments in a given case. We review many of these in this book: commonplaces, enthymemes, examples, maxims, and signs, as well as ethical and pathetic proofs. While Aristotle may have borrowed some of these proofs from other rhetoricians, he was the first to combine them into a systematic treatment of available argumentative strategies. In fact, the *Rhetoric* may have been part of a more ambitious project. Aristotle may have intended to create a comprehensive methodology, a set of intellectual tools that would help people to discover knowledge about anything whatsoever. If so, the methodology would have included his treatises on logic (the two *Analytics, Sophistic Fallacies, Topics* and *Categories*) as well as the *Poetics,* which is about the composition of drama and lyric poetry.

Aristotle's students and followers were called Peripatics (*peripatein,* walking about, from their habit of strolling up and down the halls of the Lyceum while they lectured). They were interested in rhetoric only as a sideline, which lessened the chance that they would preserve the *Rhetoric* as carefully as they did Aristotle's more philosophical works. Apparently a few copies were housed in the famous library at Alexandria, which was burned to the ground by the Roman general Octavian during the first century BCE. Fortunately, Arab scholars who had worked at Alexandria preserved copies of the *Rhetoric* intact throughout the European Middle Ages. During the Crusades, Westerners reestablished contact with Islamic scholars, and as a result the *Rhetoric* was introduced into European universities during the twelfth century CE. In modern times its popularity has eclipsed that of Cicero's works, which were the basic texts for the study of ancient rhetoric throughout the European Middle Ages and the Renaissance. Indeed, Aristotle's text on rhetoric has received more scholarly attention during the twentieth century than it did during all the rest of its long history (some 2300 years). Probably for this reason, the Aristotelian theory of rhetoric is usually what is meant when a contemporary scholar or teacher refers to classical rhetoric.

ISOCRATES

Despite Aristotle's current fame, his rhetorical theory was completely eclipsed during his lifetime by that of Isocrates. Some sources say that Isocrates studied with Gorgias, from whom he acquired his interest in style. Isocrates started out as a logographer—someone who wrote speeches for people who for some reason couldn't compose a persuasive speech for themselves. Later, he established a famous and influential school of rhetoric that was attended by ambitious young men from all the Greek city-states.

Throughout his long career, Isocrates taught young men the art of rhetoric so that they could become capable and cultured citizens. As he remarked in the epigraph that begins this chapter, rhetors should devote themselves to the "welfare of humanity and the common good." He repeatedly wrote that achieving this goal required three things: native ability, study, and practice. Some authorities credit Isocrates with establishing the public speech as an art form. Certainly his surviving speeches are highly polished works of art, and he is said to have worked on some of them for as long as fifteen years. Isocrates' *Art of Rhetoric* does not survive; but we do have most of his speeches and letters.

AN EARLY SOPHISTIC TEXTBOOK

We do have another rhetoric text available from Aristotle's and Isocrates' time; it is called the *Rhetoric to Alexander* (in Latin, *Rhetorica ad Alexandrum*). Ancient scholars thought that Aristotle had written it, since it is prefaced with a letter from Aristotle to his most famous student, Alexander the Great. But this letter is a later addition to the treatise. The *ad Alexandrum* is so different from the *Rhetoric* that it probably represents another scholarly or pedagogical tradition altogether. It is not a theory of rhetoric, as Aristotle's *Rhetoric* is; it simply lists and discusses the appropriate arguments to use in each part of a speech. The author of the *ad Alexandrum* was probably one of many teachers working at Athens who called themselves "sophists." These teachers should not be confused with the Older Sophists; Isocrates considered them to be cheats and parasites who promised to teach their students the art of living a happy life, when what they really did was hand out lists of stale formulas for putting arguments together.

HELLENISTIC RHETORIC

Aristotle, the great rhetorical theorist, and Demosthenes, the great practitioner of rhetoric, both died in the same year: 322 BCE. Scholars use this date to mark the close of the classical period of ancient Greek culture. Ancient scholars realized almost immediately that the intellectual work done during the classical period was important. During the Hellenistic period (roughly 300 BCE to 100 CE), Greek rhetoricians codified classical rhetorical lore into a coherent system which could be easily taught to young people. One of these teachers, Hermagoras of Temnos, added something new to the two rhetorical traditions—Aristotlean and sophistic—that were handed down from the classical period. Hermagoras, who lived during the second century BCE, is thought to have invented stasis theory, a means of invention which was simpler and less philosophical than Aristotle's, and which was somewhat better adapted to the needs of courtroom rhetors as well. Versions of stasis theory either replaced earlier inventional schemes or were incorporated into them in many post-Hellenistic rhetorical treatises.

We have a very full treatise on Greek rhetorical theory from this period, written in Latin. It is called the *Rhetorica ad Herennium*, because its author dedicated the work to one Gaius Herennius. Modern scholars are uncertain about its authorship, although for awhile during the Middle Ages it was thought to have been written by Cicero. In any case, this work gives us a very complete picture of Hellenistic rhetorical theory, and it is especially valuable because it includes a very full discussion of an ancient art of memory.

ROMAN RHETORIC

During the Hellenistic period of Greek culture, the city of Rome, located on seven hills in what is now south-central Italy, became the economic and military ruler of the known world. Even then, Rome was a very old city. Early on, it was governed in a fashion quite similar to that of other city-states, where all those defined as citizens (plebeians) gathered to vote on pressing issues. By the second century BCE, however, the people's assembly had become a working fiction, and the city was in fact governed by a Senate made up of persons who made more or less recent claims to the status of patrician, or aristocrat, by virtue of their ancestry or service to the state. This Senate had no legitimate constitutional authority, having wrested political control away from the plebeian assembly. Because of the political instability of this situation, terrible political turmoil wracked Rome throughout the second and first centuries BCE, until the Empire was firmly established under Octavian shortly before the beginning of the Common Era (CE).

Marcus Tullius Cicero was an important actor in the declining years of Rome's so-called Republic. He was a member of the Roman senate; but more important for our purposes, Cicero is the most influential practitioner and theorist of ancient rhetoric who ever lived. All the while he was active in Roman politics, Cicero gave many speeches and managed as well to write works on literature, philosophy, and rhetorical theory. Since Cicero's politics were unrelentingly republican, he was able to forge only temporary alliances with the succession of powerful generals who wanted to turn Rome into an empire, and it was inevitable that he would sooner or later fall afoul of some powerful pretender to the title of emperor, as he did in 43 BCE, when he was murdered by an assassin sent by Marc Antony. Some ancient sources say that the dead Cicero's hands were cut off, since he used these to write his powerful speeches; other authorities suggest that Cicero's head was displayed in the forum with a golden pin stuck through the tongue.

Cicero's rhetorical works were read in schools throughout the European Middle Ages. During the Renaissance, many thought his literary style to be the finest ever achieved, and the only one worthy of imitation. While Cicero was alive, his skill as an orator was respected and feared; indeed, even when he lost (as in his defense of Milo), his speeches were so powerful and skillful that they are still read today. We rely upon Cicero's *De Inventione* (*On Invention*), *Orator*, *Partitiones Oratoriae* (*The Parts of Speaking*), *Topica* (*The Topics*), and the magnificent *De Oratore* (*On the Art of Oratory*) in this book. The early treatise *On Invention* was heavily indebted to Hellenistic rhetoric, but Cicero's more mature rhetorical treatises were influenced by the work of Aristotle, as well as that of other Greek rhetoricians and philosophers. But the real shaping force on Cicero's work was the Roman state—its respect for authority and tradition, its political fluctuations, and its ethical dilemmas.

The other important figure in Roman rhetoric is Marcus Fabricius Quintilian, who may be the most influential teacher of rhetoric who ever lived. His *Institutio Oratoria* (*Institutes of Oratory*) was considered to be a classic work on education almost from the day he published it in 90 CE. Quintilian's influence on his contemporaries, such as the poet Juvenal and the historian Tacitus, is evident, and he influenced the work of the early Christian fathers as well. Sometime during the Middle Ages, all the complete manuscripts of the *Institutes* disappeared. But in 1416 an Italian scholar named Poggio Bracciolini rediscovered a complete copy of the work in a dusty monastery library. Poggio knew the value of what he had found. He immediately made a handwritten copy of the entire manuscript, thus preserving this ancient work for future generations to enjoy.

The *Institutes* is particularly valuable because it is a compendium of the best of ancient rhetorical theory, composed near the end of its theoretical development. Quintilian was a careful scholar, and his discussions of the competing theories of this or that ancient rhetorician often give us the best (and sometimes the only) information we have about them. Quintilian's theory of rhetoric was thoroughly indebted to Roman practical ethics. The education he prescribed for young citizens was aimed at producing speakers and writers who had the best aims of their community at heart. Many of the practices he recommended were used in Roman schools at least until the collapse of the empire, and probably beyond.

RHETORIC IN LATER ANTIQUITY

When political power was solidified within the Roman Empire, the great age of ancient rhetorical theory was past. No new theorists of the caliber of Gorgias or Aristotle appeared. The practice of rhetoric changed greatly under the restrictions imposed by the succession of Roman emperors. Rhetors no longer advocated policy; they no longer dared to blame the powerful for their shortcomings or to celebrate alternative versions of community with the people. Instead, they became performers. They used their art to create dazzling displays of highly ornamented variations on harmless themes that were hoary with age. Perhaps rhetorical study was put to its most effective and lasting use during later antiquity by the great Latin poets—Virgil, Ovid, and Horace. The only theoretical development, if it can be called that, occurred in discussions of style and literary criticism, written by such Greek rhetoricians as Hermogenes of Tarsus and Dionysus of Halicarnassus. Nevertheless, the rhetorical theories that had been forged during the immediate centuries before the Common Era remained at the center of higher education throughout later antiquity and well into the European Middle Ages and in Greek Byzantium as well.

FURTHER READING ABOUT ANCIENT RHETORICS

If you are interested in reading more about ancient rhetorics, you can look at any of several accessible histories written by modern scholars. The bibliography at the back of this book lists several of these, most of which should be available in any good public or university library. If you are interested in reading the works of the ancient rhetors and rhetoricians themselves, cheap editions of many of these can be found in the classics or literature sections of any bookstore, and they are available in libraries, too. The bibliography also lists modern editions of the major works of the most influential ancient rhetors and rhetoricians.

KAIROS AND THE RHETORICAL SITUATION

If the whole of rhetoric could be thus embodied in one compact code, it would be an easy task of little compass: but most rules are liable to be altered by the nature of the case, circumstances of time and place, and by hard necessity itself.

—Quintilian,
Institutes II xiii, 2

ANCIENT RHETORICIANS DIVIDED their art into five canons, or divisions: **invention, arrangement, style, memory,** and **delivery.** Invention is the part of the art of rhetoric that helps rhetors to find arguments. Arrangement had to do with the appropriate ordering of proofs within a discourse, style with sentence composition, memory with memorization of a completed discourse or a series of prompts, and delivery with appropriate management of the voice, gestures, and appearance. The five canons deal in turn with the activities that rhetors perform as they compose and present a piece of discourse, and so we have organized this book around them.

A few ancient rhetoricians, particularly the sophists, organized their treatises on rhetoric according to the divisions of a discourse: **exordium, narrative, proofs,** and **peroration.** Within each division, they listed topics that were appropriate for use in that part of a discourse. This organization is more common in surviving ancient texts than is the canon-oriented arrangement that we have adopted in this book. We did not use the sophists' approach because it is text-oriented. That is, it implies that the art of rhetoric deals with the pieces or parts of a discourse. This orientation may give the erroneous impression to contemporary readers that the parts of discourses are more important than the rhetorical situation for which they are composed. Ancient users of sophistic texts would not have made this error, since their cultures were far less text-oriented than ours.

We begin our study of rhetoric with the first canon: invention. We present three ancient approaches to this canon. The first, considered in this chapter, was developed during the period when the Older Sophists were speaking and teaching in the city of Athens during the sixth and fifth centuries BCE. The development of the second approach—stasis theory—is credited by ancient authorities to a rhetorician named Hermagoras of Temnos who taught rhetoric during the second century BCE. **Stasis** appears in almost all extant treatises on rhetoric, thus testifying to the high regard in which ancient teachers held this approach to invention. The third approach—the commonplaces—was probably developed by the sophists, but contemporary rhetoricians know it from its powerful presentation in Aristotle's *Rhetoric.*

We include this wealth of inventional tactics in this book in the spirit of *copia.* We hope that our readers will try all of them in order to gain facility in invention and to develop an abundance of propositions, arguments, and proofs.

SEIZING THE MOMENT (KAIROS)

Ancient rhetoricians recognized the complexity of rhetoric, and they realized that teaching such a multifarious art was a difficult task. Rhetoric cannot be reduced to a handy list of rules on writing or speaking, because each rhetorical situation presents its own unique set of challenges. One way to think about a particular rhetorical situation is to consider its **kairos.** A multi-dimensional and flexible term, *kairos* suggests a notion of space and/or time. Since American English does not have a term quite like *kairos,* a bit of explanation is in order. An important element of the rhetorical situation is the context of the issues, what Quintilian called the "time and place," or the "circumstances," what the Greeks called *kairos.*

The Greeks had two concepts of time. They used the term *chronos* to refer to linear, measurable time, the kind with which we are more familiar, that we track with watches and calendars. But the ancients used *kairos* to suggest a more situational kind of time, something close to what we call "opportunity" (as in "the *time* is ripe"). In this sense, *kairos* suggests more of an advantageous time, or, as lexicographers put it, "exact or critical time, season, opportunity" (Liddell and Scott, 859). The temporal dimension of *kairos* can indicate anything from a lengthy time to a brief, fleeting moment. In short, *kairos* is not about duration, but rather about a kind of time—quality, rather than quantity. In Roman rhetoric, the Latin word *opportunitas* was used in a similar manner; its root *port* means an opening, and from it we get our word "portal." *Kairos* is thus a "window" of time during which action is most advantageous. On Wall Street, there are *kairotic* moments to buy, sell, and trade stock to maximize gains. Victorious sprinters often accelerate at just the right time to pass their opponents. The success of a joke or funny quip depends upon its timing, or the *kairos* of its delivery. The advantage of good timing and seizing opportunities is certainly a prominent idea in our culture, and it is important for practicing rhetoric as well.

Kairos was so important for ancient thinkers that it became a mythical figure. Lysippus, the famous ancient sculptor of athletes, chose to "enroll Kairos among the gods" (Himerius, 759). It is little wonder that someone knowledge-able about competitive athletics—where timing and an awareness of the situation are critical—would render *kairos* into human form. The figure Kairos provides a good way to think about the rhetorical situation. Indeed, the rhetor is much like Kairos, bearing many different tools. Not just anybody can balance precariously on a stick while balancing a set of scales on a razorblade and de-pressing one pan; such balance takes practice. As you can see in Figure 3.1, a de-piction of a relief at Turin, Kairos is concerned about balancing the particulars of the situation, just as he perches tenuously on edge. His winged back and feet suggest the fleeting nature of time and situations. Perhaps the most remarkable and well known characteristic of Kairos, however, is his hairstyle. Kairos was said to have long hair above his forehead, suggesting that one must keep an eye out for the opportune moment and seize it by grasping the forelock before it passes.

Figure 3.2 shows another depiction of Kairos, still with wings, this time holding a wheel, suggesting movement again. In this depiction, found on a The-ban limestone relief, Kairos is flying on the back of another mythical figure—Pronoia, the figure of foresight. Sitting dejected in the background is her counterpart, Metanoia, who is the figure of afterthought or hindsight. This scene, like the forelock in Figure 3.1, suggests the importance of anticipating op-portunities and seizing them—or in this case, jumping on them—before they pass by.

These figures underscore the many dimensions of *kairos*. The ancients were certainly aware of its relevance to the art of rhetoric. Indeed, the Older Sophist

FIGURE 3.1
Kairos, from a bas-relief in Turin

FIGURE 3.2
Kairos, from a bas-relief in Thebes

named Gorgias was famed for having based his theory of rhetoric on it. Greek writer Philostratus tells us that Gorgias may have invented extemporaneous speaking:

> For coming into the theater of the Athenians, he had the boldness to say "suggest a subject," and he was the first to proclaim himself willing to take this chance, showing apparently that he knew everything and would trust to the moment (*toi kairoi*) to speak on any subject. (Sprague 1972, 30)

By privileging *kairos*, Gorgias' rhetorical theory acknowledged the contingencies of issues and situations. Gorgias chose to rely on his awareness of the particularities of each situation to help him come up with compelling things to say.

Isocrates, too, emphasized the importance of *kairos*, claiming that people need to discuss prevailing issues before their currency dissipates:

> the moment for action has not yet gone by, and so made it now futile to bring up this question; for then, and only then, should we cease to speak, when the conditions have come to an end and there is no longer any need to deliberate about them. ("Panegyricus" 5, 2)

For Isocrates, the urgency and currency of a situation demands action which calls for lively rhetorical exchanges about an issue. But if an issue has lost its immediacy, then the rhetor must not only deliberate about the issue, but also make a case for the issue's relevance.

KAIROS AND DISSONANCE

We believe, along with the sophists, that the world is always changing, and that knowledge itself is full of contradictions and uncertainties. *Kairos* draws attention to the mutability of rhetoric and discourse, of the ever-changing arguments surrounding a particular issue. Further, *kairos* points to the situatedness of arguments and the ways in which different arguments depend on many different forces: the rhetor's political views, past experiences, particular stance on the issue at the time a discourse is composed, and the views of the audience at that time and place.

One way to consider the *kairos* of a particular issue is to pay careful attention to the arguments made by various sides in order to cultivate a better understanding of why people disagree about a given issue at a particular moment. The sophists believed that every argument had at least one contrary argument. According to the ancient historian named Diogenes Laertius, "Protagoras was the first to say that on every issue there are two arguments opposed to each other" (Sprague 1972, 21). Some collections of sophistic arguments have come down to us. Characteristically, the arguments in these collections are arranged in contradictory pairs, since the sophists taught their students how to argue both sides of any question. (This pedagogical tactic distressed philosophers, who characterized it as "making the weaker case seem the stronger.") Students using these arguments learned how to create a proof favorable to one party in a litigation, or to argue for adoption of a proposal before the assembly. Then they would use a set of opposing arguments to prepare a case for the other side, or to argue for rejection of the proposal they had just supported.

The sophistic treatise called *Dissoi Logoi,* or "Countervailing Arguments" illustrated the sophists' conviction that contradictions pervade rhetorical situations. Here are some sample arguments from that treatise:

> Some say that the good is one thing and the bad another, but others say that they are the same, and a thing might be good for some persons but bad for others, or at one time good and at another time bad for the same person. I myself side with those who hold the latter opinion, and I shall examine it using as an example human life and its concern for food, drink, and sexual pleasures: these things are bad for a man if he is sick, but good if he is healthy and needs them. And, further, incontinence in these matters is bad for the incontinent but good for those who sell these things and make a profit. And again, illness is bad for the sick but good for the doctors. And death is bad for those who die but good for the undertakers and gravediggers. (Sprague 1968, 155)

The arguer continued in this way, listing examples showing that good and bad are the same, depending on circumstances and point of view. The topic in this case is "things that are good for some persons but bad for others." The rhetor simply applied this generalization to all the examples he could think of within the set he chose, in order to flesh out the argument that good and bad are the same. Then he did a turnabout, demonstrating that good and bad are different:

> I think it [would] not be clear what was good and what was bad if they were just the same and one did not differ from the other; in fact such a situation would be extraordinary. And I think a person who says these things would be unable to answer if anyone should question him as follows: "Just tell me, did your parents ever do you any good?" He would answer, "Yes, a great deal." "Then you owe them for a great deal of evil if the good is really the same as the bad.". . . Come and answer me this: isn't it the case that you are both pitying beggars because they have many evils, [and] again counting them lucky because they have many goods, if good and bad are really the same thing? . . . I shall go though the individual cases, beginning with eating, drinking and sexual pleasures. For the sick these things are [bad to do and again] they are good for them to do, if good and bad are really the same. And for the sick it is bad to be ill and also good, if good is really the same as bad. And this holds for all the other cases which were mentioned in the previous argument. (Sprague 1968, 156–157)

The topic in this case is "things that are good for some people cannot be bad for them too." The rhetor simply applied this generalization to all the specific cases he could think of, in order to amplify support for the other side of the original argument, that good and bad are different.

The abstract nature of this argument—whether good and bad are relative to each other, or not—demonstrates that the *Dissoi Logoi* were part of a school exercise. They were sample amplifications, used to show aspiring rhetors how to exploit systematically the argumentative possibilities inherent in an issue. When rhetors argued cases or debated before the assembly, of course, they dealt with much more specific issues, and they supported only one position on any issue.

For Gorgias and the other sophists, contradictory arguments provided fruitful starting points for the exploration of a particular issue. Moreover, the doctrine of *dissoi logoi* points to the situational nature of discourse recognized by *kairos.* In rhetorical situations, issues are always championed by people who disagree with one another. In other words, there are always at least two sides of every argument. The people who take those sides can and do change their minds, depending on the time and place in which they argue.

A KAIROTIC STANCE

A *kairos*-based discourse does not seek certainty prior to writing, but rather views writing and speaking themselves as opportunities for exploring issues and making knowledge. A rhetoric that privileges *kairos* as a principle of invention does not present a list of rules for finding arguments, but rather encourages a kind of ready stance, in which the rhetor is not only attuned to the history of an issue (*chronos*), but is also aware of the more precise turns the arguments surrounding an issue have taken and when they took these turns. In short, the rhetor must be aware of the issue's immediate relevance to the time, the place, and the community in which it arises.

Consider, for example, the ways Barbara Crossette creates an opening for a contemporary discussion about the term "slavery":

> Slavery has been in the news a lot lately. Last week, Mayor Rudolph W. Giuliani said a Mexico-based ring had been holding deaf Mexican illegal immigrants in "virtual slavery" in New York. A few days later, the Mayor himself was accused of condoning slavery by requiring at least some of the city's million-plus welfare recipients to work at community jobs. "Rudy, we will not be your slave drivers," said posters held by representatives of religious organizations and voluntary agencies who refused to participate in the city's workfare plan. Slavery is a label applied to low-wage workers in the garment and sportswear industries abroad and sweatshops in American cities. It is invoked to condemn the sex industry and prison labor.
>
> But what is slavery nowadays anyhow? It is a question the United Nations has been wrestling with for decades by assigning experts to look at what are called "contemporary forms" of enslavement. There have been conventions signed and conferences held, and still the word is open to considerable interpretation. When scores of Thai workers were found confined to a compound behind razor wire in a garment sweatshop in California two years ago, an American Civil Liberties Union official said the news should hardly have come as a surprise, since slave labor in the state "is one of those dirty little secrets everyone knows about." (*New York Times* 27 July 1997, 4:1)

At first glance, slavery would seem to be an issue with very little exigence or *kairos,* at least in the United States. In order to establish the contemporary use of the term as an issue with urgency and to get to her point—that the term "slavery" is currently misused—Crossette cites several examples of practices referred to as slavery, and points out that U.N. officials are concerned with definitions of slavery. After demonstrating an awareness of the various uses of the term "slavery" in contemporary discourse, Crossette moves to a history of slavery, citing its various forms in Babylon, Persia, Egypt, and the Roman Empire. Had she begun the article with the section about ancient slavery, the article might have read like history, and not had much exigence as a consequence. Yet Crossette, attuned to the various dimensions of the issue and its connections to welfare, immigrant labor, and sweatshops, makes the article's historical work relevant to the subsequent discussion of slavery as a category.

QUESTIONS RAISED BY KAIROS

Remembering that *kairos* is not only a concept of time, but also of space, a rhetor concerned about *kairos* can explore questions such as these:

1. Does the issue have a sense of urgency right now, or do I need to show its urgency or make it relevant to the present?

2. What arguments seem to be advantageous with what groups at this point in time?

3. What lines of argument might be inappropriate considering the prevailing needs and values of the audience?

4. What other issues are bound up with discourse about this particular issue right now, in this place and in this community? Why?

5. What are the particular power dynamics at work in an issue? Who has power? Who doesn't?

6. What venues give voices to which sides of the issues? Does one group or another seem to be in a better position from which to argue? Why?

7. Does one group seem to have a louder voice than the others? Why is this so? Bear in mind that *kairos* is not only a temporal but a spatial concept.

While you are considering the influence of time and place on an issue, it might help to remember that *kairos* is akin to the Latin term *opportunitas*, an opening. Is there an opening for you to begin making new arguments on a particular issue? If not, can you create such an opening?

An Example

In order to demonstrate the usefulness of the questions raised by *kairos,* we examine the issue of internet censorship. On June 16, 1997, Supreme Court justices denied the legality of the Communications Decency Act (CDA), which members of Congress had passed in 1996 in an attempt to ban the circulation of materials defined as "indecent" from the internet. Here is John M. Broder's report on the Supreme Court's judgment:

CLINTON READIES NEW APPROACH
ON INTERNET INDECENCY

WASHINGTON—When President Clinton signed the Communications Decency Act into law last year, he and his top advisers knew that the legislation, regulating indecent material on the Internet, was on shaky constitutional ground.

White House officials immediately began planning a new approach on Internet smut to replace the flawed law, even as administration lawyers were writing their brief defending the act. The result can be found in the broad new administration policy on Internet commerce and content that is to be announced by the president next week.

Clinton's answer to cyberporn: new technology allowing parents to block offensive material that might otherwise reach their children, stricter parental supervision of children surfing the Internet and stronger self-regulation by the online industry.

In a statement issued by the White House after the decency act was struck down by the Supreme Court on Thursday, the president said he would convene industry executives and groups representing parents, teachers, and librarians to seek a solution to the problem of online pornographic material. The meeting is to be held next Tuesday.

"We can and must develop a solution for the Internet that is as powerful for the computer as the V-chip will be for the television, and that protects children in ways that are consistent with America's free-speech values," Clinton said. "With the right technology and rating systems," he said, "we can help insure that our children don't end up in the red-light districts of cyberspace."

Members of congress who supported the decency law criticized the justices and vowed to redouble efforts to write a bill that would survive court scrutiny to protect children from online pornography. "The Supreme Court, in its ruling against the Communication Decency Act, has entered dangerous, unexplored territory," said one of the voided law's sponsors, Sen. Daniel Coates, R-Ind.

"A judicial elite is undermining democratic attempts to address pressing social problems. The Supreme Court is purposely disarming the Congress in the most important conflicts of our time."

Sen. Patty Murray, D-Wash., said she would soon introduce a bill that would make it a felony to exploit chat rooms designed for children, require Web site operators to rate their pages for content, and help provide filtering software for households with children and computers.

But free-speech and Internet industry groups said no law could effectively monitor and regulate content on the rapidly expanding global information network without trampling on fundamental freedoms. They said the Supreme Court, whose decision Friday was unanimous in most respects, had spoken forcefully in favor of free speech, leaving advocates of regulatory measures with little room for maneuver.

"The decision is a benchmark, establishing First Amendment for the 21st century," said Jerry Berman of the Center for Democracy and Technology, which opposed the decency law. "We think we can protect children and families in a far more effective way than any government censorship program." (*New York Times* Cybertimes, www.nytimes.com, 27 June 1997)

The Court's judgment generated a good deal of writing and talking about the issue of internet censorship and related issues. We think that the decision and the period leading up to it made the issue of internet censorship a *kairotic* one. The debates touched off arguments and wide-ranging issues such as free speech, internet expansion, child protection, and government legislation of morals. When the decision came down, however, it became apparent that the justices had no interest in inhibiting the growth of the newest, most expansive communication medium; nor were they interested in surveilling the internet and prosecuting those responsible for circulating questionable materials.

Here are excerpts from the *Newsweek* report in which writers Steven Levy and Karen Breslau considered the relationship between the Supreme Court's decision and freedom of speech:

Born of a hysteria triggered by a genuine problem—the ease with which wired-up teenagers can get hold of nasty pictures on the Internet—the Communications Decency Act (CDA) was never really destined to be a companion piece to the Bill of Rights. Last week the Supreme Court officially deleted the CDA on constitutional grounds, concluding that the act endangers free speech and "threatens to torch a large segment of the Internet community."

The decision had resonance far beyond dirty pictures. This was the first time that the highest court had contemplated the status of the key medium of the next century. Instead of regarding the Net with the caution the court usually shows while exploring new frontiers, the justices went out of their way to assure that this most democratic of mediums (where "any person . . . can become a town crier . . . [or] pamphleteer," the court gushed) would receive the highest level of protection. In-

ternet speakers will not be shackled with the regulations that limit content on television and radio; instead, they will enjoy the freedom granted to printed matter. And
it will be up to parents, not the government, to keep kids from accessing smut. "This
represents the legal birth certificate for the Internet," said Bruce Ennis, who argued
the case before the court, representing a group of plaintiffs ranging from the American Library Association to Human Rights Watch. . . .

If there was alarm in the court's response, it was not at the prospect of pimply
adolescents exposed to Hustler's Web site, but at other sorts of scenarios, like a parent going to jail for sending birth-control information to a 17-year-old son or daughter away at college. Even the partial dissent, written by Justice Sandra Day
O'Connor and endorsed by Chief Justice William Rehnquist, shared the majority's
disdain for the CDA's excesses. Unlike the majority, they felt that it was possible to
sanction indecency knowingly sent by adults to minors. . . .

Cyberspace will surely discuss all of this in its own unrestrained, long-winded
manner. Last week, though, it was celebration time, not only online but at in-the-
flesh rallies in Austin, Texas, and San Francisco. Mike Godwin, a lawyer for the Electronic Frontier Foundation, spoke for Netheads everywhere. After citing the likes of
Thomas Jefferson, he quoted a more up-to-date authority, Martha and The Vandel-
las: "Summer's here and the time is right," he said of the day when the Supreme
Court went cyberpunk. (*Newsweek* 7 July 1997, 28–30)

Levy and Breslau capitalize on the issue's *kairos* by marking the date as "the
day the Supreme Court went cyberpunk," and by carefully detailing the events
that led to the decision. The details reveal the complexity of the issue, but they
also underscore its urgency: a good deal is at stake in the issue of internet censorship for *Newsweek* readers, whose relative affluence affords them more likely
access to the internet than most Americans. Levy and Breslau also demonstrate
the issue's connection to other issues like freedom of speech and the question
of legislating morality by presenting the varying views of the defense lawyers
and dissenting justices. The exploration of an issue's history, along with its
implications for the future, can produce rich possibilities for understanding
an issue and its relationship to contemporary culture (see the chapter on
commonplaces).

The Supreme Court decision on internet censorship spawned less enthusiastic reactions as well. Conservative political analyst George Will used the decision as an opportunity to argue for individual responsibility in his *Newsweek*
column. The pieces of his column excerpted below follow a brief argument
about obesity in America, in which Will argues that "Americas are becoming
fatter because they are becoming more slothful and self-indulgent" (7 July 1997,
82). Will, too, presents a mini-history of the issue and connects it to other issues,
but he presents a much different picture than Levy and Breslau:

For now, the Internet, although an exotic technology, is in one sense mundane. It is
a redundant reminder of the law's limits in making life restful. The law can only do
so much in removing the burden of living vigilantly and responsibly, for our own
sake and our children's. So click off the Internet and go for a brisk walk. You look as
though you could use the exercise. (*Newsweek* 7 July 1997, 82)

Will presented internet censorship not as a free speech issue, but as an issue of moral responsibility and a sign that Americans are becoming less concerned about morality then they once were, and more self-serving in the bargain. Will took advantage of the *kairotic* moment opened by the Supreme Court decision as an opportunity to engage larger social concerns. He tried to convince people to view the internet as a corrupting force, as a sign of declining community standards.

A rhetor who wants to address the issue of internet censorship, then, should be aware of the various arguments in circulation for and against censorship, the alternatives proposed, and other issues raised in the discussion. Such a *kairotic* stance facilitates a more informed and interesting rhetorical approach to this or any issue.

URGENCY: HOW URGENT OR IMMEDIATE IS THE ISSUE?

Usually, urgency depends on the audience as well as the existing situation—on recent activity around the issue. For some activist groups such as the Family Research Council, a group which continually battles to censor the web, the issue of internet censorship always bears a certain degree of urgency. Likewise, people at the Center for Democracy and Technology, who continually make arguments against legislation that would limit the material allowed in the internet, are highly invested in the issue as well. An audience comprised largely of college students, on the other hand, might need to be convinced that the issue is pressing and that action needs to be taken. In this case, it would be advantageous to ask: What is going on right now that might help the audience see that now is the time for action? In 1997, for example, when the question of internet censorship was argued before the Supreme Court, the issue bore a good deal of exigence or immediacy. Activist groups encouraged people who were not as highly invested in the issue—such as people who don't even use the internet—to consider the ramifications of federal regulation of internet material. But an issue does not have to be under consideration by the Supreme Court to have a degree of urgency. For example, if administrators of an after school care program in a Chicago suburb are interrogated because children viewed pornographic material on the internet while under their care, arguments about internet censorship may receive more attention and be deemed more pressing in that community than in a rural Tennessee town where very few people own the technology necessary to access the internet. Current events are important to consider when trying to gauge the *kairos* of a particular issue.

ARGUMENTS

Another important consideration of a *kairotic* stance are the specific arguments that are currently circulating about a particular issue. Who makes what arguments and why? Why, for example, does George Will connect internet use to obesity in America? What values are privileged in his rhetoric and what groups would accept or reject his criticism? Considering the stakes in an issue can help a rhetor decide the most advantageous way to frame a particular argument for a particular audience at a particular time. A brief look at material on internet censorship shows a highly complex issue which resonates very differently among groups with divergent interests. Groups or individuals may agree on a particular issue for very different reasons. Internet access providers such as America Online, for example, have an economic investment in fighting internet censorship, while there are internet users who believe that federal regulation would inhibit the growth of a diverse global medium. For other groups, such as the American Civil Liberties Union, internet regulation violates freedom of speech and limits democratic participation. Similarly, the American Society of Newspaper Editors are more invested when the issue is framed in terms of freedom of the press. Proponents of censorship, on the other hand, who believe that legislation could keep bad influences out of the hands and minds of children, base their arguments on social as well as religious beliefs. Senator Daniel Coats, who sponsored the 1995 Communication Decency Act—a set of restrictions which covers everything from child pornography to profanity—believes, along with the Christian Coalition, that the issue of internet censorship is about protecting America's children from harmful influences. Other groups who advocate censorship are concerned about graphic depictions of violence on the net.

As you can see, concerned groups are invested in the issue of internet censorship for different ideological reasons. Before launching arguments about a hot social issue such as internet censorship, then, rhetors who wish to argue persuasively should "tune in" to the arguments already in circulation. Furthermore, they should interrogate the values and assumptions that drive those arguments. Rhetors who do this can maintain a kairotic stance that readies them to speak to various sides of the issue, supporting those that they find convincing and refuting those with which they disagree.

POWER DYNAMICS: WHO GETS TO SPEAK? WHO CAN BE HEARD?

To examine and invent arguments using *kairos* is to consider the power dynamics at work in a particular issue in addition to the recent events and arguments that press on it. The questions to ask here are:

- Which arguments receive more attention?
- Who is making these arguments?
- What arguments receive less attention?
- Who is making these arguments?

In the case of internet censorship, for example, we rarely hear or read the opinions of teenage internet users, a group which comprises a large and savvy sector of internet clientele. How do we account for the absence of their voices?

Could it be that this group is apathetic? Or does their non-voting status have something to do with the undervaluing of their position? In what venues do parents voice their stance? How powerful are these venues? It seems to us that most internet users and web page designers prefer to post material on the web without restrictions. Why has this group been less vocal about the issue of internet censorship than those who would like to impose restrictions?

A WEB OF RELATED ISSUES

Rhetorical arguments are complex, and a rhetor who is attuned to *kairos* demonstrates an awareness of the many values and the differential power dynamics that are involved in any struggle over an issue. As we demonstrated earlier, different values underlie what appear to be very similar arguments. Furthermore, the stakes in an argument can shift according to who is speaking, as is illustrated by the contrasting arguments of George Will and the Supreme Court justices. A rhetor attuned to *kairos* should consider a particular issue as a set of distinct political pressures, personal investments, and values, all of which produce different arguments about an issue. These diverging values and different levels of investment connect to other issues as well, producing a web-like relationship with (hyper?)links to other, different, new, but definitely related rhetorical situations.

The issue of internet censorship is linked to the issue of censorship in general, an issue that has been debated since ancient times. The contemporary system of movie ratings, which virtually insures that a movie with an "X" rating will not make any money, does not represent the first attempt by Americans to censor motion pictures. More recently, the issue of music censorship became a major concern for Americans, as Tipper Gore led a movement in the early 1990s to convince record companies to place warning labels on music with questionable content. As we write, concerned parents' groups and executives from the major television networks are trying to agree on a ratings system for television programming that will alert parents to programs they would prefer their children not watch.

Further, the proposed or actual censoring of any of the arts raises concerns about artistic freedom, freedom of speech, and freedom of the press. At the university where we teach, for example, a student artist exhibited a work of art that offended some members of the community. When a state senator threatened to withhold the university's budget unless the offending works were removed from display, the artist voluntarily took it down. However, a large color photograph of the work was subsequently published in the local newspaper. As far as we know, the newspaper did not receive any complaints about their photograph. What does this example say about the importance of location? About differences between freedom of artistic expression and freedom of the press? About power dynamics?

Internet censorship also raises the issue of legislating morals: Who gets to legislate and define what constitutes "harmful material"? Is the protection of children from such material a private or a public responsibility? Is it the government's duty to protect children from what they can see and hear, or should families and individuals be allowed to decide for themselves what internet users may have access to? These issues connect to other issues, forming a web with endless possibilities, or "openings," for arguments.

We are not suggesting that a rhetor should address all the facets of a particular issue at a particular time. Rather, we recommend that rhetors be aware of the issue's ever-shifting nuances, which might lead to new opportunities for rhetorical arguments. Considering the wealth of possibilities produced by attention to an issue's *kairos*, it is no wonder that Gorgias was bold enough to say to the Athenians, "suggest a subject," and remain confident that he could make a rhetorical argument about it on the spot.

WORKS CITED

Himerius. *Eclogae*, XVI, i.

Liddell, Henry George and Robert Scott. *A Greek–English Lexicon.* New York: Oxford UP, 1996.

Sprague, Rosemary Kent. *"Dissoi Logoi, or Dialexis." Mind: A Quarterly Review of Psychology and Philosophy 77* (306 [April 1968]): 155–167.

———, trans. *The Older Sophists.* Columbia: South Carolina UP, 1972.

STASIS THEORY: ASKING THE RIGHT QUESTIONS

How is Cato to deliberate "whether he personally is to marry," unless the general question "whether marriage is desirable" is first settled? And how is he to deliberate "whether he should marry Marcia," unless it is proved that it is the duty of Cato to marry?

—Quintilian,
Institutes III v, 13

STUDENTS WHO WANT a systematic way of asking questions about rhetorical situations can use **stasis theory.** This means of invention provides rhetors with a set of questions that, when asked systematically, can help them to determine where the disagreement between themselves and their audience begins. Determining the point of disagreement is an obvious starting point for rhetorical invention, which is always stimulated by some difference of opinion.

Staseis (questions or issues) were probably part of rhetorical lore as early as the fourth century BCE (Aristotle, *Rhetoric* III, 17). But the popularity of this system of questioning in Hellenistic and Roman rhetoric was probably due to Hermagoras' codification of the process during the second century BCE. His textbook is lost, so scholars have reconstructed his theory of invention from discussions by Cicero, Quintilian, and other ancient and medieval authorities.

The term **stasis** (Latin *status* or *constitutio*) is derived from a Greek word meaning "a stand." Thus a stasis can refer to the place where one rhetor takes a stand. Seen from the point of view of two disputants, however, the stasis marks the place where two opposing forces come together, where they rest or stand in agreement on what is at issue. (Hence the appropriateness of the Latin term for stasis, *constitutio*, which can be translated as a "co-standing" or a "standing together.") An agreement to disagree must occur in every rhetorical situation, since, as Quintilian put it, "every question is based on assertion by one party and denial by another" (III vi, 7). But this resting place is only temporary, suspended as it is between conflicting movements, until a skilled writer or speaker comes along to move the argument away from stasis. The most satisfactory modern equivalent for stasis seems to be the term **issue,** which we define as the point about which all parties to an argument can agree to disagree: this is what is at issue.

Determining the point of stasis is crucial to any rhetorical argument. However, figuring out the point at issue is more difficult than it may seem at first glance, and in intellectual work of this sort no process can absolutely guarantee results. The old systematic investigative procedures described in this book were used for thousands of years to help rhetors figure out what exactly they wanted to say, and we hope that they will help you to determine the issues you want to argue, as well. We recommend that you begin by trying to answer the questions outlined below. Consider all the statements you generate as you work through the stases to be potential propositions. If you work systematically and thoroughly, you should produce a full and useful analysis of the issue you have chosen to examine. Doing all of this intellectual work has several advantages. Rhetors who work through the questions raised by this heuristic in systematic fashion will find that

- It clarifies their thinking about the point in dispute.
- It forces them to think hard about the assumptions and values shared by members of their target audience.
- It establishes areas in which more research needs to be done.
- It suggests which proofs are crucial to the case.
- It will perhaps even point the way toward the most effective arrangement of the proofs.

However, this heuristic will not provide a draft of a paper. Ancient rhetors spent a good deal of time preparing to write or speak, trying out one inventional scheme or another. They did not mind if these trials produced false starts, because they knew that the false starts could perhaps be used elsewhere. It is important to remember, then, that practice with this (or any heuristic) also supplies the rhetor with *copia.* Proofs generated in practice with any heuristic system may prove useful at some other time.

WHAT HAPPENS WHEN STASIS IS NOT ACHIEVED?

Contemporary public discourse about abortion provides a stunning example of an argument that has been sustained for many years but that shows no sign of being resolved. One reason that this argument has not been resolved is that it cannot be, as long as the central propositions put forward by those involved in it are not in stasis. People who line up against the legalization of abortion offer the following statement as their major proposition:

Abortion is murder.

People who argue that abortion should maintain its current status as a legal operation put the following statement forward as their major proposition:

Women have the right to choose what happens to their bodies.

Keeping in mind that reaching stasis means finding the place where opponents agree to disagree, even a cursory examination of these statements shows that they are not in stasis. A rhetor who wishes to find stasis with someone who believes that abortion is murder should argue (a) that abortion is not murder; or (b) that abortion is legal, so, therefore, it cannot be murder because murder is illegal in America; or (c) that abortion is not murder because a fetus is not a human being, or some other proposition that defines abortion in such a way that it can be excluded from the category "murder."

Stasis Achieved: Rhetors Can Now Agree to Disagree

    A. Abortion is murder.
    B. Abortion is not murder.

A rhetor who wishes to find stasis with someone who believes that women have a right to decide what happens to their bodies, on the other hand, must argue that (a) women do not have that right, at least when they are pregnant, or (b) that the right to life of a fetus outweighs a woman's right to choose what happens to her body, or (c) that the right to life extends to potential human beings and takes primacy over any other human right, or some other similar proposition about the ranking of human rights.

Stasis Achieved: Rhetors Can Now Agree to Disagree

    A. Women have the right to decide what happens to their bodies.
    B. Women do not have the right to decide what happens to their bodies, at least when they are pregnant.

Now while the propositions that turned up in our stasis analysis do appear in contemporary discourse about abortion, they are seldom offered in the systematic juxtapositions we have listed here; that is, they are seldom put in stasis. It is not for nothing that opponents of abortion are called "pro-lifers" while those who want to keep abortion legal are called "pro-choicers." Surely those who support legal abortion do not want to be known as "anti-life," and those who oppose abortion do not want to be known as "anti-choice." As this juxtaposition of terms suggests, stasis analysis establishes that the participants in this argument are arguing right past each other. That is to say, the major propositions they put forward do not address the same issue.

    Interestingly enough, the statements that would achieve stasis in this argument are a bit shocking: pro-choice advocates do not often directly address the pro-life position by saying "abortion is not murder." Nor do pro-life advocates often say in public forums that "women do not have the right to determine what happens to their bodies." This reluctance to admit the implications of its propositions may be another reason why the argument is not in stasis. Those who frame the abortion issue as a question of murder are compelled to argue that women do not have the right to choose an abortion. They frequently support their position by making reference to religious, moral, or natural laws. Those who support legalized abortion, on the other hand, have recourse to the discourse of rights, arguing that individuals have a right to conduct private business without interference from the state. They assume further that deciding to have an abortion is a private, not a public, matter. Another way to say this is that people who oppose abortion are arguing from metaphysical assumptions about the point at which life begins; people who defend women's rights are arguing from political grounds about the rights of individuals and the relation of those rights to community goods. The point to be made here, however, is that as long as the major propositions in this discourse remain out of stasis, the argument will continue. For some reason, those who argue about this issue have been unwilling to meet one another on the same ground.

THE FOUR QUESTIONS

The process of asking questions does not conclude once the point of stasis has been identified. Ordinarily, the determination of the question for debate will give rise to other questions. Ancient rhetoricians devised a list of four questions, or stases, that would help them refine their grasp on the point of contention.

1. Conjecture (*stasis stochasmos*)—"Is there an act to be considered?"
2. Definition (*stasis horos*)—"How can the act be defined?"
3. Quality (*stasis poiotes*)—"How serious is the act?"
4. Procedure (*stasis metalepsis*)—"Should this act be submitted to some formal procedure?"

If someone is accused of theft, for example, the first question that must be raised is **conjecture:** "Did she do it or not?" If all parties agree that she took the property in question, the stasis moves to a question of **definition:** "Was it theft?" (She might have borrowed it.) And if everyone agrees that the act can be defined as theft, the stasis becomes: "Was it right or wrong?" (The theft might be justified on any number of grounds—she took liquor from the house of a friend who is an alcoholic, for instance.) And if this question is agreed upon, the stasis then becomes: "Should she be tried for the offense?"

When a rhetor begins to examine an issue, according to Cicero, he should ask:

Does the thing about which we are disputing exist? (Latin *an sit*)

If it exists, what is it? (*quid sit*)

What kind of thing is it? (*quale sit*)

Cicero said that the first is a question of reality, the second of definition, and the third of quality or value (*On the Parts* xviii, 62). If, for example, a rhetor were concerned with the theoretical issue of justice, the three questions might be:

1. Does justice exist in nature or is it merely a human convention?
2. Can justice be defined as that which benefits the majority?
3. Is it advantageous to live justly or not?

The first question forces the rhetor to conjecture about whether justice exists, and where; the second, how it can be defined; and the third, what its **value** is, and to whom. Cicero and Quintilian insisted that only the first three questions were really necessary for preparing arguments to be used outside the courtroom. Nevertheless, the fourth stasis, **procedure,** is sometimes useful in non-legal settings.[1] People who deliberate in assemblies often have to decide how to regulate practices.

Stasis theory is as useful to writers as it is to speakers, since rhetors must assess the probable response of an audience to their work. Cicero recommended that speakers and writers work through the questions in order. The process of working through questions of conjecture, definition, and quality, in order, will help rhetors find the points about which they and their audience agree; it will also establish the point from which they must begin the argument—the point where they disagree. In the first stasis, the rhetor determines whether she or he and the audience agree about the existence of some being or the commission of some act. If they do, this stasis is no longer relevant or useful, having been agreed to by both parties. In the second stasis, the rhetor determines whether she or he and the audience agree about the classification of the being or the act; if so, the stasis of definition may be passed by. Third, the rhetor determines whether she or he and the audience agree about the quality of the being or the seriousness of the act. That is, what is its relevance to the community as a whole? According to Cicero, in the third stasis, there is a controversy about the nature or character of an act when there is both agreement as to what has been done and certainty as to how the act should be defined, but there is nevertheless a question about how important it is or what kind of thing it is, or in general about its quality: for example, was it just or unjust, profitable, or unprofitable? (*De Inventione* I viii, 12).

THE FOUR STASES

Conjecture: Does it exist? Did it happen?
Definition: What kind of thing or event is it?
Quality: Was it right or wrong?
Procedure: What should we do?

Elaborating the Questions

Each of the four questions can be elaborated into other sets of questions. According to Cicero, there are four ways of dealing with a question of conjecture (*Topics* xxi, 82). One can ask any of the following questions:

1. Does the thing exist or is it true?
2. What is its origin?
3. What cause produced it?
4. What changes can be made in it?

Some modern rhetoricians call the issue of conjecture "the question of fact." However, the Greek term *stochasmos* is more literally translated as "a guess" or "an inference." Since the term "fact" connotes the sort of hard physical evidence we discussed in the first chapter of this book, it is misleading. The stasis of conjecture does not establish anything at all about the truth or fact of the matter under discussion; rather, it represents an educated guess about what might be, or what might have occurred. And since reality may be perceived very differently by people who occupy different social and political positions, people may paint very different pictures of that reality. For example, a man who tells a racy joke to his colleagues at work may think that he is only being friendly, while a woman colleague who hears the joke may think of it as an insult to women. Or, in another example of conjecture, a recipient of Aid to Families with Dependent Children might describe a welfare check as the only means she has for feeding her children. A politician who is opposed to welfare, however, might characterize that very same check as a handout to freeloaders. These people have all offered conjectures about the way the world is or how people behave. In the examples given here, each party has some stake or interest in picturing the joke or the welfare check in the way that they do. Their disagreement about these facts is what renders conjecture rhetorical.

Questions of Conjecture

Does it exist? Is it true?

Where did it come from? How did it begin?

What is its cause?

Can it be changed?

Let's return to the case being prepared by our fictitious astronomer as another example of how the stases work. Under the question of conjecture, the astronomer can ask:

Does light pollution exist in the city?

What is the origin of the pollution?

What causes it?

What will change it?

When she tries to answer these questions, the astronomer learns that she will probably need to provide evidence that light pollution does indeed exist. She will need to provide further evidence that the pollution is not natural (that is, that it doesn't originate from moonlight or starlight). She will have to establish that the pollution is caused by billboards and streetlights, and she will need to establish further that elimination of these two sources will produce a level of light that will make astronomic observation possible.

If all parties to the discussion agree about the conjecture—the description of the state of things—the search for stasis moves on to matters of definition. Definition requires that the astronomer name the particular or proper quality of light pollution, and divide it into its parts.

Questions of Definition

What kind of thing or event is it?

To what larger class of things or events does it belong?

What are its parts? How are they related?

Let's say that the astronomer defines the particular quality of light pollution as "that level of light which is sufficient to interfere with astronomical observations." She might then divide such light levels into

light caused by billboards

light caused by streetlights

light caused by home lighting

light caused by natural sources

This examination will demonstrate to her that she needs evidence that establishes the level of pollution caused by each of these sources.

Questions of quality may be asked in two ways: simply or by comparison. If asked simply, the question of quality is "Is light pollution a good or a bad thing?" According to Cicero, there are three kinds of simple questions:

1. What to seek and what to avoid.
2. What is right and what wrong.
3. What is honorable and what base. (*Topics* xxi, 84)

Questions of Quality or Value

Simple Questions of Quality or Value

Is it a good or a bad thing?

Should it be sought or avoided?

Is it right or wrong?

Is it honorable or dishonorable?

Comparative Questions of Quality or Value

Is it better or worse than something else?

Is it more desirable than any alternatives?

Is it less desirable than any alternatives?

Is it more or less right than something else?

Is it more or less wrong than something else?

Is it more honorable than something else?

Is it less honorable than something else?

Is it more base than something else?

Is it less base than something else?

Thus our astronomer might ask the following simple questions of quality:

Should lower levels of light pollution be sought or should they be avoided?

If the lower levels of light affect other situations, like citizens' safety, should they then be avoided?

That is, is it right or wrong to ask for lower levels of light?

Is it honorable to put the needs of astronomers above those of ordinary citizens?

Is it dishonorable to deprive citizens of a source of safety?

Thinking comparatively, the rhetor compares the importance of her issue to other related issues. In the astronomer's case, for example, the general comparative question of quality is:

Should the present state of affairs, which includes light pollution, be preferred to a state of affairs in which light pollution has been lessened?

The comparative specific question is:

Should the present state of affairs, which includes lighted billboards, be maintained in preference to an imagined state of affairs where lighted billboards have been eliminated so that astronomers can see better?

Since questions of comparison are of two kinds—similarity and difference—the astronomer will ask herself what differences will be brought about in her observations of the night sky if light pollution is reduced; under the head of similarity she also will consider what problems might remain even if light pollution is reduced.

The fourth stasis, procedure, is relevant in the astronomer's case as well. In questions of procedure, the rhetor proposes that some action be taken or that some action be regulated (or not) by means of a policy or law. Questions of policy or procedure are usually two-fold: they are both deliberative and forensic. That is, a rhetor who wishes to put forward a question or issue of policy must first deliberate about the need for the policy and then argue for its implementation.

Questions of Policy or Procedure

Deliberative Questions

Should some action be taken?

Given the rhetorical situation, what actions are possible? Desirable?

How will proposed actions change the current state of affairs? Or should the current state affairs remain unchanged?

How will the proposed changes make things better? Worse? How? In what ways? For whom?

Forensic Questions

Should some state of affairs be regulated (or not) by some formalized procedure?

Which procedures can be implemented? Which cannot?

What are the merits of competing proposals? What are their defects?

How is my proposal better than others? Worse?

Using the deliberative questions of procedure, our astronomer is forced to ask herself some hard questions. She has already decided that some action should be taken. She now needs to ask herself whether her proposal to enact a dark-sky ordinance can be implemented, and whether it is a good thing for the community it will affect. She needs to consider changes that its implementation might bring about—loss of revenue to Ourtown, possibly dangerous situations for citizens—and determine whether the seriousness of these changes outweighs the merits of her proposal. Turning to the forensic questions of procedure, the astronomer realizes that she can enhance both her ethical and logical appeals by presenting the Council with a draft of a proposed dark-sky ordinance. The draft demonstrates the depth of her concern about the situation, since she took the time to compose it. It also strengthens the possibility that the ordinance will be satisfactory to her, since busy people are likely to make use of work that has already been done. She can find arguments for implementing her proposal by showing how it will improve the current state of things, by showing how alternative proposals are not as satisfactory as her own, and by showing that implementation of her proposal is entirely possible. For example, she should try to counter the opposing argument that lowered levels of light can endanger citizens' safety. If possible, she should point out in her proposal that current levels of light from streetlights do not pose a problem to astronomical observation.

If you wish to recommend that a policy or procedure be implemented then, you must first compose it. Find out how similar policies are enacted in similar situations, and compose a plan for implementing the one that you suggest. You should also determine how the policy that you recommend can be enforced. If you are recommending, on the other hand, that some public practice be implemented or changed, you must first compose your recommendation. Then find out who can make the changes you suggest, and find out what procedures must be followed in order to make the recommended change. You should also try to find out how your recommended change can be implemented and enforced, and offer suggestions for achieving this.

ARE WE INTO THEORY HERE, OR WHAT?

Ancient rhetoricians divided questions into two kinds: theoretical and practical. Some questions concern what people should do (action); but these are always related to questions about why people should do something (theory). Cicero gave this example of a **theoretical issue** in his treatise called *Topics* (xxi, 82):

> Does law originate in nature or in some agreement and contract between people? This is the sort of abstract theoretical question that is discussed today by law school professors and their students when they talk about what grounds or centers the law. It is an important question, believe it or not, because certain practical actions follow from any answer that may be given. If law is grounded in nature it cannot be easily changed. If law is natural, it is also difficult to argue that a given law is incorrect or unfair; a rhetor's only option in this case is to argue that the law in question is unnatural. (To get an idea of how difficult this is, imagine yourself arguing in court that laws against speeding are unnatural. The argument from nature is used on occasion: motorcycle riders who opposed legislation requiring them to wear helmets have argued—without much success—that such laws violate the natural human desire for freedom). If law results from human contract, on the other hand, it is much easier to justify alterations to laws, because a rhetor can appeal to the expressed opinions or desires of the majority as support for an argument that a law should be changed.

Unlike theoretical questions, which address the origins and natures of things, practical questions always concern what people should do. Cicero gave this example of a **practical issue:**

> Should a philosopher take part in politics?

Notice that this question concerns what people who study philosophy ought to do; it does not raise questions about the nature or aim of philosophy or politics, as a theoretical question would.

Our word "theory" derives from a Greek word (*theorein*) which literally means "to sit in the highest row of the bleachers." More freely translated, the term means something like "to observe from afar." A theoretical question, then, allows rhetors to view questions "from afar," as though they had no immediate relevance for daily affairs and putting aside for the moment their practical effects. Many times theoretical investigations will provide positions on more practical issues. But they also take rhetors far afield from everyday events. Take this very practical (and very specific) question, for instance:

> Should Jane study this weekend?

To answer this question, a rhetor needs to consider Jane's options (partying, visiting home, and so on) and the consequences attached to each choice. But this practical question has theoretical underpinnings:

> Is studying more important than having fun or visiting family?

To answer this theoretical question is more difficult because a rhetor must take into account not only Jane's immediate desires but her longer-term goals, her values, her personal history, and so on.

Another way to think about the difference between theoretical and practical questions is to consider the level of generality at which an issue may be addressed. Greek rhetoricians used the term *hypothesis* to name a specific question that involved actual persons, places, or events. They used the term *thesis,* on the other hand, to name general questions having wide application—matters suited to political, ethical, or philosophical discussions—which don't refer to actual persons or events. The classic example of a general question was:

> Should anyone marry?

The classic specific question was:

> Should Cato marry?

Here are some contemporary examples of general and specific questions:

1. *General:* Is censorship a violation of the right to free speech?

    Specific: Does the Communications Decency Act infringe on the right of internet users to free speech?

2. *General:* Should materials that are considered indecent by the community be censored?

    Specific: Should the internet be censored or monitored so that the children of Ourtown do not have access to materials considered indecent by our community?

3. *General:* Are the needs of scientific investigation more important than the safety of citizens?

    Specific: Should Ourtown adopt a low-light ordinance to aid astronomical observation even though lower levels of light may endanger citizens?

The ancient distinction between a theoretical question and a question of action is a binary distinction—that is, it allows for only two possibilities. However, it might be more helpful to think of general and more specific questions as lying along a spectrum. There are many levels of generality and specificity at which any issue can be stated. The generality or specificity of a given claim is never absolute; rather, statements of a question are general or specific only in relation to each other. For example:

General: Is conservation of the environment more important than economic development? (*Note that this is a theoretical as well as a very general question —stated this way, the question raises issues for contemplation and discussion rather than action.*)

More Specific: Should the United States sacrifice industries that negatively impact its environment—logging, manufacture of certain chemicals and plastics, nuclear power plants—in order to conserve the environment? (*This question, while still general, is no longer simply theoretical; answers to it imply actions to be taken by the United States.*)

Even More Specific: Should the City Council of Ourtown reject an application to build a large new discount department store if this requires clear-cutting five acres of forest?

Very Specific: Should I take time to recycle plastics, paper, and aluminum even though to do so costs money and time?

The last three versions of the claim raise practical questions, insofar as they imply human actions, but each successive claim involves fewer people, so each is more specific than the one which precedes it.

The level of generality at which a question or issue is stated determines the amount of research needed and the kinds of proofs that must be composed in order to argue it persuasively. More general questions require broader knowledge, and they usually require a longer and more complex treatment. To answer the general question about conservation given above, for example, would require at least a book-length discussion. On the other hand, the very specific question, involving a personal decision, at minimum requires some private reflection and a bit of hands-on research. To answer this very specific and very practical question would only require the rhetor to recycle plastics, paper, and aluminum for awhile to see how much time and/or money is required to recycle these substances and to compare these results to the time and money required in having all the garbage hauled away by the city. A composition answering this question could simply state a proposition ("Recycling is expensive and time-consuming") and report the results of this research. As you can see, though, answers given to this very specific question depend on answers given to more generally stated questions, including the first, very general, question stated above. Whether you recycle or not depends, ultimately, on your values: Is the environment more important to you than your time or your budget? (Here we've restated the very specific question just a bit more generally.)

The relation of general to specific issues was a matter of debate among ancient rhetoricians. As Quintilian pointed out, every special issue presupposes a general one; for example, the question of whether Cato ought to marry really couldn't be answered satisfactorily unless the general question, "Should a person marry?" had also been considered (III v, 13). Too, there are questions that hover somewhere between the very general and the very specific; for example, "Should an older person marry?" For ancient rhetoricians, questions like these were ethical ones, having to do with a person's character and the right course of conduct for certain characters. Ethical questions still concern us. We regularly

read or hear arguments about whether young people ought to marry, for example, and there is a good deal of contemporary argument about when people
should have children. Often these arguments are cast as personal or financial
choices, but they have ethical aspects, too, since decisions about marriage and
reproduction affect many people, not just those who make them.

Of course, any decision you make about the level of generality at which you
will pursue an issue is always affected by the rhetorical situation for which you
are composing. Who is the audience for the composition? What is the setting?
How does the audience feel about the issue? What do they know already and
what will I have to tell them? And so on.

Putting These Distinctions to Work

Rhetors can use the set of questions developed by ancient rhetoricians as a
means of clarifying for themselves exactly what is at issue between them and
their projected audience. And if they choose and frame the question carefully,
rhetors can begin the argument from their own ground, rather than an opponent's. Let us return, for example, to the case of the astronomer who argues that
the city council should adopt a dark-sky ordinance. When she prepares her case,
she asks: are we disagreeing about a general or a specific issue? She can define
the issue specifically, as follows:

> Ourtown should adopt a dark-sky ordinance.

As stated, this is a specific issue, because it names a particular city and urges the
adoption of a particular action. It also provides an advantage to the astronomer
because it permits her to take a stand on her own ground; that is, she defines the
point at issue in such a way that the ensuing argument must revolve around
adoption of a dark-sky ordinance, rather than issues of safety or of the advertising revenue brought to the city from lighted billboards.

The astronomer might prefer, however, to state the issue in more general or
theoretical terms. In that case, she could raise a question of values:

> Which is more important to us: the accumulation of scientific knowledge made
> available by a darkened night sky or the revenue which is brought to advertisers by
> lighted billboards?

This statement of the general issue is theoretical. She could also state the more
general issue in practical terms, though:

> Should we give priority to advertisers when we pass city ordinances?

To state the issue in general terms gives the astronomer a persuasive advantage,
since her audience might view the particular statement of the issue ("Ourtown
should adopt a dark-sky ordinance so that astronomers can make night-time observations") as self-serving. Stated generally, the issues raise questions which
concern the entire community, not just astronomers.

Stating the Issue

The Question Framed Specifically

> Should Ourtown adopt a dark-sky ordinance?

The Practical Question Framed More Generally

> Should cities value scientific knowledge over advertising revenues?

The Specific Question Framed as Theory

> Should the city council of Ourtown give priority to astronomers or to advertisers when it passes city ordinances?

The Specific Question Framed in Practical Terms

> Will Ourtown profit more from a dark-sky ordinance than from revenue brought in by billboard advertising?

Very Specific, Very Practical Questions

> Will the astronomers who work at Ourtown's observatory close down the facility if they cannot get a sufficiently dark night-time sky? Can Ourtown afford to lose the prestige and money brought into town by the observatory? Does the revenue brought in by billboard advertising offset this loss of revenue?

Opponents of the astronomer's proposal can follow exactly the same procedure. For example, the city police could anticipate the astronomer's statement of the particular issue and simply state it negatively:

> Ourtown should not adopt a dark-sky ordinance.

But this tactic gives an advantage to the astronomer, since it takes up the stand on her turf, so to speak. Thus the police might prefer to begin by defining the issue so that the stand occurs on their ground:

> Lowering the level of light in Ourtown will endanger citizens who must travel the streets at night.

Once again, this is a specific statement of the issue, since it refers to a specific place and implies a single potential action. It is also practical, since it involves human activity. The police might also prepare to argue the case from the vantage point of a general, theoretical stance which addresses values:

> The safety of citizens is more important than the accumulation of scientific knowledge.

Or, they might choose a general, practical stance which counsels a principle for action:

> When the city council of Ourtown passes ordinances, its members should always give top priority to the safety of citizens.

Stating the question this way adds to the **ethos** of the police, since it shows their concern, not for the added work they must do if lower levels of light are permitted, but for the safety of the community at large.

A good way to decide which kind and level of question you may wish to argue is to imagine the kind and level of question your opponent may advance. Will he argue a theoretical question? In that case, you must be prepared to consider the question on that level, in order to meet him in stasis. The level of generality you choose will also be dictated by the rhetorical situation in which you find yourself. Do the police of Ourtown have an amicable working relationship with the city council? Are their spokespeople trusted by council members? Does their ethos outweigh that of the astronomers at the observatory? Will their concerns about citizen safety carry greater weight with the council than the scientific concerns of the astronomers? And so on.

As you have probably guessed by now, heuristics do not work as reliably as mathematical formulas. There is no guarantee that your consideration and development of theoretical and practical or general and specific questions will provide you with exactly the proposition that you wish to argue. In many cases, you will continue to refine the issue and to develop nuances of your proposition as you work through each of the rhetorical canons. In fact, invention can begin all over again during later stages of the composing process—arrangement, revision, or even editing. However, attention to the heuristics described in this book will certainly enrich your stock of arguments—your intellectual *copia*. And systematic, thoughtful consideration of the issue at hand may provide you with precisely the proposition you are looking for, if not with some of the arguments you can use to support it.

USING THE STASES

The stases still prove surprisingly useful for beating a path through the thicket of issues which often surround a controversy. We suggest that rhetors begin by asking themselves what sort of question they are facing: general or specific? theoretical or practical? Try to formulate the question in each of these terms in succession. Then compare them in order to determine which seems like the most effective approach given the rhetorical situation for which you are preparing. Once you have decided upon the level of generality at which you wish to argue and have examined possible points of stasis, you should then formulate your question in terms of each of the four questions: conjecture, definition, quality, and procedure. Again, compare these formulations: do any seem to capture the point at issue? Do any hold out the possibility of helping you with further investigation? Do any tell you something about issues that might be raised by a member of the audience, or by someone who disagrees with you? Do any help you to begin to develop an argument? Remember that this procedure is only intended to help you decide where to start. Its use does not guarantee that you will generate any useful proofs, much less that you can begin to draft a paper at this stage of your preparation.

In the sample analyses that follow, we used stasis theory to find out what issues reside in two contemporary controversies. The examples are intended to demonstrate how this heuristic can help someone who is just beginning to think about a rhetorical problem. We did no research on these issues before we began this analysis, although of course we had heard them discussed in conversation and had read news articles about them. Our examples do not include all of the potential questions that could have been raised by application of the stases. Nor should they be followed slavishly, as though they model all possible uses of the system. As you will see when you study the examples, we have used the stases very differently in each one. This happened because the rhetorical situations that gave rise to each of the controversies were very different. Because of the situatedness of rhetoric, then, stasis theory cannot be applied mechanically. The issues or problems it turns up will differ from situation to situation, so any rhetor who uses it must be alert to all the possibilities it raises in any case. Rhetors should always be ready to follow any tangent thrown up by their consideration of the stases.

The First Example: A Familiar Argument

We return to the issue of abortion as a means of demonstrating how stasis theory can work because most Americans are familiar with the terms of this argument in our public discourse. Here is an article that appeared in a recent issue of our university's student newspaper:

NEW CLINIC WILL OFFER FREE CARE

A new health care facility, mired in a recent abortion controversy, will offer free medical care once a week.

by Molly K. Fellin, *Collegian* Staff Writer

A new sign hangs on the door of suite 210 in the Uni-Mart Building, 477 E. Beaver Ave., naming the soon-to-be opened general medical practice State College Medical Services. The facility will begin to operate sometime in August as a family medical practice for all State College residents and will offer free medical care one day of every week to those who need it most, said Eric Harrah, director of administration and owner of the new facility. Harrah said he would pay for the cost of the free care out of his own pocket. "My personal philosophy is that health care should be available to everyone," Harrah said, explaining that State College does not have such a practice currently, but is in need of one. "People who are homeless . . . can receive free medical care (at State College Medical Services)." One part of the general medical services offered at the facility will be reproductive health care, specifically, abortions, Harrah said.

Controversy began to strike for Harrah and his would-be practice soon after he signed the lease with HFL Corp., owner of the Uni-Mart Building, because of the abortions that would be offered. The Centre County Citizens Concerned for Human Life began efforts to halt the opening of the facility because of their concern about

Harrah and associates of his, according to a press release. The release said Harrah owned several abortion clinics across the country, including one in Philadelphia, which were eventually shut down because of improper and illegal practices by Harrah and associates. Though he admitted to owning several medical facilities, Harrah said the offices were never closed for any illegal activity. "I've never had a facility close in my entire life. They're liars," he said. "Abortions are only a small part of the practice, and abortion is legal in this country."

Although abortion is legal in the country, Jill Dworzanski, co-director of Womyn's concerns, said they are not available or convenient enough for those women who choose to have them. The closest places to State College which offer abortions are located in Harrisburg, Williamsport, and Pittsburgh. State College Medical Services will be the first facility ever to offer abortions in Centre County. "It's not an easy decision; it's not for fun," Dworzanski said. "If this clinic goes through, it would make things easier for women—they wouldn't have to take time off of work or travel all around in order to have this done." Having a facility which offers abortions so close to campus will not cause harm to the area, Dworzanski said, it will only help women. "I don't think it's going to influence anyone (who would not normally have had an abortion) to have one," she added.

But other members of the university community say they are not interested in seeing such a facility open in State College. Father Fred Byrne, director of the Penn State Catholic Community, said the proposed clinic would "make it very convenient for young girls to kill their babies." "As Pope John Paul says, we have a culture of death," Byrne said, explaining the recent influx of infanticide by young people is a good example of the current disrespect for human life. "Human life is not a problem, it's a gift," he said. Rather than start an abortion clinic in the area, Byrne said other options must be created for those who might consider abortion. "As a university, we have to do a better job of teaching our students," he said.

Both Byrne and Harrah say that more and better education is needed for youth to help prevent difficult situations. Describing himself as a social liberal, Harrah said he does not believe abortion is always the answer. He said he does not believe in abortion for sex selection, for instance. "I believe that women have the right to choose," Harrah said. "I believe health care is a private matter—the government can't interfere." And Harrah does not want anyone to interfere in the impending opening of State College Medical Services either. "This will happen," Harrah said. "I will open this facility." (*Digital Collegian*, www.collegian.psu.edu, 7 July 1997)

We have already examined the major propositions that tend to be put forward in this argument by partisans of opposing sides, and as you can see, they appear again in this news article.

In what follows, we back up a bit and assume that a rhetor who is examining this issue has not yet developed a position on it. In other words, we use stasis theory here as a heuristic—a means of discovery. We state the issue both theoretically and practically, and consider what happens when we state its available propositions at various levels of generality. Then we subject its available propositions to Hermagoras' questions in order to see if we can discover persuasive arguments that may be useful on occasions when we wish to enter into discussions about abortion.

Step 1. *Decide whether to formulate the question in theoretical or practical terms.*

Possible Theoretical Questions

Seen "from afar," what is the nature of abortion?

What are its origins? Its ends?

Where and when do abortions occur? Who is involved?

Possible Practical Questions

Why do people practice abortion?

What and whose interests are served by the practice of abortion?

What and whose interests are denied by the practice of abortion?

Your answers to these questions may yield propositions that you wish to support or reject. If you try to answer the theoretical questions, you will probably discover that you do not know all that you need to know about this issue in order to argue responsibly about it. To answer the first theoretical question, for example, you need a dictionary (or better, a medical dictionary) that will tell you just what this procedure entails. Answers to the second require you to know something about the history and contemporary use of the practice.

Answers to the practical questions lead to lines of argument—the related issues that we discussed in chapter 2. For example, the first practical question might be answered as follows: people practice abortion as a means of birth control. This answer suggests a line of argument: since there are other means of contraception available, why do people resort to abortion for this purpose? Is there some feature of the state of affairs that keeps people from using these other means?

Step 2. *Decide whether to formulate the question generally or specifically.*

Possible General Formulations of the Question

Do abortions occur? (conjecture)

What is abortion, exactly? (definition)

Is it a good or a bad thing? (quality)

Should abortion be regulated? (policy)

Possible Specific Formulations of the Question

Do abortions occur in Ourtown? (conjecture)

Are the abortions that occur in Ourtown safe or unsafe? (definition)

Is the availability of abortion a good thing or a bad thing in Ourtown? (quality)

Should the practice be regulated in Ourtown? (procedure)

This analysis reveals something about the scope of the available arguments on this issue. To answer the theoretical question of conjecture requires a great deal of empirical research; each of the other three theoretical questions requires at least a book-length examination. The practical and specific questions cover less daunting amounts of space and time and hence require a rhetor to do less research. They may also be more interesting to the immediate community. If you reread the news article quoted above, you will see that there seems to be no disagreement about the practical questions of conjecture and definition, at least as they are phrased here. And since the question of policy has already been decided in American courts of law (abortion is legal), the question of quality seems to be the point of stasis in this argument. In other words, in this rhetorical situation the argument seems to turn on whether the ready availability of abortion is a good or a bad thing for this community. Once again, the rhetorical situation dictates which of the propositions yielded by the stases will prove most useful to a rhetor.

Step 3. *Decide which of the four stases best describes the point at issue in the rhetorical situation at hand.*

Conjecture

Is there an act to be considered? In this case no abortions have yet occurred in the proposed facility. Since all responsible parties must agree to this factual statement, a rhetor could pass by this question. However, the fact that value arguments are being made even before the clinic has opened suggests that the arguments underlying this issue are deep and complex. So perhaps an interested rhetor should investigate the questions of conjecture to see whether they yield useful propositions.

Questions to Ask about Conjecture

1. Does abortion exist? In this case it would be interesting to know, given the relative distances involved in traveling to a city where abortion clinics operate, whether illegal abortions occur in this community. If abortions are practiced in the community before the new clinic opens, this state of affairs yields some interesting conjectural arguments that could be used by rhetors on both sides of the issue. People who are opposed to abortion can conjecture that the clinic is unnecessary, since the need is already being met; people who support greater availability can conjecture that people who want or need abortions must undergo them in unsafe conditions.

2. How did it begin? Abortion has been used as a method of birth control for thousands of years. Recently, however, safer more effective means of birth control have been found, and the use of abortion as a means of contraception has become increasingly controversial. Interestingly, the specific case being examined here is about a beginning—if the clinic is allowed to open, it will be the first of its kind in the community. Those who are opposed to its opening seem to conjecture that its presence in the community will cause an increase in the number

of abortions performed there. Is this a necessary assumption? The spokesperson for Womyn's Concerns conjectures that it is not. Is she correct? How could you find out?

3. What is its cause? In some cases, of course, abortions are performed because they are required in order to save women's lives. This cause does not seem to be so controversial as cases in which abortion is used as a means of birth control. Here the question of cause asks us to consider what causes people to choose abortion rather than other available means. Those who support the legality and availability of abortion suggest a number of causes for its use: lack of education about birth control, lack of access to birth control, women's lack of control over their reproductive choices, rape, and fear of rejection, or abuse. Those who oppose abortion conjecture its causes quite differently: as irresponsibility, lack of values, and disrespect for tradition.

4. Can it be changed? Whether the practice of abortion will ever cease, and whether the number of abortions, legal or illegal, can be changed by regulation are interesting questions. Abortion has been legal in America for about twenty years, which suggests that it can be made illegal again if the correct procedures are followed. Many states have begun to limit access to abortion by mandating a twenty-four hour waiting period, for example. And on the national level, opponents of abortion rights have attempted to outlaw certain kinds of abortions. These are legal means of seeking change, as are demonstrations and parades and petitions. Conjecture about the possibility of change in this case raises further interesting questions: Can illegal procedures—such as the bombing of abortion clinics or murder of doctors who perform abortions—effect a change in law? If not, why do the perpetrators of such acts engage in them?

Definition

How can the act be defined? As we have seen, this is a crucial stasis in the debate over abortion. In this case the question of definition requires rhetors to examine their moral positions—something that is ordinarily very difficult. Perhaps the question of definition is seldom raised in public discussion about abortion because of the difficulty and seriousness of the questions it raises. If a rhetor accepts the definition of abortion as murder, she or he can only argue propositions that treat abortion like other instances of murder. It would follow that similar punishments should be meted out to those found guilty of performing the act. A rhetor who supports abortion rights cannot allow the argument to be taken up at the stasis of definition if his opponents argue that abortion is murder. Such a rhetor will inevitably occupy the unenviable and untenable position of defending acts of murder. If this rhetor accepts some other definition of abortion, certain other consequences follow.

Questions to Ask about Definition

1. What kind of a thing is it? Is abortion an act of murder? Is it a medical practice? A means of birth control? An affront to family values? A feminist issue? (See chapter 10 for help in composing definitions.)

2. To what larger class of things does it belong? Is a fetus a human being with all the rights to which humans are entitled? Or is a fetus not human if it is not viable outside the womb? What is a human being, anyway? Is abortion a crime against humanity? Is resistance to legal abortion part of a disabling set of patriarchal prescriptions against women?

3. What are its divisions? Currently, the law proscribes medical intervention into a pregnancy beyond the first trimester (three months), unless some overriding concern (such as the mother's life or health) warrants this. Is this the best temporal division that can be devised?

Quality

How serious is the act? Answers to questions of quality always depend upon the values maintained in the community. There are few issues currently under public debate that so deeply involve community values as does abortion. Obviously, for the Catholic priest quoted above, the issue of abortion is very serious indeed, since the Church sees it as part of a "culture of death." But people who support legalized abortion take the issue seriously, too, arguing that it is part of the larger issue of women's control of their reproductive lives.

Simple Questions of Quality

1. Is abortion good or bad? No one who is party to this argument thinks that abortion is a good thing. Those who oppose it want it banned completely. Those who support it want it to be safe and legal, but they would prefer that women not have to resort to it as a means of birth control. As the bumper sticker proclaims, "Keep abortion safe, legal, and infrequent."

2. Should abortion be sought or avoided? Are there any cases in which abortion ought to be sought? Or should abortion always be the choice of last resort?

3. Is abortion right or wrong? Those who oppose abortion say that the practice is always wrong. Can you imagine a hypothetical situation in which this is not the case? Are there any general situations in which abortion is the right choice?

4. Is abortion honorable or dishonorable? Those who are opposed to abortion have tried to shame doctors who perform the procedure by convincing them that it is a dishonorable act. Some doctors refuse to perform the procedure, while others consider it a mark of courage and pride that they are willing to continue performing abortions under frightening and sometimes dangerous conditions. Are they behaving honorably or dishonorably?

Comparative Questions of Quality

5. Is it better or worse than some alternative? There are only a few alternatives to abortion: abandonment, adoption, and parenthood. Keeping in mind that situations differ, try to rank these alternatives in terms of their relative goodness and badness.

6. Is it less or more desirable than any alternative? Can you think of situations in which abortion may be the most desirable alternative? The least desirable?

7. Is it more or less right or wrong than any alternative? Those who support abortion rights often argue that abortion is preferable to bringing an unwanted child into the world. In other words, they say that abortion is less wrong than giving birth to an unwanted child. Is this argument valid? With whom might it be effective?

8. Is it more or less honorable or base than some alternative?

Procedure

Abortion is currently a legal medical procedure. However, there is much contemporary debate about policies related to abortion (for example: should so-called "partial birth" abortions remain legal? Should women under the age of 18 be forced to tell their parents about a planned abortion?). As is the case with any issue, rhetors who wish to advocate or oppose adoption of a procedure must first deliberate the need for the policy or procedure, and second, they must study how it would be implemented (or removed).

Deliberative Questions of Procedure

1. Should some action be taken? Should abortion remain legal? Should it be made illegal? Should it be made illegal in some cases only? In the specific case examined above, should the proposed abortion clinic be allowed to open for business?

2. Given the rhetorical situation, what actions are possible or desirable? Is it possible to outlaw abortion? Is it desirable? In the specific case examined above, is it possible to prevent a clinic from doing business? Is it desirable to do so?

3. How will the proposed actions change the current state of affairs? Or should the current state of affairs remain unchanged? How will the presence of an abortion clinic affect the community's attitude toward abortion? Will its presence alter the numbers of abortions that are performed on citizens of the community? Is the status quo, where there are no such clinics located within hundreds of miles, satisfactory? Desirable?

4. How will the proposed changes make things better? Worse? How? In what ways? For whom? Obviously, the establishment of a clinic will benefit those in need of abortions. Presumably it will also benefit its owner economically, even though he promises to provide free health care one day a week to the indigent. Those who oppose abortion rights suggest that the presence of the clinic will make things worse ("young girls will be able to kill their babies"). Will the presence or absence of the proposed clinic benefit or harm citizens who have no direct stakes in the procedures it performs? In what ways?

Forensic Questions of Procedure

5. Should some state of affairs be regulated (or not) by some formalized procedure? The practice of abortion is currently legal, although it is regulated by a variety of state and local laws. Those who oppose abortion, obviously, would like to see it made illegal so that all the regulatory procedures that attend illegal

operations (the police, courts, prisons) can be brought to bear on those who participate in abortion.

6. Which procedures can be implemented? Which cannot? Given the current ideological climate in America, the legality of abortion must be defended against those who would outlaw it. So it does not seem likely that a proposal which recommends free abortions for everyone will be readily accepted. Rather, proposals to limit or deter access to abortion have been successful in recent years.

7. What are the merits of competing proposals? What are their defects? Those who support abortion rights have often argued that better and more widely available sex education and wide distribution of free contraceptives would markedly reduce the number of abortions that are performed in this country. Are they right? If their proposals were adopted, could abortion then be made illegal?

A Second Example: Hate Speech

Recently a number of American universities and even a few cities have adopted policies regulating the use of so-called "hate speech." In an article written for the *New York Times,* Anthony DePalma pointed to some of the controversial issues raised by speech codes:

> PROVIDENCE, RI—Douglas Hahn may have thought he was just blowing off steam when he shouted abusive words at fellow students at Brown University last fall, but to others his words constitute harassment.
>
> In any case, he was expelled last month, and the incident drew attention to a growing controversy on campuses about codes of behavior that guard civil rights by limiting freedom of speech. By one count, more than 100 colleges and universities, including Stanford, Emory, Smith, and the University of Massachusetts at Amherst, have tried in recent years to counter escalating racism and bias by enacting campus regulations that hold students to stricter standards of speech and behavior than in society as a whole.
>
> The incident that has again focused attention on these policies occurred about 2 A.M. last Oct. 18. According to a witness and reports in the campus newspaper, Mr. Hahn, who was celebrating his 21st birthday, and several members of his Delta Phi fraternity were walking down Brown Street to Keeney Quad, a freshman dormitory. Mr. Hahn started shouting anti-black comments involving a common obscenity and the word "nigger." The remarks did not appear to be directed at anyone, the witness said.
>
> When a student in the dormitory opened his window and shouted "Keep it down," Mr. Hahn reportedly shouted "What are you, a faggot? What are you, a Jew?" and an obscenity.
>
> The expulsion of Mr. Hahn, a 21-year-old junior from Pittsburgh, is believed to be the first instance in the nation in which a student has been so severely punished for violating such standards. Some praised the action as a strong message against racism; others condemned it, saying they fear that such extreme actions, when com-

bined with new campus codes against hate speech, will inhibit the free exchange of ideas that is the essential commerce of a university.

Those conflicting views have already clashed. A few of the more than 100 college codes identified by the American Civil Liberties Union have been challenged in court and at least one, at the University of Michigan, was overturned on constitutional grounds. Many institutions are reviewing and sometimes amending the codes they adopted a few years ago, to make sure they are constitutional. (*New York Times,* 20 February 1991: B10)

Examination of this issue by means of stasis theory discloses its available propositions, and suggests as well the level and extent of preparation necessary to argue any of these. Often, rhetors have opinions about controversial issues before they are ever called to write or speak about them. If this is the case, a rhetor may use stasis theory to discover whether an opinion, expressed in a proposition, can be supported with strong and persuasive arguments. Use of the stases will also disclose arguments that can be used against a position, so that they can be anticipated and refuted.

Step 1. *Decide whether to formulate the question generally or specifically.*

Possible Formulations of the Question as a Thesis

Does hate speech occur? (conjecture)

What is hate speech, exactly? (definition)

Is hate speech a bad thing? (quality)

Should hate speech be regulated? (procedure)

Possible Formulations of the Question as a Hypothesis

Does hate speech occur on my campus? (conjecture)

What forms does it take on my campus? (definition)

Is hate speech a bad thing on my campus? (quality)

Should hate speech be regulated here? (procedure)

This analysis demonstrates that very different kinds of research are necessary to argue the question as a thesis and as a hypothesis. The general questions require the rhetor to examine the state of affairs on campuses across the country, to examine American values regarding good manners and the limits of expression, and to consider whether regulation of hate speech violates other American practices and policies (such as freedom of speech, for example). A thorough discussion of the question at this level of generality would require at least a book-length treatment, and a good deal of specialized knowledge as well— knowledge about constitutional law, for instance.

The specific questions would require much less preparation and composition, although their scope is still quite large. To answer the first or second hypothetical questions would require some informal research: questioning friends or acquaintances, reading through back issues of the campus newspaper. More formal research might include compiling a list of questions to ask of people who claim to have heard hate speech, or assembling an attitude survey about its effects on the campus climate. Once a rhetor has documented a list of occurrences of hate speech, she or he can define it as it occurs on campus and classify its forms. Either of these questions could be answered in a discourse of three or four pages. Answers to the third hypothetical question, on the other hand, are more difficult to compose since they require an understanding of the educational values of the university in question and of its students. Answers to the fourth require study of the university's existing policies in this area, as well as an understanding of how such policies are generated, implemented, and enforced.

Circumstances sometimes force rhetors to use particular questions even when a general question might produce a more powerful argument. If the rhetor is president of the student body at My State University, for instance, she or he might be suspected of evading the responsibility to represent students at that particular campus if she or he chooses to argue the general question.

Circumstances may also prevent use of the particular questions. If no instances of hate speech can be documented on campus, rhetors who wish to address the issues raised by its regulation must retreat to a more general formulation. The general formulations of the question do present some rhetorical advantages. If they choose to argue any of them, they take up the stand on their own ground, which always works in a rhetor's favor. For example, a proposition based on the first general question might be constructed as follows:

> Hate speech occurs with increasing frequency on American campuses.

Anyone who disagrees with this is forced to argue negatively, which is always more difficult:

> Hate speech never occurs on American campuses.

This is demonstrably untrue, since the controversy surrounding hate speech would not arise at all unless someone, somewhere, had used it. He can modify his negative stance a bit:

> Hate speech occurs so seldom that its use is unimportant or negligible.

This is still a pretty weak proposition, since its probability is diminished by the very fact that hate speech is being discussed.

Step 2. *If you choose to treat the question generally, decide whether to state it theoretically or practically.*

Theoretical questions ask why people behave as they do; practical questions investigate actual human behavior.

General Questions, Stated Theoretically

Is the use of hate speech natural (or unnatural) to human beings?

Do people use hate speech because of their upbringing, or education, or habits, or because their friends and acquaintances use it?

General Question, Stated Practically

What happens when people use hate speech?

This analysis reveals that, as usual, the practical question would be much easier to prepare and argue (although none of these questions are simple). The practical question requires only a study of the practice and its effects, while the theoretical questions inquire into human psychology and sociology. A successful answer to the practical question requires only some empirical evidence about what happens when people use hate speech.

Steps 1 and 2 demonstrate the scope of various arguments on a given question. That is, they show the size of various questions, and hence supply a quick estimate of the work and time required to compose an argument in support of each one. Rhetors can also use stasis theory to get a quick sense of how much research will be necessary in order to argue a given issue. Practicing rhetors need to know whether they have the resources to do justice to a given formulation of an issue. Use of the stases will help them to decide very quickly.

Step 3. *Decide which of the four stases best describes the point at issue in the rhetorical situation at hand.*

Conjecture

Is there an act to be considered? That is, has someone used hate speech in some relevant situation? If hate speech has occurred, try to describe the incidents as accurately and as persuasively as possible (see Quintilian's advice for doing this in the chapter on arrangement). If no incidents of hate speech have occurred, this stasis is not relevant in this case. Move to the next stasis.

Questions to Ask about Conjecture

1. Does hate speech exist? Someone who is opposed to regulation of hate speech could very well argue that it doesn't exist. This is a weak position, however, since the regulation of hate speech would not be under discussion if it hadn't been used. This rhetor can more usefully resort to the stasis of definition, defining hate speech so narrowly or trivially that it seems nonexistent. How widespread is its use? Is it confined to a few small groups of people, or is the general climate permeated with it? A rhetor who supports the regulation of hate speech should catalogue as many incidents of its use as he can find.

2. How did it begin? Answers to this question require some empirical research. When did hate speech first occur in the relevant situation?

3. What causes it? Proponents of regulation can argue that hate speech originates in some unsavory source such as racism, sexism, or religious bigotry. Opponents of regulation can argue that it stems from less offensive sources such as
carelessness or high spirits.

4. Can it be changed? Proponents of regulation can argue that implementation
of a policy prohibiting the use of hate speech can change students' behavior,
thus stopping its use. Opponents can argue that such regulations will not
change behavior, or will only force students to utter hateful remarks in private.

Definition

How can the act be defined? If instances of hate speech have occurred in some
relevant situation, compose a definition of hate speech that describes them as accurately as possible (see the discussion of definition in the chapter on the commonplaces). Your definition should also allow you to take up your stand on
defensible ground. For example, if you define hate speech as "all utterances that
are offensive" you risk including justifiable criticism of someone's behavior
under the heading of hate speech. In case there are no relevant instances of hate
speech to be defined, move to the next stasis.

Questions to Ask about Definition

1. What kind of thing is it? Is hate speech an example of racist, sexist, or big-
oted behavior or attitudes? or is it an example of high spirits, careless good fun,
blowing off steam? Must an utterance be backed by an intent to offend in order
to be classed as hate speech? Someone who supports regulation of hate speech
might define those who oppose it as insensitive clods who underestimate the
power of language to wound and offend others. An opponent of its regulation
might define those who support regulation as extraordinarily sensitive persons
who mistake idle chatter for offensive language.

2. To what larger class of things does it belong? Perhaps hate speech belongs
among the kinds of speech protected by the first amendment to the Constitution. In this case, it can't be regulated—at least not in America.

3. What are its parts? Are racist, sexist, and religiously biased remarks the only
kinds of hate speech? Does hate speech include remarks that slur a person's sexual preferences? His abilities? His appearance? Does "offensive utterances" include pornography? Slang? Four-letter words? Does the use of racist remarks
bear any relation to the use of sexist remarks? To religiously biased remarks?

Quality

How serious is the act? This is a challenging question with regard to the issue of
hate speech. Answers to questions of quality nearly always depend on what is
valued in a given community. (See our analysis of the political and ethical values involved in this question in the chapter on the commonplaces.)

Depending on their ideology, some rhetors may hold that the use of hate
speech is very serious indeed, since it violates the American belief that everyone
has the right to be treated equally and with respect. Others may feel that even

though hate speech is serious, it is primarily a violation of good manners. Others may think it's not very serious at all. Some people may feel that some instances of hate speech are worse than others; women, for example, may feel quite offended by gender-biased representations. At Emory University, according to DePalma, "a women's group on campus charged a fraternity with sexual harassment for wearing T-shirts showing a woman's rear end." The image was accompanied by suggestive comments. Depending on their circumstances and ideology, some persons will think this is not hate speech at all, or at least that it is not as serious as the use of words like "nigger," "faggot," "kike," or "cripple." Others, like the women at Emory, take it very seriously indeed.

Questions to Ask about Quality

1. Is hate speech good or bad? Hate speech is widely regarded as a bad practice, since it breeds divisiveness and unhappiness. Conceivably, rhetors who oppose the regulation of hate speech could argue that its use is sometimes a good thing, since verbal wounds are not as serious as physical ones. That is, they could argue that people must be allowed to express their hatred verbally so that they need not resort to physical violence.

2. Should hate speech be sought or avoided? Rhetors who support regulation of hate speech can argue that rules prohibiting it will force people to avoid its use. Rhetors who oppose regulation of hate speech can argue that rules forbidding it will cause people to seek out instances of its use in the hope of bringing users to justice.

3. Is hate speech right or wrong? Answers to this question of quality depend upon a rhetor's religious or moral beliefs. For example, a rhetor might cite Christ's teaching that humans should love their neighbors as themselves; the use of hate speech is wrong in terms of this religious injunction. On the other hand, a rhetor might cite the first amendment to the American constitution, which protects the right of Americans to utter their opinions without fear of reprisal; the use of hate speech is protected by this legal injunction.

4. Is hate speech honorable or dishonorable? If a rhetor has defined hate speech as an attempt to belittle others, its use is certainly not honorable. If she has defined it as a satisfactory alternative to violence, on the other hand, its use is honorable.

Comparative Questions of Quality

5. Is the unregulated use of hate speech better or worse than a related state of affairs? An opponent of regulation might argue that, if the use of hate speech is regulated, students will not feel free to express their opinions on anything. This repressive state of affairs is certainly not preferable to a state of affairs wherein all speech, even hate speech, is tolerated.

6. Is the use of hate speech more or less desirable than alternatives? A proponent of regulation can argue that the current state of affairs, wherein hate speech runs rampant, is less preferable than one in which students think carefully before they utter remarks that offend others.

7. Is the state of affairs where hate speech is unregulated better or worse than alternatives? This question calls upon rhetors to establish priorities among their values. Is absolute freedom of speech more important than the less offensive climate brought about by regulation of speech?

8. Is the state of affairs where hate speech is unregulated more or less honorable than alternatives? People who oppose regulation can argue that the existence of policies controlling speech demonstrates that the policymakers do not trust individuals to behave honorably. People who support regulation can argue that people have demonstrated by their use of hate speech that they cannot behave honorably without regulation by external authority.

Procedure

Should this act be submitted to some formal procedure? Or, how can this policy be implemented? This stasis is relevant in this case only if a rhetor supports or rejects the implementation of a policy regarding hate speech. If you simply wish to take a position on the use, definition, or value of hate speech, careful and thorough use of the first three stases is sufficient to raise the relevant questions. If you wish to implement a policy that will regulate hate speech, however, you must compose it, and be sure to demonstrate how it will serve its intended function. To do this, you can look at the policies used at other universities. Here, for instance, is a policy that was adopted at the University of Connecticut:

> An action which disrupts or impairs the purposes of the University and its community is subject to penalty under the *Student Conduct Code.* This is the *general principle* for determining whether a violation has occurred even if the action does not violate criminal law. Behaviors which violate the *Student Conduct Code* may also violate criminal or civil law and as such subject to proceedings under the legal system.
>
> Students at The University of Connecticut are subject to the provisions of the *Student Conduct Code* while on University premises or University-related premises or when involved with off-campus University activities. A student who is found guilty of misconduct or is found guilty of being an accessory to misconduct shall be subject to the penalties authorized by this Code:
>
> Students alleged to have committed the following acts are subject to disciplinary procedures of this Code:
>
> 1. Academic Misconduct. (See Section XI of this Code for penalties and procedures related to academic misconduct.)
>
> 2. Disruption of Classes, Seminars, Research Projects, or Activities of the University.
>
> 3. Actual or Threatened Physical Assault or Injury to Persons.
>
> 4. Actual or Threatened Sexual Assault—This includes, but is not limited to, unwanted sexual touching even between acquaintances.
>
> 5. Harassment and/or Intimidation—Engaging in conduct which threatens to cause physical harm to persons or damage to their property; making unwelcome sexual advances or requests for sexual favors. This also covers harassment or intimidation of persons involved in a University disciplinary hearing and of persons in authority who are in the process of discharging their responsibilities.

The face-to-face use of "fighting words" by students to harass any person(s) on University property or on other property to which the *Student Conduct Code* applies is prohibited. "Fighting words" are those personally abusive epithets which, when directly addressed to any ordinary person are, in the context used and as a matter of common knowledge, inherently likely to provoke an immediate violent reaction, whether or not they actually do so. Such words include, but are not limited to, those terms widely recognized to be derogatory references to race, ethnicity, religion, sex, sexual orientation, disability, and other personal characteristics.

6. Disorderly Conduct—Conduct causing inconvenience and/or annoyance which includes any action which can reasonably be expected to disturb the academic pursuits or to interfere with or infringe upon the privacy, rights, privileges, health or safety of members of the University community.

7. Manufacture, Distribution, Sale, Use, Offer for Sale, or Possession of Drugs or Narcotics, or Drug Paraphernalia—The manufacture, distribution, sale, use, offer for sale, or possession of drug paraphernalia or of any illegal drug or narcotic, including barbituates, hallucinogens, amphetamines, cocaine, opium, heroin, marijuana, or any other substance not chemically distinguishable from them except as authorized by medical prescription.

8. Behavior or Activity Which Endangers the Safety of Oneself or Others. . . .

As you can see, this code covers a wide range of activities. Do you want your proposed code to be so sweeping?

If you want to implement, change, or rescind a policy or a procedure, you should find out how policies are generated and implemented at your university or in your community: that is, what committees make policy; where and how policies are published; and who enforces them once they are in place.

As you will see in ensuing chapters of this book, there are many more propositions and arguments available within these issues than those we found by using stasis theory. However, even a preliminary use of this heuristic discloses its rich argumentative possibilities, and points out as well the research and composition that are necessary to argue it persuasively.

EXERCISES

1. Select one of the issues you worked with in the last exercise of chapter 1. Try to frame the theoretical and practical questions raised by it. To determine the theoretical questions, ask yourself: What is the nature or origin of this issue? To determine the practical questions, ask yourself what effects the issue has on people, what is expected of people, what people should do.

   Now try to frame the issue in general, specific, and very specific terms. When you finish this exercise, you should have a list of questions that help you see how much work will be required to argue the issue you have chosen at any level of generality and in theoretical or practical terms. You may discover ways to argue about this issue that you had not thought about before. You should also have a sense of how much research you will need to do to argue the question you eventually choose to pursue.

2. Select one of the issues you worked with in the last exercise in chapter 1, and examine it using the questions suggested by stasis theory. The first time you try this, you may wish to use our examples as models. But since every issue is different (because every rhetorical situation is different), you will soon discover that our models don't raise all the relevant questions for your issue, while they may raise some questions that are not relevant to your issue.

3. Find a compelling letter or op-ed piece on the editorial page of your college newspaper. Write up a brief analysis of the argument that appears in this letter. Here are some questions to ask: What is the issue under debate? Given the writer's account of the issue, can you determine at what stasis the argument seems to lie? That is, does the argument rest at conjecture (X exists; X is a problem)? Definition (X is this kind of thing or event)? Value (X is a good or a bad thing)? Procedure (what should we do)? Can you determine the position that is being argued against? That is, what position or positions is the writer attacking? Can the writer achieve stasis with her opponents, given the way she has stated the issue and the ground upon which she has taken up her stand?

NOTE

1. The system of questions given here does not appear in any one ancient treatise. We have synthesized the four questions out of primary and secondary classical sources (for an illuminating, if complex, account of competing ancient traditions of stasis, see Quintilian's painstaking discussion in the third book of the *Institutes*). Our system is a hybrid, although it is the same one that George Kennedy reconstructs for Hermagoras' lost treatise (1963, 304–313). In particular, our consideration of policy or procedure along with the other three stases is a departure from ancient stasis theory, since the ancients usually classed policy with questions of law (forensic rhetoric), while the first three stases we discuss were ordinarily associated with legislative questions (deliberative rhetoric).

THE COMMONPLACES

For just as all kinds of produce are not provided by every country, and as you will not succeed in finding a particular bird or beast, if you are ignorant of the localities where it has its usual haunts or birthplace, as even the various kinds of fish flourish in different surroundings, some preferring a smooth and others a rocky bottom, and are found on different shores and in diverse regions . . . so not every kind of argument can be derived from every circumstance, and consequently our search requires discrimination.

—Quintilian,
Institutes V x, 21

PERHAPS THE INVENTIONAL device most often associated with ancient rhetoric is that referred to by both ancient and modern rhetoricians as the *topics* (Greek *topos*, "place") or the **commonplaces** (Latin *locis communis*). The word "place" was originally meant quite literally. Lists of topics were first written on papyrus rolls, and students who were looking for a specific topic unrolled the papyrus until they came to the place on the roll where that topic was listed. Later, this graphic meaning of "place" was applied conceptually, to mean an intellectual source or region harboring a proof that could be inserted into any discourse where appropriate. Even later, the terms "topic" and "place" referred to formal or structural inventive strategies, like definition, division, or classification.

Ancient rhetoricians often described the places as though they were hidden away somewhere. Quintilian, for example, defined the topics as "the secret places where arguments reside, and from which they must be drawn forth" (V x, 20). Just as hunters and fishermen need to know where to look for specific kinds of prey, rhetoricians need to be skilled at tracking down suitable proofs. Quintilian's students must have used the topics much as hikers use trail markers—to point them in the right direction to take through the wilderness of all possible proofs. As Cicero wrote to his friend Trebatius, "it is easy to find things that are hidden if the hiding place is pointed out and marked; similarly if we wish to track down some argument we ought to know the places or topics" (*Topics* I, 7).

Some modern scholars treat the commonplaces as representations of structures in the human mind. That is, they argue that the places describe the processes everybody uses to think with, such as comparing and contrasting. But this interpretation gives the commonplaces quite a modern coloring, because it focuses invention on minds or brains rather than on language. The only ancient treatises that lend themselves to such a reading are Aristotle's *Rhetoric* and *Topics.* However, Aristotle also discussed topics drawn from the operations of the Greek language (as in *Topics* I, vii, for example), and he drew as well from the ethical and political issues that confronted fourth-century Athenians (as in *Rhetoric* I, iv).

Nor should the ancient topics be confused with the modern use of the term "topic." In modern thought, topics exist either in a body of knowledge which must be learned or in a thinker's review of her experiences. When modern teachers ask students to assemble a list of topics to write about, they mean that students are to select some piece of knowledge found in books, or in original research, or in some personal experience, as subjects which can be discussed in writing. For ancient rhetoricians, on the other hand, topics existed in the structures of language or in the issues that concerned the community. That is why they were called *common*places—they were available to anyone who spoke or wrote the language in which they were couched and who was reasonably familiar with the ethical and political discussions taking place in the community. No experts need apply. Since the topics yield propositions and proofs drawn from daily discussion and debate—the common sense of a community—they cannot be easily separated from consideration of political, ethical, social, economic, and philosophical issues. And since we want to emphasize the shared aspect of commonplaces, we will use that term for them in this chapter. We use the term "topic" only in our historical discussions of Greek rhetorics, where it might cause confusion to substitute the Latin term.

COMMONPLACES AND IDEOLOGY

Contemporary rhetoricians have another way of speaking about the *sensus communis,* or the common sense that is shared among members of a community: they call it ideology. As we suggested in the first chapter of this book, ideologies are bodies of beliefs, doctrines, familiar ways of thinking that are characteristic of a group or a culture. They can be economic, ethical, political, philosophical, or religious. When we call someone a capitalist or a socialist, we assume that the person subscribes to a set of coherent beliefs about the best way to structure an economy. If we say that someone is a Christian or a Jew, we imply that the person holds a recognizable set of religious values. If we describe someone as a conservative or as a liberal, we imply that the person's political practices are guided by a distinct set of beliefs about human nature. If we refer to someone as a new-ager, a feminist, or an environmentalist, we imply that the person's ethical, economic, social, and political practices are governed by a coherent philosophical position. Capitalism and socialism, Christianity and Judaism, conservatism and liberalism, new-age philosophy, feminism, and environmentalism are examples of ideologies. Some ideologies are older or more sweeping than others, and some are highly respected in given cultures. All are subscribed to with varying degrees of faithfulness by people who are influenced by them.

Ideologies can be held by a person or a group or a culture. No doubt a personal ideology is a result of life experiences and education. But even though personal ideologies grow out of experience, they are not entirely private; experiences, and our memories of them, are influenced by prevailing cultural attitudes about ethnicity, gender, class, appearance, ability, and occupation, among other things.

Groups can coalesce around ideologies such as environmentalism (Greenpeace, The Sierra Club) or fascism (American Nazi Party, skinheads). Groups also coalesce around specific issues: members of Operation Rescue are united by their opposition to abortion; members of NOW (The National Organization for Women) are united by their desire to enact legislation that will secure equality for women. Members of each of these groups may or may not share the same ideologies, however. Some members of Operation Rescue, for example, appear to oppose abortion on religious grounds, while others oppose it for moral or political or social reasons. Members of NOW may subscribe to a variety of feminisms—liberal, radical, cultural, materialist—and it is conceivable that a member of NOW may not be a feminist at all.

Entire cultures may be said to subscribe to a common ideology. There is a perceptible American ideology that centers on values embedded in the Declaration of Independence and the Constitution of the United States. In *Cultural Literacy*, E. D. Hirsch describes America's "civil religion," as he calls it, as follows:

> Our civil ethos treasures patriotism and loyalty as high, though perhaps not ultimate, ideals and fosters the belief that the conduct of the nation is guided by a vaguely defined God. Our tradition places importance on carrying out the rites and ceremonies of our civil ethos and religion through the national flag, the national holidays, and the national anthem (which means "national hymn"), and supports the morality of tolerance and benevolence, of the Golden Rule, and communal cooperation. We believe in altruism and self-help, in equality, freedom, truth telling, and respect for the national law. Besides these vague principles, American culture fosters such myths about itself as its practicality, ingenuity, inventiveness, and independent-mindedness, its connection with the frontier, and its beneficence in the world (even when its leaders do not always follow beneficent policies). It acknowledges that Americans have the right to disagree with the traditional values but nonetheless acquiesce in the dominant civil ethos to the point of accepting imprisonment as the ultimate means of expressing dissent. (98–99)

Has Hirsch captured Americans' commonplace sense of what it means to be an American? Remember that commonplaces are not necessarily true—the distinguishing mark of a commonplace, rather, is that it is widely believed. Remember too that the commonplaces that make up an ideology sometimes contradict one another.

Take patriotism, for example. During the Vietnam war, those who opposed the United States' participation in that war were widely castigated as unpatriotic. A popular slogan, "America—love it or leave it," suggested that anyone who did not support the war did not support American values and hence was not entitled to American citizenship. Those who opposed the war, however, thought of themselves as patriots—as people who loved their country and showed as much by dissenting from its foreign policy (an act which is also quintessentially American, according to Hirsch). Some opponents of the war actually went to prison in order to express their dissent. The boxer Muhammed Ali, who was then called Cassius Clay, is probably the most famous person who was imprisoned for refusing to serve in the war. But thousands of other men were also incarcerated for burning their draft cards or otherwise refusing to be inducted into military service.

For rhetoricians, the point of this example is that while Americans may disagree about what counts as a patriotic act, the commonplace of patriotism—love of country—circulates in American discourse with such power that it affects lives and actions. Disagreements about what patriotism is or about the specific acts that can be classified as patriotic (Serving in the military? Burning your draft card?) are arguments; that is, they can be subjected to invention and rhetors can, ideally, work toward achieving agreement about them. The value of patriotism itself, on the other hand, has an altogether different status if it is a fundamental tenet of American ideology. It seems not to be an argument but a commonplace with such power and scope that its force has to be acknowledged in any discussion about national values or activities.

Here is another list of American commonplaces, written this time by Howard Zinn, whose politics are far to the left of Hirsch's:

> We grow up in a society where our choice of ideas is limited and where certain ideas dominate: We hear them from our parents, in the schools, in the churches, in the newspapers, and on radio and television. They have been in the air ever since we learned to walk and talk. They constitute an American *ideology*—that is, a dominant pattern of ideas. Most people accept them, and if we do, too, we are less likely to get into trouble.
>
> The dominance of these ideas is not the product of a conspiratorial group that has devilishly plotted to implant on society a particular point of view. Nor is it an accident, an innocent result of people thinking freely. There is a process of natural (or, rather *unnatural*) selection, in which certain orthodox ideas are encouraged, financed, and pushed forward by the most powerful mechanisms of our culture. These ideas are preferred because they are safe; they don't threaten established wealth or power.
>
> For instance:
>
> "Be realistic; this is the way things *are*; there's no point thinking about how things *should be*."
>
> "People who teach or write or report the news should be *objective*; they should not try to advance their own opinions."
>
> "There are unjust wars, but also just wars."
>
> "If you disobey the law, even for a good cause, you should accept your punishment."

"If you work hard enough, you'll make a good living. If you are poor, you have only yourself to blame."

"Freedom of speech is desirable, but not when it threatens national security."

"Racial equality is desirable, but we've gone far enough in that direction."

"Our constitution is our greatest guarantee of liberty and justice."

"The United States must intervene from time to time in various parts of the world with military power to stop communism and promote democracy."

"If you want to get things changed, the only way is to go through the proper channels."

"We need nuclear weapons to prevent war."

"There is much injustice in the world but there is nothing that ordinary people, without wealth or power, can do about it."

These ideas are not accepted by all Americans. But they are believed widely enough and strongly enough to dominate our thinking. (3–4)

Zinn's list shows that commonplaces do change. For instance, commonplaces about the threat of communism are not so powerful or widespread now as they were prior to the collapse of Soviet Communism, and the threat of nuclear war does not now seem so menacing as it once did. Nonetheless, all the commonplaces Zinn lists have enjoyed currency within American discourse, and many still harbor the power to stir people to action.

Even though Hirsch and Zinn do not agree precisely about what beliefs constitute an American ideology, they do agree that it exists. Whether we can list its contents precisely or not, everyone who lives in America is affected by its ideology, since its values are embedded in our public discourse. Our coinage says "from many, one" and "in God we trust"; our elementary schoolbooks tell us that "all men are created equal"; our national anthem tells us that America is "the land of the free and the home of the brave." Action movies tell us that life's problems can be solved by violence—the more spectacular the better. Whether we believe these commonplaces or not, they provide the terms within which American discourse works. Rhetors cannot escape the commonplaces of American public discourse, and they overlook them at their peril.

An understanding of ideology, of the common sense of a group or a whole culture, is important to rhetors because people do not respond to a rhetorical proposition out of context. Their responses are determined by the ideologies to which they subscribe. People use commonplaces to express ideological positions. Contemporary commonplaces range from well-worn slogans ("tax and spend," "family values," "when guns are outlawed only outlaws will have guns") to sophisticated texts that encapsulate key beliefs of a given ideology (the platform of a political party, the Bible, a constitution). The persuasive power of rhetorical commonplaces depends upon the fact that they express assumptions held in common by people who subscribe to a given ideology. For example: a first principle of environmental philosophy is preservation of the earth's ecosystem. Within the environmentalist community, people have developed commonplaces that express this principle: "Earth first"; "Think globally,

act locally"; "Good planets are hard to find." These slogans represent the received wisdom of the environmental community in a shorthand that reminds
them of their shared beliefs. They can be deployed whenever the group needs
to be energized or reminded of their ideological commitments.

Rhetorical commonplaces have heuristic potential as well, since they give
rise to an inexhaustible supply of proofs. They can be used as major premises for
arguments (see our discussion of enthymemes), and, like all rhetorical proofs,
they can also be used to persuade others to join the community and to accept its
commitments. For instance, the appeal to traditional family values is currently a
well-worn commonplace. Even though it was initially put into circulation by
conservatives, it has since been adopted by people who subscribe to other political ideologies. A first principle of contemporary American conservativism is
that morality is best transmitted across generations when people live in a traditional nuclear family headed by two parents, where moral authority rests with
the father. Hence a conservative rhetor is likely to argue that Americans could
solve problems as diverse as high rates of teenage pregnancy, drug abuse, or inadequate public schools if only we would return to traditional family values.
The commonplace of family values is a shorthand way for conservatives to express their dismay that most Americans no longer live in traditional nuclear families; its use also strengthens their sense of community. Like all commonplaces,
however, the appeal to family values is very general—which explains why it has
so easily been appropriated by liberals. Nor is it necessarily a good causal explanation for issues such as dilapidated schools and drug abuse, issues which
may or may not be caused by the perceived decline in so-called "family values."
Nevertheless, this commonplace seems to be very persuasive. In fact, it has been
so successful with American audiences in general, we might argue, that it has become a national commonplace. It has even appeared on a bumper sticker (a sure
sign of its status as a commonplace): "Hatred is not a family value."

Like most commonplaces, the commonplace of "family values" also has
heuristic potential. Using it, a rhetor can think through his position on almost
any political issue, from AIDS research (does AIDS threaten families?) to abortion (is this practice anti-family?) to defense systems (how much and what kind
of defense is required to keep American families safe?).

The power of ideology and commonplaces stems from the fact that they reside in the very language we speak and the symbols we rely on. For that reason,
many of our ideological values are hidden from our conscious awareness, just
as Quintilian said they were. Take, for example, the response of the American
people to President George Bush's declaration of war against Iraq in 1991. People who remembered the country's negative reaction to the Vietnam war pre-
dicted that Americans would not support another interventionist war. But
President Bush's rhetoricians succeeded in associating the war with American
values by arguing that it would restore democracy and freedom to the Kuwaiti
people. They invoked powerful symbols of American patriotism—the flag and
yellow ribbons—and suggested that anyone who did not support the war did
not support American soldiers. This strategy, focusing on traditional American
values and symbols, diverted attention away from the hard facts of war itself—
death and destruction, hunger and privation. For a time, the president's popu-

larity soared, thanks to his rhetoricians' skillful use of commonplaces drawn from the rhetoric of American patriotism.

ANCIENT TOPICAL TRADITIONS

Humans have used commonplaces for a very long time. Some historians of rhetoric think they may be related to a memory device used during very ancient times by poets called *rhapsodes,* who traveled about the countryside reciting epic and lyric poetry and telling stories of the gods. Before the time when writing was readily available to most people, rhapsodes recited long poems from memory, and they accomplished this partly by relying on bits of lines or images that they could insert into any recitation wherever they needed a transition or a description or a way to fill out the meter of a line. The poets, who are now known collectively as "Homer," probably repeated phrases like "rosy-fingered dawn" and "the wine-dark sea" to help them remember what came next while they recited lengthy poems (see the chapter on memory).

By the sixth or fifth centuries BCE, rhetoricians might have used commonplaces in the same way, memorizing a stock of arguments that were general enough to be inserted into any speech. Because they had this stock, rhetors were ready to speak on the spot whenever necessary simply by combining and expanding upon the appropriate commonplaces. By including several commonplaces, and amplifying each one, rhetors could lengthen any speech to fit the time allotted them by a rhetorical situation. In the dialogue called *Menexenus,* Plato gives us a glimpse of how this might have been done:

> yesterday I heard Aspasia composing a funeral oration about these very dead. For she had been told, as you were saying, that the Athenians were going to choose a speaker, and she repeated to me the sort of speech which he should deliver—partly improvising and partly from previous thought, putting together fragments of the funeral oration which Pericles spoke, but which, as I believe, she composed. (236b)

In other words, Aspasia used parts of an earlier, similar, speech she had composed in making up a new one. These fragments may have been what were later called commonplaces. They would certainly include arguments that praised the dead, such as Aspasia would need for her funeral oration, and there would be commonplaces of blame as well. Probably there were also commonplaces appropriate for use in the courtroom and in the assembly.

After writing became readily available, lists of commonplaces that had previously served as memory devices could more easily be preserved. Ancient rhetoricians produced at least three topical traditions. One of these is ordinarily identified with sophistic teachers like Tisias and Corax, Theodorus, or Thrasymachus, who may have written the first rhetorical handbooks. No one knows for sure whether any of the Older Sophists wrote handbooks, but if they did, the sections on invention probably contained lists of stock arguments—commonplaces—that could be inserted into any discourse. Aristotle developed this sophistic tradition into a full-blown topical theory of invention.

Two topical traditions were in use during the Hellenistic period and in Roman rhetoric, and both were based on Aristotelian texts. The first was drawn from the *Rhetoric*, the second from the *Topics*. The second tradition appeared prominently in works by Cicero, Quintilian, and minor rhetoricians, and is the system most often referred to by modern rhetoricians when they discuss the classical commonplaces. Some of the commonplaces delineated in this tradition —definition, comparison, and contrast—survive in modern composition textbooks, where they are usually treated as means of arrangement rather than invention. We call them "formal topics," and we discuss them in the chapter of that name.

ARISTOTLE'S COMMON TOPICS

The topical system delineated in Aristotle's *Rhetoric* is tightly bound to the huge system of logical proofs that he erected in his treatises on logic, dialectic, and poetry as well as those on rhetoric and the topics. These treatises taken together reveal in great detail his assumptions about how language can be put to work as a heuristic, a method of finding proofs to use when debating any issue. Like the sophistic topics, Aristotle's common topics comply with intellectual assumptions that are far distant in time and space from our own. Thus they display the foreignness of ancient rhetorical thought more graphically than many of its other features. Nevertheless, Aristotle's topical system is still useful, when updated to account for the commonplaces used in contemporary ideologies.

Aristotle probably did not invent the topics that appear in the *Rhetoric*. They had most likely been in circulation for many years among traveling sophists and teachers. His contribution was to devise a classification scheme for the topics that made sense of them. He divided rhetorical commonplaces into two kinds: those which were suited to any rhetorical argument at all (the *koina* or **common topics**), and those which belonged to some specific field of argument (the *eide*, or **special topics**) (*Rhetoric* I ii, 21). The three common topics are:

1. whether a thing has (or has not) occurred or will (or will not) occur;
2. whether a thing is greater or smaller than another thing, and
3. what is (and is not) possible.

Scholars call these common topics **past/future fact; greater/lesser** or magnitude; and **possible/impossible.** We refer to them here as **conjectures, values,** and **possibilities.**

According to Aristotle, the common topics belonged exclusively to rhetoric because they do not discuss any particular class of things; rather, they are useful for discussing anything whatever. The special topics, on the other hand, dealt with specific arts and sciences: medicine, geometry, physics. Aristotle apparently developed the category of common topics in order to support his argument that, like dialectic, rhetoric was a universal art of investigation. Some authorities on the *Rhetoric* argue that the common topics represent all the kinds of rhetorical questions that can be debated. In other words, an issue has to fall into one of these three categories in order to be available for discussion at all. Other scholars argue that the common topics help people to invent proofs for propositions drawn from the specific arts, chiefly politics and ethics, to which the universal art of rhetoric is most closely related (I ii, 1356a).

Past/Future Fact (Conjecture)

The English word "fact" is ordinarily used to translate the Greek term for "conjecture." However, the facts that can be uncovered by this topic are not irrefutable physical facts in the modern sense; rather, they are educated guesses about something that probably took place in the past or present or about something that will take place in the future. The common topic of past fact is useful in courtrooms, where it is often necessary to speculate about whether something happened or did not happen, while the common topic of future fact is often used in deliberative assemblies, such as legislatures, which have the responsibility to make policy that will be binding on future generations.

Contemporary rhetors resort to the topic of conjecture in order to describe the way things are: what people are like, what the world is like, what society is like.[1] Such conjectures may include portraits of a community's history (past fact), as well as predictions of its future (future fact). Proponents of a given political position can use this topic to argue that certain features of a given society exist, while others don't. For instance, proponents of the current state of affairs can conjecture that the national economy is in great shape: the stock market is thriving, unemployment is low, inflation has been held at bay. Critics of the current state of affairs, on the other hand, can conjecture that the stock market is dangerously out of control, that the figures used to calculate unemployment are misleading, that inflation is occurring on a very small scale.

The Common Topic of Conjecture

What exists.

What does not exist.

The size or extent of what exists.

How things used to be (past fact).

How things will be in the future (future fact).

Strange as it may seem, rhetors disagree vigorously about what exists and how extensive it is. For instance, one of us recently taught a class about the rhetoric of political correctness. A few students in the class argued that there is no such thing as political correctness, while others argued that political correctness did indeed exist on our campus, and that it exerted pressure on students to be careful not to say anything that offended identifiable groups of people. When asked to define "political correctness," members of the class settled on this definition: "Political correctness means not giving offense." We read some books about political correctness, whose authors agreed that it exists but disagreed both about what it is and about its extent or seriousness. In *Illiberal Education*, Dinesh D'Souza argues that political correctness is "an unofficial ideology" that generates pressure to conform among students and faculty at American universities (xv). According to John K. Wilson, however, conservatives like D'Souza use the term "to convey the image of a vast conspiracy controlling American colleges and universities" (4). When used by contemporary conservatives, according to Wilson,

> political correctness described a broad movement that had corrupted the entire system of higher education. By this transformation the conservatives accuse universities of falling under the influence of extremist elements. For conservatives, "I'm not politically correct" became a badge of honor, a defense against a feared attack—even though no one had been seriously accused of being politically incorrect. (4)

In other words, D'Souza conjectures political correctness as a powerful ideology that stifles freedom of speech on American campuses. Wilson, on the other hand, conjectures political correctness as itself a rhetoric mounted by conservatives in order to brand universities as hotbeds of coercive liberal or leftist thought. Both of these conjectures take the issue of political correctness far more seriously than did the students who conjectured it to be a matter of etiquette— a way of speaking that doesn't give offense.

From a rhetorician's point of view, nothing is to be gained by trying to determine which of these conjectures about political correctness is true. Persons who accept either of them believe they are true because each stems from and affirms a world view—an ideology. It is important for rhetors to understand the commonplaces and arguments deployed in each of these conjectures and how they are implicated in ideological positions, and to determine the actual or potential effects of each conjecture in order to decide which causes the least public harm.

Here is another example of the way conjecture works in contemporary American discourse. Stephanie Coontz, who teaches courses about the history of the family, asked her students to write down images of "the traditional family." In her book called *The Way We Never Were*, Coontz lists some of those images:

> One is of extended families in which all members worked together; grandparents were an integral part of family life, children learned responsibility and the work ethic from their elders, and there were clear lines of authority based on respect for age. Another is of nuclear families in which nurturing mothers sheltered children from premature exposure to sex, financial worries, or other adult concerns, while fathers taught adolescents not to sacrifice their education by going to work too early. Still another image gives pride of place to the couple relationship. In traditional families, my students write—half derisively, half wistfully—men and women remained chaste until marriage, at which time they extricated themselves from competing obligations to kin and neighbors and committed themselves wholly to the marital relationship, experiencing an all-encompassing intimacy that our more crowded modern life seems to preclude. (8)

Needless to say, all of these images are conjectures that are associated with the commonplace of "traditional family values." Coontz argues in her book that the rhetorical conjecture of the traditional family had practical, real-life downsides for both men and women, downsides that never appeared on *Leave It to Beaver* and *The Donna Reed Show*:

> All women, even seemingly docile ones, were deeply mistrusted. They were frequently denied the right to serve on juries, convey property, make contracts, take out credit cards in their own name, or establish residence. A 1954 article in *Esquire* called working wives a "menace"; a *Life* author termed married women's employment a "disease." Women were excluded from several professions, and some states even gave husbands total control over family finances. There were not any permissible alternatives to baking brownies, experimenting with new canned soups, and getting rid of stains around the collar.
>
> Men were also pressured into acceptable family roles, since lack of a suitable wife could mean the loss of a job or promotion for a middle-class man. Bachelors were categorized as "immature," "infantile," "narcissistic," "deviant," or even "pathological." Family advice expert Paul Landis argued: "Except for the sick, the badly crippled, the deformed, the emotionally warped and the mentally defective, almost everyone has an opportunity (and, by clear implication, a duty) to marry." (32–33)

Of course, Coontz' argument is itself a mixture of conjectures and the extrinsic proofs called "testimony." For rhetoricians, it is worth asking what rhetorical and actual, practical effects would have occurred if Coontz' conjecture about family life in the 1950s had been portrayed in the media more frequently than it was.

Greater/Lesser (Values)

Aristotle anchored his discussion of the topic of greater and lesser in his notion of the golden mean. We know that which is great, he wrote, when it is compared to the normal; likewise for that which is small (I vii, 1363b). "Greater" and "smaller" are always relative to each other: greatness can be measured by the fact that it exceeds something else, while smallness is always exceeded by something else. The relation of these terms is easy enough to illustrate with examples from the physical world: if the average person is about five feet eight inches tall, then the average basketball player will be taller since this class of people is marked to some extent by the requisite of tallness. But more difficult, and more interesting, applications of the topic occur when we move to the realm of values. To call someone "a great leader" implies a norm against which greatness is measured—the average leader. The implied existence of such a norm also permits us to contemplate the existence of lesser leaders.

Athenian citizens of ancient times apparently agreed on a list of common public values. At any rate, ancient rhetoric texts regularly list goodness, justice, honor, and expediency as important values. While these terms obviously do not mean the same thing to us as they meant to Aristotle, we can still use them to name values that are supposedly common in our own public discourse. Certainly, contemporary rhetors resort to the common topic of value in order to establish what is good, just, honorable, or expedient. These values can be phrased in terms of their opposites, as well—what is bad, unjust, dishonorable, or inexpedient. The common topic of greater/lesser can also be used to establish the relations between degrees of goodness, justice, and so on. Rhetors can argue that some state of affairs is better, more just, more honorable, or more expedient than another, or less so. They can also argue that changes in these values have occurred over time: Some state of affairs is less good than it used to be, or will deteriorate in the future.

To return to our example about economics: Using the common topic of greater/lesser, all parties in a discussion may agree that economic prosperity exists; however, they may disagree about whether or not this is relatively a good, just, honorable, or expedient state of affairs. Using the topic of greater/lesser, for example, a proponent of the current state of affairs can argue that economic prosperity is better than recession, since prosperity allows more people to be employed, to feed and clothe their families, and to save for retirement. A critic of the current state of affairs, using the topic of greater/lesser, can argue that the good brought about by general prosperity is offset by the fact that the very rich are profiting from good times far more than are the poor. As this example demonstrates, the topic of greater/lesser can be applied generally or selectively: A rhetor can argue that what is good for one segment of the community is good for all; or he can argue that what is good for one group isn't necessarily good for everyone, or isn't good for other groups in the community.

The Common Topic of Greater/Lesser

What is greater than the mean or norm.

What is lesser than the mean or norm.

What is relatively greater than something else.

What is relatively lesser than something else.

What is good, just, beautiful, honorable, enjoyable, etc.

What is better, more just, etc.

What is less good, less just, etc.

What is good, etc., for all persons.

What is good, etc., for a few persons or groups.

What has been better, etc., in the past.

What will be better, etc., in the future.

The topic of greater/lesser obviously lends itself to questions of value. Let us return, then, to the issue of abortion in order to illustrate its argumentative possibilities. The analysis which follows touches on only a few of the many arguments opened by this rich commonplace.

Using greater/lesser, rhetors who oppose the legal status of abortion can argue that more abortions are performed when the practice is legal (that is, the number of abortions is greater under the current circumstances); a rhetor who supports legalization can argue, though, that there are fewer unsafe abortions performed when the operation is legal. But greater and lesser are not only relative to each other; there are relative degrees of magnitude and minuteness. So, the first rhetor could rejoin that if abortions were illegal, fewer abortions would be performed overall; this decrease in turn would reduce the relative number of unsafe abortions.

Tying the topic of greater/lesser to values, an opponent of abortion can argue that legal abortion is not a good thing; nor is it just, or enjoyable, or beautiful. Furthermore, relative to other means of birth control, abortion is less good. Her opponent can argue, on the other hand, that abortion is better than bringing unwanted children into the world; that justice means extending the same rights to women that are extended to men (on the ground that men's reproductive practices are not legislated by the state); that while abortion is of course neither enjoyable or beautiful it is sometimes the only available practical alternative. An opponent of abortion can argue that while abortion may be good for individual women, it is obviously not good for the fetus; less obviously, it is not good for members of an immediate family or for society at large; a rhetor who supports legalized abortion can argue that the availability of the practice is nonetheless better for women, who currently constitute a majority of the population. A rhetor who is opposed to abortion can argue that things were better (and more just and more honorable) in the past when abortion was not legal and women were forced either to bear every pregnancy to term or to undergo an illegal abortion. A rhetor who supports legalized abortion, on the other hand, can argue that things were worse in the past when alternative means of birth control were not available and women were forced either to bear every pregnancy to term or to seek out some back-alley abortionist. Finally, a rhetor who opposes abortion can argue that legal abortion is not good for future generations, who will lack the proper respect for human life if abortion becomes a routine option. A rhetor who supports legalized abortion, on the other hand, can argue that the future will be better if unwanted and uncared-for children are never brought into the world.

Our balanced list of value arguments about abortion may give the impression that we are indecisive or heartless (see the chapter on ethos). We are not indecisive about this issue, and we are sensitive to the emotional costs of abortion. If we were actually arguing the issue of abortion for an audience we would never present all of the arguments produced by the common topic of greater/lesser. We would not even present all of the arguments in favor of our own positions (see the chapter on arrangement). Here, however, for purposes of demonstration we have used the topic of greater/lesser as a heuristic, to discover the wide range of arguments that are available on this or almost any issue. Our analysis also demonstrates that if rhetors examine all available arguments raised by the common topics, they will come across arguments that follow from their position which may be distasteful to them. In other words, rhetors who use the common topics vigorously and thoroughly must be prepared to discover arguments that they do not like. This is why thorough examination of an issue sometimes brings rhetors to change their minds.

Possible/Impossible (Possibilities)

Rhetors resort to the common topic of possible/impossible in order to establish that change either is or isn't possible, now or in the future. For example, proponents of the current state of affairs might use this topic to argue that it is impossible for inflation to occur during a period of economic prosperity. Critics can argue the opposite position, that it is possible for inflation to occur at such times. Rhetors using this topic can argue that it is impossible for this period of prosperity to become unstable today, but it might become so in six months or a year. A critic, on the other hand, can argue that it is entirely possible that current economic strategies will bring about instability in the marketplace. Strange as it may seem, rhetors can also argue about past possibilities: Anthropologists do this when they argue about whether it was possible for some hypothetical set of events to have occurred in the past—was it possible for *homo sapiens* to have developed a larger brain without an opposable thumb? Without an upright posture? Writers of popular nonfiction are especially fond of the topic of the past possible: Is it possible that an extraterrestrial vehicle crashlanded in the desert around Roswell, New Mexico in 1949? Is it possible that President Kennedy was killed not by a lone assassin but by a band of conspirators?

Use of this topic also admits degrees of possibility/impossibility. While it may not be possible to stabilize economic prosperity for all groups, it may be more (or less) likely that this can be done in the future.

The Common Topic of Possible/Impossible

What is possible.

What is impossible.

What is more or less possible.

What is possible in the future.

What is impossible in the future.

What was possible or impossible in the past.

We return the issue of hate speech to illustrate the uses of this rich Aristotelean commonplace. Is it possible that hate speech occurs on our campus? A rhetor who opposes the implementation of a speech code could argue that it is impossible that students at Our State University would be tactless or insensitive enough to use language that offends people. An opponent could argue that, given the strain of student life, it is possible that ordinarily tactful and sensitive people could, on occasion, utter an offensive remark unless they were aware that the possibility exists that they could be punished for saying offensive things. Or, noting the existence of some group that is known for its opposition to certain other groups, a rhetor could argue that it is quite possible that members of this group could utter offensive remarks. Or, noting the currency of racism or sexism in our culture, a rhetor could argue that it is quite possible that hate speech would be used on some occasion. Rhetors who oppose implementation of a speech code could argue that it is possible that such a code will stifle free speech. Arguing from relative possibilities, those who support a code could argue, alternatively, that its implementation increases the possibility that those who might otherwise utter offensive remarks will keep these to themselves.

The topic of probabilities is also used regularly in discussions of abortion. Proponents of legalized abortion argue that it is not possible to stop women from having abortions by means of legislation against it. Opponents argue that it is possible to stop women from having abortions, and they seek to do so either by passing laws against it or by bringing the moral authority of the community to bear.

THE TOPICS AND AMERICAN IDEOLOGIES

A rhetor's persuasive use of topics is affected by the ideologies or networks of interpretation through which they are filtered and received. Ideologies vary because people are differently located in terms of gender, age, ethnicity, class, economic situation, religious beliefs, education, and the political or cultural power they possess. A rhetor who uses the topics as a means of invention should take careful account of whether or not her discourse will be well received by an audience whose ideological affiliations may prescribe very different versions of what exists, what is good, and what is possible than the versions of these commonplaces that are espoused by the rhetor.

Conventionally, political and ethical ideologies may be distinguished from one another if they are placed along an imaginary line or spectrum:

An Ideological Spectrum

Left   Center   Right

Political theorists decide whether to place a given position on the left or right side of this spectrum depending on its adherents' views about a number of issues. Political positions such as socialism, democratic socialism, some versions of communism (Castroism, for example), and liberalism are conventionally placed on the left wing of the ideological spectrum. We list these positions in order of their decreasing leftward leaning: socialism is farthest left, while liberalism is only slightly left of center. On the right wing of the spectrum are fascism, American neo-conservatism (the "new right"), and traditional conservatism. We list these ideologies in order of their decreasing rightward leaning: traditional conservatism—which today seems very close to nineteenth-century free-market liberalism—is just right of center on the political spectrum, while fascism is farthest to the right. Of course the range of political possibilities is much more complex than we have suggested here. Many more positions on the spectrum are represented in the world than appear in the United States; Italy, for example, has over one hundred political parties, each representing a slightly different position on the spectrum:

An Ideological Spectrum

In current American rhetoric there is debate about the following issues, stated very generally.

1. What is the appropriate foreign policy (nationalism, internationalism, interventionism, pacifism)?
2. What is the role of the federal government in making legislation as opposed to the roles of state and local governments?
3. What level of fiscal responsibility do citizens bear toward federal, state, and local government?
4. What social and economic relations should appropriately maintain among citizens (more or less personal freedom? more or less economic equality among classes, races, and genders?).
5. What levels of political and legal equality should exist among genders, races, classes, and sexualities (none, some, full equality)?
6. What is the appropriate relation to authority (acceptance, questioning, skepticism, rejection)?
7. What is the appropriate role for government to play in legislating moral issues (none, some, a lot)?
8. What is or should be the relation of human beings and governments to the environment?[2]

The answers given to these questions by individuals or groups give clues about the ideologies to which they subscribe, although these clues are not infallible.

Two ideologies dominate contemporary political and ethical discourse in the United States: liberalism and conservatism. There are fascists, anarchists, libertarians, social democrats, and socialists in this country, but their views are generally not sufficiently widespread within mainstream discourse to generate national commonplaces. In what follows, we attempt to describe commonplaces that are generally accepted by persons who subscribe to liberalism or conservatism. These lists are not meant to imply that all persons calling themselves "liberal" or "conservative" subscribe to every commonplace named in those categories. Nor are they meant to imply that someone who subscribes to one or more liberal or conservative commonplaces is necessarily a liberal or a conservative. In short, "conservative" and "liberal" do not refer to identities; rather they depict positions on an ideological spectrum. That is to say: What follows is a series of conjectures about contemporary American political discourse.

Contemporary American liberalism tends to support capitalism, but people who subscribe to liberal politics usually feel more secure if business can be regulated by government. Sometimes people who accept liberalism will support policies that lean toward socialism—for instance, some argue that there should be free health care for all citizens who cannot afford it. Liberalism tends to be internationalist insofar as its supporters want to maintain good relations with other countries. Those who subscribe to liberalism may, in fact, oppose war of any kind. The core of American liberalism, however, is support for a high degree of individual freedom and advocacy of social and economic equality for all. Liberalism promotes a positive view of human nature; its proponents believe that human beings are naturally good or at least tend toward good action. If people do not behave well, the liberal assumption is that there is or has been some impediment or lack in their lives and environment that has kept them from fulfilling their potential. Liberalism tends to be skeptical of authority (this is in keeping with the high value that it places on individuality). Those who accept liberalism usually advocate government intervention in social and economic issues to correct what they perceive as unfair distribution of wealth, but they generally resist intervention by any authority into moral choices, which they tend to characterize as "private" matters in keeping with their emphasis on individual freedom and their skepticism about authority.

People who accept the tenets of American conservatism part company with liberalism on most of these issues. Support of capitalism and business are traditional conservative values. Conservatism tends to be nationalist insofar as its adherents want the United States to be the most important nation in the world, and people who accept conservatism will sometimes support military intervention in the affairs of other nations in order to further the goal of U.S. supremacy (unless they are isolationists). People who subscribe to conservative commonplaces support personal freedom, but they care less about individual rights than liberals do, since they think that the greater good of the group is more important than individual desire. This is in keeping with conservative respect for tradition and authority, especially that of the family and of religion. Conservatism is skeptical about the perfectibility of human nature—its adherents generally do not assume that everyone is naturally good at heart. Nonetheless, a central tenet of conservatism is that people must take responsibility for their actions. Conservatism also assumes that people who do not take such responsibility must accept the community's decisions regarding their actions. People who subscribe to traditional conservatism do not care for government intervention in social or economic matters, arguing instead that free enterprise will take care of poverty and social inequality. At present, however, people who subscribe to the collection of commonplaces called "neo-conservatism" do advocate government intervention in moral matters. In fact, those who accept neo-conservatism believe that political struggles must be waged in the cultural arena. The neo-conservative pundit Pat Buchanan put it this way: "Culture is the Ho Chi Minh trail of power; you surrender that province and you lose America."

The positions we ascribe to conservatives and liberals are commonplaces within those discourses. Thus, in conservative rhetoric, appeal to traditional family values is a commonplace, while appeal to personal freedom for individuals—

now usually cast in the discourse of "individual rights"—is a commonplace in liberal rhetoric. For heuristic purposes, we now explore how people who accept liberal and conservative commonplaces, respectively, would answer the questions named above as major issues in American rhetoric. Remember that we are operating on the level of the commonplace. The positions we delineate are positions that follow ideologically from liberal and conservative rhetoric. As such, they may not apply at all times and in all places to people who identify themselves as liberals or conservatives.

1. *What is the appropriate foreign policy?*
Generally, liberalism favors peaceful interaction with other countries. Liberals ordinarily support the United Nations and other global political organizations. Conservatism is not so inclined to favor global political efforts, especially if these efforts are perceived to interfere with America's political preeminence in the world. Liberalism is not inclined to support military intervention into the affairs of other countries, while conservatism will support intervention into foreign affairs if such intervention can be characterized as necessary to the preservation of America's position as a world leader. There are exceptions, of course, as there are to any commonplace. Liberals in the Kennedy and Johnson administrations maintained and escalated the Vietnam War, for instance.

2. *What is the role of the federal government in making legislation as opposed to the roles of state and local governments?*
Currently, people who describe themselves as conservative say they are opposed to "big government," and conservatives in the United States Congress have recently supported legislation that passes fiscal responsibility for social programs such as welfare onto state and local governments. Conservative rhetoric typically depicts liberals as favoring federal intervention into many aspects of cultural and social life. Conservative rhetors have argued, for instance, that liberals restricted Americans' personal freedom when they imposed affirmative action and environmental regulations. Conservative rhetors would prefer that individuals and corporations assume responsibility for any initiatives that are necessary to protect the environment and to care for those who cannot care for themselves; conservatism assumes that market pressures will urge individuals and corporations to ensure that these things happen. Liberalism, on the other hand, typically supports legislation that is intended to correct what its adherents perceive as social wrongs. Social security, civil rights legislation, affirmative action, medicare and medicaid were all sponsored by liberals.

3. *What level of fiscal responsibility do citizens bear toward federal, state, and local government?*
Currently, rhetors who subscribe to conservatism argue that the tax burden on citizens should be lessened, while rhetors who accept liberal beliefs argue that certain initiatives are so important to social and economic progress that taxpayers must continue to shoulder the burden of financing them (hence the conservative commonplace used to describe liberal administrations: "tax and spend"). Rhetors who accept liberalism generally argue that these social initiatives should include at least social security and medicare.

4. *What social and economic relations should appropriately exist among citizens?*
The rhetoric of liberalism champions social and economic equality. In fact, the American doctrine that "all men are created equal" is borrowed from eighteenth-century liberal thought. Given its distrust in the perfectability of human nature, conservatism is not sure that all people are created equal to one another in intelligence and ability. However, contemporary conservatives (usually) defend the principle that all citizens are equal before the law.

5. *What levels of political and legal equality should exist among genders, races, classes, and sexualities?*
In keeping with their faith in equality, those who accept liberalism profess that all citizens—no matter their gender, race, class, sexuality, ability, or age—should be treated equally, at least in law. For those who accept conservatism, on the other hand, and especially for those who respect tradition and authority—equality among genders, races, and sexualities is a more complicated and vexed issue. Strict adherence to traditional beliefs requires an American conservative to assume that men best fulfill their social and moral duties, if not their nature, when they take care of and protect women. Traditional conservatism assumes further that heterosexuality is a norm. Hence people who accept this position are not sure that full legal equality should apply to women or to homosexuals.

6. *What is the appropriate relation to authority?*
In keeping with their respect for instituted authority and their emphasis on personal responsibility, conservative rhetors tend to take tough stands on crime and punishment and on enforcement of the law. In keeping with their respect for individual rights and the potential perfectibility of human nature, on the other hand, liberal rhetors tend to advocate prevention and rehabilitation rather than punishment for offenders. It makes ideological sense that people who subscribe to liberalism would be more skeptical of received religious wisdom or traditional notions about family structure than are those who subscribe to conservative positions.

7. *What is the appropriate role for government to play in legislating moral issues?*
People who subscribe to liberalism tend to resist government intervention into realms that they define as "private." This is why liberal rhetors generally support legal abortion, and why many persons of liberal persuasion think that the use of marijuana and perhaps other proscribed drugs should be legalized. These days conservative rhetors, if they share conservatism's elevation of the good of the community over individual rights, tend to support legislative intervention into realms that liberals define as "private." Hence, they are generally opposed to the legalization of drugs and abortion on the ground that drug use and abortion negatively affect the community at large, even though they may benefit specific individuals. Liberal rhetors tend to argue against censorship on the ground that censorship is a restriction of the individual right to free speech. Conservative rhetors, on the other hand, tend to support censorship, on the ground that the circulation of some materials—pornography, for example—is deleterious to the public good. It is not always easy to predict liberal and conservative positions on moral issues, however. For instance, some liberal

feminists support restrictions on the distribution of pornography. Liberal rhetors tend to support restrictions on smoking in public areas, while conservative rhetors tend to oppose such measures.

8. *What is or should be the relation of human beings and governments to the environment?*
It is hard to delineate conservative and liberal positions on environmental issues. The term "conservation" is etymologically related to the term "conservative," which suggests that the desire to conserve or preserve natural phenomena is or should be a conservative position. Protection of the common good is also a conservative goal, and preservation of the environment would seem to serve that goal as well. However, in today's political economy, environmentalists tend to be liberals or even left-of-liberal. Conservative disinterest in this issue may have to do with conservatism's general support of business, which often finds itself at odds with environmental protection. Liberal rhetors, on the other hand, have traditionally favored legislative intervention to correct what they perceive to be wrongs, and so it is they who have typically proposed environmental regulations. However, support for environmentalism can place liberals in difficult rhetorical positions, since environmentalists would like to place limits on the use of automobiles (thus restricting the individual right to freedom of movement) and on human reproduction (thus restricting the freedom of individuals to have as many children as they wish).

THE POLITICAL AND ETHICAL COMMONPLACES

Aristotle would have called liberal and conservative commonplaces "special topics," since they have to do with ethics and politics. He thought of these arts as more specialized than rhetoric, which he treated as a universal art of inquiry. Given that we have chosen to use the Latin term "commonplace" in our discussion, to adopt Aristotle's terminology here would cause some confusion, since we would be forced to call the places that are specific to political and ethical issues something like "special places." So we will persist in using the more general term "commonplace" as a sort of blanket to cover arguments that are generated through use of all of Aristotle's topics, both common and special. Using the commonplaces that appear in contemporary versions of conservativism and liberalism, then, we can now work out how advocates of each position might use Aristotle's common topics of conjecture, values, and possibilities to find proofs for pressing issues. We first present very brief lists of arguments that may be found on a variety of issues by using the topics. Then we apply them more extensively and systematically to two exemplary issues.

We recommend that, after studying our examples, readers choose some issue that interests them and work slowly through Aristotle's topics, using them to probe for proofs on the issue. As Quintilian warned, not all of the topics will be appropriate for use on every issue. Practice and experience are the best guides to their proper use.

Conjecture

Disagreement often stems from the fact that rhetors interpret the same reality differently. Conservative rhetors interpreted the Vietnam War as a fight against the spread of international communism, while liberal rhetors viewed America's role in the conflict as an intrusion into a local civil war. Liberal rhetors interpret welfare as necessary support for those who cannot support themselves; conservative rhetors interpret it as an oppressive system that keeps people from achieving self-reliance. After an outbreak of disturbances in south-central Los Angeles in the summer of 1992, liberal rhetors argued that people who lived in the area were frustrated because poverty and underemployment were rampant in the area. Conservative rhetors denied that description of reality. Instead, they blamed the disturbances on past fact—people who lived in south-central Los Angeles were frustrated with the failure of liberal administrations during the 1960s to make good on their promises to help them develop economic opportunities.

Rhetors' depictions of the present state of affairs necessarily affect their descriptions of future facts. Liberal rhetors argued from their depiction of the present state of affairs in Los Angeles that poverty and unemployment would continue in the south-central portion of the city unless the federal government intervened with social programs aimed at changing this state of affairs. Conservatives argued that this would only perpetuate liberal policies that had already been shown to be inadequate, and argued instead that intervention should be left to free enterprise.

Greater/Lesser

Using this topic, a rhetor can argue that even though poverty exists in the United States, it isn't as severe as that experienced in other countries. She or he can argue as well that it is relatively easy (or relatively difficult) to solve the problem of poverty, compared to other problems we face. A liberal rhetor may argue that it is better to address poverty than to fund defense spending. A conservative rhetor may argue that it is better for poverty to be addressed by local or state agencies or by free enterprise, while defense spending is necessarily a federal priority because it protects the nation as a whole. If a rhetor is forced by circumstances to admit that a given situation is less good, or right, or just, or preferable than some other state of affairs, this commonplace can be used to argue that these negative features are actually a relative good. Conservative rhetors who are forced to acknowledge the existence of poverty and unemployment sometimes argue that the poor deserve their lot, since they refuse to take responsibility for themselves. Liberal rhetors counter this conjecture by arguing that since a capitalist economy dictates that a certain percentage of the citizenry will inevitably suffer from poverty, government is obligated to support its poorer citizens. Finally, using the topic of greater/lesser, a liberal rhetor can argue that the achievement of financial equity for all people is more important than accumulation of wealth by the few. Conservative rhetors can argue that free enterprise is preferable to socialist desires to redistribute wealth, since a free market enhances initiative and fosters community growth.

Possibilities

This topic is regularly put to use in contemporary discussions about environmental protection. Corporations and factory owners often argue that it is not possible for them to conform to clean-air regulations and maintain their present levels of production. Sometimes they argue that while conformity may be possible in the future, it is not possible at the present time. Environmentalists argue, on the other hand, that it is entirely possible that human activity is causing global warming. They argue further that it is impossible for the environment to survive present levels of pollution and degradation.

An Example

In order to give an extended illustration of how Aristotle's topics aid invention, we return to the issue we analyzed in the previous chapter: the regulation of hate speech. This is primarily an ethical issue, although it can become political when hate speech is defined as speech protected by the First Amendment. In any case, rhetors who address it can use liberal and conservative commonplaces having to do with personal freedoms, relationship to authority, and social equality. As was demonstrated by our application of stasis theory to this issue in the previous chapter, a rhetor can treat hate speech as an issue of conjecture, definition, or quality, depending upon the rhetorical situation. Here we treat it as a procedural question. Two broad procedural positions are available on this issue: a rhetor may either favor or oppose regulating the use of hate speech. Our example does not use all the available commonplaces, although all are theoretically available for use with any issue.

Using the Topic of Conjecture

What exists?

What does not exist?

What is the size or extent of what exists?

Did it exist in the past?

Will it exist in the future?

Using the commonplace of "what exists," rhetors who wish to regulate hate speech can paint a picture of the university as beset by an epidemic of slurs against certain groups. They can mention epithets painted on walls, shouted from windows. Using the topic of size or extent, they can try to show that the problem is widespread, and that it represents a general climate of hatred on campus. Using the topic of past conjecture, they may argue that the climate is worse than it used to be, and may use the topic of future conjecture to show that the situation contains little promise of improvement unless something is done. Rhetors who oppose regulation, on the other hand, can describe the campus scene as peaceful and harmonious, or can argue that incidents of hate speech are isolated and do not occur very often, or that they are the work of just a few people who can be disciplined and removed from the scene, if necessary. They may argue that the situation is better than it was in the past, since a few guilty persons have been removed from the scene. They can point out that this local action mitigates the need for a blanket policy regarding hate speech which, after all, anticipates that a need for regulation will arise in the future. If the rhetors who oppose regulation are conservative, they may conjecture that students are responsible people who do not need policies to keep them from behaving badly. A conservative who favors regulation, on the other hand, can point out that groups often need to adopt rules and enforce them in order to regulate the behavior of individuals who, inevitably, cannot restrain themselves. Liberal rhetors who favor regulation have much precedent for their argument, since liberal procedure historically has been to adopt regulations that are intended to protect defenseless people from harm. These rhetors, then, can conjecture the campus as a scene where frequent belittling remarks injure students' self-esteem. A liberal who opposes regulation, of course, can always appeal to the individual right to free speech.

Using the Topic of Value

What is greater than the mean or norm.

What is lesser than the mean or norm.

What is relatively greater than something else.

What is relatively lesser than something else.

What is good, just, beautiful, honorable, enjoyable, etc.

What is better, more just, etc.

What is less good, less just, etc.

What is good, etc., for all persons.

What is good, etc., for a few persons or groups.

What has been better, etc., in the past.

What will be better, etc., in the future.

Rhetors who favor regulation of hate speech can use the topic of values to show why hate speech should be regulated. Generally, they can take the position that hate speech is bad, unjust, dishonorable, or inexpedient, and that regulation of it is therefore good, just, honorable, and expedient. Not all of these topics will be useful or necessary in any given case, of course, but in general each should produce arguments for any case. For example, rhetors can argue that the use of hate speech is unjust on the ground that it discriminates among persons according to unacceptable criteria such as gender or appearance. Or they can argue that the use of hate speech is inexpedient since it can foment uneasiness and even violence on campus.

Relative value arguments are also available: rhetors can argue that regulation of hate speech, even though it impedes personal freedom, is better than unbridled expression of racist or sexist opinions, for example. Or they might argue that regulation is not a good idea since it affects everyone on campus, while the expression of hate speech affects only a few. If rhetors who favor regulation are liberals, they face a quandary, given that liberals think of individual freedoms (including freedom of speech) as good, just, and expedient. However, liberals also think of social equality as a good, and hate speech can be construed as an attack on the right of equal access for certain groups. This dilemma can be resolved by using the topic of greater/less: in other words, rhetors can decide which liberal value—freedom of speech or social equality—is more important. Or, they can argue that hate speech is so disruptive and so immoral that an exception must be made to their general support for freedom of speech. Whether they can support regulation of hate speech depends on whether they define it as a political or ethical issue, since liberals generally support intervention that regulates matters of social equity, but they do not approve of legislation of moral matters.

If rhetors who favor regulation are conservatives, they also face a value dilemma. They are not likely to be impressed by the argument that hate speech impedes progress toward social equality, since this is not high on their list of goods. However, they may favor regulations that curtail abusive verbal behavior by individuals in the interests of maintaining harmony in the wider community.

Using the topic of values, rhetors who oppose regulation of hate speech may argue that such regulation is neither good, just, honorable, nor expedient. It would be difficult for them to argue that hate speech is good, just, and honorable, but use of this topic shows that such positions are available if they wish to defend any of them. A more defensible argument is available to these rhetors, however. They may argue that a policy of regulation imposes the values of some on the entire group, and for that reason, regulation is unjust. If the rhetors are liberals, they can characterize those who use hate speech as exercising their right to free speech, although they face the same dilemma as liberal rhetors who favor regulation, insofar as they have to decide whether individual freedom is more important than social equity in this case. If rhetors who oppose regulation are conservatives, they can use the topic of values to argue that university policies are not appropriate means for regulating hate speech, which should be policed instead by family and religious authority; these rhetors can also argue that students have a personal responsibility to behave respectfully toward others.

Using the Topic of Possibilities

What is possible.

What is impossible.

What is more or less possible.

What is possible in the future.

What is impossible in the future.

What was possible or impossible in the past.

Using the topic of possibilities, rhetors who favor regulation of hate speech must consider whether it is possible to curtail hate speech by such means. They must also examine whether such a policy will have the desired effect in the future as well. Rhetors who oppose regulation, of course, can argue that it is not possible to regulate verbal behavior; they can suggest as well that it was impossible for hate speech to have occurred in the past since the term itself is a recent invention.

Another Example

Recently, a student at our university invented an organization that he called STRAIGHT. The acronym stands for Students Reinforcing Adherence In General Heterosexual Tradition. The mission of the organization, according to a draft of its constitution, is as follows:

> The purpose of STRAIGHT is to provide students with an official and formal organization in which they can express their views regarding the refusal to accept or support homosexuality, as well as provide peer support for inter-heterosexual matters. STRAIGHT will also function as a lobby organization providing such students the ability, and means, to participate in furthering their related political agendas. Furthermore, STRAIGHT is committed to deterring the inclinations of intolerant individuals who engage in any actions that are not purely political, or in any way suggest animosity.

The founder and president of STRAIGHT, Darin Loccarini, was quoted by the student newspaper as saying that STRAIGHT "will promote education and pride in the tradition and appropriateness of heterosexuality in society" (*The Daily Collegian*, 6 November 1996, 2). According to the paper,

> Loccarini said he had two reasons for starting the organization. "The first reason," he said, "is equal representation for all students. . . . There should always be two sides to an issue." LGBSA (Lesbian/Gay/Bisexual Student Alliance) is a very active group on campus, and Loccarini believes heterosexuals need a group of their own to balance out different viewpoints. He said his group and LGBSA will naturally oppose each other ideologically, but not hate each other. "People are going to automatically think pro-heterosexual is anti-homosexual, but it is not," he said. "It's not a person thing, it's an ideology. It has to do with beliefs. I may be accused of being homophobic—that's nonsense." Loccarini illustrated the second reason his group is necessary by relaying the story of a friend. This friend wanted to join STRAIGHT but did not. "He was afraid it will get dug up in the future and effect him when he wants to run for political office," he said. "This is what's wrong with America—he's saying he's afraid to pronounce his membership in the overwhelming majority for fear of what the overwhelming minority will do to him." (2)

Loccarini subsequently applied to the Student Government for permission to register STRAIGHT as an official student organization. Official recognition of the group would allow its members to use the university logo and to meet in university facilities. After considering the group's application, the justices of the student court rejected it.

Here are excerpts from the majority opinion of the student court, written by Associate Justice Jit Chatterjee:

> The job of the Court is to be objective, unbiased, and determine what groups would better the University community. The Court looks down upon approving organizations that define themselves, in their purpose, as being against another group, culture, or lifestyle. In the eyes of the Court, STRAIGHT is not defining itself as for promoting the heterosexual tradition, but against homosexuality. To its credit, with over 400 student organizations under its jurisdiction, the Supreme Court has indeed been committed to building a structure whereby every organization and individual can promote their views, without having to fear being directly opposed by an organization created for that purpose.
>
> *Intolerance was not an issue regarding this decision.* The Court did not feel that STRAIGHT would exclude homosexuals from joining the group. Also, the Court did not feel that STRAIGHT is, or would become a hate group, encouraging "gay-bashing." However [citing a university policy], the USG Supreme Court has been given a mandate to "provide educational programs and activities to create an environment in which diversity and understanding of other cultures are valued." In the eyes of the Court, we would not be fulfilling our duties in this regard if we were to have approved STRAIGHT.
>
> Homosexuality is a lifestyle that is accepted by a great number of people in the Penn State community, and the fact that STRAIGHT says that its purpose is to "provide students with an official and formal organization in which they can express their view regarding the refusal to accept or support homosexuality" is very troubling. Approval of STRAIGHT would have created much bitterness and tension in the Penn State community, as well as exacerbating anxiety and fears among the lesbian, gay, and bisexual community and their supporters.
>
> For the reasons stated above, the Court feels that the impact of this organization and their actions would not have fostered a positive image for, or have been a benefit to the University community in any substantial way. Indeed, the Court feels that the purpose of this organization came close to being detrimental to the University community.
>
> The decision of the Court is in no way infringing upon the rights of individuals to exercise the First Amendment guarantees to free speech and freedom of assembly. The denial of STRAIGHT does not squelch the right of free speech or political agendas of individuals. It is not a right to be registered as a student organization, but more of a privilege. When a group is approved as an official Penn State University organization by the court, the power and prestige of the University is put behind the recognized organization. In the case of STRAIGHT, the Court felt that to put the power and prestige of the University behind STRAIGHT by approving the group would have put the University in a bad light. The Court is dedicated to at least maintaining the good name of the University.

Loccarini subsequently appealed this negative decision to the Student Organization Appeals Board, which overturned the decision of the student justices. This board decided that STRAIGHT "does not discriminate in its membership, and its purpose does not conflict with university policies" (*Centre Daily Times,* 7 March 1997, 13A). In a letter discussing its decision, members of the Appeals Board wrote:

> The Appeals Board, while believing that STRAIGHT's purpose might well be phrased in a more positive manner, which we encourage it to do, nonetheless affirms that a university community should be open to a wide range of conflicting and diverse viewpoints. . . . This open exchange of ideas and viewpoints goes to the heart of the university and should not be abridged. (13A)

This incident raised a number of issues that are deeply affective in contemporary American discourse. The overarching issue was sexuality, of course, but the struggle over STRAIGHT's official recognition also raised the issues of free assembly and the limits of tolerance. In the following analysis, we use Aristotle's topics to discover just a few of the arguments that can be made in connection with this series of events.

Using the Topic of Conjecture

What exists?

What does not exist?

What is the size or extent of what exists?

Did it exist in the past?

Will it exist in the future?

Using the topic of "what exists," the founder of STRAIGHT painted his university community as a place wherein heterosexuals were under-represented. Hence they needed an official voice and a place to assemble. The proposed constitution also implied that individuals exist who are "intolerant" and who engage in behavior that is not political but is—we must assume—threatening, coercive, or even violent. The newspaper account suggests that the group's founder believes in a hearing for "both sides" of an issue; readers are left to draw the conclusion that the unnamed "sides" in this case are positions taken by heterosexuals and homosexuals. The founder of the group also implied that prejudice against heterosexuals now exists, and his story about a friend indicates concern that such a prejudice will be more widespread in the future than it currently is.

Even though definition was not one of the topics delineated by Aristotle, arguments about definition were crucial in this event. The founder of STRAIGHT took pains to assure readers that "pro-heterosexual" did not mean "anti-homosexual" or "homophobic" (while he persisted in defining the issue as having only two sides, he was correct to point out that those who support different "sides" in an argument need not necessarily be opposed to those who hold other available positions). The Supreme Court also used arguments from definition, classifying its views as objective and unbiased. Furthermore, they disagreed with STRAIGHT's definition of the issue, arguing that a pro-heterosexual stance was indeed anti-homosexual. The court also took pains to define its decision as a tolerant one that did not violate STRAIGHT members' rights to free speech and freedom of assembly. Crucially, they defined group representation as a privilege, rather than a right, implying that such representation must be earned rather than granted.

Using the Topic of Value

What is greater than the mean or norm.

What is lesser than the mean or norm.

What is relatively greater than something else.

What is relatively lesser than something else.

What is good, just, beautiful, honorable, enjoyable, etc.

What is better, more just, etc.

What is less good, less just, etc.

What is good, etc., for all persons.

What is good, etc., for a few persons or groups.

What has been better, etc., in the past.

What will be better, etc., in the future.

Values were at the heart of this conflict. The overriding question at issue was whether there ought to be a sexual norm. Secondary questions which follow from this were very much at issue: Is heterosexuality still the norm, as it has been in the past? If not, is this a good or a bad thing? Is it a good or a bad thing for everyone? The argument of STRAIGHT's founder rested on the implication that homosexuality has become so valued that its privilege threatens the traditional heterosexual norm, even though homosexuals are in the minority. He also appealed to a traditional American commonplace—the will of the majority—when he asserted that the minority position has "overwhelmed" the position of the majority, so much so that the majority is afraid to express its views.

Appropriately enough, the Supreme Court's major appeal was to the value of justice, although they also concerned themselves with fairness and tolerance. They represented their denial of STRAIGHT's charter as an act of justice that would maintain a climate free from fear, bitterness, intolerance, and tension on campus. The appeals board, obviously, disagreed that the recognition of STRAIGHT would interfere with the maintenance of such values.

Using the Topic of Possibilities

What is possible.

What is impossible.

What is more or less possible.

What is possible in the future.

What is impossible in the future.

What was possible or impossible in the past.

The founder of STRAIGHT made several arguments from possibility, arguments that are implied in the group's constitution and in the newspaper account. He assumed that it is possible to achieve equality among groups or positions through equal representation (this commonplace is typical of liberal ideology). He also apparently believed that it is possible for the will of the majority to be eclipsed by that of a minority. The Supreme Court justices, on the other hand, argued that it is possible that a group organized to protect the rights of a majority may infringe on the rights of a minority. They also took the position that is possible that a majority may oppress a minority unless they are prevented from doing so.

We hope that our readers will find it useful to search for the many other commonplaces that we have not listed but which are nonetheless at work in this argument. All of the arguments advanced in this situation are open to contest, as is true of any rhetorical argument, and we hope that readers will use Aristotle's topics to develop the available arguments that contest those actually used by the participants in this debate.

EXERCISES

1. Reread the descriptions of American ideology given by E. D. Hirsch and Howard Zinn in this chapter. Whose description seems more accurate to you? Can you tell from these descriptions whether Hirsch and Zinn lean toward the right or left of the political spectrum? How can you justify your placement of either writer on the political spectrum?

2. Find a large parking lot. Copy down the bumper stickers that you see on the vehicles parked there, such as "Rush is Right," "My Other Car is a Lawn Mower," "Abortion—Safe, Legal, and Infrequent," "If You Can Read This, Thank a Teacher." Each of these commonplaces implies an argument and an ideology. Try to figure out the arguments and ideologies that underlie the bumper stickers you found. If a vehicle sports several bumper stickers, does the collection suggest contrary or conflicting ideologies? This exercise also works with vanity license plates, such as "FLYNHI," "BIGDOG," "PDFOR." What do these phrases suggest about the ideologies of their owners? What happens when a commonplace is not commonplace enough? What happens, for example, if a reader of a bumper sticker doesn't know who, or what, "Rush" refers to?

3. Think about a specific rhetorical situation in which you recently participated. Writing as fast as you can, describe this situation: the people who participated, their relationships to each other (friends, family members, and so on), the place, the time, the issue. Now examine the position taken by one participant in the rhetorical situation (not yourself). Write down as many of his or her arguments as you can remember. What beliefs or values undergird the position he or she took in the argument? See if you can list these. Do any of them look like conservative or liberal commonplaces? Is the person open to persuasion on any of them? If so, how might a rhetor persuade that person to change his or her mind about any of his or her arguments?

4. Use Aristotle's topics to analyze some issue that you want to understand better. Ask each of the questions listed in this chapter under the topics of conjecture, values, and possibilities. Take your time, and write down all of

the answers that come to you. Remember, the point of a heuristic is to help you find all of the available arguments. If you are thorough, systematic use of the topics should turn up more arguments than you need.

5. Read the front page of a daily newspaper that covers both local and national news. Read this week's news magazines, watch the news on TV, listen to radio news programs, or surf the internet. This ought to familiarize you with the issues that are currently being debated in the American public sphere. Then read some magazines that are avowedly partisan in order to see how they treat currently controversial issues. *The New Republic, The American Spectator,* and the *Wall Street Journal* are conservative; *The Nation, Dissent,* and *The Village Voice* are liberal or left-of-liberal. Compare the treatments of the same issue that appear in conservative and liberal magazines. Now try to answer these questions: What is the ideological bias (if any can be detected) of your hometown newspaper? Of the news desk of your local TV station? Of the *New York Times?* Of *USA Today?* Of *Time* magazine? Of *Newsweek?* Of CNN? Of network television news? Of Oprah? Of Geraldo Rivera? Of Dr. Laura? Of Rush Limbaugh?

This exercise will help you to compile an inventory of the commonplaces that appear in American rhetoric. You may draw on this list in two ways: It should help you to understand the ideology that undergirds the arguments presented to you, and you can use it to build your own arguments.

NOTES

1. We relied in part on Goran Therborn's *The Ideology of Power and the Power of Ideology* (London, NLB: 1980) for the analysis that follows.
2. We do not pretend that this list is exhaustive. And it will change with the passage of time (see the chapter on *kairos*). In the first edition of this book, for example, our list began with this question: "What is the appropriate kind of economy?" We removed that question from this edition since virtually all American political ideologies that have a public voice currently accept capitalism as the preferred economy for America. (There is only one socialist serving in the United States Congress.)

WORKS CITED

Coontz, Stephanie. *The Way We Never Were: American Families and the Nostalgia Trap.* New York: Basic Books, 1992.

D'Souza, Dinesh. *Illiberal Education: The Politics of Race and Sex on Campus.* New York: Vintage, 1992.

Hirsch, E. D. *Cultural Literacy: What Every American Needs to Know.* Chicago: Chicago UP, 1987.

Wilson, John K. *The Myth of Political Correctness: The Conservative Attack on Higher Education.* Durham: Duke UP, 1995.

Zinn, Howard. *Declarations of Independence.* New York: HarperCollins. 1990.

ETHICAL PROOF

As regards the orator,
the qualities which will
most commend him are
courtesy, kindliness,
moderation and
benevolence. But, on the
other hand, the opposite
of these qualities will
sometimes be becoming
to a good man. He may
hate the bad, be moved
to passion in the public
interest, seek to avenge
crime and wrong, and,
in fine, as I said at the
beginning, may follow
the promptings of every
honorable emotion.

—Quintilian,
Institutes XI i, 42

ANCIENT RHETORICIANS KNEW that good arguments were available to them from sources other than the issues. As early as the fourth century BCE, Greek teachers of rhetoric gave suggestions about how a person's character (ethos) could be put to persuasive uses, and rhetorical theorists continued to discuss the uses of ethical proofs throughout the history of ancient rhetoric.

We use the terms "character" and "ethical proof" in this chapter to refer to proofs that rely on a rhetor's personality or reputation. According to Webster's dictionary, the English word "character" retains three of the important senses it carried for ancient rhetoricians: (1) "the pattern of behavior or personality found in an individual or group"; (2) "moral strength, self-discipline, fortitude, etc."; (3) "a good reputation." Our term "personality" does not quite capture all the senses of the ancient Greek term "ethos," since it carried moral overtones, and since, for the Greeks, a character was created by a person's habits and reputation rather than by experience.

To give you a sense of how effective this proof can be, and of how important it was to ancient orators, we quote at length from the opening of Isocrates' Panegyricus:

> Many times have I wondered at those who first convoked the national assemblies and established the athletic games, amazed that they should have thought the prowess of human bodies to be deserving of so great bounties, while to those who had toiled in private for the public good and trained their own minds so as to be able to help also their fellow humans when they apportioned no reward

whatsoever, when, in all reason, they ought rather to have made provision for the latter; for if all the athletes should acquire twice the strength which they now possess, the rest of the world would be no better off; but let a single man attain to wisdom, and all men will reap the benefit who are willing to share his insight. Yet I have not on this account lost heart nor chosen to abate my labors; on the contrary, believing that I shall have a sufficient reward in the approbation which my discourse will itself command, I have come before you to give my counsels on the war against the barbarians and on concord among ourselves. I am, in truth, not unaware that many of those who have claimed to be sophists have rushed upon this theme, but I hope to rise so far superior to them that it will seem as if no word had ever been spoken by my rivals upon this subject. (1–3)

Contemporary rhetors may shy away from such unabashed praise of themselves. Nevertheless, it must be admitted that in this passage Isocrates established his character as a very serious man whose important work is underestimated. At the same time he separated himself from persons who had spoken less well than he does.

To create a persuasive ethos is not easy. This difficulty is compounded by the fact that ethos always manifests itself to listeners or readers, whether a rhetor is aware of it or not. Consider, for example, the following letter that appeared in the daily newspaper of Flagstaff, Arizona. The writer was participating in a discussion about the county sheriff's refusal to give a permit to a group who had asked for the use of a county fairground:

> To the editor:
>
> I would like to remind some people that [the county sheriff] executed the requirements of his position correctly and legally in regard to the requested homosexual "festival" that was held at Fort Tuthill. As an elected official he was required to sign his name to their petition. He could have denied them permission and, I am sure, he would have been supported by the people of Flagstaff, with, of course, some few exceptions.
>
> I would also remind you narrow-minded people that as a citizen of this country he has some constitutional rights of his own, for instance, the right of free speech, one which certain new citizens wish to deny him. [The sheriff] is guaranteed the right to think for himself and the right to express his thoughts to ANYONE he wishes; these inalienable rights are not revoked upon his being elected.
>
> Most citizens should remember something called AIDS and homosexuals like [Jeffrey] Dahmer before they start clamoring for their rights. Consider that the non-homosexual population has the homosexuals to thank for our ability to contract the AIDS virus.
>
> If you have moved to Flagstaff and are disturbed or uncomfortable with the way of life you have found, I sincerely welcome you to go back where you came from. Flagstaff is far too good for you. (*Arizona Daily Sun,* 46:355 [August 4, 1992] p. 6)

Whether they agree with him or not, readers inevitably build up an impression of the sort of person this writer is. It isn't hard to see where his ethos began to go wrong. Most Americans would not be offended by anything in the first or second paragraphs, since these sections of the letter express commonplaces from American ideology. Perhaps sensitive readers were put off by the quotation marks around "festival" and the use of the term "narrow-minded," but these usages do not do serious damage to the writer's ethos as a sensible and reasonable American. In the third paragraph, however, the writer began to lose control of his ethos when, without further proof or elaboration, he connected AIDS and the mass murderer Jeffrey Dahmer to homosexual activity. Of course, the association of AIDS with homosexual activity is a commonplace in homophobic communities, and so, conceivably, this audience might read the third paragraph without being offended. In the final paragraph, however, the writer implied that homosexuals are not welcome in his city, and he implied further that all newcomers to the city must fit in with its traditional ways. No doubt, these comments alienated even those citizens who are indifferent to the sexual practices of other people, since the writer showed himself to be not only homophobic but provincial as well.

ETHOS IN ANCIENT RHETORICS

The term "ethos" was used in several ways over the long history of ancient rhetoric. The author of the *Rhetoric to Alexander* cautioned rhetors to be careful about their personal conduct, "because one's manner of life contributes to one's powers of persuasion as well as to the attainment of a good reputation" (XXXVIII 1445b, 30). This passage implies that a rhetor's ability to persuade is connected to his or her moral habits—a connection that was more fully developed by Roman rhetoricians. Aristotle, on the other hand, was not so concerned about the way rhetors lived as he was about the appearance of character that they presented within their discourse (*Rhetoric* I ii, 1356a). Perhaps in keeping with Plato's injunction that rhetors must know what types of souls men have (*Phaedrus,* 271d), Aristotle also provided a long list of the "characters" of audiences, depending on their age, station in life, and so on.

Aristotle's student, Theophrastus, wrote descriptions of possible character traits, a practice that critics later called *ethopoeia* ("fabricating character"). These descriptions typically began with a definition and listed examples of behavior that typified the character being described. Here, for instance, is Theophrastus' account of the character of a tactless person:

> Now tactlessness is a pain-giving failure to hit upon the right moment; and your Tactless person . . . will accost a busy friend and ask advice, or serenade a sweetheart when she is sick of a fever. He will approach someone who has gone bail and lost it, and ask that person to be his security for a loan; and will come to bear witness after the verdict is given. Should you bid him to a wedding, he will inveigh against womankind. Should you be but now returned from a long journey, he will invite you to a walk. He is given to bringing you a merchant who, when your bargain is struck, says he would have paid more had you asked; and to rising from his seat to tell a tale all afresh to such as have heard it before and know it well. He is forward to undertake for you what you would not have done but cannot well decline. If you are sacrificing and put to great expense, that is the day he chooses to come and demand

what you owe him. At the flogging of your servant he will stand by and tell how a servant of his hanged himself after just such a flogging as this; at an arbitration he will set the parties against each other when both wish to be reconciled; and when he would dance, lay hold of another who is not yet drunk enough to behave foolishly. (XII)

Theophrastus' characters were probably used to teach students how to analyze character, and they provided moral instruction as well. Later on, Hellenistic teachers of rhetoric encouraged their students to compose "characters" for historical or fictional persons as part of their rhetorical exercises (see the chapter on the progymnasmata).

Aristotle recognized two kinds of ethical proof: invented and situated. The distinction probably depends on Aristotle's prior distinction between intrinsic and extrinsic proofs, or invented and found proofs (1355b). According to Aristotle, rhetors can invent a character suitable to an occasion—this is invented ethos. However, if rhetors are fortunate enough to enjoy a good reputation in the community, they can use it as an ethical proof—this is situated ethos. But it is, nevertheless, a proof that is extrinsic to the issue, that is simply found in a rhetorical situation. Interestingly enough, this distinction parallels two primary senses of the term "character" in ancient Greek: character could be invented by means of habitual practice; but it also referred to the community's assessment of a person's habitual practices. Thus a given individual's character had as much to do with the community's perception of her or his actions as it did with actual behavior.

Today we may feel uncomfortable with the notion that rhetorical character can be constructed, since we tend to think of character, or personality, as fairly stable. We generally assume as well that personalities are shaped by an individual's experiences. The ancient Greeks, on the other hand, thought that character was constructed not by what happened to people but by the moral practices in which they habitually engaged. An ethos was not finally given by nature, but was developed by habit (*hexis*). Thus it was important for parents and teachers not only to provide children with examples of good behavior, but to insist that young persons practice habits that imprinted their characters with virtues rather than vices. The notion that character was formed through habitual practices endured throughout antiquity. Quintilian devoted many pages of the *Institutes* to the importance of carefully selecting a teacher for very young children, a teacher whose character would set a suitable example for them and whose practices would develop positive moral habits in them (I i, v).

Since the Greeks thought that character was shaped by one's practices, they considered it to be much more malleable than we do. Within certain limits imposed by class and gender restrictions, one could become any sort of person he or she wished to be, simply by engaging in the practices that produced that sort of character. It followed, then, that playing the roles of respectable characters enhanced one's chances of developing a respectable character.

According to Quintilian, Roman rhetoricians who relied on Greek rhetorical theory sometimes confused ethos with pathos—appeals to the emotions—because there was no satisfactory term for ethos in Latin (VI ii, 8). Cicero occasionally used the Latin term *persona* ("mask"), and Quintilian simply borrowed the Greek term. This lack of a technical term is not surprising, because the requirement of having a respectable character was built into the very fabric of Roman oratory. Early Roman society was governed by means of family authority, and so a person's lineage had everything to do with what sort of ethos he could command when he took part in public affairs. The older and more respected the family, the more discursive authority its members enjoyed. Under the Republic and the Empire the family requirement softened a bit, but it was still necessary for someone to maintain a reputation for good character in order to be heard. In fact, Quintilian equated the skillful practice of rhetoric with a good character: "no person can speak well who is not good" (II xv, 35). Cicero, the practitioner, was more sympathetic to the Greek position that a suitable ethos could be constructed for a rhetorical occasion, although he makes Antonius remark in *De Oratore* that "merit, achievements, or reputable life" are "qualifications easier to embellish, if only they are real, than to fabricate where non-existent" (II xlii, 182).

In later antiquity, ethos became associated almost wholly with style. Hermogenes of Tarsus, for example, furnished a long list of the virtues or characters of different styles—simplicity, modesty, solemnity, vehemence, and so on—that was read and used by students well into the Renaissance.

Contemporary discussions of rhetoric often overlook the role played by ethical proofs, despite the fact that Americans are very much interested in the character and personal habits of public figures. Americans don't talk as much as they used to about persons having a good character, but apparently they still care about such things. The "character issue" is regularly raised in presidential elections, although in this case "character" ordinarily refers to a candidate's personal moral choices: Has he been faithful to his spouse? Has he used drugs? Ancient rhetoricians were not so interested in private moral choices like these as they were in the virtues that counted in public affairs: courage, honesty, trustworthiness, modesty, intelligence, fair-mindedness.

The ancient interest in character is still useful because it highlights the role played by this important kind of proof in contemporary rhetorical exchanges. In this chapter, we review the ancient rhetorical advice about ethos that is still useful or interesting to modern rhetors, and we freely adapt some of it for contemporary use. Ethical rhetorical effects are varied and subtle, and we have not attempted to exhaust the enormous lode of ancient teachings about them. We have tried to give a sufficiently full treatment to alert our readers to the persuasive potential contained in this sort of rhetorical proof.

INVENTED ETHOS

Contemporary discourse is often composed for very large audiences, and so it is often the case that rhetors do not know the people to whom they will speak or write. Thus they cannot use whatever situated ethos they enjoy among those who know them as a means of ethical proof. So they must rely upon invented ethos.

A rhetor who uses invented ethos, you will recall, constructs a character for herself within her discourse. In an essay entitled "Finding My Place in Black America," Gloria Nauden invented an ethos for herself by recalling remarks made to her by others:

> "Excuse me, what are you?" As a person of mixed heritage, Black and Korean, I get asked this question several times a day. Sometimes rudely, most of the time innocently. But I'm always open to educating others about what it means to be Black and Asian.
>
> Among Blacks, I get this kind of reaction: "You look so exotic and different" (pickup line); "It's not too often you see an Asian person at a Black function" (ignorantly curious); "You know, I just got back from China" (So what?); and "My ex-girlfriend was Black and Philipino" (So you have an Asian fetish?). Then there are the rude taunts. They go like this: "She thinks she's Black"; "I can't stand when Chinese people try to act Black."
>
> The worse incidents are when I'm called a "war baby," a reference to the children who were fathered by American soldiers and left behind in the streets and orphanages of Vietnam. In fact, my mother, who is Korean-born, met my father, an Army man, in her homeland, and came to the United States with me when I was a year old. They have been married for 30 years.
>
> Among the worst of all scenes is when I am called a "chink." Recently, I was at a new hot spot among young Black professionals, the BET SoundStage restaurant in Largo, Md., which is owned by BET Holdings Inc. I am the entertainment director and helped develop the restaurant. But one guest felt comfortable in trying to make me feel unwelcome.
>
> I was in "his" house, he said, taking great pride in this Black-owned venture. Chinese people have slanted eyes "because you're always squinting, being in everyone's business," the brother said. He complained that he was sick of "chinks" like me coming to the United States and trying to take over and that his people are responsible for building this country. Shocked and angry and hurt, as usual, I wanted to deck him. I wanted to let him know that I was the "sista" who had given the restaurant all its "flava." But even as I told him, "My father is Black, I am Black," he jeered and walked away while making an obscene jesture.
>
> I want people like him to know that I am a very confident, proud and passionate person. I want people to know that my generic code is Black and Korean, but I consider myself an African-American. This mostly has to do with how I was reared. Unlike Tiger Woods, who grew up in a predominantly White neighborhood, I grew up in a public housing complex in the Hill District of Pittsburgh. It was a Black neighborhood and my mother and I stuck out like sore thumbs. (*Emerge*, August 1997, 67)

By implication, Nauden established that her identity is quite different from and much more complex than the ethnic identities that others attempt to construct for her. She demonstrates her own ability to shift among personas. Her use of first person and her frank admissions about her feelings construct an ethos which indicates that she is an honest and trustworthy narrator whose mixed heritage nonetheless causes confusion in insensitive others, which in turn brings difficulty and pain to her.

Aristotle taught that the character conveyed by a rhetor was most important in cases where the facts or arguments were in doubt, "for we believe fair-minded people to a great extent and more quickly [than we do others] on all subjects in general and completely so in cases where there is not exact knowledge but room for doubt" (I ii, 1356a). In other words, people tend to believe rhetors who either have a reputation for fair-mindedness or who create an ethos that makes them seem fair-minded. This is especially true in cases where, as Aristotle said, there is room for doubt.

Aristotle saw three possible ways in which rhetors could make ethical mistakes. First, "through lack of practical sense they do not form opinions rightly." That is, rhetors could be so inexperienced or so uninformed that they simply don't draw the right conclusions. Second, "though forming opinions rightly they do not say what they think because of a bad character." That is, even though rhetors know the right answer or the right course they may hide it from people because of some character flaw, such as greed or dishonesty. Third, "they are prudent and fair-minded but lack good will, so that it is possible for people not to give the best advice although they know what it is." That is, rhetors may not care about what happens to the people they represent, and so they do not give good advice even when they could. These, Aristotle wrote, are the only possibilities for a failed invented ethos.

The first ethical lapse still afflicts rhetors, but it doesn't seem nearly so serious as violations of the second and third requirements. These mistakes describe behavior that is unethical in a much stronger moral sense than failure to develop a persuasive character. Dishonesty, greed, and selfishness were (and still are) considered immoral when practiced by anyone, rhetor or not. Unfortunately, it is possible for these vices to be reflected in a discursive ethos. A rhetorician named Ken Macrorie fabricated the following example of a failed invented ethos:

> Unquestionably the textbook has played a very important role in the development of American schools—and I believe it will continue to play an important role. The need for textbooks has been established through many experiments. It is not necessary to consider these experiments but, in general, they have shown that when instruction without textbooks has been tried by schools, the virtually unanimous result has been to go back to the use of textbooks. I believe too, that there is considerable evidence to indicate that the textbook has been, and is, a major factor in guiding teachers' instruction and in determining the curriculum. (177)

The ethos in this piece fails all three of Aristotle's tests. Since the rhetor does not cite any of the "many experiments" that supposedly support his arguments, there is no evidence that he has done the necessary homework. His good will toward an audience can be questioned, as well, since he suggests that while evidence exists which supports his position, he has not bothered to cite it so that readers could find and read it for themselves. In this passage, he paints himself as both lazy and assertive—not an attractive character at all.

To put Aristotle's ethical requirements in positive terms, rhetors must seem to be intelligent, to be of good moral character, and to possess good will toward their audiences. Rhetors can construct a character that seems intelligent by demonstrating that they are well-informed about issues they discuss. They project an appearance of good moral character by describing themselves or others as moral persons and by refraining from the use of misleading or fallacious arguments. Rhetors project good will toward an audience by presenting the information and arguments that audiences require in order to understand the rhetorical situation.

Demonstrating Intelligence by Doing the Homework

Rhetors can create a character that seems intelligent by demonstrating that they are informed about the issues they discuss, and by refraining from using arguments that are irrelevant or trivial. General audiences can be assumed to be relatively uninformed about difficult or technical issues, so in this case rhetors must take special care to convince an audience that they are well informed without overwhelming them with details. Here is Sheryl Gay Stolberg, writing for the *New York Times* about a report on deaths from AIDS:

> The headlines last week trumpeted the good news: Deaths from AIDS had dropped 19 percent in the United States, continuing a decline first reported in May. The disease, it appears, has turned a corner in this country, changing from a death sentence into a chronic, treatable illness. As the Centers for Disease Control and Prevention declared, "We have entered a new era in the H.I.V. epidemic."
>
> Yet in the fine print of the Government's statistics was a less cheerful tale. Between 1995 and 1996, deaths of women decreased by just 7 percent, as against 22 percent in men. And while the number of deaths dropped 28 percent for whites, the drop was 10 percent for blacks and 16 percent for Hispanic victims.
>
> The turnaround, in other words, has primarily benefitted white men. (20 July 1997, 4–1)

In this critical evaluation of a complex report, Stolberg established her ethos as a good reporter by adding details to the already published statistics on deaths from AIDS. The details she mentioned tell a very different story from previous reports, which focused on the overall decline in deaths without considering gender and ethnicity. Stolberg's ethos is thus defined against that of other, presumably more careless or less insightful journalists who did not report on what she calls "the fine print" which, according to her, suggests that the treatment and prevention of AIDS are discriminatory practices. The concluding sentence confirmed Stolberg's character as one who examines data from different angles and delivers the news and is willing to draw conclusions even though they are distressing. She therefore made her report seem better informed than the others, for it offered the previously cited statistics about AIDS deaths in general as well as the grimmer details apparently overlooked in previous news stories.

To seem well informed is especially important when the audience is relatively well informed themselves about the issue at hand. In this case, the rhetor must quickly assure them that he knows what he is talking about. He may do so by using language that suggests he is an "insider," by sharing an anecdote that indicates he has experience or knowledge in a particular area, or by describing his qualifications. Thomas Landauer, author of *The Trouble With Computers* (1995), chose to describe his qualifications as follows:

> I started doing research and prototype development with computers about fifteen years ago at Bell Laboratories. Before that, I'd done psychological research on human learning, memory, and thinking. I belonged to a department called Human Information Processing Research. Along with many others, I was captivated by the idea that computers offered a technology that could finally underwrite the kinds of power tools for human minds that motors have provided for our hands. (xi)

The title of Landauer's book suggests that he will discuss problems with computer technology, so it is important that he quickly demonstrate his level of expertise. He does so by recounting his considerable experience in the area. This way, readers are more likely to seriously engage his critiques of technology than they might if he launched into his arguments without establishing his ethos as a knowledgeable and experienced person.

Rhetors may also use specialized language to demonstrate their adeptness in a particular field, hence reassuring informed readers that what they have to say is worth their time. Jeff Bowers, an undergraduate student writing for expert readers of *Technology Review*—a periodical published by the widely known and respected Massachusetts Institute of Technology—does just that:

> The Superconducting Supercollider was to be the most powerful particle accelerator in the world. The 53-mile underground tunnel, lined with 11,000 superconducting magnets, would accelerate two beams of protons in opposite directions around a gigantic ring, slamming the beams together to create a spectacular fireworks display of subatomic particles. Physicists expected that by mimicking the conditions thought to exist in the primordial plasma of the early universe, the supercollider would reveal new exotic species of particles, thereby providing significant insight into the fundamental structure of matter. ("A Particular Passion," August/September 1997, 50)

Bowers managed to make the scientific terms come to life as he described the cultural moment in science when he decided to enter the field of physics. Because he details the supercollider's activity with such precision, Bowers establishes himself as someone who knows a good deal about the subject under discussion and, as a result, readers are more likely to pay attention to what he has to say.

We remarked earlier that rhetors who wish to appear intelligent and well informed must demonstrate that they have done whatever research and contemplation is necessary to understand an issue, and they must avoid making irrelevant or trivial arguments as well. A rhetorical disaster may ensue when rhetors fail to establish themselves as well informed about the issues they discuss. While campaigning for the Presidency in 1996, for example, then Senator

Bob Dole repeatedly criticized Hollywood values. Here is an account of one such incident from *USA Today:*

> Senate Majority Leader Bob Dole Wednesday said Hollywood is "mainstreaming deviancy," and accused the entertainment industry of promoting rape, violence, and casual sex.
>
> At a Los Angeles fund-raiser, Dole—front-runner for the GOP presidential nomination—said, "It will only stop when the leaders of the entertainment industry recognize and shoulder their responsibility."
>
> Dole is going after Hollywood because advisers say it's good politics. He's hoping to appeal to mainstream voters, as well as conservatives.
>
> Dole called his outrage more than a "codgy old attempt of one generation to steal the fun of another."
>
> He said R-rated movies, like *Natural Born Killers* and *True Romance* "revel in mindless violence and loveless sex."
>
> Dole singled out recording groups Cannibal Corpse, Geto Boys and 2 Live Crew, and a "culture business that makes money from music extolling the pleasures of raping, torturing, and mutilating women." And he said Time Warner, which owns Interscope Records, was on the "leading edge of coarseness and violence."
>
> "Bob Dole finds it easier to put the blinders on and attack Hollywood for political points," said Arthur Kropps of People for the American Way.
>
> Dole's Hollywood denunciation is not his first. In April he was criticized for attacking the movie *Priest* while acknowledging he had never viewed the film, which portrays sexual misconduct by Roman Catholic priests. (1 June 1995: A1, 6)

When asked if he had seen the films under discussion, Dole admitted that he had not. His admitted failure to do his homework negatively affected the reception of his later speeches on violence in the media. Failed ethos in one situation can carry over into subsequent situations, shaping a rhetorical character that can hinder the reception of future messages, especially if the rhetor is under intense and constant public scrutiny. In this case, those who recalled his previous mistake might not regard Dole's views as informed evaluations.

Here is an example of failed ethos produced by another rhetor who did not do the necessary research on the issue at hand:

> Many students go to college to find a husband or wife. While there are some who attend for the purpose of getting themselves an education, these are few and far between. The majority of companion seekers are men because by the time they reach college most of them are ready to settle down after the bebop life of high school. In most cases, men are tied to home, security, and have problems in adjusting to being completely on their own. In the opinion of this author, men are looking to fulfill their need of security by finding a wife in college.

There is no hint here that the author did any research on this subject, even to the extent of asking one or two college men whether or not his conclusions were true. Audiences whose experiences and aims do not match the generalizations made here will feel excluded by the rhetor's assertive tone, while others may be offended by it. This tone is mitigated somewhat in the last sentence, where the rhetor tells us that these generalizations are his "opinion." Here is a revision of the passage:

> Although I have some friends who are here to get themselves an education, I know many students who come to college to look for a husband or a wife. For instance, my roommate is having problems adjusting to being completely on his own, and I think he's still tied to home and security. In fact, he has admitted to me that he is looking to find a wife in college who will give him the security he misses. This need for security seems to be the case with many of my male friends.

While talking with the author, his classmates discovered that the generalization about wife-seeking men was based on only one example—his roommate. They encouraged him to limit his generalization to what he knew from experience. As a result, the second version manifests a character who does not make claims about which he is uninformed.

Establishing Good Character

There are probably as many ways to demonstrate good moral character as there are virtues—and vices. Cicero encouraged rhetors to extol their "merits or worth or virtue of some kind, particularly generosity, sense of duty, justice, and good faith" (*On the Parts* viii, 28). He also suggested that rhetors weaken charges or suspicions that had been cast on their character, and to elaborate on misfortunes or difficulties that had befallen them in order to strengthen their audience's estimate of their ability to bear suffering (*On Invention* I xvi, 22). When Cicero defended a man named Lucius Murena, he was accused of having a double standard—of holding other men to higher standards of conduct than he held for Murena. He responded by commenting on his own character:

> I have always gladly shown the restraint and forgiveness which nature herself has taught me; I have not been eager to wear the mask of dead seriousness and hardness, but I wore it willingly when the crisis of state and the solemn requirements of my office demanded. If, then, when the republic wanted force and uncompromising severity, I overcame my nature to become as ruthless as I was forced into being, not as I wished, may I not now respond to the sympathetic and humane qualities which all the motives in the case prompt in me and accord them my characteristic degree of energy and enthusiasm? (*Pro Murena*, 3)

Here Cicero pictured himself as a sympathetic and softhearted man, forced by his duties into seeming hardhearted. On this occasion, however, he portrayed himself as a more human and sympathetic character.

Contemporary rhetors are more subtle about displaying moral character than Roman rhetors were, but they still use moral standards as means of proof. Opponents of abortion characterize pro-choice advocates as "baby killers" and "murderers"; public officials are often charged with immoral behavior such as infidelity or harassment. Apparently, some news writers believe that even actors should demonstrate good moral character, at least when they are not acting, as is suggested by this *Newsweek* review of the film *Men in Black:*

> The key ingredient in getting the movie made was Tommy Lee Jones. No one wanted to make the movie without him. He had approval of the script and director, and everyone lived to please him. . . . The Texas-bred, Harvard-educated Jones has a reputation for being difficult and blunt. "Tommy is like the original cactus," says (producer Laurie) McDonald. . . . Perhaps apprehensive about playing comedy again after going *mano a mano* with Jim Carrey in the unfortunate *Batman Forever,* Jones fired off a blistering six-page critique of the script. It wasn't funny. Why did it have to be funny? Why Men in Black? Why not Man in Black? ("The Odd Squad," 7 July 1997, 62)

The writers of this review assumed that readers are interested not only in the power of Jones' ethos but in his character and background as well. Do Americans associate a certain kind of character with Texas or with a Harvard education? In any case, *Newsweek's* dwelling on the actor's character traits suggests that moral character still matters to Americans.

In order to establish their good moral standing, rhetors may cite approval of their character from respected authorities. Ordinary people establish their character in this way when they ask teachers or employers for letters of reference. References are often asked about the same qualities of character in prospective employees that concerned ancient rhetoricians: intelligence, honesty, and trustworthiness. Rhetors can also shore up an audience's sense of their character simply by refraining from the use of unfair discursive tactics: faulty reasoning or non-representative evidence, threats, name-calling, or lies.

A slightly different interpretation of good character seems to be very persuasive in modern discourse. This is the ethos that conveys a person as an authority, either by virtue of respectable credentials or long experience in some activity. The covers or inside pages of books often list "other works by the same author," in order to establish the writer's history as a published author (and to sell more copies of the older books). Advertisements for movies often list actors' credits for other films, thus demonstrating that they have done good work previously. This usually happens when the producers think that the actors' name recognition isn't tied closely enough to their face recognition—two kinds of ethos that are very important in the movie industry.

The following passage introduced an article in *Emerge* magazine about attorneys who were influential in the development of civil rights legislation. One of them, Fred D. Gray, is introduced as follows:

> Gray is senior partner in the law firm of Gray, Langford, Sapp, McGowan, Gray & Nathanson, which has offices in Montgomery and Tuskegee, Ala. He was Dr. Martin Luther King Jr.'s first civil rights lawyer; represented Rosa Parks after her refusal to give up her seat to a White man touched off the Montgomery bus boycott in 1955; and helped the NAACP win a suit, which eventually was decided in the U.S. Supreme Court, against the state of Alabama's decision forbidding the organization to operate there. He also represented victims of the Tuskegee syphilis exper-

iment. Gray, a former president of the Nation Bar association, is author of *Bus Ride to Justice.* ("Dedicated Lives," July/August 1997, 35)

This history of good work associates Gray with several important moments in the civil rights movement, thus indicating to readers why they should be interested in learning more about him.

Sometimes reviewers will allude to a rhetor's history in order to reinforce their estimates of his abilities. Here, for example, is Roger Ebert's review of *Batman & Robin*, the fourth in the Batman movie series:

> Because of my love for the world of Batman, I went to Joel Schumacher's *Batman & Robin* with real anticipation. I got thrilled all over again by the Gothic towers of Gotham City. I was reminded of how cool the Batmobile is (Batman has a new one), and I smiled at the fetishistic delight with which Batman and Robin put on their costumes, sheathing themselves in shiny black second skins and clamping on lots of belts, buckles, shields, hooks, pulleys, etc. (How much does that stuff weigh? How do they run while they're wearing it?)
>
> But my delight began to fade at about the 30-minute mark, when it became clear that this new movie, like its predecessors, was not *really* going to explore the bizarre world of its heroes, but would settle down safely into a special effects extravaganza. *Batman & Robin,* like the first three films in the series, is wonderful to look at, and has nothing authentic at its core. . . . Watching it, I realized why it makes absolutely no difference who plays Batman: There's nobody at home. The character is the ultimate Suit. Garb him in leather or rubber, and he's an action hero—Buzz Lightyear with a heartbeat. Put him in civilian clothes, and he's a nowhere man. (*Chicago Sun-Times Online*, www.suntimes.com, 20 June, 1997)

The opening paragraph establishes Ebert's ethos as a fan of Batman. His child-like delight at the costumes and props in the movie suggests that Ebert's review will be positive—that is until the second paragraph when he discusses his disillusion with Batman films in general and with the character of Batman in particular. The contrasting opening paragraphs make Ebert's argument seem more earnest and his disappointment more poignant. His comparison of Batman to Buzz Lightyear, an animated action figure in the movie *Toy Story*, subtly reminds the readers that Ebert is an expert on all sorts of movies, has viewed an array of heroic characters, and is therefore qualified to place Batman on a continuum of movie superheroes. Ebert assumes that most of his readers know the plots of the films in the Batman series, and so he gives them no attention at all, thus subtly diminishing their importance through neglect.

Achieving Good Will

Cicero wrote that good will could be won "if we refer to our own acts and services without arrogance; if we weaken the effect of charges that have been preferred, or of some suspicion of less honorable dealing which has been cast upon us; if we dilate on the misfortunes which have befallen us or the difficulties which still beset us; if we use prayers and entreaties with a humble and submissive spirit" (*On Invention* I xvi, 22). While ethical tactics like these were persuasive to Roman audiences, they may be a bit too flamboyant for modern tastes. Modern rhetors can demonstrate their good will toward an audience by carefully considering what readers need to know about the issue at hand in order to follow the argument. They should supply any necessary information that audiences might not already have, but should be careful not to repeat information that the audience already knows.

Movie reviewers usually operate on the ethical principle of good will: they must assume that people will listen to or read their reviews in order to decide whether to see a given film. Since people put their trust (and their money) on the line when they take reviewers' advice, movie reviewers are obligated to have good will toward their audiences. They demonstrate this good will by telling audiences just enough about the plot or characters or direction to allow them to decide whether to see a film, but they don't give away the ending. They also demonstrate good will by providing audiences with their frank opinion about a film.

The ethical criterion of good will poses interesting problems for writers of weekly news magazines like *Time* and *Newsweek.* These writers are obligated to include the facts of the news in their stories, but their stories sometimes appear a week to ten days after the same events have been thoroughly covered in newspapers and television. How do such writers manage to present the necessary facts—in case some reader has been hiding in a cave—and yet do so without boring their readers? Many Americans watched the extensive news coverage of the bombing of the Murrah federal building in Oklahoma City on April 19, 1995. How are writers after the fact to compete with the gripping images that appeared on television? Here is an excerpt from *Newsweek's* lead story the following week:

> Dan Webber was happy to be away from Washington, with its petty rivalries, its crime, its world-weariness. The onetime Senate aide had come home to Oklahoma City to clerk for a judge and raise his family in the normalcy of the heartland. He had just dropped off his 3-year-old son, Joseph, at the America's Kids day-care center when the force of the explosion hurled him across his desk in the courthouse. Stunned, wild with fear, Webber ran down the street, to the smoking, shattered shell that had, until a few minutes before, been a federal office building. There was just rubble where the day-care center had been. He found a group of children huddled with rescue workers—but his own was not among them. He ran to fetch his wife, who worked nearby. Twenty minutes later, miraculously, he found a policeman carrying his boy. Joseph's face had been slashed by flying glass, his eardrums had been ruptured by the blast and his arm was broken. But he was alive. (1 May 1995, 28)

This piece is very like fiction; in fact, Aristotle would have called it an argument from example (see the chapter on rhetorical reasoning). The writers used the third person point of view to describe the details of the blast as it affected one man and his family, before giving other details about the larger effects of the bombing. They presented Webber as a victim of a tragic irony: he and his family moved away to Oklahoma city on the presumption that they would be safer in the Midwest than in Washington DC. Moreover, the writers characterized Webber as "stunned" and "wild with fear," thus creating dramatic character like those in novels. These details and effects create ethical interest where a simple rehearsal of the facts could not.

As another means of securing good will, rhetors can say why they think their presentation of an argument is important, and what benefits will accrue to those who read or listen to it. We made an ethical appeal of this sort at the beginning of this book when we suggested that the study of ancient rhetorics would, in essence, turn people into better citizens. Of course, this ploy works only if audiences do not suspect ulterior motives on a rhetor's part. Television advertisements for life insurance often begin with scenarios depicting loved ones whose lives have been disrupted by the death of a provider who left no insurance. While the companies that sponsor these ads seem to have good will toward their audience insofar as they wish to protect people from harm, viewers know that these companies also want to sell insurance. In this case, they do it by frightening people—a tactic that is marginally ethical.

Establishing good will is especially difficult to manage when students write for teachers, since in this case the audience is usually better informed than the rhetor. The best way to demonstrate good will in this case is to follow teachers' instructions.

VOICE AND RHETORICAL DISTANCE

We have been arguing that rhetors can create a character within a discourse, and that such self-characterizations are persuasive. Ancient rhetoricians realized that very subtle ethical effects were available through the manipulation of stylistic features. Here is Hermogenes of Tarsus, for example, on how to convey an appearance of anger by means of word choice:

> Rough and vehement diction and coined words are indicative of anger, especially in sudden attacks on your opponent, where unusual words that seem to be coined on the spur of the moment are quite suitable, words such as "iamb-eater" or "pen-pusher." All such words are suitable since they seem to have been dictated by emotion. (*On Types of Style*, 359)

Rhetors can still create self-characterizations by means of certain stylistic choices: modern rhetoricians give the name "voice" to this self-dramatization in style.[1] Of course voice is a metaphor in that it suggests that all rhetorical situations, even those that use written or electronic media, mimic the relation of one person speaking to another. Written or electronic discourse that creates a lively and accessible voice makes reading more interesting. Like the characters of style, the repertoire of possible voices is immense: there are cheerful voices, gloomy ones, stuffy ones, homey ones, sincere ones, angry ones—the list is endless.

Voices affect the rhetorical distance that exists between rhetors and their audiences. Once again, the term "distance" is a metaphor representing the degree of physical and social distance that exists between people speaking to one another. But even in written or electronic discourse rhetors can narrow or widen the rhetorical distance between themselves and their audiences by means of stylistic choice. When creating a voice, rhetors should consider the situation for which they are composing: how much distance is appropriate, given their relationship to an audience; how much distance is appropriate, given their relationship to the issue. As a general rule, persuasion occurs more easily when audiences can identify with rhetors. Identification increases as distance decreases.

Intimate distance = Closer Identification, More Persuasive Potential

Formal Distance = Less Identification, Less Persuasive Potential

Rhetors who know an audience well, or whose audience is quite small, can use an intimate distance (unless some factor in the rhetorical situation prevents this). The distance created in personal letters, for example, is ordinarily quite intimate, while that used in business correspondence is more formal since rhetors either do not know their correspondents personally or because convention dictates that such relationships be kept at arm's length, so to speak. However, rhetorical situations can create exceptions to the distance–intimacy equation. Formal language is ordinarily appropriate in a courtroom, for example, even though an attorney, a defendant, and a judge constitute a very small group. In addition, the attorney may know both the judge and the defendant well. Nonetheless, she probably ought to use formal language in her conversations with both, given the official and serious nature of courtroom transactions. And sometimes very large groups are addressed in quite intimate language: performers at concerts and television evangelists, whose audiences number in the thousands or even millions, nonetheless occasionally address their audiences quite personally and intimately.

A rhetor's attitude toward the issue also influences distance. Where rhetors remain as neutral as possible, expressing neither a supportive nor rejecting attitude, distance tends to be greater. On the other hand, rhetors' strong expression of an attitude—approval or disapproval, for example—closes distance.

Attitude = Intimate Distance

Less Attitude = More Formal Distance

Compare the implied distance between writer and audience in the following statements. The first is excerpted from an article written by Rich Lowry, which appeared in the partisan *National Review:*

> The clearest indication yet that democrats hope to decapitate the House Government Reform and Oversight committee came on Thursday, April 10, in the *Wall Street Journal*—an Al Hunt column vilifying the committee's chairman, Dan Burton (Ind.). In the media food chain, Al Hunt is in the spot closest to Washington's Democratic apparatus, feasting on its handouts. The Democratic target *du jour* is Burton, and so Hunt hit him for his "fringe views and theories," called one of his staffers "wacko," and warned that a campaign-finance allegation against Burton "could prove dreadfully serious." (5 May 1997, 20)

Here is our revision, which attempts to use more neutral language to describe the same event:

> Last week, *Wall Street Journal* columnist Al Hunt criticized Indiana congressman Dan Burton for wavering in his perspectives and for maintaining an unstable support staff. Burton, an eight-term Indiana congressman and chair of the House Government Reform and Oversight Committee, is leading investigations into allegations made against the Clinton administration. Hunt's column suggests that he and other Washington journalists are trying to protect the Clinton administration by refracting ethical questions back onto investigation.

Whether readers are charmed or repelled by Lowry's ethos, it is difficult to feel neutral toward him. His use of disapproving language ("media food chain," "feasting on handouts," "wacko") creates a far more intimate distance than the neutral language of our revision, where the authors' voices are remote to the point of disappearing from view.

Grammatical Person

The prominent features of style that affect voice and distance are: grammatical person, verb tense and voice, word size, qualifiers, and—in written discourse— punctuation. There are three grammatical persons available in English: first person, where the person or persons speaking or writing refer to themselves as "I" or "we"; second person, where the audience is addressed by means of "you"; and third person, where the rhetor mentions agents or issues but does not allude directly to herself or her audience.

First Person Reference

"I will veto this bill when it comes to my desk." (The President speaks, referring to himself as "I.")

Second Person Address

"You'll see . . . I'll veto this bill." (The President speaks to someone else, referring to that person in second person.)

Third Person Reference

"President Smith will veto the bill sent him by Congress today." (Another person speaks about the President.)

or "Today the White House announced that it will veto the bill. (Someone speaking about the President uses **metonymy** to increase distance even more by referring not to the President's person but to the place where he lives.)

Composition textbooks (and teachers) often tell their students never to use first-person ("I" or "we") or second-person ("you") pronouns in the papers they write in school. We think that this rule is far too simple and inflexible to respond to the great variety of rhetorical situations that people encounter.

Generally, first- and second-person discourses create less distance between a rhetor and an audience than does third-person discourse, because the participants in the action are referred to directly. In third-person discourse, the issue or subject is foregrounded instead, and references to the rhetor or her audience tend to disappear. Thus third-person discourse creates the greatest possible rhetorical distance. First- and second-person discourses are used in situations where rhetors are physically proximate to audiences—in conversation, and in more formal speech situations as well. In settings where spoken discourse is used, "I" and "you" actually refer to participants in the situation, even when the audience is very, very large, as it is at football games and open-air concerts. Third-person is generally used by speakers only within quite formal contexts, or if convention dictates that it be used—at a conference of scientists, for instance.

First-Person Discourse

First- and second-person have interesting and complex ethical effects in writing and in electronic discourse, since the persons participating in these rhetorical acts are not physically proximate to each other. Here is a fictional example of first-person discourse, from Charles Dickens' novel *David Copperfield:*

> Whether I shall turn out to be the hero of my own life, or whether that station will be held by anybody else, these pages must show. To begin my life with the beginning of my life, I record that I was born . . .

Here is a version of the passage revised into third-person discourse:

> Whether or not David Copperfield turns out to be the hero of his own life will be shown in these pages. To begin the story of his life at its beginning, records show that he was born . . .

The third person version demonstrates how that choice increases the distance between reader and writer as well as that between readers and the subject of this novel, the life of David Copperfield.

We used the first-person pronoun throughout this book, even though to do so is unconventional in textbooks. We did so for three reasons. First of all, this voice seemed to be more honest, since much of what we have to say here has developed from our own thinking about the usefulness of ancient rhetoric. As a result, writing in first-person was easier for us since we didn't have to go searching for circumlocutions like "in the opinion of the authors" to express what we think. Second, when we took a position on a matter that is debated by scholars of ancient rhetoric, the first-person voice allowed us to take responsibility for that position; third-person made flat statements about disputed matters seem far too authoritative and decisive. Third, we hoped that readers would identify more readily with a first-person voice. The material in this book is foreign and difficult, and by itself puts quite a little distance between us and our readers. The use of a third-person voice would only widen that distance. Our choice of first-person did create one problem, one that some readers may have noticed by now. The first-person voice often led us to want to write in second person as well, as in phrases like "Notice how . . . " and "you should do. . . ." Since we wanted to avoid the instructional tone conveyed by the second person, we were often forced to substitute third-person circumlocutions for "you"— "the rhetor," "the writer," and so on.

There is yet another rhetorical problem inherent in the use of a first-person voice. Its use can create an ego-centered voice that excludes an audience. Whether this happens or not depends on the care taken by the rhetor to establish a respectable ethos and on his attitude toward his subject. Here is an example— taken from an article by Lewis H. Lapham and published in *Harpers*—of a first-person voice that may cause readers to feel excluded:

> Were I to believe what I read in the papers, I would find it easy to think that I no longer can identify myself simply as an American. The noun apparently means nothing unless it is dressed up with at least one modifying adjective. As a plain American I have neither voice nor authentic proofs of existence. I acquire a presence only as an old American, a female American, a white American, a rich American, a black American, a gay American, a poor American, a native American, a dead American. The subordination of the noun to the adjectives makes a mockery of both the American premise and the democratic spirit, but it serves the purposes of the politicians as well as the news media, and throughout the rest of this election year I expect the political campaigns to pitch their tents and slogans on the frontiers of race and class. For every benign us, the candidates will find a malignant them; for every neighboring we (no matter how eccentric or small in number), a distant and devouring they. (284:1700 [January 1992] p. 43)

Interestingly enough, the effectiveness of this first-person voice depends on whether or not readers share Lapham's desire that all Americans be identified as similar to one another simply because they live in the same country. Readers whose identity customarily has an adjective placed in front of it (whether they want this to happen or not) might wonder whether the author represented by this voice understands how difficult it is for some persons to be thought of "simply as an American."

First-person discourse always implies the presence of a hearer or a reader, a "you" who is listening or reading, whether that "you" is explicitly mentioned or not. Prose that relies on an "I–you" relation indicates to members of an audience that a rhetor feels close enough to them to include them in a relatively intimate conversation:

> Dear folks: I know you may be worried about me, so I'm writing to say that I arrived safely. Please send money. Love, your son.

The author of this note gives no details at all about his arrival—when, where, how. He obviously feels so close to his audience that he assumes they need no more information than he supplies.

In relationships that are not intimate, the "I–you" voice has complex ethical effects. Novelist Fyodor Dostoevsky's "Underground Man" provides a good instance of the ego-centeredness that may result from the use of first-person discourse, even when the rhetor is a fictional person, as he is in this case:

> I am a sick man . . . I am a spiteful man. I am an unpleasant man. I think my liver is diseased. However, I don't know beans about my disease, and I am not sure what is bothering me. I don't treat it and never have, though I respect medicine and doctors. Besides, I am extremely superstitious, let's say sufficiently so to respect medicine. (I am educated enough not to be superstitious, but I am.) No, I refuse to treat it out of spite. You probably will not understand that. Well, but I understand it. Of course, I can't explain to you just whom I am annoying in this case by my spite. (1)

Here is a complaining neighbor, wrapped so deeply in his own troubles that he seems at first to be engaging in an ego-centered, aimless, and self-contradictory monologue. But suddenly he acknowledges the presence of an audience ("you probably will not understand"), a move that establishes a sort of back-fence intimacy. And the final sentence in the passage suggests that the relationship will become "us" against "them" before very long. The intimate "I–you" relationship includes Dostoevsky's audience, whether they want to be this man's companion or not.

The ethical possibilities opened by a grammatical person are endless. In *Desert Solitaire*, Edward Abbey used a combination of third and first persons to separate "us" from "them."

> There may be some among the readers of this book . . . who believe without question that any and all forms of construction and development are intrinsic goods, in the national parks as well as anywhere else, who virtually identify quantity with quality and therefore assume that the greater the quantity of traffic, the higher the value received. There are some who frankly and boldly advocate the eradication of the last remnants of wilderness and the complete subjugation of nature to the requirement of—not man—but industry. This is a courageous view, admirable in its simplicity and power, and with the weight of all modern history behind it. It is also quite insane. I cannot attempt to deal with it here.
>
> There will be other readers, I hope, who share my basic assumption that wilderness is a necessary part of civilization and that it is the primary responsibility of the national park system to preserve intact and undiminished what little still remains. (1968, 47)

Abbey referred to those who don't share his opinions in the third person, perhaps because he was pretty sure they wouldn't be among his readers. This tactic created a "we–they" relationship that gave Abbey's readers a sense of being allied with him against those who do not share his position.

"We," the plural first-person pronoun, shares in the complex rhetorical effects created by the use of "I." "We" may establish a cozy intimacy that presumes much in common between rhetor and audience. Joe Bob Briggs is a master of the conspiratorial "we." Here he is having fun with the "Iron John" branch of the men's movement:

All right, guys, listen up.

It hasn't been our century, has it?

We kinda blew it, didn't we?

Even though you don't know exactly what I'm talking about, you kinda *know what I'm talking about*, don't you?

Haven't you had that morning where you wake up, look around and go, "Do I have to do this again?" And maybe you can't describe exactly what it is that's missing, but *something* is missing, right?

I'm here to tell you what's missing.

Your Ancient Spear is missing.

Obviously I don't mean that you need to go out and buy a spear. If it was that easy, I'd be selling you a spear. Instead, I'm selling you a book.

No, what I'm talking about is something deeper, much deeper than a plain wooden spear or one of those spears with a lot of feathers hanging off it like Cochise had. Yes, what I'm talking about is richer than that, *richer even than Michael Ansara's spear.* I'm talking about the Golden Spear that lies at the bottom of the Soggy Gooey Lake. . . .

We men fought an entire war in Europe so that a New Man could emerge in America, and what did we end up with?

Ward Cleaver.

Gimme a break.

Let's face it, it's been all downhill since then, hasn't it?

We're weenies.

We've been weenies.

Women have known this for a long time. (*New York Times Book Review* [31 May 1992]: 44)

In addition to his repeated assertion that men "know" what he is talking about, Briggs uses allusions to popular TV shows, short sentences, questions, and colloquialisms ("gimme a break") to reinforce the impression he wants to give: that he and the reader have a lot in common by virtue of their being men during the late twentieth century.

And so the use of "we" may exclude readers depending upon whether they are included in the group of persons it designates, and whether or not their inclusion/exclusion matters in some way. Compare the relative inclusiveness of the following uses of "we":

We the people of the United States . . .

We shall overcome.

"We weren't always old and conservative. We used to be young and conservative." (New York Life Insurance Company)

In the first example, "we" refers to the Americans who established their colony as an independent nation; "we" was intended to consolidate group feeling among Americans against the British, who were very definitely excluded from its scope. On the other hand, the "we" in "we shall overcome" has a generally inclusive effect. Anybody can join the singers. Compare the original version to the distancing effect, for anyone who is not African-American, of "African-Americans will overcome." In the third example, "we" refers, presumably, to the people who run an insurance company, who want to project an ethos of wise, risk-free management. This reference to a group of persons that does not include the reader is something of a departure for advertising, which generally uses a second-person voice. Whether or not readers will do as they are asked in the last paragraph ("call your New York Life agent") depends upon whether or not they wish to be included in a group of investors who are "set in our ways" and who "weather the storms" because of their conservative financial philosophy.

Second-Person Discourse

Second-person discourse is the province of advertising. "Come fly the friendly skies"; "Just do it"; "Remember when you dreamed of becoming a man? How's it going?" (BVD); "You're in good hands." Advertisers want their audiences to feel close to the companies they represent and the products they sell. The cozy second-person voices they establish cover over the fact that every ad gives instructions to its audience: use this, buy that. In other words, a rhetorical problem is potentially inherent in second-person discourse, because rhetors who adopt it are giving directions. Obviously, this is true of recipes and directions for using or assembling something: "Add just a pinch of marjoram to the boiling sauce"; "Join tab A to slot B." The person who gives directions assumes a position of superiority to audiences. If readers are ready to be dictated to, as users of recipes usually are, this voice works. When readers or hearers are not receptive to instruction, use of the second-person pronoun can increase distance rather than closing it. For example, political activist and Presidential candidate Ross Perot goofed in his address at the annual convention of the National Association for the Advancement of Colored People when he referred to the audience several times as "you people." Perot's grammatical separation created a palpable and alienating distance between himself and his audience.

Third-Person Discourse

Third-person voice establishes the greatest possible distance between writer and reader. Use of this grammatical person announces that its author, for whatever reasons, cannot afford too much intimacy with an audience. Third person is appropriate when rhetors wish to establish themselves as authorities or when they wish to efface their voice so that the issue may seem to be presented as objectively as possible. In third-person discourse the relationship of both rhetor and audience to the issue being discussed is more important than the relation between them.

Here is a passage from Fredrich A. Hayek's *The Constitution of Liberty* that is written in third person:

> The great aim of the struggle for liberty has been equality before the law. This equality under the rules which the state enforces may be supplemented by a similar equality of the rules that men voluntarily obey in the relations with one another. This extension of the principles of equality to the rules of moral and social conduct is the

chief expression of what is commonly called the democratic spirit—and probably that aspect of it that does most to make inoffensive the inequalities that liberty necessarily produces.

Hayek did not qualify the generalizations put forward in this paragraph with an "I think" or even with an "Experience shows that . . . ". He may have had several reasons for choosing to write in this distancing fashion: to seem objective, to seem authoritative and therefore forceful, or to keep his subject—equality—in front of readers, rather than his personality. Since Hayek is a well-known political theorist, his status as an authority (his situated ethos) may be such that he doesn't have to qualify his generalizations.

Here's another example of third-person discourse from the first page of *How Institutions Think,* written by a well-known anthropologist, Mary Douglas:

> Writing about cooperation and solidarity means writing at the same time about rejection and mistrust. Solidarity involves individuals being ready to suffer on behalf of the larger group and their expecting other individual members to do as much for them. It is difficult to talk about these questions coolly. They touch on intimate feelings of loyalty and sacredness. Anyone who has accepted trust and demanded sacrifice or willingly given either knows the power of the social bond. Whether there is a commitment to authority or a hatred of tyranny or something between the extremes, the social bond itself is taken to be something above question. Attempts to bring it out into the light of day and to investigate it are resisted. Yet it needs to be examined. Everyone is affected directly by the quality of trust around him or her.

This third-person voice is a bit less distancing than Hayek's, because it does refer to people, rather than to abstractions. However, Douglas takes great pains not to name anyone, even though she is writing about intimate issues ("feelings of loyalty and sacredness"). Use of the third-person forces Douglas to put rather vague words in the grammatical subject positions of her sentences: "writing," "solidarity," "it," "they," "anyone." We have revised the passage into first person, making the author ("I") the grammatical subject of most of the sentences:

> If I write about cooperation and solidarity, I must write at the same time about rejection and mistrust. I define "solidarity" as the readiness of individuals to suffer on behalf of the larger group and their expecting other individual members to do as much for them. I have difficulty talking about these questions coolly, because they touch on intimate feelings of loyalty and sacredness. Since I have accepted trust and demanded sacrifice, and have willingly given them as well, I know the power of the social bond. I take the social bond to be above question; my commitment to authority or my hatred of tyranny are irrelevant to this question. Every time I attempt to bring it out into the light of day and to investigate it, people resist my efforts. Yet we need to examine it, because all of us are affected by the quality of trust around us.

We think the revision makes the passage clearer and more lively as well. Use of the first person also forces the author to take responsibility for the large generalizations she makes about the touchiness of this question. However, our use of first-person discourse does lessen the authority carried by the original passage, because the generalizations made in the revision are less sweeping in scope. That is, they apply to "I" rather than to people in general.

Scientists, social scientists, and other scholars use third-person discourse in order to reinforce the impression that the facts speak for themselves, that human beings have had as little influence in these matters as possible. The warning label on cigarette packages, for example, used to read as follows: "Warning: The Surgeon General Has Determined That Cigarette Smoking Is Dangerous To Your Health." Even though the Surgeon General probably did not conduct the research that discovered the connection between smoking and lung cancer, the message relied on the authority of that office to underscore the seriousness of the message. A later version of this warning reads: "Quitting Smoking Now Greatly Reduces Serious Risks To Your Health." While the newer version is a bit more specific, it is also firmer, because it omits reference to an author and addresses the audience directly. It is probably safe to predict that this warning will never be couched in a first-person voice: "I think that smoking cigarettes is bad for you, and you ought to stop it. Mary Jones, M.D." The intimacy of first-person simply undermines the authority that this serious message requires.

Students often use third person when they write for teachers, on the correct assumptions that the formal distance lends authority to their work, and that it is appropriate for the rhetorical situation that obtains in most classrooms. A curious thing sometimes happens within third-person prose, however: people write phrases like "the writer of this paper feels" or "in the opinion of this author." If these constructions emerge during the writing process, it may be that the issue demands that the rhetor express some opinions and take responsibility for them. In this case, first person may be a better choice. Third-person statements tend to have an authoritative flavor. When rhetors find themselves trying to add qualifiers about their opinions or attitudes, it may be the case that the third-person voice is inappropriate or even dishonest. Of course, dishonesty is disastrous if a reader detects it.

Verb Tense and Voice

The choice of grammatical person is the most influential element in establishing voice and distance. However, other stylistic choices, such as verb tense and voice, affect an ethos as well. Present tense has more immediacy than past tense; use of the present tense gives an audience a sense of participation in events that are occurring at the moment, while past tense makes them feel like onlookers in events that have already occurred. Compare your response to the following phrasings:

Present Tense: Quintilian teaches his students to . . .

Past Tense: Quintilian taught his students to . . .

The second example distances readers from Quintilian because it explicitly places his teaching in the past.

In English, verbs may assume one of two "voices"—active and passive. Passive verb constructions betray themselves through an explicit or implicit "by

_____" phrase, as in "The door was left open (by _____)." Phrasing such a construction in active voice requires the rhetor to supply somebody (or some thing) who can act as an agent upon the door: John, for example, as in "John left the door open." Active verb constructions tend to lessen distance, since rhetors using them are forced to name either themselves or somebody or something else as an actor in the sentence; usually this rhetorical subject (the actor) is also the grammatical subject of a sentence with an active verb construction. Passive constructions, on the other hand, tend to create distance between rhetor and issue, since the grammatical subject of the sentence is usually not its rhetorical subject.

Active Voice: Mary did the dishes.

Passive Voice: The dishes were done.

Active Voice: I take responsibility for these actions.

Passive Voice: Responsibility must be taken for these actions.

Active constructions force rhetors to betray their presence as creator of the discourse; it also forces them to take overt responsibility for their assertions. Passive constructions permit rhetors to avoid taking responsibility for their statements. "The police were misled" is a passive construction that avoids mentioning the person who did the misleading.

Sometimes this strategy is useful, depending upon the rhetorical situation. If rhetors do not know what they need to know, they may want to disguise their ignorance by using passive constructions. Rhetors who do so, however, run the risk of damaging their audience's estimate of their intelligence, honesty, and good will. Take this passive sentence, for example:

> Sometimes ridiculed for directing their presentation to the non-intellectual, television news coverage is obligated to give a concise, easily understandable, factual news report.

In this case, the use of third person creates distance between author and audience, since the passive construction allows the rhetor to disappear completely. Since nobody is around to take responsibility, readers might wonder just how authoritative this statement is. A reader might wonder: "Well, who obligates television news coverage to be concise, factual, and so on? Who says so? In my experience, Cokie Roberts and Dan Rather and the rest don't always stick to the facts. . . ." If this happens, the rhetor might as well have never written at all, because important aspects of ethos—that the rhetor appears well informed and honest, and that the rhetor appears to have the audience's interest in mind—have been compromised. Active voice might have been a better choice, although it requires naming some names and taking some responsibility for assertions:

> Critics sometimes ridicule television news coverage for directing their presentation to the non-intellectual. News writers couch the news in simple terms, however, because their duty as journalists obligates them to give a concise, easily understandable, factual news report.

Word Size

Other stylistic resources help to establish voice, as well. Word size seems to affect voice and distance. American audiences tend to assume that polysyllabic words (big words with lots of syllables, like "polysyllabic") indicate that the user is well-educated. Hence, they are likely to confer authority on a rhetor who uses them. Compare the effect of "It will be my endeavor in this analysis . . . " to that of "Here I will try to analyze . . . ".

When used carefully, polysyllabic words are generally more precise than smaller words: "polysyllabic" is more specific than "large" or "big"; "deconstructing" is both more impressive and precise than "taking apart"; "chloroflourocarbons" is more precise, but less intimate, than "the stuff that causes holes in the ozone layer." Because of their greater accuracy, larger words tend to appear in formal discourse, where rhetors are more concerned with accuracy than with establishing an intimate relation with readers. However, big words can have the disadvantage of making their user sound pompous; too many polysyllabic words can also discourage people from making the effort to plow through them, especially if their meanings are obscure to the intended audience. Here is a brief passage written by philosopher Jacques Derrida:

> On what conditions is a grammatology possible? Its fundamental condition is certainly the undoing of logocentrism. But this condition of possibility turns into a condition of impossibility. In fact it risks upsetting the concept of science as well. Graphematics or grammatography ought no longer to be presented as sciences; their goal should be exorbitant when compared to a grammatological knowledge. (*Of Grammatology* [1976], 74)

While Derrida writes simple sentences, he nonetheless litters his pages with polysyllabic terms whose meanings are unfamiliar to many readers (chiefly because Derrida coined many of them himself). One has to be very committed to read Derrida's work because it takes a long time to learn the meanings of the terms he employs.

Familiar words are effective in informal discursive situations where the audience is on fairly close terms with the rhetor; everyone shares common understanding that lessens the rhetor's obligation to be precise. "Cool!" or "This Rocks!" are examples wherein precision of meaning is absolutely sacrificed to the establishment of intimacy. (As you can see, these phrases, which are ordinarily used in conversation, lose much of their effect in print.)

Qualifiers

Qualifiers like "some," "most," "virtually," and "all" affect voice and distance. A qualifier is any term (usually an adverb or an adjective) or phrase that alters the degree of force or extent contained in a statement. Compare the relative distance achieved by the use of qualifiers in the following statements:

All humans are created equal.

It may be that some humans are created equal.

Actually, very few humans are created equal.

Virtually no humans are created equal.

The first statement is quite distant, because it makes a sweeping, authoritative judgement. No authors are present to identify with readers. The other statements are more intimate because they betray the presence of an author, modifying the extent or intensity of her or his judgement in each case.

As a general rule, the more qualifiers, and the more intensity they convey, the more intimate the distance between rhetor and audience. Qualifiers have this effect because they indicate, however subtly, that someone is present, making judgements about degrees of intensity. Compare this unqualified statement to the heavily qualified one that follows it:

> Three months after announcing it had settled a lawsuit filed against it by Bread and Butter Corporation, the City Council of Ourtown made the agreement public today.

> Three long months after announcing it had tentatively settled one of the most expensive civil lawsuits in the city's history, today the City Council of Ourtown, with some trepidation, made public a proposed agreement between it and the gigantic Bread and Butter Corporation.

The first version creates more distance between author and readers because the writer expresses few judgements about the event under discussion. The author of the second version, on the other hand, is willing to qualify events by using adjectives and adverbs that express degree ("tentatively," "expensive," "gigantic").

Composition textbooks sometimes caution writers against the use of qualifiers, calling them "weasel words." However, *cautious* rhetors *often* find it necessary to use a *few* qualifiers in order to represent a position as *accurately* as possible. (The italicized words in the preceding sentence are qualifiers.) Moreover, qualifiers can be effective in reducing distance between a rhetor and an audience in situations where an intimate distance is more persuasive than a more formal one.

Here is a passage about Newt Gingrich, who was Speaker of the House of Representatives in 1997. It was composed by the editors of the *National Review.* We have italicized the qualifiers that appear in it.

> The leader of a *reformist, populist* party in a *representative* government must stay on the offensive to survive. He should not pick *quixotic* fights and need not eschew *tactical* compromises, but he must continue to make *strategic* advances across a broad front. Instead, Gingrich has narrowed the *Republican* agenda and adopted a *defensive* posture. The decision to get the President's signature on a *balanced* budget at any cost has enabled Clinton to extort concession after concession from a *demoralized* GOP. That is surely not Gingrich's fault *alone.* But he should not be surprised that troops without a mission will *sometimes* direct their energies against one another. (11 August 1997, 14)

Some of the italicized qualifiers are necessary to convey the meaning of the passage ("representative," "Republican," "balanced"). However, the other italicized terms work to convey Buckley's opinion of the Republican party ("reformist," "populist"). These terms are conjectures about the party's agenda; not everyone will agree that they appropriately describe the party's goals. Other qualifiers convey Buckley's opinion of the Speaker's recent actions: "quixotic," "defensive," and, obviously, not everyone will agree with this assessment, either.

Punctuation

Punctuation is an extremely subtle means of establishing voice and distance in written discourse. The more exotic punctuation marks work to close distance between writers and readers; they do the work that gestures, facial expressions, tone, and pitch do for speakers. Dashes convey breathlessness or hurry—or a midthought—or an afterthought. Parentheses (like these) decrease distance, because they have the flavor of an interruption, a remark whispered behind the hand. Exclamation points indicate strong emotions at work! *Underlining* or **bold** or CAPS convey emphasis or importance, and all of these graphic signals close the distance between rhetor and audience. Textbooks say that quotation marks should only be used to represent material that has been quoted from another source, but increasingly quotation marks are being used for emphasis. This example shows them doing both jobs: "We don't "cash" checks."

People who use computers are developing a lexicon of punctuation marks, called "emoticons," to indicate ethos. Among these are the use of asterisks on either side of a word to indicate some action on the rhetor's part: *blush* *wink*. A wink can also be indicated by this creative combination of punctuation marks ;-). Here is an example of the use of punctuation to enhance ethos:

> Sharon:
>
> Our meeting yesterday proves that two heads definitely make more stuff ;-). To recap: I will plow through my list, edit the chapters on extrinsic proof and formal logic and deliver the ms to you. Then you will add the remaining items on the list, do a final edit, and we'll be DONE with draft one (*big exhale*). Then we can put on our party hats. @:-)
>
> Deb

These innovative marks of punctuation seem to make e-mail less distant by bringing author's personality into their posts.

If you doubt that such small things do influence distance, note whether you are offended or not the next time you see them in a posting e-mailed to you by someone you do not know. Contemporary decorum seems to dictate, in short, that fancy or innovative punctuation should be used in intimate situations while discourse composed for more formal rhetorical situations should feature only the standard punctuation marks to distinguish sentences and indicate possession (see the chapter on delivery).

SITUATED ETHOS

Because rhetoric is embedded in social context, the relative social standing of participants in a rhetorical situation can effect a rhetor's persuasiveness. A differential power relation is inherent in any rhetorical situation simply because rhetors have the floor, so to speak. As long as they are being read or heard they have control of the situation. But audiences have power too, particularly in the case of written rhetoric, where readers are relatively free to quit whenever they please. Few rhetors enjoy absolute power over either hearers or readers. We all know how easy it is to mute television commercials or to skip to the end of a murder mystery to see how it turns out.

But differential power relations exist outside of rhetorical situations, and these affect the degree to which an invented ethos can be effective. In other words, exceptions to Aristotle's generalizations about ethos occur in rhetorical situations where a rhetor's ethos is either bolstered or compromised by her or his reputation and position in the community. Such exceptions apply most strongly to well-known people, and especially to those who are well known because they hold some authoritative or prestigious position in the community. Ministers generally enjoy more cultural authority than bartenders, at least in rhetorical situations where they are considered to have expertise. A prior reputation as an "A" student, or as a goof-off, may effect a teacher's reception of a student's work, no matter how carefully that student crafts an invented ethos.

Rhetors and audiences may exist in unequal social relations to one another for a variety of reasons. Within classrooms, for example, teachers have more power than students, and usually teachers can interrupt students whenever they think it's necessary or proper to do so. Within the culture at large, in general, older people have more authority than younger people, and wealthy people have more power than poorer people (when E. F. Hutton speaks . . . people listen!). According to a modern rhetorician named Wayne Brockriede (1968), there are three major dimensions in any rhetorical situation: interpersonal, attitudinal, and situational.

The interpersonal dimension—the relations among persons who participate in a rhetorical act—has three characteristics: liking, power, and distance. *Liking* has to do with how well the people who are engaging in a rhetorical situation like each other. During the years when the United States and the Soviet Union were negotiating a peaceful co-existence, reporters made much of the fact that the leaders of the two countries, Boris Yeltsin and Bill Clinton, actually seemed to like each other. According to Professor Brockriede, this personal relationship should have smoothed their discussions of the difficult issues that these two leaders had to face.

Under the head of "liking," then, rhetors should ask: Are the feelings of liking or disliking mutual among participants in this rhetorical situation or in arguments about this issue? How intense are these feelings? Are these feelings susceptible to rhetorical change?

Brockriede defines *power* as "the capacity to exert interpersonal influence." Power may be the focus of a rhetorical act (as in "a power struggle"), or it may be a by-product of the act. A person may have power in a rhetorical situation for several reasons: charisma, position within the social system, control over the channels of communication or other aspects of the rhetorical situation, influence over sources of information and/or the participants' ideology, or access to powerful people. President Ronald Reagan, who was frequently referred to as "the great communicator," was thought by his supporters to have great personal charm, or charisma (which was to be expected, perhaps, given his experience as an actor). John F. Kennedy was also thought to be a charismatic person, and many television evangelists owe their success to their personal charisma.

But not everyone has this mysterious quality called charisma. And so it is also important for rhetors to think about the power structure inherent in any rhetorical situation. Power is usually unequally shared between rhetors and their audiences. Few rhetors enjoy absolute power over their hearers or readers, even those, like the President of the United States, who can exert enormous power in other situations.

Rhetors who control the channels of communication have great situated power, because in extreme situations they can force people to become their audiences. When the President schedules a news conference on an important issue, for example, television networks are obligated to carry it, even though this costs them money. People are obligated to listen and watch, unless they take rhetorical power into their own hands and turn the television off. A film about the murder of John F. Kennedy apparently influenced the U.S. Senate to open secret government files on his assassination. In this case, the director of the film, Oliver Stone, has a controversial reputation as a filmmaker, and he is well financed and can make almost any film he wishes. His reputation gave him access to a communication channel that was much more rhetorically powerful than any of the many books about the assassination had been.

Rhetorical power is obviously tied to access. Access (or lack of it) can either facilitate communication or disable certain possibilities for fruitful exchange. The issue of access came to the fore during the 1995 controversy over the national budget when Republican leaders claimed to have been denied opportunities to discuss budget concerns with President Bill Clinton. Here is an account of an incident from the *Detroit News:*

> House Speaker Newt Gingrich said Wednesday that he decided to toughen the Republican position on the budget after being "stiffed" by President Clinton aboard Air Force One.
>
> Gingrich, R-Ga., and Senate Majority Leader Bob Dole, R-Kan., were among dozens of dignitaries who flew to Israel last week with Clinton to attend the funeral of Prime Minister Yitzhak Rabin.
>
> The GOP leaders were insulted that their only contact with Clinton during the 25-hour round-trip flight was when he walked by twice to thank them for coming, Gingrich said. A chat with White House Chief of Staff Leon Panetta lasted only a few minutes.
>
> Gingrich said he and Dole assumed at least part of the journey would be spent trying to work out the imminent budget crisis.

Then the guests were told to exit the rear ramp of Air Force One when it returned to Andrews Air Force Base outside of Washington, while Clinton exited the main steps in full view of waiting media.

"Was it just a sign of utter incompetence and lack of consideration or was it a deliberate strategy of insult?" Gingrich said Wednesday.

He said he concluded at that point that the White House wasn't interested in compromising, and they shared no common ground. Consequently, he said, Congress would have to pass important budget-related legislation without Democratic votes.

"That's part of why you ended up with us sending down a tougher continuing resolution," he said. The continuing resolution, a short-term spending measure needed to keep the government operating until a budget is adopted, was vetoed by Clinton. As a result, large chunks of the government shut down Tuesday.

"This was not petty," Gingrich said. "This was an effort on our part to read the White House strategy. . . . It was clear coming out of that airplane that they wanted a confrontation." (16 November 1995, 6A)

Here issues of power and access came to the fore, radically influencing the rhetorical strategies that followed. Because Gingrich and Dole read their limited contact with the president as a controlled measure of avoidance, a standoff ensued, and for weeks to come the government did not function as usual. Indeed, federal agencies all over the country closed their doors, leaving 800,000 federal employees temporarily out of work because they had no operating budgets.

Here are some questions to ask about the power structure of a rhetorical situation: how disparate are the power positions of the various participants of a rhetorical act, and does the act increase, maintain, or decrease the disparity? How rigid or flexible is the power structure, and does the rhetorical act function to increase, maintain, or decrease the stability?

As we have been saying, the rhetorical principle of distance examines how far apart, socially or situationally, participants are from one another in a rhetorical situation. When choosing a voice for a discourse, a rhetor should ask: Is this the optimal distance for persuasion, or should it be closed or opened up?

The attitudinal dimension of rhetorical situations determines what predispositions exist among the participants in a rhetorical act that will influence their response to the situation. We can predict, roughly, that people will respond to a rhetorical proposition in one of three ways: acceptance, indifference, or rejection. Rhetors who are preparing to argue a case should ask: what would it take to move someone who is indifferent toward acceptance or rejection of my position? Can I move someone from a position of acceptance toward rejection, or vice versa? People who do research on rhetorical situations have found that the more ego-involved participants are, the less likely it is that they will be persuaded. Is this true in the situation you are analyzing?

People do not respond to a proposition out of context; their responses are determined by their ideology. Rhetors enjoy situated power if they are in a position to influence the ideology of participants in a rhetorical situation, as parents and clergy usually are. Rhetors also have situated power if they can suppress or divulge information that is crucial to understanding or deciding an issue. Press secretaries, spokespeople, and spin doctors enjoy this sort of power. What sorts of beliefs or ideological responses will your audience bring to your rhetorical situation?

An Example

Two novelists—John Irving and Andrea Dworkin—once engaged in an interesting exchange in the pages of the *New York Times Book Review.* Irving wrote the first essay in the exchange, in which he condemned attempts to censor pornography. His essay relied for the most part on ethical and logical appeals. However, Dworkin's response to that essay, and Irving's response to Dworkin, relied for their effectiveness almost entirely on ethical appeals.

Here is Irving's essay:

> These are censorial times. I refer to the pornography victims' compensation bill, now under consideration by the Senate Judiciary Committee—that same bunch of wise men who dispatched such clearheaded, objective jurisprudence in the Clarence Thomas hearings. I can't wait to see what they're going to do with this maladroit proposal. The bill would encourage victims of sexual crimes to bring civil suits against publishers and distributors of material that is "obscene or constitutes child pornography"—*if* they can prove that the material was "a substantial cause of the offense," *and if* the publisher or distributor should have "forseen" that such material created an "unreasonable risk of such a crime." If this bill passes, it will be the first piece of legislation to give credence to the unproven theory that sexually explicit material actually *causes* sexual crimes.
>
> At the risk of sounding old-fashioned, I'm still pretty sure that rape and child molestation predate erotic books and pornographic magazines and X-rated videocassettes. I also remember the report of the two-year, $2 million President's Commission on Obscenity and Pornography (1970), which concluded there was "no reliable evidence . . . that exposure to explicit sexual material plays a significant role in the causation of delinquent or criminal sexual behavior." In 1986, not satisfied with that conclusion, the Meese commission on pornography and the Surgeon General's conference on pornography also failed to establish such a link. Now, here they go again.
>
> This time it's Republican Senators Mitch McConnell of Kentucky, Charles Grassley of Iowa and Strom Thurmond of South Carolina; I can't help wondering if they read much. Their charmless bill is a grave mistake for several reasons; for starters, it's morally reprehensible to shift responsibility for any sexual crime onto a third party—namely, *away* from the actual perpetrator.
>
> And then, of course, there's the matter of the bill running counter to the spirit of the First Amendment of the United States Constitution; this bill is a piece of backdoor censorship, plain and simple. Moreover, since the laws on obscenity differ from state to state, and no elucidation of the meaning of obscenity is presented in the bill, how are the publishers or distributors to know in advance if their material is actionable or not? It is my understanding, therefore, that the true intent of the bill is to make the actual creators of this material think very conservatively—that is, when their imaginations turn to sex and violence.
>
> I recall that I received a lot of unfriendly mail in connection with a somewhat explicit scene in my novel "The World According to Garp," wherein a selfish young

man loses part of his anatomy while enjoying oral sex in a car. (I suppose I've always had a fear of rear-end collisions.) But thinking back about that particular hate mail, I don't recall a single letter from a young woman saying that she intended to rush out and *do* this to someone; and in the 14 years since that novel's publication, in more than 35 foreign languages, no one who actually *has done* this to someone has written to thank me for giving her the idea. Boy, am I lucky! . . .

It dismays me how some of my feminist friends are hot to ban pornography. I'm sorry that they have such short memories. It wasn't very long ago when a book as innocent and valuable as "Our Bodies, Ourselves" was being banned by school boards and public libraries across the country. The idea of this good book was that women should have access to detailed information about their bodies and their health, yet the so-called feminist ideology behind the book was thought to be subversive; indeed, it was (at that time) deplored. But many writers and writers' organizations (like PEN) wrote letters to those school boards and those public libraries. I can't speak to the overall effectiveness of these letters in regard to reinstating the book, but I'm aware that some of the letters worked; I wrote several of those letters. Now here are some of my old friends, telling me that attitudes toward rape and child molestation can be changed only if we remove offensive *ideas*. Once again, it's ideology that's being banned. And although the movement to ban pornography is especially self-righteous, it looks like blacklisting to me.

Fascism has enjoyed many name changes, but it usually amounts to banning something you dislike and can't control. Take abortion, for example. I think groups should have to apply for names; if the Right to Life people had asked me, I'd have told them to find a more fitting label for themselves. It's morally inconsistent to manifest such concern for the poor fetus in a society that shows absolutely no pity for the poor child after it's born.

I'm also not so sure that these so-called Right to Lifers are as fired up about those fetuses as they say. I suspect what really makes them sore is the idea of women having sex and somehow not having to *pay* for it—pay in the sense of suffering all the way through an unwanted pregnancy. I believe this is part of the loathing for promiscuity that has always fueled those Americans who feel that a life of decency is slipping from their controlling grasp. This notion is reflected in the unrealistic hope of those wishful thinkers who tell us that sexual abstinence is an alternative to wearing a condom. But I say how about *carrying* a condom, just in case you're moved to *not* abstain?

No one is coercing women into having abortions, but the Right to Lifers want to coerce women into having babies; that's why the pro-choice people are well named. It's unfortunate, however, that a few of my pro-choice friends think that the pornography victims' compensation bill is a good idea. I guess that they're really not entirely pro-choice. They want the choice to reproduce or not, but they *don't* want too broad a choice of things to read and see; they know what *they* want to read and see, and they expect other people to be content with what they want. This sounds like a Right to Life idea to me.

Most feminist groups, despite their vital advocacy of full enforcement of laws against violence to women and children, seem opposed to Senate Bill 1521. As of this writing, both the National Organization for Women in New York State and in California have written to the Senate Judiciary Committee in opposition to the bill, although the Los Angeles chapter of NOW states that it has "no position." I admit it is perverse of me even to imagine what Tammy Bruce thinks about the pornography victims' compensation bill; I hope Ms. Bruce is not such a loose cannon as she appears, but she has me worried. Ms. Bruce is president of the L.A. NOW, and she has lately distinguished herself with two counts of knee-jerk overreaction. Most recently, she found the Academy of Motion Picture Arts and Sciences to be guilty of an "obvious exhibition of sexism" in not nominating Barbra Streisand for an Oscar for best director. Well, maybe. Ms. Streisand's other talents have not been entirely overlooked; I meekly submit that the academy might have found "The Prince of Tides" lacking in directorial merit—it wouldn't be the first I've heard of such criticism. (Ms. Bruce says the L.A. chapter received "unrelenting calls" from NOW members who were riled up at the perceived sexism.) . . .

Do we remember that tangent of the McCaran-Walter Act of 1952, that finally defunct business about ideological exclusion? That was when we kept someone from coming into our country because we perceived that the person had *ideas* that were in conflict with the "acceptable" ideas of our country. Under this act of exclusion, writers as distinguished as Graham Greene and Gabriel Garcia Márquez were kept out of the United States. Well, when we attack what a publisher has the right to publish, we are simply applying the old ideological exclusion act at home. Of all people, those of us in the idea business should know better than that.

As for the pornography victims' compensation bill, the vote in the Senate Judiciary Committee will be close. As of this writing, seven senators have publicly indicated their support of the bill; they need only one more vote to pass the bill out of committee. Friends at PEN tell me that the committee has received a lot of letters from women saying that support of the bill would in some way "make up for" the committee's mishandling of the Clarence Thomas hearings. Some women are putting the decision to support Justice Thomas alongside the decision to find William Kennedy Smith innocent of rape; these women think that a really strong antipornography bill will make up for what they perceive to be the miscarriage of justice in both cases.

The logic of this thinking is more than a little staggering. What would these women think if lots of men were to write the committee and say that because Mike Tyson has been found guilty of rape, what we need is *more* pornography to make up for what's happened to Iron Mike? This would make a lot of sense, wouldn't it?

I conclude that these are not only censorial times; these are stupid times. However, there is some hope that opposition to Senate Bill 1521 is mounting. The committee met on March 12 but the members didn't vote on the bill. Discussion was brief, yet encouraging. Colorado Senator Hank Brown told his colleagues that there are serious problems with the legislation; he should be congratulated for his courageous decision to oppose the other Republicans on the committee, but he should also be encouraged not to accept any compromise proposal. Ohio Senator Howard Metzenbaum suggested that imposing third-party liability on producers and distributors of books, magazines, movies and recordings raises the question of whether the bill shouldn't be amended to cover the firearms and liquor industries as well.

It remains to be seen if the committee members will resist the temptation to *fix* the troubled bill. I hope they will understand that the bill cannot be fixed because it is based on an erroneous premise—namely, that publishers or distributors should be held liable for the acts of criminals. But what is important for us to recognize, even if this lame bill is amended out of existence or flat-out defeated, is that *new* antipornography legislation will be proposed.

Do we remember Nancy Reagan's advice to would-be drug users? ("Just say no.") As applied to drug use, Mrs. Reagan's advice is feeble in the extreme. But writers and other members of the literary community *should* just say no to censorship in any and every form. Of course, it will always be the most grotesque example of child pornography that will be waved in front of our eyes by the Good Taste Police. If we're opposed to censorship, they will say, are we in favor of filth like this?

No; we are not in favor of child pornography if we say no to censorship. If we disapprove of reinstating public hangings, that doesn't mean that we want all the murderers to be set free. No writer or publisher or *reader* should accept censorship in any form; fundamental to our freedom of expression is that each of us has a right to decide what is obscene and what isn't.

But lest you think I'm being paranoid about the iniquities and viciousness of our times, I'd like you to read a description of Puritan times. It was written in 1837—more than 150 years ago—and it describes a scene in a Puritan community in Massachusettes that you must imagine taking place more than 350 years ago. This is from a short story by Nathaniel Hawthorne called "Endicott and the Red Cross," which itself was written more than 10 years before Hawthorne wrote "The Scarlet Letter." This little story contains the germ of the idea for that famous novel about a woman condemned by Puritan justice to wear the letter A on her breast. But Hawthorne, obviously, had been thinking about the iniquities and viciousness of early New England morality for many years.

Please remember, as you read what Nathaniel Hawthorne thought of the Puritans, that the Puritans are not dead and gone. We have many new Puritans in our country today; they are as dangerous to freedom of expression as the old Puritans ever were. An especially sad thing is, a few of these new Puritans are formerly liberal-thinking feminists.

"In close vicinity to the sacred edifice [the meeting-house] appeared that important engine of Puritanic authority, the whipping-post—with the soil around it well trodden by the feet of evil doers, who had there been disciplined. At one corner of the meeting-house was the pillory, and at the other the stocks; . . . the head of an Episcopalian and suspected Catholic was grotesquely incased in the former machine; while a fellow-criminal, who had boisterously quaffed a health to the king, was confined by the legs in the latter. Side by side, on the meeting-house steps, stood a male and a female figure. The man was a tall, lean, haggard personification of fanaticism, bearing on his breast this label—A WANTON GOSPELLER—which betokened that he had dared to give interpretations of Holy Writ unsanctioned by the infallible judgment of the civil and religious rulers. His aspect showed no lack of zeal . . . even at the stake. The woman wore a cleft stick on her tongue, in appropriate retribution for having wagged that unruly member against the elders of the church; and her countenance and gestures gave much cause to apprehend that, the moment the stick should be removed, a repetition of the offence would demand new ingenuity in chastising it.

"The above-mentioned individuals had been sentenced to undergo their various modes of ignominy, for the space of one hour at noonday. But among the crowd were several whose punishment would be life-long; some, whose ears had been cropped, like those of puppy dogs; others, whose cheeks had been branded with the initials of their misdemeanors; one, with his nostrils slit and seared; and another, with a halter about his neck, which he was forbidden ever to take off, or to conceal beneath his garments. Methinks he must have been grievously tempted to affix the other end of the rope to some convenient beam or bough. There was likewise a young woman, with no mean share of beauty, whose doom it was to wear the letter A on the breast of her gown, in the eyes of all the world and her own children. And even her own children knew what that initial signified. Sporting with her infamy, the lost and desperate creature had embroidered the fatal token in scarlet cloth, with golden thread and the nicest art of needlework; so that the capital A might have been thought to mean Admirable, or anything rather than Adulteress.

"Let not the reader argue, from any of these evidences of iniquity, that the times of the Puritans were more vicious than our own."

In my old fashioned opinion, Mr. Hawthorne sure got that right. ("Pornography and the New Puritans," 29 March 1992)

Irving employed the commonplace of cause and effect to argue that no causal link has ever been established between the use of pornography and sexual violence. When he wrote that the sexual violence depicted in novels did not cause people to commit similar acts in real life, for example, he tried to sever any cause/effect relation between language and reality by arguing that spoken or written words (or visual images for that matter) do not effect the attitudes or habits of those who consume them. He concludes his argument with a **fable**, which his readers are supposed to take as an analogy to the current situation (see the chapter on the *progymnasmata* for information about the rhetorical uses of fables).

Dworkin responded with a long letter. This letter relies almost wholly on ethical appeals and is particularly explicit about the author's moral standards.

To the Editor:

As a woman determined to destroy the pornography industry, a writer of 10 published books and someone who reads, perhaps I should be the one to tell John Irving ("Pornography and the New Puritans," March 29) who the new Puritan is. The old Puritans wouldn't like her very much; but then, neither does Mr. Irving.

I am 45 years old now. When I was a teen-ager, I baby-sat. In any middle-class home one could always find the dirty books—on the highest shelf, climbing toward God, usually behind a parched potted plant. The books themselves were usually "Ulysses," "Tropic of Cancer" or "Lady Chatterley's Lover." They always had as a preface or afterword the text of an obscenity decision in which the book was exonerated and art extolled. Or a lawyer would stand in for the court to tell us that through his mighty efforts law had finally vindicated a persecuted genius.

Even at 15 or 16, I noticed something strange about the special intersection of art, law and sex under the obscenity rubric: some men punished other men for producing or publishing writing that caused arousal in (presumably) still other men. Although Mrs. Grundy got the blame, women didn't make these laws or enforce them or sit on juries to deliberate guilt or innocence. This was a fight among men—but about what?

Meanwhile, my life as a woman in prefeminist times went on. This means that I thought I was a human being with rights. But before I was much over 18, I had been sexually assaulted three times. Did I report these assaults (patriarchy's first question, because surely the girl must be lying)?

When I was 9, I told my parents. To protect me, for better or worse, they did not call the police.

The second time, beaten as well as raped, I told no one. I was working for a peace group, and I heard jokes about rape day in and day out. What do you tell the draft board when they ask you if you would kill a Nazi who was going to rape your sister? "I'd tell my sister to have a good time" was the answer of choice.

The third time, I was 18, a freshman in college, and I had been arrested for taking part in a sit-in outside the United Nations to protest the Vietnam War. It was February of 1965. This time, my experience was reported in the New York Times, newspapers all around the world and on television: girl in prison—New York's notorious Women's House of Detention—says she was brutalized by two prison doctors. Forced entry with a speculum—for 15 days I had vaginal bleeding, a vagina so bruised and ripped that my stone-cold family doctor burst into tears when he examined me.

I came out of the Women's House of Detention mute. Speech depends on believing you can make yourself understood: a community of people will recognize the experience in the words you use and they will care. You also have to be able to understand what happened to you enough to convey it to others. I lost speech. I was hurt past what I had words for. I lived out on the streets for several days, not having a bed of my own, still bleeding; and finally spoke because Grace Paley convinced me that she would understand and care. Then I spoke a lot. A grand jury investigated. Columnists indicted the prison. But neither of the prison doctors was charged with sexual assault or sexual battery. In fact, no one ever mentioned sexual assault. The grand jury concluded that the prison was fine. In despair, I left the country—to be a writer, my human dream.

A year later I came back. I have since discovered that what happened to me is common: homeless, poor, still sexually traumatized, I learned to trade sex for money. I spent a lot of years out on the street, living hand to mouth, these New York streets and other streets in other hard cities. I thought I was a real tough woman, and I was: tough-calloused; tough-numb; tough-desperate; tough-scared; tough-hungry; tough-beaten by men often; tough-done it every which way including up. All of my colleagues who fight pornography with me know about this. I know about the lives of women in pornography because I lived the life. So have many feminists who fight pornography. Freedom looks different when you are the one it is being practiced on. It's his, not yours. Speech is different, too. Those sexy expletives are the hate words he uses on you while he is using you. Your speech is an inchoate protest never voiced.

In my work, fiction and nonfiction, I've tried to voice the protest against a power that is dead weight on you, fist and penis organized to keep you quiet. I would do virtually anything to get women out of prostitution and pornography, which is mass-produced, technologized prostitution. With pornography, a woman can still be sold after the beatings, the rapes, the pain, the humiliation have killed her. I write for her, on behalf of her. I know her. I have come close to being her.

I read a lot of books. None of them ever told me the truth about what happens to women until feminists started writing and publishing in this wave, over these last 22 years. Over and over, male writers consider prostituted women "speech"—their speech, their right. Without this exploitation, published for profit, the male writer feels censored. The woman lynched naked on a tree, or restrained with ropes and a ball gag in her mouth, has what? Freedom of what?

I lost my ability to speak—became mute—a second time in my life. I've written about being a battered wife: I was beaten and tortured over a period of a few years. Amnesty International never showed up. Toward the end, I lost all speech. Words were useless to the likes of me. I had run away and asked for help—from friends, neighbors, the police—and had been turned away many times. My words didn't seem to mean anything, or it was O.K. to torture me.

Taken once by my husband to a doctor when hurt, I risked asking for help. The doctor said he could write me a prescription for Valium or have me committed. The neighbors heard the screaming, but no one did anything. So what are words? I have always been good with them, but never good enough to be believed or helped. No, there were no shelters then.

But I am talking about speech: it isn't easy for me. I came to speech from under a man, tortured and tormented. What he did to me took away everything; he was the owner of everything. He hurt all the words out of me, and no one would listen anyway. I come to speech from under the brutalities of thousands of men. For me, the violence of marriage was worse than the violence of prostitution; but this is no choice. Men act out pornography. They have acted it out on me. Women's lives become pornography. Mine did. And so for 20 years now I have been looking for the words to say what I know.

But maybe liberal men—so open-minded and intellectually curious—can't find the books that would teach them about women's real lives. Maybe, while John Irving and PEN are defending Hustler, snuff films and "Deep Throat," the direct product of the coercion of Linda Marchiano, political dissidents like myself are anathema—especially to the free-speech fetishists—not because the publishing industry punishes prudes but because dissenters who mean it, who stand against male power over women, are pariahs.

Maybe Mr. Irving and others do not know that in the world of women, pornography is the real geography of how men use us and torment us and hate us.

With Catharine A. MacKinnon, I drafted the first civil law against pornography. It held pornographers accountable for what they do: they traffic in women (contravening the United Nations Universal Declaration of Human Rights and the Convention on the Elimination of All Forms of Discrimination Against Women); they eroticize inequality in a way that materially promotes rape, battery, maiming and bondage; they make a product that they know dehumanizes, degrades and exploits women; they hurt women to make the pornography, and then consumers use the pornography in assaults both verbal and physical.

Mr. Irving refers to a scene in "The World According to Garp" in which a woman bites off a man's penis in a car when the car is accidentally rammed from behind. This, he says, did not cause women to bite off men's penises in cars. I have written (in my novels, "Ice and Fire" and "Mercy," and in the story "The New Womans Broken Heart") about a woman raped by two men sequentially, the first aggressor routed by the second one, to whom the woman, near dead, submits; he bites viciously and repeatedly into her genitals. When I wrote it, someone had already done it—to me. Mr. Irving uses his imagination for violent farce. My imagination can barely grasp my real life. The violence, as Mr. Irving must know, goes from men to women.

Women write to me because of our shared experiences. In my books they find their lives—until now beyond the reach of language. A letter to me dated March 11 says in part: "The abuse was quite sadistic—it involved bestiality, torture, the making of pornography. Sometimes, when I think about my life, I'm not sure why I'm alive, but I'm always sure about why I do what I do, the feminist theory and the antipornography activism." Another letter, dated March 13, says: "It was only when I was almost [raped] to pieces that I broke down and learned to hate. . . . I have never stopped resenting the loss of innocence that occurred the day I learned to hate."

Male liberals seem to think we fight pornography to protect a sexual innocence, but we have none to protect. The innocence we want is the innocence that lets us love. People need dignity to love.

Mr. Irving quoted Hawthorne's condemnation of Puritan orthodoxy in the short story "Endicott and the Red Cross"—a graphic description of public punishments of women: bondage, branding, maiming, lynching. Today pornographers do these things to women, and the public square is a big place—every newsstand and video store. A photograph shields rape and torture for profit. In defending pornography as if it were speech, liberals defend the new slavers. The only fiction in pornography is the smile on the woman's face.

—Andrea Dworkin
Brooklyn (*New York Times Book Review,* 3 May, 1992)

We can find only one logical argument in this letter. Dworkin tries to show that pornography should not be classified as speech, but rather as violence against women. She also makes an appeal to pathos when she argues that men cannot understand the effects of pornography on women. The rest of the letter depends entirely upon ethical arguments for its persuasiveness.

The passage is ethically interesting because Dworkin is not concerned to secure Irving's good will. And although her ethos may be off-putting to men (especially "liberal-minded men") she risks this, because she is concerned that people read a woman's point of view about pornography. She supplies her credentials in an unusual way: she shows that she has been involved in the sexual violence that is usually pictured in pornography. She demonstrates her moral character by showing sympathy with women who are forced to participate in the production of pornography, and she repeatedly expresses her moral outrage at this state of affairs. Irving replied to Dworkin as follows:

It is impossible for me to summon much irritation toward Andrea Dworkin; I would rather beg Ms. Dworkin to understand that it is possible for me to feel great sympathy for her—for the atrocities she's suffered in her life—without feeling even in the slightest inclined to accept the absurd remedies she proposes for her pain. In truth, it is painful for me (and an irony utterly missed by Ms. Dworkin) that I have often created, in my fiction, women characters who have suffered from the violence and the laws of men as much as Ms. Dworkin has; yet Ms. Dworkin says that "Mr. Irving uses his imagination for violent farce." How strange, then, that in reading about Ms. Dworkin's life, I am reminded of a character in a John Irving novel. (*New York Times Book Review,* 7 June 1992, p. 34)

Irving makes no substantive arguments in this letter. Even though he sets up what looks like an **enthymeme** (I can accept Dworkin's suffering, but I can't accept the remedy she proposes for it), he makes no connections between these two statements about his feelings. Irving attempts to recoup his position entirely by means of ethical arguments—I am a sympathetic person, I am pained that Dworkin overlooked the depiction of women in my fiction, my fiction represents life as Dworkin paints it. We leave our readers to evaluate the success of this ethical response.

EXERCISES

1. Find six short pieces of professional writing. These can be selections from books, newspapers, or magazines, fiction or non-fiction. Read each passage carefully. How do the authors establish an ethos? Specifically, how do the authors convince you that they are intelligent and well informed? What tactics do the authors use to establish their good character? Their good will toward readers? Make lists of these tactics for future reference. Do any of the pieces display an ethos that is not successful?

2. Now analyze the pieces in terms of the rhetorical distance created by their authors' voices. Do the authors assume they know readers well, or do they establish a formal distance? How do they achieve this distance? Look at their uses of grammatical person, verb voice and tense, word size, qualifiers, and punctuation.

3. For practice, try to alter the voice and rhetorical distance of two or three of the pieces. Change the grammatical person, the word size, the voice and tense; use more or fewer qualifiers; use more or less and different kinds of punctuation. What happens? That is, is the author's ethos altered? How? Does the distance change? How? Is your revision more or less effective than the original? Why?

4. Look at several articles in a popular newspaper or news magazine such as *USA Today* or *Newsweek*. Who seems to be speaking? How do the authors of these articles establish an ethos? Do they attempt to seem intelligent and well informed? How do they get access to the information they pass along?

5. To practice creating an effective ethos, write a letter to someone who is very close to you—a spouse, parent, or friend. Now write a letter that says the same thing to someone who is less close to you—a teacher, for example. Now write the letter to a company or corporation. What happens to your voice in each case? What features of your writing are altered?

6. Write a letter in someone else's voice: someone you know, or better yet, a famous person such as a politician, a TV anchorperson, a movie star. You may have to watch and listen awhile to the person whose ethos you are imitating before you can do this successfully.

7. Try imitating the voice used by some writer you admire. How does the writer achieve ethical effects? (For more exercises of this kind, see the chapter on imitation.)

NOTE

1. We are indebted to Walker Gibson's *Persona: A Style Study for Readers and Writers* (New York: Random House, 1969); and *Tough, Sweet, and Stuffy: An Essay on Modern American Prose Styles* (Bloomington: Indiana UP, 1966).

WORKS CITED

Abbey, Edward. *Desert Solitaire.* Tucson: Arizona UP, 1968.

Brockriede, Wayne. "The Dimensions of Rhetoric," *Quarterly Journal of Speech* 54 (1968): 1–12.

Dostoevsky, Fyodor. *Notes from Underground.* New York: E. P. Dutton, 1960.

Douglas, Mary. *How Institutions Think.* Syracuse: Syracuse UP, 1986.

Hayek, Friedrich. *The Constitution of Liberty.* Chicago: Chicago UP, 1960.

Lowry, Rich. "Burton Huntin." *National Review* (5 May 1997): 20.

Macrorie, Ken. *Writing to be Read.* 3rd. Rev. ed. Portsmouth: Boynton Cook, 1984.

PATHETIC PROOF

Speech is a powerful guide, which by means of the finest and most invisible body effects the divinest works: it can stop fear and banish grief and create joy and nurture pity. . . . Fearful shuddering and tearful pity and grievous longing come upon its hearers, and at the actions and physical sufferings of others in good fortunes and in evil fortunes, through the agency of words, the soul is wont to experience a suffering of its own.

—Gorgias, "Encomium of Helen," 8

RHETORS CAN FIND arguments in the issue itself (*logos*), and a rhetor's character (*ethos*) can be persuasive as well. According to Aristotle, a third kind of intrinsic proof is also available: rhetors can appeal to human emotion (*pathos*). The Greek term *pathos* meant, among other things, "experience," "emotion" and "suffering." Pathos is still used in English to refer to any quality in an experience that arouses emotions, and many English words are borrowed from the Greek term, including "sympathy" and "empathy" (to feel what another person feels). Speakers of modern English generally use an adjective form, "pathetic," to refer to anything that is pitiful or unsuccessful, as in the phrase "that's a pathetic excuse." But "pathetic" also refers to the arousal or expression of emotions, and that's the sense in which we use it here.

Of all the ancient kinds of rhetorical proofs, the appeal to the emotions seems strangest to contemporary rhetors, and perhaps a little bit shoddy as well. That is because of the modern reverence for reason and our habit of making a sharp distinction between reason and the emotions. In our culture, if you're emotional, you're irrational. Reason is associated with the mind, and connotes a calm, studied, masculine approach to issues. Emotions are associated with the body, and are thought to be superficial, dangerous, and feminine. Contemporary skepticism about the legitimacy of emotional appeals also stems from the assumption that emotions are private. Because emotions are often experienced in private, people tend to think of emotions as belonging to individuals. This attitude depicts emotional response as both unimportant and inappropriate for public discussion.

Despite the popular ideology that characterizes emotions negatively, modern rhetors make emotional appeals all the time. Apparently, such appeals are still as persuasive as Aristotle said they were. The most obvious modern use of emotional appeals appears in advertisements that appeal to consumers' desire for success ("be all you can be") or their fears of losing status in their communities ("ring around the collar"). Obviously, commonplaces can appeal to pathos.

Here is a letter to the editors of *USA Today* that makes overt emotional appeals:

SELF-DEFEATING EVIDENCE

Fashion is known to be outrageous, as evidenced by last week's Alexander McQueen show in Paris where some writers and others drooled and gushed over the brazen display of animal bodies.

McQueen would get thrown in prison for dangling human parts from his clothes, so he settles for those of animals—heads, feathers, skulls, skin, even a goose's neck wound around a model's neck.

Actually, McQueen is doing a favor for People for the Ethical Treatment of Animals (PETA) and the entire animal-rights movement.

He's showing people clearly that animals suffer and die for the whims of some desperate fur designers and their customers.

So show it all, McQueen. Dip a dress in blood that warmed a living masterpiece; fasten to the lapel a heart that pounded in joy and fear and pain; and button the garment with eyes that saw this world as no others ever have or will again.

Please decide now which side you will support. The line has been drawn.

Carla Bennett

Senior writer, PETA (18 July 1997)

The persuasiveness of the emotional appeals made here depend in part on whether the **irony** used in the first paragraph works; its effectiveness depends on whether readers know that there is a history of conflict between the fashion industry and animal-rights activists. The effect of the emotional appeals depends more directly, of course, on whether readers agree that animals feel emotion, as Bennett maintains.

Since there is a gap between our attitudes toward emotional appeals and the reality of their widespread use, it is important for rhetors to know how to recognize such arguments and how to use them effectively as well.

ANCIENT TEACHERS ON THE EMOTIONS

Greek orators could find examples of the persuasive use of emotion in the texts of the poet Homer, whose two great epic poems, the *Iliad* and the *Odyssey*, were well known among the Greek people. In the last book of the *Iliad*, Homer depicted the Trojan king, Priam, appealing to Achilles, the Achean hero, to return the body of his son, Hector:

> Remember your own father,
> Achilles, in your godlike youth: his years
> like mine are many, and he stands upon
> the fearful doorstep of old age. He, too,
> is hard pressed, it may be, by those around him,
> there being no one able to defend him
> from bane of war and ruin. Ah, but he
> may nonetheless hear news of you alive,
> and so with glad heart hope through all his days
> for sight of his dear son, come back from Troy,
> while I have deathly fortune. Noble sons
> I fathered here, but scarce one man is left me.
> Fifty I had when the Acheans came,
> nineteen out of a single belly, others
> born of attendant women. Most are gone.
> Raging Ares cut their knees from under them.
> And he who stood alone among them all,
> their champion, and Troy's, ten days ago
> you killed him, fighting for his land, my prince,
> Hector. It is for him that I have come
> among these ships, to beg him back from you,
> and I bring ransom without stint. Achilles,
> be reverent toward the great gods! And take
> pity on me, remember your own father.
> Think me more pitiful by far, since I
> have brought myself to do what no man else
> has done before—to lift to my lips the hand
> of one who killed my son. (XXIV, 485–506)

Priam first arouses Achilles' sense of filial love by reminding him of his own father, and tries to arouse his pity for the plight of lonely old men whose sons are missing or dead. Then he tells how his many children have been slain, hoping to rouse Achilles' pity for his misfortunes, and he mentions ransom, hoping to stimulate Achilles' greed. He reminds Achilles of the gods; this is a subtle attempt to make Achilles fearful, since he committed a serious religious transgression by refusing to bury Hector's body. Finally, he asks Achilles to pity him for the shameful position in which he, a king, has been placed by being forced to beg a mere hero to return his son's body.

As this passage makes clear, emotional appeals are based on the assumption that human beings share similar kinds of emotional responses to events: fathers everywhere weep for lost sons; an old man who has lost his family is pitied by everyone, even his enemies. While this may not be true across wide cultural differences, it certainly is the case that people who live in the same community have similar emotional responses. If this were not true, governments would not be able to incite great numbers of people to volunteer for military service during wartime (which is an irrational thing to do, after all). In his history of the Peloponnesian War, Thucydides reported a speech made by Pericles, who had incited the Athenians to war against the Spartans. When this war did not go well, the people became angry. Pericles "called an assembly, wanting to encourage them and to convert their angry feelings into a gentler and more hopeful mood" (II, 59). Pericles was only partially successful in quelling the anger of the people, because the war had brought them great suffering. As this passage indicates, Pericles was quite aware that rhetoric could arouse or dispel emotional responses, and that communities could share emotional responses to public events.

Ancient rhetoricians also treated the emotions as ways of knowing, thus associating them with intellectual processes rather than with bodily responses, as moderns do. During Gorgias' lifetime, the Western philosophical distinction between mental and bodily responses had not yet been firmly made. Thus, he argued in the "Encomium of Helen" that the persuasive effect of verbal seduction is no different from physical force; Helen was blameless no matter whether she was abducted or whether her seducer simply persuaded her to flee her husband and country. Indeed, early rhetorical theorists like Gorgias and Plato characterized rhetoric as a *psychagogia,* a leader or enchanter of souls. Gorgias argued that, given the right circumstances (*kairos*), a rhetor could alter an audience's emotional state of mind and thus change their assessment of reality, in essence helping them to see the world in new ways.

In other words, the ancients taught that emotions held heuristic potential. This seems reasonable enough. That emotions are a means of reasoning seems obvious: If someone becomes afraid, realizing that she is in a dangerous situation, she quickly assesses her options and takes herself out of danger as quickly as she can. Emotions can also move people to action: If someone feels compassion for someone else, he helps the suffering person.

Early sophistic treatises on rhetoric included topics for appealing to the emotions. For example, the *Rhetoric to Alexander* discussed appeals to friendliness, kindliness, and the like as a means urging an audience to act on behalf of the needy (1439b, 15ff). Since sophistic manuals were organized according to the parts or divisions of a discourse, they gave no systematic advice about arousing the emotions but rather included it in their discussions of introductions and conclusions.

Aristotle seems to have been the first rhetorician to provide a systematic discussion of emotional proofs. In Book II of the *Rhetoric,* he defined emotions as "those things through which, by undergoing change, people come to differ in their judgments" (i, 1378a). This sounds very much like Gorgias' argument that emotional responses help people to change their minds. When people experience emotions such as anger, pity, or fear, they enter new states of mind in which they see things differently. If a person has become angry at someone, for example, she or he sees that person in a different light than she or he previously did. Perhaps a woman is angry with her supervisor because he mistakenly blamed her for something that was not her fault. Her angry reaction to this event will change her attitude toward her supervisor. She may even be moved by this new way of thinking to change her behavior toward him: she may, for example, vow to speak up for herself the next time she is unfairly accused; she may even decide to quit her job. Aristotle also realized that emotions are communal in the sense that they are usually excited by our relations with other people. We do not become angry in some general or vague way; ordinarily we are angry at someone else. We do not feel love toward nothing; we feel love for some persons or creatures. We can also communicate emotions to others—people who are afraid can make others fearful as well.

Most postclassical rhetorical treatises employed the sophistic habit of treating the emotions as suitable proofs only in the introduction and conclusion of a discourse. Cicero's *De Oratore* and Quintilian's *Institutes* are exceptions to this general rule. While both rhetoricians adopted Aristotle's tripartite division of rhetorical proofs, neither added much of theoretical value to his discussion of pathos. However, their treatises do supply many examples of successful emotional appeals and give helpful suggestions on how to compose these. For these reasons, we rely on Aristotle for the theoretical part of our discussion of pathos, and turn to Cicero and Quintilian for advice on how to compose emotional appeals.

EMOTIONS AS RHETORICAL PROOFS

Emotions should not be confused with appetites such as pleasure or pain, nor should they be confused with values such as justice and goodness. However, people hold values with more or less intensity, and this is where the rhetorical force of emotional appeals resides, since people respond emotionally when their values are reinforced or threatened. Aristotle and Cicero discussed the following sets of emotions: anger/calm, love/hate, fear/confidence, shame/shamelessness, compassion, pity/indignation, envy/emulation, joy, and hope (*Rhetoric* II, 2–12; *De Oratore* II i, 203).

According to Aristotle, three criteria must be met if rhetors wish to understand how emotions are aroused or quelled. First, they must understand the state of mind of people who are angry, or joyful, or indignant; second, they must know who can excite these emotions in people; third, they must understand the reasons for which people become emotional (II 1, 1378a). People do not enter the state of mind called "anger" without a reason; they become angry *at* someone, even if they don't know who the person is. If a man leaves his workplace feeling perfectly calm, this state of mind changes when he discovers in the parking lot that someone has put a dent in his car. He becomes angry because this situation leaves him with choices that are unpleasant: don't repair the dent, in which case it may rust and become worse, thus lowering the car's value; do repair the dent and pay for it out of his own pocket, since the repair will probably cost less than the deductible on his insurance. Note that his anger is not irrational in this case; it is a perfectly reasonable response to events.

Aristotle's first criterion is that rhetors must know the emotional states of mind of their hearers or readers. An audience may bring a certain emotional state of mind to a rhetorical situation, and if so, the rhetor needs to decide whether this state of mind is conducive to their acceptance of her proposition. If it is not, she needs to change this state of mind. Aristotle thought that emotional change came about through changes in the level of intensity with which emotions are felt (II ii, 1377b–1378a). Emotional intensity alters in accordance with the spatial and temporal proximity of the people or situations that arouse them.[1] When the person with whom someone becomes angry is close, either physically or relationally, anger will be felt more intensely. If the person who dented the car is still in the lot when its owner arrives there, the owner focuses his anger more intensely on the culprit than if he can only be diffusely angry in general with people who dent parked cars and run. (In this case he may even refocus his anger on another car or on the traffic as he drives home.) If the culprit happens to be someone known to the owner of the dented car, the owner's emotional response will be intensified, as well, and the quality of their relationship may evoke other emotions in addition to anger. If the two are co-workers who don't like each other very much, the owner of the dented car may be more intensely angry than if the culprit is a friend. Their relationship may deteriorate even more. If the culprit is a supervisor, however, the owner of the dented vehicle may try to temper his anger with mildness. If the two are spouses or partners, however, things become even more complex emotionally.

As this example demonstrates, the relation of spatial proximity to emotional intensity depends upon social hierarchy, as well. As Aristotle noted, "people think they are entitled to be treated with respect by those inferior in birth, in power, in virtue, and generally in whatever they themselves have much of" (1378b). According to Aristotle's reasoning, people are less prone to be angry with those above or equal to them on a scale of social authority, while they are more prone to be angry with those below them on that scale. If the supervisor who dented the car is a foreman, the car's owner may be more angry than he would be if the culprit were the president of the company.

Some emotions are also more intensely felt if people nearby are experiencing them as well. This feature of emotional intensity is what makes horror fiction and films work, of course, since the audience fears for the characters. The feeling of fear is intensified in a theater because others are sharing it. Joy and anxiety appear to be shareable emotions, and mob violence can be stimulated by shared hatred or rage. Communities can feel hope, as when it seems likely that a war is about to end, and they can also feel despair, as Americans did during the Great Depression.

The intensity with which emotions are felt depends on the nearness of their objects in time, as well. Love tends to grow with time, but so can hatred. The intensity with which people feel joy depends very much on the temporal proximity of a joyful event, while sadness seems to linger through time. Anger tends to fade with time, unless the object of that anger is nearby in space. The car owner's anger toward the person who dented his car will lessen over time, unless for some reason he fails to get the dent fixed. In that case, every time he see it he may get angry all over again.

The intensity with which people feel fear is closely dependent on both the spatial and temporal proximity of a fearful person or event. During wartime, or when relations between nations are tense, governments try to stimulate fear of the enemy by bringing their images close to the people, altering them into objects of fear and thus disguising the fact of their spatial and temporal distance.

In 1987, when relations between Iran and the United States were very tense, American media portrayed the Iranian leader, the Ayatollah Khomeini, as a crazed religious fanatic. Pictures of his stern, angry countenance were prominently featured on television and in news magazines. At the same time, Iranian media portrayed the President of the United States, Ronald Reagan, as an idiotic warmonger, using close-up photographs of his vacantly smiling face. In other words, both parties to the conflict tried to personalize it for their citizens, because it is easier to make people afraid and angry toward a person than it is to make them afraid and angry toward an abstraction.

THE CHARACTERS OF AUDIENCES

> Since the function of oratory is in fact to influence mens' souls, the intending orator must know what types of soul there are. Now these are of a determinate number, and their variety results in a variety of individuals. To the types of soul thus discriminated there corresponds a determinate number of types of discourse. Hence a certain type of hearer will be easy to persuade by a certain type of speech to take such and such action for such and such reason, while another type will be hard to persuade. (Plato, *Phaedrus,* 271d)

Some authorities think that Aristotle followed Plato's advice in Book II, chapters 12–17 of the *Rhetoric*, where he developed some general guidelines for evaluating the emotional states of audiences. He listed lots of Greek commonplaces about the differing attitudes held by young, middle-aged, and old people. For example, young persons are more passionate than older people, Aristotle wrote, but their emotions pass quickly. Older people, on the other hand, tend to be suspicious because their hopes have often been dashed. He also provided commonplaces about the differing attitudes of rich and poor, powerful and powerless, and those who have good or bad luck.

In *De Oratore*, Cicero made Antonius say that it is desirable for an audience to "carry within them . . . some mental emotion that is in harmony with what the advocate's interest will suggest. For, as the saying goes, it is easier to spur the willing horse than to start the lazy one" (XLIV, 185–186). He continued:

> This indeed is the reason why, when setting about a hazardous and important case, in order to explore the feelings of the tribunal, I engage wholeheartedly in a consideration so careful, that I scent out with all possible keenness their thoughts, judgments, anticipations and wishes, and the direction in which they seem likely to be led away most easily by eloquence. . . . If . . . an arbitrator is neutral and free from predisposition, my task is harder, since everything has to be called forth by my speech, with no help from the listener's character. (187)

In this passage Cicero anticipated the findings of some contemporary research about audiences. Roughly speaking, members of an audience may hold one of three attitudes toward an issue or a rhetor's ethos: they may be hostile, indifferent, or accepting. Communication researchers have found that it is easier to move people who are enthusiastic about an issue than it is to influence those who are indifferent. Interestingly enough, it is also sometimes easier to bring about a change of mind in those who are accepting or hostile than in those who are indifferent.

During the Vietnam War, people who opposed the war were called "doves" while those who approved it were called "hawks." Extreme doves wanted the war stopped and American soldiers brought home immediately. Extreme hawks wanted not only to escalate the war but to win it by whatever means were necessary. Many Americans subscribed to neither of these extremes, but held more moderate positions. For instance, some dovish people wanted to scale down America's war effort, limiting it to guerilla skirmishes that would protect vital supply or communication lines. Other doves argued that a limited war should continue while peace was negotiated. Some hawkish people approved of bombing vital targets, but stopped short of recommending large-scale bombing or the use of nuclear weapons. Early on in the war, many Americans were simply indifferent to it; that is, they held no position regarding it. These people presented both doves and hawks with their most difficult audiences, since they first had to be convinced that the war was somehow important to them. Indeed, it might be said that the war was finally ended, not because doves won the national argument about it, but because a sufficient number of Americans finally abandoned their indifference toward the war when they saw the toll it took on American lives.

Researchers have also discovered that people's willingness to change their minds depends on two things: the emotional intensity with which they cling to an opinion; and the degree to which their identities—their sense of themselves as integrated people—are wrapped up with that opinion. People who are intensely invested in a position are less likely to change their minds than those who are not.

People who were hawkish on Vietnam, for example, might have been so for intellectual reasons: perhaps they saw the strategic importance of the Vietnamese peninsula to American rubber production. This commitment to rubber production and thus to capitalism is a value rather than an emotion, and so it is only partially relevant to an emotional state. Its relevance depends upon the emotional intensity with which people value capitalism, as well as the degree to which their identities and personal fortunes depend on its maintenance. Theoretically, these people would be easier to move away from hawkishness than those who were emotionally invested in the position, who feared for example that an American pullout in Vietnam would exacerbate the spread of dangerous communist values across Asia. And if a hawkish person's identity were wrapped up with this position, theoretically at least it would be very difficult to move that person away from it. This was apparently the case for some high-level military and state department personnel whose careers depended on successful maintenance of the war.

In sum, rhetors need to assess the emotional states of their audiences as well as the intensity with which they cling to those states. Rhetors need to decide as well whether those emotional states render their audiences receptive to them and their propositions. Next, they should decide whether or not an audience can be persuaded to change their minds, and, if so, whether they will be moved by appeals to their current emotional states or to a different one induced by a rhetor.

COMPOSING PATHETIC PROOFS

Let us return to the issue we've been pursuing throughout this book: the regulation of hate speech. Suppose that a rhetor who supports regulation wishes to compose some suitable emotional appeals to use in an argument. The rhetor first needs to consider whether the audience will have an emotional response to this issue. This is not likely unless members of the audience are users or victims of hate speech, or are for some other reason very much interested in the issue. (Members of the ACLU, for example, will be interested, because that organization has a long record of defending speech protected by the first amendment.) If the audience makes light of the use of hate speech, emotional appeals should be directed at opening their eyes to its serious effects—the pain it causes, the hatred and anger it creates and sustains. If they are very emotional about the issue (perhaps they have been victimized by the use of hate speech), they will be receptive to the rhetor's proposition, and no emotional appeals are required. But what about an audience who opposes the regulation of hate speech? Are there any emotional appeals that might persuade such an audience?

Using Enargeia

In *De Oratore*, Cicero's characters argued that emotional appeals are equal in importance to ethos and logos (II xliv, 185ff). Antonius argued further that it is important for rhetors to feel the emotions they want to arouse in their audiences. He exemplified this point by recalling his defence of Manius Aquilius, who was accused of extortion:

> Here was a man whom I remembered as having been consul, commander-in-chief, honored by the Senate, and mounting in procession to the Capitol; on seeing him cast down, crippled, sorrowing and brought to the risk of all he held dear, I was myself overcome by compassion before I tried to excite it in others. (xlvii, 195)

Cicero's rendering of this scene, through the mouth of his character Antonius, is so powerful that it still evokes compassion in people reading it two thousand years later. Cicero insisted that rhetors must somehow bring themselves to feel the emotions they wish to arouse in their audience.

Quintilian echoed this advice in his discussion of pathos, and he gave a useful hint about it. If rhetors do not actually feel the requisite emotions while they are composing, they can draw on humans' shared emotions, their natural empathy with other human beings. Using these, they can imagine how events must have affected those who suffered them:

> I am complaining that a man has been murdered. Shall I not bring before my eyes all the circumstances which it is reasonable to imagine must have occurred in such a connection? Shall I not see the assassin burst suddenly from his hiding-place, the victim tremble, cry for help, beg for mercy or turn to run? Shall I not see the fatal blow delivered and the stricken body fall? Will not the blood, the

deathly pallor, the groan of agony, the death-rattle, be indelibly impressed upon my mind? (*Institutes* VI ii, 31)

Rhetors who can imagine the emotions evoked by a scene may stimulate similar emotions in their audiences by deploying the power of *enargeia*, a figure in which rhetors picture events so vividly that they seem actually to be taking place before the audience. Vivid depictions of events, Quintilian argued, stir the emotions of an audience exactly as if they had been present when it occurred. Perhaps Shakespeare had this advice in mind when he imagined Marc Antony's funeral oration for Julius Caesar, which, historians say, whipped the Roman people into a fury of anger at Caesar's murderers. Shakespeare imagined his fictional Antony as standing before the crowd, holding up Caesar's bloodstained cloak for all to see. He put these words into Antony's mouth:

> You all do know this mantle. I remember
> The first time ever Caesar put it on.
> 'Twas on a summer's evening, in his tent,
> That day he overcame the Nervii.
> Look, in this place ran Cassius' dagger through.
> See what a rent the envious Casca made.
> Through this the well-beloved Brutus stabbed,
> And as he plucked his cursed steel away,
> Mark how the blood of Caesar followed it,
> As rushing out of doors, to be resolved
> If Brutus so unkindly knocked, or no.
> For Brutus, as you know, was Caesar's angel.
> Judge, O you gods, how dearly Caesar loved him!
> This was the most unkindest cut of all,
> For when the noble Caesar saw him stab,
> Ingratitude, more strong than traitors' arms,
> Quite vanquished him. Then burst his mighty heart,
> And, in his mantle muffling up his face,
> Even at the base of Pompey's statue,
> Which all the while ran blood, great Caesar fell. (*Julius Caesar* III, ii)

It is easy for readers to imagine this scene—Antony holding up the torn, bloodstained cloak, putting his hands through the holes made by the daggers that killed Caesar. Note also that he dwells on the emotional relationship between Brutus and Caesar—Antony implies that it was Brutus' ingratitude that killed Caesar, along with the assassins' knives. By playing upon the crowd's shock and outrage at the bloody murder, he roused them to anger against the murderers.

We composed this *enargeia* for possible use by a rhetor who supports the regulation of hate speech:

> A small child walks jauntily home from school, swinging her backpack in time with her steps. Her eyes sparkle with happiness—school is out for the day—and her smile indicates her sheer happiness at being alive on this beautiful autumn afternoon.

Suddenly, three girls from her class at school appear on the sidewalk in front of her. Giggling, they point at her in unison and the tallest one yells "Fatso! Go on a diet." They run away.

This *enargeia* is structured in such a way as to elicit sympathy for victims of hate speech—in this case, for a happy young girl whose fine mood is shattered by the cruel words of her classmates.

Using Honorific and Pejorative Language

Another way to evoke emotions is to use words that are honorific or pejorative. Honorific language treats people and things respectfully, while pejorative language disparages and downplays them. Here is *Newsweek's* introduction to Madeleine Albright, published shortly after she became Secretary of State:

> As a working mother, she's got fabulous juggling skills. She knows how to pay attention to everything all the time. That might help her as secretary of state, but otherwise, I don't think being a woman will make any difference. She'll be as determined as any of her predecessors in the job. She's going to conduct the foreign policy of the United States as it should be conducted. She's a tough, gutsy lady, and she's extremely talented; she always taught us that being charming and attractive is not inconsistent with being smart and aggressive. But the real secret of her success is that she works like a dog. (10 February 1997, 26)

The author of this piece (Albright's daughter, Anne) uses honorific terms ("fabulous," "determined," "tough," "gutsy") to evoke an attractive picture of her mother. We mentioned some of the honorific language in this passage, and there is much more. If you cross out the emotive terms and read the passage without them, you will see that much of the emotional appeal of the passage disappears.

Here is an introduction to an essay about the Federal Bureau of Investigation, written by the editors of *The Nation*.

> The Federal Bureau of Investigation is the most powerful and secretive agency in the United States today. Despite the bureau's influence over a broad terrain of American life, independent examinations of the "B," as special agents refer to it, have been rare. (In the sixties *The Nation* published a special issue on the bureau by Fred Cook, which became *The FBI Nobody Knows*.) No Congressional committee has mustered the political will and staff to carry out a comprehensive review. With the bureau's political power greater than at any time in its eighty-nine-year history, an examination of the questions of how well it is performing its crime-fighting mission and safeguarding civil liberties is overdue. Beyond the recent series of F.B.I. problems—the tragedy at Waco, the shootout at Ruby Ridge, the Atlanta Olympic Park bombing, the flawed investigations by its scientific lab—are there broader kinds of defects that demand attention? We asked David Burnham, a reporter who has specialized in law-enforcement issues for thirty years, to review the current state of the F.B.I. With research support from The Nation Institute's Investigative Fund, Burnham availed himself of an entirely new kind of information—internal administrative data main-

tained by the Justice Department, which tracks every instance an investigative agency like the F.B.I. refers a matter for prosecution and the ultimate disposition of these referrals. Data tapes containing this detailed information, from the mid-seventies to fiscal year 1996, were obtained under the Freedom of Information Act by the Transactional Records Access Clearinghouse (TRAC), a research organization formed in 1989 by Burnham and Susan Long, a professor at Syracuse University. They then verified and analyzed the data. The F.B.I. did not respond to our request for comment on the findings of this article.

—The Editors (11/18 August 1997, 11)

The editors use pejorative language ("secretive," "tragedy," "shootout," "flawed") to cast a negative pall over their subject. We suggest that you find and cross out these and the other pejorative terms that appear in the passage. Read it again without those terms. Does their absence change your rhetorical relation to its subject?

Examples

The following passage introduces a book entitled *Gathering Storm: American's Militia Threat*, written by attorney Morris Dees.

Louis Beam minced no words.

"I warn you calmly, coldly, and without reservation that over the next ten years you will come to hate government more than anything in your life," Beam, a spokesman for the Aryan Nations, told his audience of 160 white men. They ranged from white supremacists to pro-gun extremists, meeting at an invitation-only gathering two months after FBI sharpshooters killed Randy Weaver's wife and son on Ruby Ridge in Idaho. They called themselves patriots.

"The federal government in north Idaho has demonstrated brutally, horribly, and with great terror how it will enforce its claim that we are religious fanatics and enemies of the state," added Beam, his voice rising with each word. "We must, in one voice, cry out that we will not tolerate their stinking, murdering, lying, corrupt government.

"Men, in the name of our Father, we are called upon to make a decision, a decision that you will make in the quietness of your heart, in the still places of the night," Beam continued. "As you lie on your bed and you look up at the ceiling tonight, you must answer the question: Will it be liberty or will it be death?"

"As for me," he concluded in the words of Patrick Henry to thunderous applause, "give me liberty or give me death."

At this gathering, now known as the Rocky Mountain Rendezvous, held on October 23–25, 1992, at a YMCA in Estes Park, Colorado, plans were laid for a citizen's militia movement like none this country has known. It is a movement that already had led to the most destructive act of domestic terrorism in our nation's history. Unless checked, it could lead to widesperad devastation or ruin.

"We bear the torch of light, of justice, of liberty, and we will be heard," Beam shouted over the cheers of his audience. "We will not yield this country to the forces of darkness, oppression, and tyranny."

His face pockmarked, his hair slicked down, and speaking in a manner that evoked images of Adolf Hitler, Beam continued, "So if you believe in the truth, if you believe in justice, then join with us. We are marching to the beat of the same drum. The beat of that drum, like those heart at Valley Forge and at Gettysburg, has called good men everywhere to action."

Dees' point in this book is that paramilitary groups, incited to violence by men like Beam, are a growing threat to the peace of the United States. His opening remarks, then, appeal directly to readers' emotions, particularly fear.

Enargeia

Here is a passage from W. Charisse Goodman's *Invisible Woman* that illustrates the use of *enargeia:*

No one can deny that America is currently in the throes of a gender-specific obsession with thinness, but what does that mean in terms of the quality of everyday life for large women in this country? Let's take a look at an average day in the life of a composite average large lady in an average city.

As she reads the morning newspaper, she sees ads and articles glorifying the slender figure and relegating her own body type to the weight-loss ads. The message: lose weight. You're not a real woman unless you're thin. While taking public transportation to work, she may have to cope with seats designed for much thinner people, some of whom will clearly resent her presence should they have to share a seat with her.

Once at work, she must listen to other women discuss at painful length their diets, their own perceived weight problems, and their anxiety and self-reproach at not being more disciplined. She winces as they express to one another, or her, their disgust and contempt for fatness as a general concept. Eating her meals in the lunch-room results in criticism or comments about her appetite and choice of foods. Perhaps she is even the object of coarse jokes made right to her face, and thinner co-workers who are prejudiced gossip smugly about her. (One man in my former workplace reportedly reacted to news of a relationship between two fellow employees with the immortal words, "That's impossible. She's fat.") She may be discreetly or unconsciously excluded from office or extracurricular social interaction. She may be automatically passed over for promotions, even paid less than thinner people for equal work, solely because her size does not reflect a lean, fashionable corporate image. The message: lose weight. You're not acceptable as you are, and you make us uncomfortable.

Should she have a hairdresser's appointment after work and scan magazines or the salon's catalogues for new hairstyle ideas, she finds few, if any, large women in one volume after another of photographs. Message: your type doesn't belong among pictures of beautiful women. On a clothes-shopping trip, she discovers she must shop in a separate department which is often tucked floors away from the smaller sizes; often she must go to a separate store altogether. When she checks out clothing ads in flyers or newspapers, she finds that garments advertised in sizes ranging from 4–14 or –16 invariably portray a woman at the smaller end of the spectrum modeling the product, and that even clothes for sizes 16 and up may be modeled by thin women.

When she turns on her TV or goes to a movie, she finds a seemingly endless number of slick commercials, programs and plots portraying thin women as attractive, lovable, successful, and glamorous while usually presenting heavy women, when they are included at all, as loud, aggressive, oafish, raw, alienated, etc.; in short, as *un*attractive, *un*lovable, *un*successful, and decidedly *un*glamorous. Practically the only television programming that addresses her directly consists of weight-loss ads. True, sometimes there will be a "special" talk show about large-size fashions or the "special" problems big women face; if she makes enough of an effort, she can even find "special" magazines that actually depict the big woman as normal and attractive, or advertisements for "special" social events or "special" exercise classes geared to large people so they, too, can meet potential mates or exercise in peace. The message? She is set apart from a world that acknowledges only thin people. She is not permitted to "fit in."

Should our lady exercise in public, she will be fortunate indeed if she does not encounter harassment in the form of snickers, pitying or contemptuous looks, or even outright jeering from complete strangers passing by who feel they have every right to comment on her body's size and shape. The irony here, of course, is that weight bigots are quite fond of condemning fat people for their supposed sloth; but when a heavy person does make an effort to engage in exercise, she needs a huge dose of courage and self-confidence to cope with such negative remarks.

Upon arriving home, she may face a companion or family that hounds her about her weight. If she attends parties to try and meet new people, she may find that men are often polite but distracted as they jockey for the attention and favors of thinner, conventionally sexy "babes." Indeed, any public appearance is fraught with unpleasant possibilities. (4–6)

If Goodman is correct when she argues that there is widespread "weight prejudice" in this country, and if she wants to eradicate that prejudice, she is arguing a distinctly minority view. And so she resorts to *enargeia* to depict the effects of this prejudice as vividly as she can so that thin people can learn what it is like to be fat. In other words, she is trying to elicit sympathy for the plight of large people in order to change cultural attitudes about weight. Of course, the effectiveness of her appeal to pathos depends in part on whether people accept her ethos. Often enough, ethical and pathetic appeals depend closely on one another for their effects. In fact, it is sometimes difficult to disentangle the ethical from the pathetic in a successful argument.

Pejorative and Honorific Language

Here is the opening passage from a *New Republic* article about hate speech. Although its author took a position on the issue of regulation later on in the article, he or she limited the paragraphs quoted here to the presentation of information:

One year ago Robert Viktora, white and 18 years old, was arrested for burning a cross on the lawn of the only black family in his St. Paul, Minnesota, neighborhood. Rather than booking him for trespassing or disturbing the peace, police charged him under a local ordinance prohibiting "bias-motivated disorderly conduct." The law makes it illegal to place "on public or private property a symbol, object, appellation, characterization, or graffiti, including but not limited to, a burning cross or Nazi swastika, which one knows or has reasonable grounds to know arouses anger, alarm, or resentment of others on the basis of race, color, creed, or religion or gender."

A Minnesota District Court judge struck down the ordinance as unconstitutional, citing the 1989 Supreme Court decision establishing that flag burning was a constitutionally protected form of expression. The court found that the ordinance was "content-based" (it depended on the message of a given action), failed to serve a "compelling state interest," and was overly broad. Six months later the Minnesota Supreme Court reversed the decision, saying that cross burning was "deplorable conduct the City of St. Paul may without question prohibit." Last week the Supreme Court agreed to hear the case, *R.A.V.* v. *St. Paul.*

The issue [divided] those who usually find themselves in the same corner on First Amendment questions. The Anti-Defamation League has sided with the prosecution, claiming that the burning of a cross is not "expressive or symbolic conduct" protected by the First Amendment. The ADL supports the Minnesota Supreme Court in its application of the "fighting words" doctrine, which says that words "which by their very utterance inflict injury or tend to incite an immediate breach of the peace" are not protected by the First Amendment. On the other side is the American Civil Liberties Union, which argues that the St. Paul law is unconstitutional both because it is based on message; not action, and because it is "hopelessly vague," and thus subject to abuse and arbitrary enforcement.

The Court's decision will hinge on the question of whether hate speech is one of the few kinds of expression not protected by the Bill of Rights. The two relevant exceptions recognized by law are "fighting words" (*Chaplinsky* v. *New Hampshire*) and speech that provokes "imminent lawless action" (*Brandenburg* v. *Ohio*). Proponents of legislation banning hate speech use these exceptions to argue that hate speech is not a protected freedom under the First Amendment. ("Breaking the Codes," *The New Republic* [8 July 1991] 7–8)

This passage represents an unemotional rendering of material that is potentially inflammatory. The author of the passage achieved this effect by avoiding the use honorific or pejorative language. We suggest that you revise the passage, using honorific or pejorative language that intensifies readers' reactions to the events recounted there.

EXERCISES

1. Try creating an emotional appeal to use in an argument you are working on. If you are not working in a specific rhetorical situation at the moment, invent one. That is, describe an audience and an issue. Now decide what the emotional state of your designated audience is likely to be. Decide what emotions would rouse them to action, or at least move them to change their minds. Create an *enargeia*, a vivid scene, that is calculated to rouse the requisite emotions.

2. Select a proposition from your own repertoire of beliefs—that is, from your ideology. For example, perhaps you believe that the United States ought to intervene the affairs of other countries for humanitarian reasons. Perhaps you support the legal status of abortion, or perhaps you oppose the recognition of groups such as STRAIGHT. Now imagine an audience of one or more persons who are either hostile or indifferent to your proposition. Write a description of a rhetorical situation in which you attempt to persuade this audience to accept your proposition. Try to figure out why your audience is hostile or indifferent to you or to your proposition. List some proofs you might use to persuade its members to accept your premise, or at least to examine it. Don't overlook available ethical and pathetic appeals.

3. Aristotle and Cicero discussed the following sets of emotions: anger/calm, love/hate, fear/confidence, shame/shamelessness, compassion, pity/indignation, envy/emulation, joy, and hope (*Rhetoric* II, 2–12; *De Oratore* II i, 203). Think of a rhetorical situation in which an appeal to anger is appropriate. Compose the appeal. Now try your hand at composing appeals to the other emotions listed here. Advertisers often rely on fear—particularly the fear of losing status in the community—to get people to buy things. Do advertisers exploit other emotional appeals?

4. Are Aristotle and Cicero's lists of emotions complete? That is, can you think of other emotions that are used in contemporary emotional appeals? For example, desire is often appealed to in contemporary rhetoric. Politicians say that "The American people want" this or that, and advertisers create extremely subtle appeals to desire, especially sexual desire (perfume and clothing ads are good examples here). Can you think of other examples? Is desire an emotion?

5. Keep a list of the honorific and pejorative terms that you come across in your reading. Once it has become long enough (fifty examples each of honorific and pejorative terms should do), study the list to determine whether they tell you something about community values. For example, Anne Albright used the word "tough" to describe her mother honorifically. Do we admire toughness in all women or just in those who become Secretary of State? Do we honor toughness in all men?

NOTE

1. We are indebted in part to Craig R. Smith and Michael J. Hyde, "Rethinking 'the Public': The Role of Emotion in Being-with-others," (*Quarterly Journal of Speech* 77 [November, 1991], 446–466) for our analysis of emotional appeals.

REASONING
IN RHETORIC

In some oratorical styles examples prevail, in others enthymemes; and in like manner, some orators are better at the former and some at the latter. Speeches that rely on examples are as persuasive as the other kind, but those which rely on enthymemes excite the louder applause.

—Aristotle,
The Rhetoric I ii, 20

ARISTOTLE DEVELOPED FOUR methods of reasoning to help people argue their way through complex issues: scientific demonstration, dialectic, rhetoric, and false or contentious reasoning. Aristotle taught that in each of these kinds of reasoning the arguer began with a statement called a **premise.** This word is derived from Latin words which mean "to send before." Thus a premise is any statement laid down, supposed, or assumed before the argument begins. Premises are then combined with other premises in order to reach conclusions. Arguers can insure that their arguments are valid (that is, correctly reasoned), if they observe certain formal rules of arrangement for the premises. Conclusions reached by this means of reasoning are true only if their premises are true.

In scientific demonstration, according to Aristotle, argument begins from premises which are true, or which experts accept as true. The premises of scientific argument or demonstration must be able to command belief without further argument to support them. For example: "Water freezes at 32 degrees Farenheit" and "The moon orbits the earth" are simple scientific premises. In dialectical reasoning, the arguers are less certain about the truth of the premises; here the premises are accepted by the majority of people, or by those who are supposed to be especially wise. For example, Socrates' dictum that "the unexamined life is not worth living" is a dialectical premise, as is Jesus' teaching that human beings ought to love each other. In rhetorical reasoning, premises are drawn from beliefs accepted by all, or most, members of a community. False or contentious reasoning differs from scientific, dialectical, and rhetorical reasoning because it relies on premises that only appear to be widely accepted. False reasoning also uses premises that are mistakes or lies.

The premises in rhetorical reasoning always involve human action or belief. Many rhetorical premises are so taken for granted that they are not articulated very often. For example, "Convicted criminals should be punished" and "All Americans ought to register and vote" are rhetorical premises. Note that not everyone believes these premises. Nor do people always practice them. Nevertheless, they are commonplaces in American ideology, and that qualifies them as rhetorical premises.

PROBABILITIES

For our purposes, the salient difference among scientific, dialectical, and rhetorical premises has nothing to do with some external criterion for truth. Rather, the difference among them depends upon the degree of belief awarded them by the people who are arguing about them. Ancient teachers of rhetoric began the reasoning process with premises which were widely accepted as certain, and moved to those which were less certain. In fact, Quintilian defined arguments in rhetoric and logic as methods "of proving what is not certain by means of what is certain" (V x, 8). Thus, such arguments enable "one thing to be inferred from another"; they also confirm "facts which are uncertain by reference to facts which are certain" (11). Without some way of moving from the certain to the uncertain, Quintilian argued, we would have no way of proving anything.

Greek rhetoricians called any kind of statement which predicts something about human behavior a statement of **probability** (*eikos*). Probabilities are not as reliable as certainties, of course, but they are more reliable than chance. Furthermore, rhetorical probabilities differ from mathematical probabilities in that they are both more predictable and less easy to calculate. Compare, for example, the relative probability that you will draw a winning poker hand to the relative probability that your parents, spouse, or partner will be upset if you get home late from the game. The chances of drawing to an inside straight are relatively remote, although they can be mathematically calculated. The chance that parents or a spouse or partner will be upset if you arrive home later than you promised are relatively greater than your chance at drawing to an inside straight, but this chance cannot be calculated by mathematical means. If you want to estimate the probability of their reaction, you need to know something about their attitudes toward promise-keeping, the quality of their relationship to you, and the record of promise-keeping you have built up over the years.

The reason for the relative certainty of statements about probable human action is that human behavior in general is predictable to some extent. Aristotle wrote that people can reason about things that happen "as a rule." As a rule, family members become upset when promises made to them are broken. Moreover, people cannot reason about things that happen by chance, like drawing to an inside straight. Since rhetorical statements of probability represent the common opinion of humankind, we ought to place a certain degree of trust in them. Thus statements of probability are pieces of knowledge, and as such they provide suitable premises for rhetorical proofs.

Plato credited the legendary Tisias with the invention of the argument from probability (*Phaedrus,* 273b). Whether this attribution is correct or not, probability must have been a sophistic tactic, given its emphasis on human behavior rather than human nature (which is what Plato would have preferred). Since the premises used in rhetoric deal with human action, they are only usually or contingently true. In antiquity, the most famous argument from probability was the following:

> A small, weak man will not physically attack a large, strong man.

This is a rhetorical premise, since it articulates some common sense about the way people generally behave. In this case, it is not certain that the weaker man will leave the stronger man alone; it is only probable. The smaller man could hire others to act for him, or he could be so driven by desperation or anger that he attacks a man who is sure to injure him anyway. A sophist would likely argue the argument from probability in the other direction as well: a small weak man might attack a larger more powerful man, even though he was bound to be injured, since no one would suspect that he had done such a dangerous thing. His doing so, in other words, was not probable. Quintilian named four kinds of premises that could be regarded as certain:

> those which involved things perceived by the senses;
>
> those which involved things about which there is general agreement, such as children's duty to love their parents;
>
> those which involved things that exist in law or in custom, such as the custom of punishing convicted criminals;
>
> those which are admitted by either party to the argument. (V x, 12–14)

A sophist might have disagreed with Quintilian about this, however. As we noted earlier, things perceived by the senses are not always certain, since our senses may not be functioning properly: When someone has a cold, it is difficult for her or him to smell the coffee. Moreover, observers may not be in a position to use their senses properly, or they might not be paying attention. Nor is it true that things existing in law always have certain outcomes; these days, even if someone is convicted of a heinous crime, it is not certain that she or he will serve the designated sentence. Executions are even more uncertain. Customs are not always adhered to, either, because they change quite rapidly. Men no longer open doors for women, as a rule; women may now ask men for a date, as a rule. Neither of these was even a probability 30 years ago. Last, parties to an argument may have extrinsic reasons for accepting a premise as a given: they may have been bribed, or they may think that a premise is irrelevant to their case. In insanity defenses, for example, the defense attorneys sometimes admit that their clients are guilty of the crime they have been charged with. This admission has no bearing on the certainty or likelihood that a client did indeed commit a crime.

In short, very little is certain in the realm of human action. Quintilian regarded three sorts of statements as probable:

those which involved what usually happens (children are usually loved by their parents)

those which were highly likely (a man who is healthy today will be alive tomorrow)

those in which nothing worked against their probability (a household theft was committed by some resident of the household). (16–17)

These sorts of premises are suitable for use in rhetoric, because they are statements about the probable conduct of human beings.

ARISTOTLE ON REASONING IN RHETORIC

For Aristotle, argument took place in language. Arguers placed premises in a sequence in order to determine what could be learned from the procedure. He wrote that "a statement is persuasive and credible either because it is directly self-evident or because it appears to be proved from other statements that are so" (I ii, 11). Aristotle taught his students how to reason from knowledge which was already given to that which needed to be discovered. People who wished to discover knowledge in any field did so by placing premises in useful relations to one another.

Deduction

In rhetoric, as well as in dialectic and science, the discovery process moves in two directions. Aristotle called these directions reasoning (*syllogismos*) and induction (*epagoge*). He defined reasoning (also called **deduction,** from a Latin word meaning "to lead down") as "a discussion in which, certain things having been laid down, something other than these things necessarily results through them" (*Topics* I, i). The most famous example of this sort of reasoning goes as follows:

1. All people are mortal.
2. Socrates is a person.
3. Therefore, Socrates is mortal.

The first statement is a general premise accepted by everyone. This premise is general because it makes an observation about an entire class: all people. In syllogisms set up like the example about Socrates, the first general premise is called the **major premise.** The second statement is a **particular** premise accepted by everyone. This premise is particular because it refers to only one person out of the class of people. This premise is called the **minor premise.** The last statement is a **conclusion,** arrived at by comparing the premises: if Socrates fits in the class "people" he also fits in the class "mortal," and thus his death is inevitable. The reasoner has moved from a generalization ("all people are mortal") to statements concerning a particular person, Socrates.

Aristotle assumed that premises did two kinds of work: they named classes of things (generalizations or classifications) and they named particulars (one instance of a thing). A **class** is any number of people or things grouped together because of certain likenesses or common traits (see Figure 8.1). All members of this class share certain traits: they are predatory flesh-eating mammals, usually soft-furred, having whiskers, four legs each with five toes, and so on. The cheetah has many feline (cat-like) characteristics, but it has many dog-like characteristics as well. So it is a marginal member of the class "cats."

When logicians make classes or categories, they like to know how completely its members have been enumerated. So any premise beginning with the word "all" must designate a class for which all the members are known or can be found. When a complete class is put into a premise in logic, whatever is predicated of it should be true of every member of the class, as well, as in "All people are mortal." These general classifications can be further divided into subclasses and particulars (see Figure 8.2). Syllogisms worked in classical logic, because classical logicians thought that the relations between classes and the particulars were a fundamental element of human thinking. So they often began by naming classes, groups that belonged to those classes, and individuals that belonged to those groups (see Figure 8.3). Rhetors are not so concerned as logicians are that the members of classes be completely enumerated, since rhetorical classes are intended to be persuasive rather than mathematically accurate. Complete enumeration of every item in a class would soon put audiences to sleep (*Rhetoric* I i, 1357a). For persuasive purposes, almost any items can be grouped together into a class, depending on the rhetorical situation. The class "politicians" logically includes anyone who runs for public office; but a rhetor might want to include campaign managers or spin doctors in this class as well, in order to make a more sweeping judgement about the whole group.

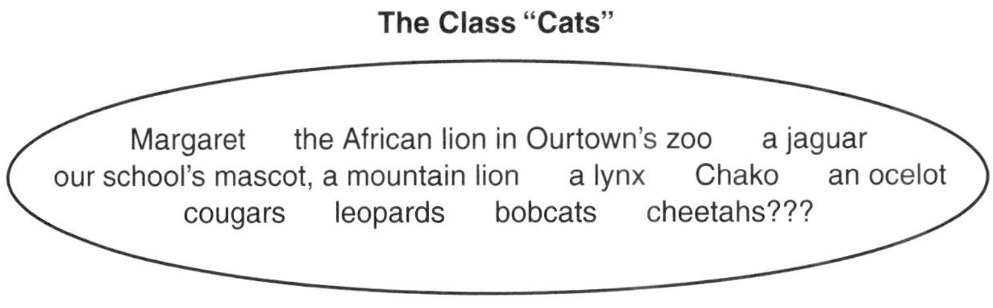

The Class "Cats"

FIGURE 8.1
General classification

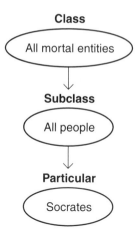

FIGURE 8.2
Subdivisions of a general classification

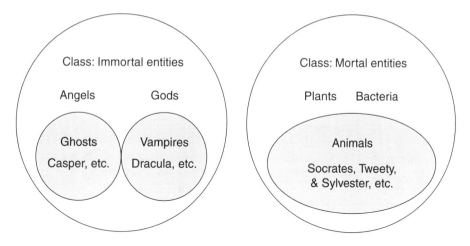

FIGURE 8.3
Relationships between classes, subclasses, and particulars

Induction

Aristotle recognized another movement between premises, and he defined it as "the progress from particulars to universals." Later logicians called this movement **induction** (Latin *inducere,* "to lead into." Induction leads away from particulars and to a general conclusion). A particular is any individual that can be put into a class. Particulars are also called "instances" or "examples." Aristotle supplied this example of inductive reasoning: If the skilled pilot is the best pilot (particular premise) and the skilled charioteer the best charioteer (particular premise), then, in general, the skilled man is the best man in any particular sphere (general conclusion) (*Topics* I, 12). Of course the inductive reasoner could continue to pile up particulars that would reinforce the conclusion by naming skilled athletes, weavers, flute players, engineers, and so on. Induction provides certainty only when all the particulars that belong to a class have been enumerated—something that would be difficult to do in this example, which would require a rhetor to name every sphere of human work. However, rhetoricians do not require complete enumeration of particulars, since a piece of inductive reasoning may be persuasive if enough particulars have been named to convince most people that the conclusion is valid.

Aristotle had a good deal more to say about reasoning in rhetoric, all centered on the relation of general premises to particular ones. Using this scheme, he invented four types of reasoning that are special to rhetoric: **enthymemes, examples, signs,** and **maxims.**

Enthymemes

The premises used in constructing rhetorical proofs differ from those used in dialectic and science only in the degree of certainty we can attach to them. In dialectic and science, deductive arguments are called syllogisms. In rhetoric, they are called enthymemes. The word "enthymeme" comes from Greek *thymos*, "spirit," the capacity whereby people think and feel. Ancient Greeks located the thymos in the mid-section of the body. Quite literally, then, an enthymematic proof was a visceral appeal. To put this in more graphic terms, enthymemes were supposed to grab people in the gut.

Generally, major enthymematic premises represent commonsense beliefs about the way people behave. Rhetors ordinarily use some widely held community belief as the major premise of their argument. Then they apply that premise to the particular case in which they are interested. The major premises of enthymemes are probabilities concerning human action, rather than certainties, as they are in scientific demonstration.

Here, for example, is an enthymeme that could be used to develop the argument about hate speech:

Major Premise: Racist slurs directed against innocent people are offensive and ought to be punished.

Minor Premise: John stood on the commons and shouted racist epithets at people who happened to pass by.

Conclusion: John engaged in offensive behavior and ought to be punished.

Here the major premise is a rhetorical probability, since it is not certain that everyone is offended by the use of racist slurs. The rhetor counts on the fact that most people accept this premise. Those who do not accept it may be reluctant to admit as much; if so, the rhetor's major premise has a greater chance of winning acceptance by an audience.

There are many sorts of relations that may obtain among premises. Sometimes, a minor premise is an example of the major premise, as it is in the above enthymeme about John's offensive behavior. Sometimes, though, the minor premise states a reason for acceptance of the conclusion:

Major Premise: Studies of the effects of smoking have shown that exposure to secondhand smoke can cause lung cancer.

Minor Premise: Because people are allowed to smoke in our workplace, secondhand smoke is present there.

Conclusion: Smoking should be banned from our workplace.

The relations between major and minor premises, then, often take one of these two forms:

1. Y (minor premise) is an example of X (major premise).
2. Y (minor premise) is a reason for X (major premise).

And, as is the case in our examples about hate speech and smoking, the conclusion of an enthymeme often has the relation of "thus it follows that," a relation that can by indicated by the word "therefore."

Standard Enthymematic Patterns

Y is an example of X.

Therefore, it follows that Z.

or

Y is a reason for X.

Therefore, it follows that Z.

Here is an argument built on the first pattern, arguing from a single example:

My brother-in-law spends his welfare check on booze.

All welfare recipients are cheats.

As you can see, this argument is neither logical nor convincing. That doesn't stop people from making similar arguments every day. Here is an instance of an argument built on the second pattern, arguing from a reason:

Men have the power in Hollywood.

That's why there are so few good roles for actresses.

The suppressed middle premise of this argument is that "Men in power aren't interested in finding good roles for women." In order to determine whether this argument from a reason is accurate or convincing, the middle premise must be articulated and supported.

The enthymematic patterns of example and reason are not and need not be followed slavishly. Sometimes an enthymematic argument begins with its conclusion:

Because alternative music usually finds its way into pop culture, suburban kids like hip-hop, and Garth Brooks drew a million people to his concert in Central Park.

The pattern here, then, is

Because Z, X, and Y.

The slogan for Nike products—"Just do it!"—is a highly truncated enthymeme in which only the conclusion is stated. The other premises are presented in images of skilled athletes who wear Nikes while they perform incredible athletic feats. Nonetheless, the entire enthymeme can be articulated in language:

Successful athletes wear Nikes.

These successful athletes wear Nikes.

If you want to be a successful athlete, you should wear Nikes (or, You Can't Do It Without a Pair of Nikes!).

This enthymeme depends for its impact on a number of American commonplaces and attitudes: our reverence for sport, for athletes, for beautiful bodies, for activity, assertiveness, and self-reliance. All of these commonplaces could be adduced as a chain of major premises that underlie the Nike ad. Furthermore, its generalized conclusion ("Just Do It!") can be read to mean "Just buy our product!" This is the implicit or explicit conclusion offered by most advertising.

In the presidential campaign of 1988, the ad writers employed by one candidate devised an enthymeme which is now notorious as an example of the "dirty tricks" that are used in such campaigns. In "Voters Are Pack Rats," rhetorician Kathleen Jamieson tells the story of the ad campaign in which the damaging enthymemes appeared as follows:

VOTERS ARE PACK RATS

The role that ads, Bush rhetoric, news, and audience psychology played in transforming William Horton's name for some into a symbol of the terrors of crime and for others of the exploitation of racist fears shows the powerful ways in which messages interact and the varying responses they evoke in individuals. Like pack rats, voters gather bits and pieces of political information and store them in a single place. Lost in the storage is a clear recall of where this or that "fact" came from. Information obtained from news mixes with that from ads, for example.

Although Bush had been telling the tale on the stump since June, in the second week in September 1988, the Horton story broke into prime time in the form of a National Security Political Action Committee (NSPAC) ad. The ad tied Michael Dukakis to a convicted murderer who had jumped furlough and gone on to rape a Maryland woman and assault her fiancé. The convict was black, the couple white.

The ad opens with side-by-side pictures of Dukakis and Bush. Dukakis's hair is unkempt, the photo dark. Bush, by contrast, is smiling and bathed in light. As the pictures appear, an announcer says "Bush and Dukakis on crime." A picture of Bush flashes on the screen. "Bush supports the death penalty for first-degree murderers." A picture of Dukakis. "Dukakis not only opposes the death penalty, he allowed first-degree murderers to have weekend passes from prison." A close-up mug shot of Horton flashes onto the screen. "One was Willie Horton, who murdered a boy in a robbery, stabbing him nineteen times." A blurry black-and-white photo of Horton apparently being arrested appears. "Despite a life sentence, Horton received ten weekend passes from prison." The words "kidnapping," "stabbing," and "raping" appear on the screen with Horton's picture as the announcer adds, "Horton fled, kidnapping a young couple, stabbing the man and repeatedly raping his girlfriend." The final photo again shows Michael Dukakis. The announcer notes "Weekend prison passes. Dukakis on crime."

When the Bush campaign's "revolving door" ad began to air on October 5, viewers read Horton from the PAC ad into the furlough ad. This stark black-and-white Bush ad opened with bleak prison scenes. It then cut to a procession of convicts circling through a revolving gate and marching toward the nation's living rooms. By carefully juxtaposing words and pictures, the ad invited the false inference that 268 first-degree murderers were furloughed by Dukakis to rape and kidnap. As the bleak visuals appeared, the announcer said that Dukakis had vetoed the death penalty and given furloughs to "first-degree murderers not eligible for parole. While out, many committed other crimes like kidnapping and rape."

The furlough ad contains three false statements and invites one illegitimate inference. The structure of the ad prompts listeners to hear "first-degree murderers not eligible for parole" as the antecedent referent for "many." Many of whom committed crimes? First-degree murderers not eligible for parole. Many of whom went on to commit crimes like kidnapping and rape? First-degree murderers not eligible for parole.

But many unparoleable first-degree murderers did not escape. Of the 268 furloughed convicts who jumped furlough during Dukakis's first two terms, only four had ever been convicted first-degree murderers not eligible for parole. Of those four not "many" but one went on to kidnap and rape. That one was William Horton. By flashing "268 escaped" on the screen as the announcer speaks of "many first-degree murderers," the ad invites the false inference that 268 murderers jumped furlough to rape and kidnap. Again, the single individual who fits this description is Horton. Finally, the actual number who were more than four hours late in returning from furlough during Dukakis's two and a half terms was not 268 but 275. In Dukakis's first two terms, 268 escapes were made by the 11,497 individuals who were given a total of 67,378 furloughs. In the ten-year period encompassing his two completed terms and the first two years of his third term (1987–88), 275 of 76,455 furloughs resulted in escape.

This figure of 275 in ten years compares with 269 who escaped in the three years in which the program was run by Dukakis's Republican predecessor, who created the furlough program.

Jamieson charts some of the enthymematic conclusions that voters were expected to supply. The first ad asked viewers to create the following enthymeme:

Major Premise: Convicted criminals ought to be kept in prison.

Minor Premise: Our opponent (Dukakis) allows convicted criminals to take weekend furloughs outside of prison.

Minor Premise: One prisoner committed a horrible crime while on furlough.

Conclusion: Our opponent does not keep convicted criminals in prison where they belong (or, more subtly, "Dukakis is soft on crime").

The first statement is a general premise, drawn from commonsense beliefs held by the community. The minor premises are particular premises, since they refer to individuals—our opponent and one prisoner. The third statement is a conclusion derived from comparing the premises. And, as Professor Jamieson demonstrates, voters were then asked to connect this enthymeme to another, constructed in the "revolving door" ad.

As is apparent from this example, the placement of premises in rhetoric does not require the rigorous formal analysis that is necessary in logic. Thus other conclusions could be drawn from the premises of this enthymeme: that our opponent does not share beliefs which are widely held within the community, and that, as a result, the community should not vote for him. Obviously, the ad writers hoped that voters would draw these further conclusions. Nor are rhetors obligated to offer only two premises and a conclusion, as logicians are. Rather, an enthymeme may contain as many premises as are needed to secure the audience's belief in the conclusion.

Ordinarily, rhetors do not state all of the premises and conclusions of an enthymematic argument. The ad writers who devised the enthymeme about furloughed criminals omitted its first general premise (convicted criminals ought to be kept in prison), and they did not explicitly state its conclusion in their television advertisements. In the second ad, they carefully constructed the enthymeme so that it was ambiguous, allowing viewers to draw conclusions that were not true.

From the winning candidate's point of view, this was a very successful argument. From a rhetorician's point of view, however, it is an example of what Aristotle called "false reasoning," because its premises were not true. Rhetoricians are ethically obligated to avoid using premises that are not true.

Some ancient rhetoricians preferred to use a separate name for enthymematic arguments which had more than two premises and a conclusion: *epicheireme.* Ordinarily the *epicheireme* contained four or five statements. The extra one or two statements contained reasons for accepting the major and minor premise.

Here is an example of an *epicheireme* from Quintilian. A rhetor is defending a man who killed a robber who was lying in wait for him. The rhetor knows that Roman law permitted persons traveling on unprotected roads to arm themselves against bandits and predators. He might attempt to mitigate the charge of murder with the following major premise: "It cannot be unjust to kill a robber who lies in wait for a victim." Still, the audience might be reluctant to admit that murder is ever just, and their acceptance of the major premise is, of course, crucial to the success of the argument. So the rhetorician might attach a legal reason for accepting it, as follows: "after all, we are allowed to carry weapons." The minor premise would remind the audience of the circumstances surrounding the accused person's killing of a robber: "Quintus Flaccus killed an assailant who had lain in wait for him on the Damascus Road." Support for the minor premise might be given by a companion of the accused: "Fabulus the Cretan witnessed the vicious attack in which Flaccus inflicted a deadly wound on the assailant in order to protect his own life and those of his family." The conclusion would then draw on Roman law, rather than appealing to moral grounds: "We certainly should not be permitted to have weapons if we were absolutely forbidden to use them" (V xiv, 19).

Major Premise: It is just to kill a robber who lies in wait for a victim.

Reason: Roman law allows people to carry weapons precisely in order to protect themselves from marauders.

Minor Premise: Q. Flaccus killed an assailant who lay in wait.

Support for Minor Premise: Fabulus the Cretan says the death occurred in self-defense.

Conclusion: The act of Q. Flaccus was justified by Roman law.

Strictly speaking, then, an enthymeme may consist of from three to five statements. In a three-part enthymeme, the rhetor supplies two premises and a conclusion; the first (major) premise relies on some common sense about probable human action; the second (minor) premise applies the major premise to the case at hand. In a four-part enthymeme, the rhetor offers a reason to support one of the premises. In a five-part enthymeme, she offers support for both premises.

Cicero pointed out that practiced rhetoricians often do not work out enthymemes according to the strict arrangement of their premises but simply chain them together in the most effective way, sometimes beginning with premises, sometimes with conclusions, and often omitting premises that are self-evident. He maintained that a few practice sessions would demonstrate just how easy it is to compose effective enthymemes (*De Inventione* I xli, 76).

Enthymemes are powerful because they are based in community beliefs. Because of this, whether the reasoning in an enthymeme is sound or whether the statements it contains are true, sadly enough, often make little difference to the community's acceptance of the argument. Enthymemes work when listeners or readers participate in constructing the argument—that is, if their prior knowledge is part of the argument, they are inclined to accept the entire argument if they are willing to accept the rhetorician's use of their common, prior knowledge. For this reason, enthymematic arguments do not have to be spelled out completely. The rhetorician may omit premises or conclusions. The audience will enjoy supplying the missing premises for themselves, and may be more readily persuaded by the argument because they have participated in its construction.

Take this enthymeme, for example: "Good people do not commit murder; Ethica is a good person; therefore Ethica did not commit murder." While delivering this argument, the rhetor might omit the minor premise, saying only this: "Since good people do not commit murder, obviously Ethica is not guilty." Or the rhetor might omit the conclusion: "Good people do not commit murder, and Ethica is a good person." It is easy for the audience to supply the implied conclusion. As is true of all rhetorical premises, the major premise of this enthymeme is a probability, rather than a certainty, and thus exceptions to it do exist. Both Brutus and Cassius were widely regarded as good men before they planned and participated in the murder of Julius Caesar.

Examples

Aristotle's word for example was *paradeigma* ("model"). A rhetorical example is any particular which can be fitted under the heading of a class, and which represents the distinguishing features of that class. Sharon's cat, Margaret—a grey, white, and brown calico with one eye—is an example of the class "cat," for instance. So are lions and tigers (but not bears).

As Quintilian defined it, an example adduces "some past action real or assumed which may serve to persuade the audience of the truth of the point which we are trying to make" (V xi, 6). If, for instance, a rhetor wants to convince her neighbor that he should keep his dog inside the fence which surrounds his property, she can remind him of a past instance when another neighbor's dog, running free, spread another neighbor's garbage all over both our front yards. Rhetorical examples should not be confused with the particulars used in inductive reasoning. This rhetor has no interest in generalizing about all dogs in the neighborhood, but is only concerned to compare the actual behavior of one dog running free to the probable behavior of another in similar circumstances. A rhetor who uses examples is reasoning only from part to part, or like to like, or like to unlike, and not from a particular to a generalization as he does in induction.

Rhetorical examples are persuasive because they are specific. Since they are specific, they call up vivid memories of something the audience has experienced. This effect works well if the rhetor gives details which evoke sensory impressions, that mention familiar sights, or sounds, or smells, or tastes, or tactile sensations. In the following passage, Victor Villanueva, a teacher himself, gives us a portrait of a teacher who influenced him:

> An appreciation for literacy comes from Mr. Del Maestro. He teaches drama, though he ventures into poetry on occasion. A Robert Culp-like fellow, square jawed, thin but not skinny, reading glasses halfway down his nose, thin brown hair combed straight back, large hands. He had been a makeup man in Hollywood, he says. Brings movie-making to life. And for me, he brings Julius Caesar to life, removes the mist from "Chack-es-piri," as *abuela* would say it. And for those in the room not as fascinated by Julius Caesar or Prince Hamlet or poor Willy Loman as I am, those who are—in teacher talk—disruptive, Mr. D forgoes the pink slip to the principal, meets the disrupter downstairs, in the gym, twelve-ounce gloves, the matter settled. He has a broad definition of art. He knows the world—and he understands the block, *el bloque,* what kids today call "the hood." Mr. D was as close to color as any teacher I had known in school.

Notice how the details in this example evoke readers' memory of their own teachers.

Examples also work well when they evoke memories of specific historical events which are fresh in the memories of members of the audience.

> Sept. 15, 1963, was Youth Day at Birmingham's Sixteenth Street Baptist Church. Four African-American girls in white dresses and shoes had left Bible class early and were

about to go upstairs to help run the adult service. But before they got there, a timed-explosive device planted under the church steps ripped massive holes in the side of the building, sending stone, glass and metal flying in every direction. Denise Mc-Nair, Cynthia Wesley, Addie Mae Collins and Carol Robertson—ages 11 to 14—died in the blast. Even during the bloodiest days of racial conflict in the South, even in a city so beset by explosives that it was nicknamed Bombingham, this was a uniquely shocking crime. Recalls Representative John Lewis of Georgia, a civil rights veteran who was in Alabama at the time: "It was one of the darkest hours of the civil rights movement."

The author of this passage, Adam Cohen, depicted this horrible example of racist politics in graphic detail, thus gripping his readers' attention.

When rhetors reason by means of example, they ordinarily use a well-known instance to illuminate or explain one that is less well known. Aristotle, Cicero, and Quintilian all use this illustration of reasoning from example:

To prove that Dionysius is aiming at a tyranny, because he asks for a bodyguard, one might say that Pisistratus before him and Theagenes of Megara did the same, and when they obtained what they asked for made themselves tyrants. All the other tyrants known may serve as an example of Dionysius, whose reason, however, for asking for a bodyguard we do not yet know. (*Rhetoric* I ii, 1357b)

If a rhetor wishes to turn this argument from example into an inductive argument, he can mention as many examples as he needs to be convincing, and then assemble them under a universal proposition: "one who is aiming at a tyranny asks for a bodyguard." He could immediately apply this generalization to new particulars if he wished: "We should beware, then, when Pericles asks for a bodyguard."

Historical Examples

Aristotle pointed out that successful examples may be drawn from history. For instance, people who opposed the Persian Gulf War in 1991 used the historical example of Vietnam to argue that America should not become involved again in a localized quarrel in which America had no direct involvement. Later, Presidents Bush and Clinton both used the example of Vietnam as a reason for their hesitation to intervene in a local war between ethnic groups in Bosnia. If a rhetorician were interested in arguing that politicians ought not to be trusted, she could mention a number of examples taken from history—Nathan Hale, Benedict Arnold, or Richard Nixon, who, whether fairly or not, was tagged with the commonplace "Tricky Dick."

Using a procedure called "extended example," rhetors mention only one of these figures and establish their untrustworthiness by naming and describing several instances of it. For instance, Nixon lied to the American people on at least two occasions, he broke several laws, and he destroyed evidence which would implicate him in illegal acts. A rhetor can give as many vivid details as possible in order to evoke the audience's memory of the incident and thus to induce their sympathy with his argument.

Fictional Example

Aristotle pointed out that successful examples can also be found in fiction. He drew his fictional examples from Aesop:

> A horse was in sole occupation of a meadow. A stag having come and done much damage to the pasture, the horse, wishing to avenge himself on the stag, asked a man whether he could help him to punish the stag. That man consented, on condition that the horse submitted to the bit and allowed him to mount him javelins in hand. The horse agreed to the terms and the man mounted him, but instead of obtaining vengeance on the stag, the horse from that time became the man's slave. (II xx, 1393b)

According to Aristotle, Aesop used this fictional example to warn people that they should not give power to a dictator simply because they wished to take revenge on an enemy.

Fictional examples include fables and analogies (*paraboge,* "comparisons"). Fables may be drawn from literature or film, or rhetors may compose their own stories for illustrative purposes. Aristotle wrote that fables are easier to use than historical examples, because fables may be invented when no historical parallels are available that fit the rhetor's case. Fabulous examples work best if the narratives from which they are drawn are well known and liked by the audience. A rhetorician who is interested in establishing the possibility that UFO's are piloted by friendly extraterrestrials, for example, might revive his audience's memory of the vivid scenes of visitations portrayed in popular films such as "Close Encounters" or "E.T." Fables are most effective when morals, or generalizations, can be drawn from them. So the rhetor who utilized the movie fables mentioned above should point out that both films reinforce the notion that the intentions of extraterrestrial visitors are friendly. Nor should he fail to connect the lessons taught by the films with the point of his own argument—there is at least a probability that the passengers aboard UFOs are friendly.

Analogy

In an **analogy,** the rhetorician sets one hypothetical example beside another for the purposes of comparison. Aristotle borrowed his illustration of comparison from Socrates: it is as silly to argue that leaders should be chosen by balloting as it would be to argue that Olympic athletes should be chosen by ballot rather than for their athletic prowess or to argue that the pilot of a ship should be chosen by lot, rather than because he or she is the most knowledgeable sailor.

In complex analogies, two examples exhibit a similar relation among their elements. The physician William Hervey, who is credited with discovering the circulation of the blood in human beings used an analogy of this type. He reasoned that if sap circulates in vegetables and keeps them alive, it was reasonable to assume that blood circulates in animals and performs a similar function for them. Here the similarity lies in the relationship of circulation, rather than between the items mentioned—sap and blood, vegetables and animals.

Cicero included an complex example of analogical reasoning in the *De Inventione.* He told a story about Aspasia, who used the mode of reasoning to convince a couple to be satisfied with their marriage. First Aspasia prompted the wife to admit that, while she would prefer to have the gold ornaments and fine dresses possessed by a neighboring woman if they were better than her own, she would not covet that woman's husband, even though he be a better husband. In other words, since ornaments and fine dresses are not the same sorts of possession as a husband, they do not bear the same relation to a woman's well-being or happiness. Aspasia then used the same method of reasoning to demonstrate to the husband that, while he might prefer to own the better horses and the better farm possessed by a neighboring man, he would not prefer the man's wife, even though she be a better wife than his own. Aspasia concluded:

> You, madam, wish to have the best husband, and you, Xenophon, desire above all things to have the finest wife. Therefore unless you can contrive that there be no better man or finer woman on earth you will certainly always be in dire want of what you consider best, namely, that you be the husband of the very best of wives, and that she be wedded to the very best of men. (II xxxi, 52)

Cicero pointed out that the force of this conclusion is undeniable, since it is very like the undisputed conclusions about jewelry and horses which preceded it. He noted further that Socrates used this method "because he wished to present no arguments himself, but preferred to get a result from the material which the interlocutor had given him—a result which the interlocutor was bound to approve as following necessarily from what he had already granted" (53).

Similar and Contrary Examples

Quintilian distinguished between examples which work by comparing two like instances, which he called "simile," and those which work by comparing unlike cases or "contraries." His example of simile was: "Saturninus was justly killed, as were the Gracchi" (V xi, 7). The Gracchi were famous brothers, Tiberius and Gaius, who led revolts against constituted Roman authority. Quintilian's comparison implied that the lesser known and less respected Saturninus belonged in the class of persons who are important enough to pose a threat; it also implied that even though he was a lesser person, he nevertheless deserved a punishment similar to that meted out to the members of the famous Gracchi family. A contemporary rhetorician who is skeptical about official explanations of the assassinations of public figures might update this simile by arguing as follows: If it was possible to capture and imprison the assassin of Robert Kennedy, it ought to be possible to capture and imprison the assassins of Martin Luther King, Jr., and John F. Kennedy as well. All three men are generally respected. However, some people suspect that the actual killers of John F. Kennedy and Martin Luther King have not yet been brought to justice. The comparative analogy suggests that justice has not yet been done in these cases.

To argue from example by contrary is trickier, but nevertheless effective. Quintilian's illustration of contrary example was this: "Marcellus restored the works of art which had been taken from the Syracusans who were our enemies, while Verres took the same works of art from our allies." This example reflects very negatively on the character of Verres, who, in contrast to Marcellus' generosity to former enemies, stole from friends. A contemporary version of this contrary example could be employed as follows: "The Surgeon General and the American Medical Association long ago warned that smoking was dangerous to human health; the executives of tobacco companies made this admission only when forced to do so by the courts."

Using Examples

Aristotle preferred enthymemes to examples as a kind of proof, no doubt because enthymemes were similar to the fundamental unit of proof in his logical system—the syllogism. However, he wrote that if no enthymemes are available, a rhetor must use examples since they do produce conviction (II xx, 9). If enthymemes are available, he recommended that a rhetor support them with examples, and that the examples be presented last since they are likely to induce belief. If rhetors must begin with examples, they should include several; however, if they use examples last, in support of an enthymeme, one will do.

Aristotle's preference for logical reasoning seems to have overtaken his usual good sense at this point. Most audiences are very much impressed by examples, perhaps because of their specificity. Many contemporary journalists and writers of nonfiction begin their arguments with extended examples. The argument from example is also a favorite of advertisers—think, for instance, of the ad for coffee that simply shows a group of attractive people gathering at a table to drink coffee. And of course the notorious Joe Camel and Marlboro Man are fictional examples used to sell cigarettes. There is a good deal of argument over whether these figures actually cause people to buy cigarettes, but certainly they do contribute to name recognition of the products they represent.

If well chosen, examples cause audiences to recall similar circumstances in which they have participated, or in which they would like to participate. The rhetorician can hope that the vividness of the comparison will also cause his audience to draw the conclusions at which she has only hinted. The rhetors who designed the coffee ad obviously hoped that people would connect use of the product with the contented and attractive people shown in the ad.

Maxims

Maxims are wise sayings or proverbs which are generally accepted by the rhetorician's community. Ancient maxims were often drawn from poetry or history, as with Aristotle's "There is no man who is happy in everything," by the playwright Euripides, or "The best of omens is to defend one's country" from the poet Homer (II 21, 2 and 11). But maxims also arise from the common wisdom of the people: the proverb "Birds of a feather flock together" was old even when Quintilian cited it 1900 years ago (V xi, 41). Modern examples of maxims include such hoary sayings as "a stitch in time saves nine," "better late than never," and "rolling stones gather no moss."

In ancient times, where literacy was not widespread, much popular wisdom was contained in oral sayings. Many of these were drawn from lines composed by respected poets, especially Homer. A rhetorician could utter a line from Homer, and his audience would immediately recognize the context and the point of the quotation. To a certain extent, this is still possible, although modern audiences are not as well acquainted with lines from poetry as people once were. However, many of us do know maxims taken from the Bible, like "an eye for an eye," and most of us have heard the line "To be or not to be" at least once in our lives, although fewer people know that it is the first line of a speech uttered by a character created by Shakespeare, named Hamlet. This phrase could well serve as the opening line of a defense attorney's opening speech; a rhetor could use it to organize a list of options in any paper urging that some action be taken. We do remember lines from speeches, such as Martin Luther King Jr.'s "I have a dream" or John F. Kennedy's "Ask not what your country can do for you." These lines serve speakers and writers as a sort of rhetorical shorthand which can evoke whole political philosophies and memories of times gone past.

According to Aristotle, maxims are general statements which deal with human actions that should be chosen or avoided (II xxi, 2). The first two modern maxims listed above recommend actions: "A stitch in time saves nine" counsels us to be as well prepared as possible in order to save ourselves extra trouble; "Better late than never" implies that doing something too late is better than never doing it at all. The "rolling stones" maxim implies that people who submit to wanderlust don't pile up responsibilities; since wanderlust as a way of life might be either appealing or repulsive to a given audience, the action recommended here is ambiguous, and the rhetorician would do well to clarify which interpretation is intended.

Using Maxims

Maxims can be found in dictionaries of proverbs or collections of quotations. Their rhetorical force derives from their commonness. Since they are commonly held, they seem to be true. As Quintilian pointed out, "sayings such as these would not have acquired immortality had they not carried conviction of their truth to all mankind" (V xi, 41). And, as Aristotle noted, somewhat cynically, maxims are especially convincing to audiences who like to hear their beliefs confirmed. Aristotle's example is this: a man who happened to have bad neighbors or children would welcome any one's statement that nothing is more troublesome than neighbors or more stupid than to beget children (II xxi, 15). This feature of maxims provides a clue as to how to hunt for appropriate ones: A rhetor should try to determine whether the audience has any preconceived opinions that are relevant to the point. If so, the rhetor should find an appropriate maxim that generalizes these preconceived opinions. For example, the maxim "rolling stones gather no moss" would be appropriate for an older audience who disapproves of the way young Americans tend to move frequently from community to community and from job to job. Their very general nature makes maxims applicable to a wide variety of situations. In fact, part of their persuasive force lies in their generality—when applied to a specific case, a maxim can impart its own persuasive force to that case. For example, Marine officers use the motto of the corps, "Semper fidelis" ("always faithful") to breed camaraderie among their troops and to convince them to go into battle. The motto is an abbreviated reference to the entire history of the Marine Corps—it reminds the troops of its martial history and of its tradition of brotherhood under fire. Thus, though general, the motto can be effectively used in any specific situation when the troops need to be urged forward.

Aristotle noted that maxims are often the premises or conclusions of an enthymeme. Here are two chained enthymemes; the last one employs the maxim "better late than never" as its conclusion:

Major Premise: Unfortunately, the United States and the Soviet Union were enemies for most of the twentieth century.

Minor Premise: This enmity brought about the Korean War, the Vietnam War, the Bay of Pigs, and a proliferation of nuclear weaponry.

Conclusion: The enmity between the United States and the Soviet Union caused a great deal of bloodshed and fear.

Major Premise: Fortunately, this enmity ended with the collapse of the Soviet Union.

Minor Premise: The United States will no longer have to fight strategic hot wars against the Soviets, and nuclear weapons can be dismantled.

Conclusion: Better late than never.

Here is another enthymeme that concludes with the same maxim:

Major Premise: Uncontrolled use of fluorocarbons increases the size and number of holes in the ozone layer, which exacerbates the "greenhouse effect," the gradual warming of the earth's surface.

Minor Premise: Even though severe damage has already been done, public attention has finally been drawn to the deleterious potential of the greenhouse effect, and pressure is being put on politicians to decrease the manufacture of fluorocarbons.

Conclusion: Better late than never.

Maxims can serve effectively as the major premises of enthymemes as well, since they represent the common wisdom of a community. Here is an example:

Major Premise: A stitch in time saves nine.

Minor Premise: There is a small crack in the windshield of Felix's car.

Conclusion: Felix should have the crack buffed out or else it will spread and he will have to replace the entire windshield.

Note how, in this case, the maxim predicts the particular conclusion so readily that the rhetorician could safely omit the conclusion when presenting the argument.

One cautionary note is in order: Aristotle warned that maxims should not be used by young people, who run the risk of appearing to espouse something in a maxim that they have not learned through experience.

Signs

Signs are physical facts or real events which inevitably or usually accompany some other state of affairs. For example, if someone has a fever, this is a sign of illness; if someone bears a physical scar, this is a sign of a previous injury. If, as in these examples, the connection between the sign and the inferred state of affairs always exists, we have what Aristotle called an infallible sign (*tekmerion*) (I ii, 16). But not all signs are infallibly connected to some state of affairs. We can argue, for instance, that bloody clothing is a sign that a defendant committed the murder for which she or he is being tried. However, the defense attorney could plausibly argue that the defendant suffers from frequent nosebleeds, and thus that the bloodied clothing is a sign of that problem, rather than participation in a murder.

The argument from sign can be very effective in an argument for the same reason that examples are effective. Arguments from sign appeal to the daily experiences that we share with members of our audience. The trick for rhetors who use the argument from sign is to convince an audience that the sign in question is (or is not) inevitably connected to the state of affairs they are trying to establish. Because of this difficulty, Quintilian recommended that the argument from sign be accompanied by other support (V ix, 9). If the prosecuting attorney can prove that the defendant was an enemy of the murdered man, and had threatened his life, and was in his house at the time of the murder—all of these strengthen the connection of the bloody clothing to murder, rather than to a bloody nose.

We rely on arguments from sign more than we perhaps realize. We take a cloudy sky as a sign of an impending storm; if a friend is listless and uninterested in his surroundings, we take that as a sign of depression; when the pilot of an airplane in flight turns off the light that says "fasten seat belt" we take that as a sign that it is safe to get out of our seats. But as these examples suggest, it is not always safe to rely on signs as though they were infallible. A darkened sky may result from pollution; our listless friend may be coming down with the flu; sudden unexpected turbulence may make us wish we hadn't taken the pilot's message so casually. If someone who is accused of making hateful remarks has made them on previous occasions, this may or may not be a sign that she or he harbors racist or sexist attitudes.

The argument from sign has a kairotic element, insofar as signs change over time. In the 1960s, a man's long hair was taken as a sign that he was a hippie who believed in free love and used drugs. These days, however, the length of a man's hair does not reliably signify much of anything. Indeed, an important part of contemporary rhetorical argument involves the disassociation of signs from their commonplace referents. Today, rhetors are at pains to point out that tattoos or body piercings are not necessarily a sign of rebelliousness, or that being on welfare is not necessarily a sign of laziness or unwillingness to work. Some extremely conservative groups are trying to establish that refusing to pay one's taxes is a sign of patriotism. Signs differ from place to place, as well. In the midwestern and southern states, people ask strangers about their parents and family as a sign of friendliness. In eastern states, however, such curiosity may be taken as a sign of nosiness or even of very bad manners.

EXERCISES

1. Rhetors who use enthymemes, examples, maxims, and signs need to be alert to attitudes that are widely held in the culture that surrounds them. They need to watch television, read newspapers and books, listen to popular music, political speeches, and the conversations of their friends and relatives. This attentiveness should generate a long list of enthymematic premises, examples, maxims, and signs that can be used to good effect in arguments.

2. Find an article from a popular magazine or newspaper and examine its use of enthymemes, examples, maxims, or signs. How effective are these arguments?

3. Create an enthymeme and an argument from sign to use in some composition you are currently working on. Find a maxim that supports your proposition and work out the argument that connects the maxim to your position. Find a historical example that supports your position, and include it. Find or invent a fictional example that supports your position, and include it (see the chapter on the *progymnasmata* for advice about writing fictions).

4. Some slogans are conclusions or premises of enthymemes. The statement "Elvis has left the building" is part of a long enthymematic argument whose other premises are never stated. Can you articulate them?

EXTRINSIC PROOFS

The material at the rhetor's disposal is twofold, one kind made up of the things which are not thought out by himself, but depend upon the circumstances and are dealt with by rule, for example documents, oral evidence, informal agreements, examinations, statutes, decrees of the Senate, judicial precedents, magisterial orders, opinions of counsel, and whatever else is not produced by the rhetor, but is supplied to him by the case itself or by the parties: the other kind is founded entirely on the rhetor's reasoned argument.

—Cicero, *De Oratore* II xxvii, 116–117

EXTRINSIC PROOFS DO not need to be invented by a rhetor because they are found in the rhetorical situation. Modern rhetoricians place a much heavier emphasis on extrinsic proofs than the ancients did. Today rhetors often assume that whatever is written down and published is accurate and trustworthy since, in a sense, it represents someone's testimony about something. The version of rhetoric that is taught in school assumes that accounts based on empirical investigation are absolutely reliable. As a result, students are often taught that there are only two kinds of acceptable rhetorical proofs, **testimony** and **data.** Testimony provides audiences with accounts composed by people who for some reason have special access to relevant facts or arguments. The English word "testimony" derives from a Latin phrase meaning "standing as a third," that is, serving as a witness. Hence testimony is a statement given by a witness about some event or state of affairs.

Data, on the other hand, include any facts or statistics that are relevant to the rhetorical situation. This is the only place in this book where the term "fact" is used in its current sense to mean something that has been empirically demonstrated. In this sense, facts are grounded in experience. That is, the validity of a fact can be tested by personal observation, or at least we can imagine how such a test might be done. If someone remarks that the temperature has fallen below freezing, we can test this statement of fact by stepping outdoors; if we desire more accuracy, we can look at a thermometer.

Ancient teachers would have categorized both testimony and data as extrinsic to the art of rhetoric, because they are not invented according to its principles. Rhetors need only to find, select, and assemble the relevant extrinsic proofs.

EXTRINSIC PROOFS IN ANCIENT RHETORICS

Scholars doubt that Aristotle invented the distinction between intrinsic and extrinsic proofs, even though most ancient authorities credit it to him. However, it also appears in the roughly contemporaneous *Rhetorica ad Alexandrum* (vii, 1428a), which suggests that Aristotle may have found it in one or several of the treatises he gathered and studied in order to compose the *Rhetoric.*

Quintilian, noting that "the division laid down by Aristotle has met with almost universal approval," translated the Greek terms as "artistic" and "nonartistic" (V i, 1). Translators have abandoned these terms, however, since "art" carries connotations of "high" or "creative" art to contemporary ears. In the chapter on ethos we called these two kinds of proof "invented" and "situated," since, as Aristotle wrote, intrinsic proofs have to be invented with the aid of rhetoric, while extrinsic proofs are situated within the circumstances of a case or issue, and have only to be used (I 2, 1355b).

Cicero stated that all extrinsic proofs rely chiefly on the authority granted by the community to those who make them (*Topics* IV, 24). In other words, Cicero defined all extrinsic proof as testimony. In keeping with Cicero's remark, we might argue that facts are a kind of testimony, since their accuracy depends on the care taken by the person who establishes them as facts and on his reputation in relevant communities as well.

In any case, ancient authorities listed the following items as extrinsic proofs: laws or precedents, rumors, maxims or proverbs, documents, oaths, and the testimony of witnesses or authorities. Some of these were tied to ancient legal procedures or religious beliefs. The fact that someone had refused to take an oath about a disputed issue could be introduced in Athenian courts as evidence, for example, and the sayings of oracles were also cited as extrinsic support for arguments. Ancient teachers considered written documents to be extrinsic proofs because they were composed by someone other than the rhetor—usually a court official.

Ancient teachers knew that extrinsic proofs are not always reliable. For instance, they were quite aware that written documents usually required careful interpretation, and they were skeptical of their accuracy and authority as well. In Plato's *Phaedrus*, Socrates warned Phaedrus that written documents cannot always be trusted:

> written words . . . seem to talk to you as though they were intelligent, but if you ask them anything about what they say, from a desire to be instructed, they go on telling you just the same thing forever. And once a thing is put in writing, the composition, whatever it may be, drifts all over the place, getting into the hands not only of those who understand it, but equally of those who have no business with it; it doesn't know how to address the right people, and not address the wrong. And when it is

ill-treated and unfairly abused it always needs its parent to come to its help, being unable to defend or help itself. (275d)

The problem with written words, according to Plato, is that we don't always know their author: who his family was, what sort of work he did, what his reputation or ideological affiliation were. Because we don't know these things about authors, we cannot simply take their work at face value. Rather, we need to interpret it.

Furthermore, written documents that are central to a culture's definition of itself accrue a sediment of interpretation as time passes. Plato's *Dialogues* are themselves central to Western culture. When contemporary readers use very old documents like these, they must interpret them through thousands of years of readings. There is no way to retrieve their original or authoritative meaning, if, indeed, they ever had one.

A few years ago, a man named Robert Bork was nominated to fill a vacancy on the Supreme Court of the United States. There was a fierce fight in the Senate over Mr. Bork's nomination, not because anyone doubted his qualifications— nobody did—but because he is a strict constructionist of the American Constitution. This means that he interprets the Constitution according to the letter of the law; that is, he tries to read the Constitution to mean exactly what the people who wrote it wanted it to mean. His opponents argued that many things have occurred since the Constitution was ratified that the founding fathers could not have foreseen. Opponents of strict construction argued further that the Constitution must be interpreted in light of changes in American history and culture, and particularly in light of laws that have been written since the Constitution was ratified. This debate pointed up the difficulty entailed in relying on written documents as accurate representations of reality.

A related kind of extrinsic proof—law—provides good examples of the need to interpret written documents. In American jurisprudence, laws are written in general terms; that is, they describe the actions a community should take in case an instance occurs that fits within the general situation they describe. The legal debate over regulation of hate speech hinged on whether uses of offensive speech should be interpreted as speech that is protected by the First Amendment, or whether it should be read as "fighting words" or as speech that provokes "imminent lawless action." In the first case, of course, it cannot be regulated at all. On the other hand, if it is interpreted as "fighting words" that "tend to incite an immediate breach of the peace," the courts may decide to allow its regulation. It all depends on how the law is read and how any instance of the use of hate speech is interpreted.

The case of written documents suggests that Aristotle's distinction between intrinsic and extrinsic proofs is not absolute. Often, extrinsic proofs cannot simply be inserted into an argument without art or skill. Rhetors must interpret and evaluate the worth of such proofs, especially when they contradict one another. Rhetors must also determine whether or not such proofs will be persuasive. By and large, the ancients recommended that rhetors follow this procedure in composing an extrinsic proof: state it, comment on its relevance to the issue, comment on its effectiveness, make any arguments that are necessary to support it. This is good advice.

TESTIMONY

Ancient rhetoricians generally distrusted the testimony of ordinary persons, especially those who testified in legal cases. The author of *ad Alexandrum* pointed out that "what is stated in evidence must necessarily be either probable or improbable or of doubtful credit, and similarly the witness must be either trustworthy or untrustworthy or questionable" (14). Rhetors could insert testimony into their discourse without comment, he wrote, only when a trustworthy witness stated a probability. Any combination of an untrustworthy or questionable witness with improbable or doubtful testimony required rhetors to supplement the testimony with an account of its worth. Aristotle developed a rule of disinterestedness for determining which witnesses were reliable: persons who had nothing to gain by testifying were more credible than those who stood to profit by doing so (I xv, 16). Quintilian argued that rhetors need to know whether or not a witness favors or opposes a point of view, and whether the witness has held this position for a long time or has only recently adopted it (V vii, 13). In short, ancient rhetoricians never took anyone's testimony at face value. Instead, they examined the motives of witnesses in order to determine whether or not their testimony was reliable.

Since testimony is a report made by someone about some state of affairs, it is valuable to the extent that audiences accept the authority and credibility of the witnesses who provide it. Today, audiences award authority to two sorts of witnesses: persons who are respected in the relevant community and persons who were in a position to observe some disputed state of affairs. We call the first kind community authorities and the second proximate authorities.

Community Authorities

Community authorities are persons whose words or actions have earned them respect within a given community. Rhetors use the words or examples of such persons to lend credibility to their ethos and authenticity to their positions. Aristotle wrote that "witnesses are of two kinds, ancient and recent" (I xv, 1375b). In Aristotle's time, ancient witnesses were "the poets and men of repute whose judgments are known to all"—Homer, for example. Recent witnesses were "well-known persons who have given a decision on any point"—for example, Solon, who was a famous lawmaker (1376a).

Modern rhetors still rely upon the testimony of ancient witnesses, just as we have quoted or cited texts by Aristotle, Quintilian, and other ancient rhetoricians throughout this book to validate our interpretation of their theories and practices. It was important that we do so, because some of our interpretations are controversial among scholars and historians of ancient rhetorics. If we can support a doubtful or controversial position with a quotation from Cicero, we demonstrate that at least one ancient rhetorician took a position similar to ours. The quotation also suggests that we have read ancient rhetorical authorities carefully, which reinforces our ethos. Thus, citation of relevant authorities is a means of proof, albeit an extrinsic one.

American rhetors often quote historical figures like Thomas Jefferson or Abraham Lincoln in support of a point of view, since both of these men are important figures in American mythology. The following passage from President Gerald Ford's inauguration speech illustrates the rhetorical usefulness of such authorities:

> Those who nominated and confirmed me as Vice President were my friends and are my friends. They were of both parties, elected by all the people, and acting under the Constitution in their name. It is only fitting then that I should pledge to them, and to you, that I will be the President of all the people. Thomas Jefferson said, "The people are the only sure reliance with the preservation of our liberty." And down the years Abraham Lincoln renewed this American article of faith asking, "Is there any better way for equal hope in the world?"

Ford assumed the presidency under difficult circumstances: his predecessor, Richard Nixon, had resigned under threat of impeachment. Thus it was important for Ford to reassure Americans that their democratic tradition of popular government was still intact. He did this by quoting Jefferson, the architect of American democracy, and Lincoln, whose most famous utterances argue for the importance of government by the people.

Study of a community's choice of authorities often discloses the values held by its members. During one session of a recent Democratic National Convention, for example, speakers cited or quoted the following persons: Fannie Lou Hamer, John F. Kennedy, Robert F. Kennedy, Martin Luther King, Jr., Abraham Lincoln, Rosa Parks, Eleanor Roosevelt, Franklin Delano Roosevelt, Adlai Stevenson, and Harry S Truman. Hamer was a civil-rights activist and a member of an African American delegation to the 1964 Democratic convention that challenged discriminatory rules for delegate seating. Parks refused to give up her seat on a bus, and her example inspired the bus boycott of 1955–1956. Martin Luther King, Jr., was a well-known activist in the civil rights movement, an advocate of nonviolent resistance who was assassinated in April, 1968. John F. Kennedy, Franklin D. Roosevelt, and Harry S Truman were Democratic presidents, while Adlai Stevenson was the party's nominee for president and ambassador to the United Nations during the 1950s. Eleanor Roosevelt was an activist and philanthropist; Robert Kennedy, brother of John, was assassinated while running for president on the Democratic ticket in 1968.

All of these persons, with the notable exception of Lincoln, were or are Democrats. Democrats revere them for their dedication to party ideals, particularly the furthering of civil rights, which was a central theme of this convention. Even though Lincoln was a Republican, his cultural authority is so great that he can be cited, even by Democrats, in support of a strong position on civil rights. It is important to note that cultural authorities are invoked in support of a position only if they enjoy good reputations in the relevant community. Since reputations represent a community's evaluation of someone's behavior, they do not always accurately represent that person's actual behavior. Two recent Democratic presidents (Lyndon Baines Johnson and Jimmy Carter) were not cited as authorities on this occasion, even though both were active in furthering civil rights legislation during their terms in office. Their omission suggests that they, or their politics, were in disfavor among Democrats or among the Americans being wooed by Democrats at the time they held this convention.

A slightly different use of community authority appears in scholarly writing, including student writing, which relies heavily on the authoritative testimony of professionals or experts. In this case, the relevant community is a profession or discipline, such as physics or medicine or psychology or philosophy. Within communities of this kind, witnesses are ordinarily expected to hold the scholarly and research credentials authorized by the community: an M.D. for medical doctors, a D.V.M. for veterinarians, a Ph.D. for some scientists and for all scholars in the social sciences and humanities. Scholarly witnesses also accrue authority from the quality and extent of their research and publication, while their receipt of awards and prizes, such as a Nobel or a Pulitzer, increases their authority.

Rhetors who compose discourse to be used in professional or disciplinary communities are expected to cite persons who are defined as authorities within those communities. Such citations can easily be inserted into any discourse:

> Jane Doe, author of several books and many articles, winner of the coveted Status Prize for Weighty Authorities, agrees with my position.

Since we write chiefly for scholarly communities (students and colleagues), we try to cite an authority whenever we make a point that might be misunderstood or contested by an audience. We also try to comment immediately on every quotation we use. Commentary can include an interpretation of the quotation, or it can show how the quotation is relevant to the argument in progress.

The scholarly habit of invoking authorities often frustrates students who have not yet studied a discipline thoroughly enough to recognize the names of its authorities or to know their work. Here, for example, is an excerpt from the opening paragraphs of an article by cultural studies author Kuan-Hsing Chen:

> Current debates on post-marxism have centred around the works of Ernesto Laclau and Chantal Mouffe . . . Before entering into the debate, let me point out that the version of postmodernism discussed here is different from what I shall call "dominant" ones. Elsewhere, through the post-1968 works of Michel Foucault, Gilles Deleuze, Felix Guattari, and Jean Baudrillard, a "critical" postmodernism has been proposed (Chen, 1988). This critical postmodernism distances itself from a dominant "aesthetic" criticism which privileges art works as its central site of analysis (Lyotard, 1984); it departs from a philosophical criticism which locates itself within the history of philosophy (Habermas, 1987); it supersedes a cultural criticism which centres on the elite sectors of cultural lives (Huyssen, 1986); it diverges from a social criticism which reduces the ("postmodern") social worlds to a reflection of the ("late capitalist") economic mode of production (Jameson, 1983, 1984); it differs from a "moral

criticism" which calls for a return to a ("postpragmatist") ("bourgeois") social solidarity (Rorty, 1984); and it also breaks away from a popular culture criticism which
focuses on the unravelling of new cultural texts. (35–51)

Here, the author cites a dizzying list of postmodern theorists (including himself)
in order to situate his argument within a particular community. Anyone not
schooled in cultural studies or critical theory would probably be lost in the sea
of names, despite the handy parenthetical keywords from each theorists' work.

This passage exemplifies yet another scholarly habit: using a person's name
as shorthand for an ideology or a body of intellectual work. Within a given
scholarly community, some thinkers are awarded such high status that they are
no longer quoted but only named. Aristotle and Isocrates enjoy this status
among historians of rhetoric, and the same is true of Emile Durkheim and Karl
Marx in sociology or Claude Levi-Strauss and Margaret Meade in anthropology.

Evaluating Community Authorities

Since most scholarly and intellectual work relies heavily on the testimony of authorities, rhetors ought to know whether the authorities they cite or quote possess whatever credentials are required for entry to a discipline. A scholar's
credentials often appear on book jackets or at the end of books, and scholarly articles ordinarily list authors' credentials and accomplishments as well. If there
is any doubt about the extent of a scholar's research, an author search in library
holdings will show how often and where she or he has published. References to
someone's work by other scholars in the same field also suggest that she or he
is considered an authority.

Rhetors must also be concerned about an authority's accuracy. Authorities
may produce inaccurate work for at least two reasons: either they were ignorant
of some relevant information, or their ideological bias compromised their accuracy. The accuracy of a scholarly or intellectual authority is sometimes difficult
to ascertain, especially for students who are new to a field of study. One way to
check the accuracy of a source is to read reviews about it. Reviewers should indicate whether or not an authority is trustworthy, and they may indicate
whether a work is controversial, as well. Another way to insure that authorities
represent a reasonably accurate state of affairs in their work is to compare it with
that of other scholars who discuss the same issues. Another is to use more recent
accounts that correct errors in older works.

Students are sometimes surprised to learn that scholars disagree with one
another. But they do. For example, historians of rhetoric argue over whether it
is appropriate or accurate to group historical figures like Protagoras, Gorgias,
and Isocrates together into a coherent rhetorical school called "the Sophists."
Sometimes these arguments become quite heated. Arguments like these are important because their outcomes are ideological. In the case of the Sophists, if
scholars can prove that their work was consecutive and widely recognized as
such during the fifth century BCE, they have grounds for modifying Plato's negative comments about rhetoric, comments which have lent a negative coloring
to rhetoric throughout the history of Western philosophy.

Some scholars believe that accuracy is insured if authorities are objective. Supposedly, authorities are objective if they have detached themselves emotionally or ideologically from issues, and when they write or speak without bias or prejudice. We are skeptical about the ideal of objectivity, however. People ordinarily choose a field of study because they are interested in the issues raised within it. If people are interested in something, they have already denied the possibility of their being objective about it. And since scholars also subscribe to ideologies, just like everybody else, their ability to approach any issue without bias is open to question. Given the role played by ideology in all thought, even in scholarly and intellectual rhetoric, objectivity is sometimes another name for orthodoxy ("straight thinking")—support of the intellectual status quo. That is, the so-called objective scholarly authority is thought to be so because she or he does not depart radically from the tenets held by her or his scholarly or intellectual community.

Like ancient rhetoricians who examined the motives of witnesses, then, modern rhetors ought also to inspect the motives and ideologies of even the most respected authorities, if they plan to use them as extrinsic proofs. Some authors acknowledge their motives and prejudices in a forward or a preface.

> The first person ever to slap me on the ass was a federal employee. He was the army doctor at Fort Benning, Georgia, who brought me into this world. My daddy was serving there at Fort Benning as an infantry officer, so he and my momma were able to start me off with some fine federal health care.
>
> You'd have to say that the federal government made a big impression on me early in life. I grew up in a town in southern Louisiana by the name of Carville, and that's no coincidence; the town got that name because my family provided the town with its most indispensable federal employee—its postmaster. Three generations of Carvilles served as postmaster, starting with my great-grandmother Octavia Duhon. Believe it or not, working for the federal government was a source of family pride.
>
> You see, the federal government was not considered a bad thing when I was growing up. First of all, it kept my feet dry. Before I was born, the Mississippi River used to overflow its banks every spring and flood the whole town of Carville and many other towns like it. It was a Washington bureaucrat who got the idea that we could build a levee system to stop the flooding, and the federal taxpayers helped us do it. It was the heavy hand of government at work.
>
> In my hometown, the federal government also cared for a group of people no one else was willing to care for—folks from all over the country who came down with Hansen's disease, a condition more commonly known as leprosy. Carville was world famous as the home to the Gillis W. Long Hansen's Disease Center, where doctors developed the multidrug treatment that now allows people with Hansen's to lead a near-normal life. Only the federal government had the resources and inclination to do that.
>
> Washington bureaucrats also came up with the idea that black children should be able to go to school with white children. Integration was *the* searing issue when I was a kid. After the *Brown* v. *Board of Education* decision in 1954, people in Carville, which was 85 percent black, stopped talking about football and the weather. All they wanted to do was scream about race. Like most whites, I took segregation for granted and wished the blacks just didn't push so damn hard to change it.

But when I was sixteen years old I read *To Kill a Mockingbird,* and that novel changed everything. I got it from the lady who drove around in the overheated old bookmobile in my parish—another government program, I might add. I had asked the lady for something on football, but she handed me *To Kill a Mockingbird* instead. I couldn't put it down. I stuck it inside another book and read it under my desk during school. When I got to the last page, I closed it and said, "They're right and we're wrong." The issue was literally black and white, and we were absolutely, positively on the wrong side. I've never forgotten which side the federal government was on.

Federal and state governments helped me get an education and a start in life. They offered me all kinds of loans and the G.I. Bill so I could earn myself undergraduate and law degrees at Louisiana State University. They picked up my salary when I served as a corporal in the United States Marine Corps and again when I taught eighth-grade science at a tiny little public school for boys in South Vacherie, Louisiana.

Government did right by me. I'm the first one to admit that fact. No, let's back up for a minute. I don't just admit that fact—I savor it. I hold it up as an example of what government should be in the business of doing: providing opportunity. You will never catch me saying that I am a self-made man. I am not. My parents gave me their love, their example, and the benefit of their hard work. And the government gave me a big hand.

Students can look for passages like these in order to evaluate the bias of an authority. Students should also get into the habit of reading the acknowledgments pages at the beginning of books, where writers cite the people to whose work they are indebted. A list of acknowledgments often tells a discerning reader who the authors studied with, who their colleagues are, and whose scholarship they use, admire or disagree with.

Students can also determine a writer's ideological standpoint by looking for lists of the foundations or institutions that funded the work. These are usually listed in the acknowledgments or on the title page. Liberal or socialist foundations include Common Cause, Brookings Institute, the Institute for Policy Studies and the Center for the Study of Democratic Institutions; conservative or neo-conservative foundations include the American Enterprise Institute, the Heritage Foundation, the Olin Foundation, the Scaife Foundation, and the Center for Strategic and International Studies. Publishing houses and magazines also have ideological biases. Sometimes they make these explicit, sometimes not. Among English-language publishing houses, Pantheon, South End Press, Beacon Books, International Publishers, Routledge and Methuen are liberal or socialist, while Freedom House, Reader's Digest Books, Paragon House and Arlington House are conservative or neo-conservative. A book published by any of these houses is likely to reflect its ideological orientation.

In America at present, most mass-circulation media are centrist or just right of center; this is true of *Newsweek* and the major television networks, for example. (People whose politics lean to the right of ours may object to our assessments of the ideological leanings of these media, arguing that the major commercial TV networks are liberal rather than conservative.) The *Washington Post* and the *New York Times* are left-leaning, while *Time* is further to the right, as are *U.S. News and World Report,* the *Wall Street Journal,* and *Reader's Digest.* Some magazines are explicit about their ideological affiliation: *The Nation, Mother Jones, Z Magazine,* and the *Village Voice* are solidly leftist, while *Commentary,* the *National Review,* and the *New American* are solidly ensconced on the right. Some cable television programming is ideologically oriented as well. For example, the Family Channel is a Christian network. Students can sometimes determine the ideology of authorities by looking for their use of the commonplaces associated with certain ideologies (see the chapter on commonplaces).

Proximate Authorities

Contemporary rhetoric includes a kind of testimony that was absent from ancient considerations: statements by persons who were physically present at an event. The authority of proximate witnesses derives not from their wisdom or their professional expertise, but from the modern presumption that evidence provided by the senses is reliable and credible. A rhetor who wishes to establish the existence of hate speech on a campus, for example, can cite the testimony of a roommate, friend, or professor who claims to have witnessed its use.

Evaluating the worth of this sort of testimony is difficult. Rhetors can ask whether witnesses to an incident of hate speech, for example, were in a position to observe the incident carefully: perhaps it was snowing or raining, preventing them from seeing or hearing clearly; perhaps they were hurrying to class, distracted with worry about an exam. They can investigate the witnesses' freedom to report: perhaps some powerful campus group has urged them to come forward, when they would rather not become involved. They can compare testimony offered by various witnesses. They can examine the witnesses' motives: perhaps for some reason they wish to exaggerate the incidence of hate speech on campus.

In short, the worth of testimony offered by proximate witnesses must pass several tests. First, a witness must be in a position to observe the events in question. Second, conditions must be such that a witness can adequately perceive an event. Third, the witness's state of mind at the time must be conducive to accurate observation and reporting. If this is not the case, the testimony must be modified accordingly. Fourth, in keeping with modern faith in empirical evidence, testimony offered by a proximate witness is more valuable than evidence offered by someone who was not present. If the proximate witness gave his testimony to someone else (a police officer or reporter, for example), tests one through three must be applied to any testimony offered by the second person as well.

DATA

Sometimes statements of fact are reliable and sometimes they are not. Rhetors who use them should be sure that facts come from a reputable and qualified source. They should also be sure that the facts were arrived at by means of some standard empirical procedure, such as random sampling. They should insure as well that any facts they use are current. They should provide all of this information—sources, method, date—to their audiences, especially if the issue they are arguing is controversial. Polling agencies qualify the results of their polls by telling audiences how the results were obtained ("We made 400 telephone calls to registered voters living in the New York City area between December 16 and 17, 1992"; "the poll is accurate to within plus or minus 3 percentage points").

Political commentator Rush Limbaugh is known for his controversial stands on current issues. Here is an excerpt from a piece published in *The Limbaugh Letter:*

> A study in *The Archives of General Psychiatry* claims that women who smoke while pregnant are more likely to give birth to boys prone to "conduct disorder." According to the study, these boys turn into persistent liars; they set fires; they commit vandalism, physical cruelty, sexual aggression, and they steal. (And, I guess, later go into politics.)
>
> So if you smoke, goes to this latest wisdom from academia, you can produce young lying, thieving, sexual predators who set things on fire.
>
> Folks, this is where the anti-tobacco hysteria has brought us. We are now blaming criminal behavior on cigarettes. Not cigarettes smoked by the criminal himself, mind you—on his *mother's* cigarettes.
>
> Then there's Louis Farris and his family, who are suing a West Des Moines, IA, apartment complex. The Farrises claim they were made sick by secondhand smoke filtering into their apartment . . . through the electrical outlets. They are seeking medical expenses and other damages because their *neighbors* were cigarette smokers.
>
> The emotional frenzy concerning this whole tobacco issue is such that millions of Americans have allowed themselves to become convinced that the most dangerous entity on the planet is a cartoon figure: Joe Camel. So they cheer when the federal government steps in to give an American company a direct order not to use a certain *drawing,* for goodness sake, when they advertise. They celebrate when an American industry is targeted with unprecedented fines, taxes, and regulations. "Hip, hip, hooray! The government killed Joe Camel. Rah, rah! Punish those eeevil cigarette makers. Hit 'em again, harder, harder!"
>
> Which is why the tobacco companies surrendered in June, agreeing to pay $368.5 billion—in what has been called the tobacco "deal." But it isn't a deal. It's a shakedown. (August 1997, 3)

Limbaugh cites the source of the study he is discussing (*The Archives of General Psychiatry*), but he does not give sufficient data for readers to track down the study itself (the name of the article, the date of its publications, volume number of the journal and page numbers would all be necessary to find this study quickly). Nor does he quote directly from the study to support the generalizations he makes. How convincing is Limbaugh's reading of the data and findings of this study?

In recent years it has become fashionable to determine the quality of a film by the level of its box office receipts. Here, for example, is *USA Today*'s account of the weekend receipts for newly released films:

> *Conspiracy Theory* led the weekend box office with an estimated $19.4 million take.
> "That's not a *bad* opening for August," says John Krier of the box office-tracking firm Exhibitor Relations Co. Inc. "But I was a little surprised it wasn't bigger."

> Final figures are out today.
>
> "*Conspiracy Theory* did respectably," says industry analyst Harold Vogel of Cowen & Co. "But it was supposed to be a gigantic picture" because of the pairing of leads Mel Gibson and Julia Roberts.
>
> Adds industry analyst Dennis McAlpine of Josephthal, Lyon & Ross, "I would have expected it to open more like $25 million."
>
> Close on *Conspiracy's* heels was the Harrison Ford hijack thriller *Air Force One* with $18.2 million.
>
> "*Air Force One* was big enough that it drew away from *Conspiracy*," McAlpine says. "Given the choice, people were going to see *Air Force One* instead."
>
> And, Vogel says, for *Air Force One* to be just a million dollars behind *Conspiracy* after three weeks in release "makes it look a lot stronger than *Conspiracy*."
>
> Overall, the weekend was good, Krier says.
>
> Comic book-inspired *Spawn* was No. 3 with $9.1 million.
>
> Holding up well: *George of the Jungle* was No. 4 with $6.3 million after four weeks in release, and *Men in Black* was No. 5 with $5.7 million after six weeks in release.
>
> *How to Be a Player* opened eighth with $4.1 million.

The amount of gross earnings brought in by the movies named here is a statement of fact. But such facts are used to support an inference that is not always warranted—that movies which make lots of money must be worth seeing. The industry analyst inferred that *Air Force One* is a "stronger" film than *Conspiracy Theory* because it made almost as much money on a given weekend even though it had been in release for a longer time. This inference overlooks the possibility that people choose to see films that have been widely advertised. The commentators also seem to assume that American moviegoers operate on a herd instinct. In any case, box-office receipts may or may not reflect a film's quality; they only reflect its popularity.

In short, rhetors should never accept facts at face value. All data, and this includes statistics, were discovered and assembled by someone. Rhetors who use data as proof should always ascertain who discovered the data and who vouches for its accuracy. Most important, rhetors should examine the networks of interpretation through which data are filtered. Networks of interpretation gives meaning to facts; without such networks, facts are pretty much unintelligible—and uninteresting as well.

EXERCISES

1. Listen to the propositions you hear advanced by friends and family or commentators in the media. How often are these propositions supported by testimony or data? From this investigation, can you determine whether testimony and data are considered necessary in popular rhetoric? If they are not, should they be? Reread something you have recently written. Did you use testimony and data? Were any available? Would their use have strengthened your argument?

2. In *Illiberal Education: The Politics of Race and Sex on Campus* (1992), Dinesh
   D'Souza told the following story:

On February 9, 1988, Stephan Thernstrom, Winthrop Professor of history at Harvard
University, opened the campus newspaper to read the headline, "Students Criticize
Class as Racially Insensitive." Thernstrom discovered that the class in question was
"The Peopling of America," a course on the history of ethnic groups that he jointly
taught with another eminent Harvard scholar, Bernard Bailyn. Three of his black students had charged him with "racial insensitivity." Wendi Grantham, a junior and
chair of the Black Students Association political action committee, alleged that Thernstrom "said Jim Crow laws were beneficial," and that he "read aloud from white
plantation owners' journals" that painted a "benevolent" picture of slavery. The students took their complaints to Harvard's Committee on Race Relations, and administrative committee set up by President Derek Bok to arbitrate such matters. . . .
   "I was absolutely stunned when I read this," Thernstrom recalled. "None of the
students had come to me with their complaints. And the comments they attributed
to me were a ridiculous distortion of what I said in class. I simply did not know what
to make of it." . . .
   Stung by what he viewed as a meretricious and baseless attack, Thernstrom wrote
a letter to the *Harvard Crimson* observing that, both in class and during office hours,
he was "open to any student who wants to speak to me." By attempting to adjudicate
their grievances through administrative committees and in the media, Thernstrom
warned, students were engaging in a "McCarthyism of the left" which could exert a
"chilling effect" both on academic freedom and on freedom of expression. . . .
   On February 18, 1988, a few days after the Thernstrom incident, Dean of the College Fred Jewett issued an open letter to the Harvard community. Without mentioning Thernstrom, Jewett said that "recent events" compelled him to "speak out loudly
and forcefully against all kinds of prejudice, harassment and discrimination." The
most common incidents, Jewett said, "occur in comments or actions where the students or faculty members involved may be partly or wholly unaware of the import of
their words." Jewett added, "While such incidents may not require formal college discipline, they should elicit from appropriate college officials and from the community
warnings and clear messages about the inappropriateness and insensitivity of such
behavior. Every member of this community must be alert to this most insidious kind
of intolerance and be ready to state publicly that it can have no place at Harvard."
   In short, far from coming to his defense, Jewett appeared to give full administrative sanction to the charges against Thernstrom. . . .
   It was not until a month later, on March 9, 1988, that Dean of the Faculty Michael
Spence clarified that Thernstrom's academic freedom would be protected; no disciplinary action would be taken against him. Spence did, however, praise the course
of action of Thernstrom's accusers as "judicious and fair," because they had followed university grievance procedures. A couple of weeks later, Harvard president
Bok said Thernstrom had a right to teach as he wished, but professors should be
aware of "possible insensitivity" in lecturing. Bok wished the whole matter hadn't
got so much press, because "public controversy often leads to rigid positions."
   Thernstrom read these statements as equivocal at best: according to Harvard, he
had the right to be racist, if he wished; but by defending himself publicly, he was
being unreasonable and inflexible; he should try to be more "sensitive" in the future.
Meanwhile, the integrity of his critics and their charges remained unquestioned. As

for Stephan Thernstrom, he had decided, for the foreseeable future, not to offer the course. "It just isn't worth it," he said. "Professors who teach race issues encounter such a culture of hostility, among some students, that some of these questions are simply not teachable any more, at least not in an honest, critical way." (194–197)

This account is filled with extrinsic proofs. There are names and dates; its author read associated documents and quoted them; he interviewed Professor Thernstrom and quoted him.

Here is an account of D'Souza's account of this incident, written by Jon Wiener:

In fact, almost every element of the story D'Souza tells is erroneous. "I talked with one of the students who had complained about Thernstrom," says Orlando Patterson, professor of sociology at Harvard. "She was genuinely upset about one of his lectures. This was not an ideological reaction, it was a personal and emotional one. She said she did not want to make it a political issue, and had deliberately rejected attempts by more political students to make it into a cause. She was trembling with rage at the *Crimson* for making this public. She said that when Thernstrom was lecturing on black family, she understood him to be asking why black men treat their women so badly. I assumed that he had offered a straightforward statement of sociological fact. I told her it's increasingly problematic to have an objective discussion of the black family. We talked for a long time, and in the end she came around to seeing what I was trying to say. I told her I was sure Steve wasn't racist, and suggested she go talk to him about how she felt. She did. They had a long talk, shook hands and that was the end of it. But the *Crimson* had made it into a political issue."

Paula Ford is one of the students who complained about Thernstrom; today she is enrolled at Harvard Law School. D'Souza never interviewed her, she says. Although he reported that the students never complained directly to Thernstrom, she says she and several of her friends talked to Thernstrom after class "a couple of times"—especially after his lecture on the black family. . . .

Regarding Thernstrom's decision not to teach the course again, Ford said she was "surprised" and "not happy" to hear it. "That was not our goal. Our goal was to point out areas in his lectures that we thought were inaccurate and possibly could be changed. To me, it's a big overreaction for him to decide not to teach the course again because of that."

Wendi Graham is quoted by D'Souza as one of the students who complained about Thernstrom. She graduated in 1989; today she is studying drama in New York City. D'Souza never interviewed her, she says. "If he had, I would have made it clear to him that I was not one of the students who filed the complaint. I didn't even know they were filing a complaint. A reporter for the *Crimson* led me to believe this complaint was public, which turned out not to be true. All I said was that I could see that their complaint might have some basis. . . ."

Jewett today remains Dean of the College of Harvard. D'Souza never interviewed him, Jewett says: "My statement had nothing to do with Thernstrom. As I recall, it was distributed in registration envelopes at beginning of term, a couple of weeks before anything about Thernstrom became news. It was titled 'Open Letter on Racial Harassment.' There had been some incidents on campus of swastika paintings, and a few incidents involving the police that had created some concerns. So we felt we needed a strong general statement on harassment. Obviously the Thernstrom case was not in that category. When students disagree with the ideas presented by a professor, they are not dealing with harassment, they are dealing with academic freedom. That's not something that the university should interfere with."

The other administrator criticized in the book and the reviews, Spence, is today graduate dean of the business school at Stanford. Woodward repeats D'Souza's claim that Spence "praised [Thernstrom's] accusers as 'judicious and fair.' " Woodward left out the crucial part of the dean's statement, as did D'Souza: the dean said that the students who complained "have avoided public comment. . . . That course of action seems to me judicious and fair." It was not the criticism of Thernstrom that was "judicious and fair" but rather the students' decision not to go public with their criticism that the dean praised.

According to D'Souza, in the same statement the dean declared that "no disciplinary action would be taken" against Thernstrom. In fact, the issue of disciplinary action against Thernstrom was not mentioned in the dean's statement; on the contrary, the dean declared that "[in] disputes over classroom material . . . instructors exercise full discretion over the content of lectures and the conduct of classroom discussion," and "in the classroom, our students are entitled to question views with which they disagree," and finally, "the University cannot prevent all of the conflicts that a commitment to free inquiry may provoke." Thernstrom found this statement to be "equivocal at best," D'Souza reports, interpreting it to mean that "he had the right to be racist, if he wished," . . .

As for the three students who took their complaint to the university's Advisory Committee on Race Relations, they were advised that the committee had no jurisdiction over professors' teaching, and that they should take their complaint to Thernstrom—which they did. ("What Happened at Harvard," *The Nation* [30 September 1991])

This writer has also quoted people and looked at documents. List the extrinsic proofs cited by each writer, and try to determine whether each proof constitutes data or testimony. Is this distinction easy to make? A comparison of these two accounts of the same incidents suggests that extrinsic proofs are entirely at the service of whoever wishes to exploit them. Which author do you believe? Why? Did you base your decision on his use of extrinsic or intrinsic proofs?

3. In modern rhetoric, the evidence of the senses—taste, touch, hearing, sight, smell—is sometimes regarded as indisputable. Can you think of instances where such evidence might be unreliable? List some of these. Why do you think the evidence of the senses—empirical evidence—is so convincing in modern rhetoric, given the ancients' skepticism about such evidence?

4. In modern rhetoric, the argument from experience also carries a good deal of rhetorical weight. People can stop arguments by saying something like this: "Well I'm a Catholic and so I ought to know the Catholic position on abortion." The argument from experience assumes that persons who have lived through a series of experiences are authorities on any issues that are relevant to those experiences. What weight do you attach to such arguments? How can they be refuted?

5. Read the arguments you are working on. Do any require testimony or data? How reliable is the testimony or data you have assembled?

ARRANGEMENT

ANCIENT AUTHORITIES ON rhetoric agreed that arrangement was the second part of rhetoric and second in importance only to invention. In ancient rhetoric, arrangement primarily concerned two processes: selecting the arguments to be used, and arranging these in an order that was clear and persuasive.

Ancient attitudes toward arrangement were very different from modern ones. In modern thought, the proper arrangement of a piece of discourse is often dictated by genre: there are formulas for arranging business letters, papers written in school, scientific reports, and even romance novels. The formulas are intended to insure that anyone who is used to reading these kinds of discourse can follow the argument without difficulty, since they know what comes next if they know the conventions.

While ancient discussions of arrangement were formal and prescriptive to some extent, ancient rhetors paid much more attention to rhetorical situations than to formal rules. For example, the composition of an introduction was determined by a rhetor's guess about the attitude of the targeted audience toward his or her ethos and subject. Were they hostile to the rhetor or the position? In this case the rhetor needed to diffuse this hostility somehow. If they were receptive, the rhetor could begin more directly. If audiences were familiar with the case the rhetor did not need to tell them about its history. If they were uninformed and there was no skilled opponent, there was no need to anticipate and answer opposing arguments; thus a refutation was unnecessary. In other words, the composition and arrangement of the parts of a discourse were determined by a rhetor's informed guess about how listeners or readers would react to it and its author.

Arrangement, then, depends in large part on the rhetorical situation, so the *kairos* questions given in chapter 2 might prove to be useful aids to arrangement. Thus far, we've addressed *kairos* as a temporal concept, but for the ancients, *kairos* had a spatial dimension as well. In ancient literature, the term was used to indicate a vital part of the body. Indeed, *kairos* indicated the critical spots where wounds are fatal. In book 8 of the *Iliad,* for example, Nestor shot Alexander "with an arrow upon the crown of the head where the foremost hairs of horses grow upon the skull, and where is the deadliest spot" (84, 326). The spatial dimension of *kairos* can be traced to the sport of archery, where it meant "a penetrable opening or an aperture" (White, 1987, 13). It is easy to see how these earlier spatial meanings came to be used in the art of rhetoric as well; in Aeschylus's play *The Suppliant Maidens,* the King compared the act of speaking to archery, proclaiming that when a "tongue has shot arrows beside the mark," another speech may be necessary to make up for the words that weren't exactly on target (446).

Another way the spatial dimension of *kairos* informs the art of rhetoric is its usefulness for the canon of arrangement. The Greek term for arrangement, *taxis,* was originally used in military contexts to denote the arrangement of troops for battle. When considered this way, the connections between *kairos* and arrangement become clear: attention to *kairos* in arrangement means knowing when and where to marshal particular proofs. *Kairos* suggests the possibility of achieving an advantage with optimal placement of arguments, propitious timing, or a combination of the two. We believe that it is crucial to consider the spatial dimension of kairos along with Cicero's advice to weigh proofs and place them strategically. He wrote in *Orator* that "the results of [the orator's] invention he will set in order with great care." Rhetors thus need to give careful attention to questions such as: Which of the arguments produced by invention should I use? Which should come first and which last? How should I order the others? Do I need to rehearse any information about the subject? Where should I do this? Do I need to address the audience? Where? What do I say to them?

ANCIENT TEACHINGS ABOUT ARRANGEMENT

Ancient discussions of arrangement were often lengthy and quite subtle, given the enormous range of possible rhetorical situations. As early as the fifth century BCE, sophistic rhetoricians may have realized that any discourse required several sections, and that the need for certain sections of a discourse to perform certain tasks remained fairly constant in almost any situation. If so, they probably taught their students that a discourse required four parts: *prooemium* (**introduction**), **narrative** (statement of the issue), **proof,** and **conclusion.**

In keeping with his general preference for simplicity of expression, Aristotle told his readers that a discourse really needed only two parts: a statement of the case and proof (*Rhetoric* III 13, 1414a). The other parts were sometimes appropriate in certain kinds of discourse, but not in all. He dismissed the work of sophists like Theodorus and Licymnius, who, according to Aristotle, distinguished all sorts of "empty and silly" divisions of discourse, such as "narrative, additional narrative, preliminary narrative, refutation and additional refutation" (1414b). Aristotle agreed in this regard with his teacher Plato, who complained about the fancy elaborations of arrangement that had been invented by sophists, such as:

> the exposition accompanied by direct evidence . . . indirect evidence . . . probabilities; besides which there are the proof and supplementary proof . . . and we are to have a refutation and supplementary refutation both for the prosecution and defense . . . and covert allusion and indirect compliment and . . . indirect censure in mnemonic verse. (Phaedrus, 266d–267a)

Perhaps intentionally, in this passage Plato confused sophistic topics, used in invention, with the sophists' teaching on arrangement. This was possible because sophistic treatises did not separate invention and arrangement, as Aristotle did; rather, they organized their treatises according to the parts of discourse and discussed the appropriate topics to be used within each part.

Aristotle's departure from this sophistic habit may have caused some confusion in later texts on rhetoric. Quintilian hovered between the two approaches. In books IV and V of the *Institutes,* he followed sophistic practice, discussing the topics that are appropriate to each part of a discourse. Then, in book VII he started all over again, this time announcing that he would discuss arrangement as something separate from invention. But book VII turned out to be a discussion of stasis theory rather than of arrangement.

When Cicero was a young rhetoric student, rhetoric teachers apparently agreed that six parts were more or less standard in courtroom discourse. However, this division was often suggested for other sorts of discourse as well. The six parts were an **exordium,** or introduction; a *narratio,* or statement of the issue; a *partitio,* or division of the issue into its constituent parts; a *confirmatio,* where the rhetor's strongest arguments are made; a *refutatio,* where arguments that can damage a rhetor's case are anticipated and refuted; and a *peroratio,* or conclusion.

Cicero's earliest work on rhetoric, *De Inventione,* included a clear and orderly exposition of this six-part division, and it adopted the sophistic habit of discussing appropriate topics within each part. Quintilian's approach was similar to Cicero's, although his treatment of arrangement is much fuller, since he gave rhetors subtle advice about artful arrangements that pointed up their rhetorical effects. As they did with invention, ancient commentators provided much more advice about arrangement than can ever be used in a given situation.

THE EXORDIUM

The term *exordium* comes from Latin words meaning "to urge forward." The English verb "to exhort," meaning "to urge earnestly," is descended from this term. Ancient rhetoricians gave elaborate advice for *exordia,* since rhetors use this first part of a discourse to establish their ethos as intelligent, reliable, and trustworthy people. Indeed, Quintilian wrote that "the sole purpose of the exordium is to prepare our audience in such a way that they will be disposed to lend a ready ear to the rest of our speech" (IV i, 5). However, in book III of the *Rhetoric,* Aristotle contended that the main purpose of the introduction was "to make clear what is the end (*telos*) of the discourse" (1415a). Other functions of introductions, according to Aristotle, include making the audience well disposed toward the rhetor and the issue, and grabbing their attention. In any case, it is clear that ancient rhetoricians found many more uses for introductions than simply presenting the issue.

Apparently, ancient students sometimes tried to compose introductions before they had written a discourse to introduce, because Cicero warned his readers about the futility of composing the introduction first: "it does not follow that everything which is to be said first must be studied first; for the reason that, if you wish the first part of the discourse to have a close agreement and connection with the main statement of the case, you must derive it from the matters which are to be discussed afterward" (I xiv, 19). In other words, you can't introduce arguments that haven't yet been composed. We suggest that you compose at least the narrative and the **confirmation** before you consider whether to include an exordium. Not all compositions require an introduction, and, as we shall see, determining the kind of introduction to be used depends upon the rhetorical situation.

Cicero suggested that, in general, *exordia* ought to be dignified and serious. They should not be vague or disconnected from the issues or the situation. Quintilian warned that students sometimes assume that audiences are acquainted with the facts of the case, when they are not. If there is any doubt as to how much an audience knows about a situation, the wisest course is to review the situation in the exordium, in order to secure good will from the audience.

The quality of the rhetor's case determines the kind of exordium required. Cicero discriminated five kinds of cases: **honorable, difficult, trivial, ambiguous,** and **obscure.** An honorable case needs no introduction, since audiences will support it at once. All other sorts of cases need exordia, since for some reason audiences will not receive them favorably. According to Cicero, a difficult case "has alienated the sympathy" of audiences, while audiences regard the trivial case as "unworthy of serious attention" (*On Invention* I, 20). In an ambiguous case, "the point for decision is doubtful, or the case is partly honorable and partly discreditable so that it engenders both good and ill will." Last, a case is obscure either because the audience is too slow to understand it, or because the case itself "involves matters which are rather difficult to grasp."

The Kinds of Cases

1. *Honorable:* has immediate support from audience.
2. *Difficult:* audience is unsympathetic to rhetor or to issues.
3. *Trivial:* audience regards the rhetor or the issue as unimportant or uninteresting.

4. *Ambiguous:* audience is unsure about what is at issue; or issue is partly honorable and partly difficult.

5. *Obscure:* issue is too difficult for audience to understand because they are uninformed or because it is complex.

Cicero recommended two sorts of exordia to handle this variety of cases: the introduction and the **insinuation.** An introduction "directly and in plain language makes the audience well-disposed, receptive and attentive." Introductions may be used in trivial, ambiguous and obscure cases, since here an audience is not hostile but only confused or uninformed. Insinuation, on the other hand, should be used only in difficult cases, where an audience is hostile to a rhetor or to her position. Cicero wrote that insinuation "unobtrusively steals into the mind" of audiences. Using Cicero's definitions of the available kinds of cases, rhetors should be able to figure out whether they need to compose an introduction or an insinuation.

Introductions

As Cicero pointed out, honorable cases need no introduction of any kind, because in such cases the rhetor is respected, the issue is not controversial, and the audience is interested and attentive. Most other kinds of cases require an introduction. Difficult cases, however, may require insinuation rather than introduction.

In trivial cases, rhetors must use the introduction to convince their audiences that their positions on the issues are important to them, and hence make them attentive. For instance, rhetors who oppose the use of hate speech on campus may find themselves facing an audience that denies the contribution of hate speech to a negative overall climate on campus. In this case, they need to impress their audience with the seriousness of this matter. They might do so by alluding to the wider effects of hate speech on the community at large. They could also point out that every student on campus is affected by hate speech even if they are not victims of it.

SAMPLE INTRODUCTION TO A TRIVIAL CASE

Hate speech affects every student on this campus, since its unregulated use spreads a climate of hatred, fear, and disgust. In such a climate, students who are often the targets of hate speech must be fearful and watchful wherever they find themselves: in the cafeteria, walking to class, at parties, and even in classrooms themselves. And even though you think that you might never be a victim of such speech, someone among your friends and acquaintances surely will be.

Notice how this introduction both underlines the seriousness of the issue and demonstrates to the audience that they are affected by it.

An ambiguous case is one where there is some doubt about the issue—that is, the audience for some reason does not understand the issue or has confused it with another issue. Or there is doubt about the morality of the issue; that is, the audience must be shown that the issue can be defended on moral grounds. In such a case, a rhetor should begin by clarifying the ambiguity. For instance, an audience may be confused about whether a rhetor who disapproves of hate speech also opposes its regulation. If such confusion exists, it should be cleared up immediately in an introduction, as follows:

SAMPLE INTRODUCTION TO AN AMBIGUOUS CASE

> While I am utterly opposed to the use of hate speech on moral grounds, I neverthe-less am also opposed to its regulation, on constitutional grounds.

This move, which separates the moral from the legal issue, establishes a rhetor's good will toward an audience because it shows that the rhetor makes careful distinctions. However, if the case is ambiguous because it is partly discreditable, a rhetor should emphasize its honorable side in the exordium and thereby try to win good will. Perhaps a rhetor favors hate speech and hence opposes its regulation. Here is a case that is partly discreditable for some audiences, since most people disapprove of the use of hate speech. This rhetor can delay making an argument in favor of hate speech by emphasizing the other point of the case in the introduction—that the rhetor opposes regulation of hate speech. The rhetor can reserve mention of the reason for a later point in the discourse. Or the rhetor can introduce it up front, and promise to justify it later.

SAMPLE INTRODUCTION TO A MORALLY AMBIGUOUS CASE

> I am opposed to the regulation of hate speech on campus. I think that the free ex-pression of hate should be allowed, since its use may forestall more serious expres-sions of group hatred. I know that this position is controversial, and I will justify it later on in my remarks.

Once again, the rhetor establishes good will by being honest with the audience.

In an obscure case, the audience for some reason cannot follow the arguments used in support of an issue. In this case, an audience may be made receptive if a rhetor states the case in plain language and briefly explains the points to be discussed. This should make the audience receptive, even though the arguments may be difficult for them to follow.

SAMPLE INTRODUCTION TO AN OBSCURE CASE

> I am aware that many of my readers may not understand why regulation of hate speech has become a hot topic of discussion on college campuses across the country. Briefly, the facts are these: because students have begun openly to use language found offensive by other students, a few universities in the country have adopted policies regulating the use of such language. Penalties for violations range from a reprimand to expulsion.

This rhetor shows good will by taking into account the audience's need to know the relevant data.

Topics for Making Audiences Attentive

It is ordinarily necessary to explain to an audience why they should pay attention to a discourse if the issue taken up in the discourse is ambiguous, trivial, or obscure. Cicero composed a list of topics for making an audience attentive in such cases. He recommended that rhetors show that "the matters we are about to discuss are important, novel, or incredible, or that they concern all humanity or those in the audience or some illustrious people or the immortal gods or the general interest of the state" (23). Notice how the author of the following excerpt from an article in *Time* (David Van Biema) carefully sets a scene so that audiences want to continue reading:

> In Salt Lake City, Utah, on a block known informally as Welfare Square, stands a 15-barreled silo filled with wheat: 19 million lbs., enough to feed a small city for six months. At the foot of the silo stands a man—a bishop with the Church of Jesus Christ of Latter-day Saints—trying to explain why the wheat must not be moved, sold or given away.
>
> Around the corner is something called the bishop's storehouse. It is filled with goods whose sole purpose is to be given away. On its shelves, Deseret-brand laundry soaps manufactured by the Mormon Church nestle next to Deseret-brand canned peaches from the Mormon cannery in Boise, Idaho. Nearby are Deseret tuna from the church's plant in San Diego, beans from its farms in Idaho, Deseret peanut butter and Deseret pudding. There is no mystery to these goods: they are all part of the huge Mormon welfare system, perhaps the largest nonpublic venture of its kind in the country. They will be taken away by grateful recipients, replaced, and the replacements will be taken away.
>
> But the grain in the silo goes nowhere. The bishop, whose name is Kevin Nield, is trying to explain why. "It's a reserve," he is saying. "In case there is a time of need."
>
> What sort of time of need?
>
> "Oh, if things got bad enough so that the normal systems of distribution didn't work." Huh? "The point is, if those other systems broke down, the church would still be able to care for the poor and needy."
>
> What he means, although he won't come out and say it, is that although the grain might be broken out in case of a truly bad recession, its root purpose is as a reserve to tide people over in the tough days just before the Second Coming.
>
> "Of course," says the bishop, "we rotate it every once in a while."

Topics for Making Audiences Receptive

Cicero also provided a list of topics for securing good will from the audience so that they will be receptive to the rhetor. He wrote that good will "is to be had from four quarters: from our own person, from the person of the opponents, from the persons of the jury, and from the case itself" (22). Rhetors' ethos may be a source of good will if they refer to their actions and services to the community; if they weaken any negative charges that have been made against them; if they elaborate on their misfortunes or difficulties; or if they humbly ask an audience for their attention. For example, rhetors discussing the regulation of hate speech can say why they are interested in this issue. They can mention any experience they have had with it. If they are members of a group that is interested regulating such speech, they can mention that, too. If they have been the victim of hate speech, they should mention that, especially if their case is trivial or obscure. Or, they can simply ask their audience to pay attention to the issue.

Rhetors can weaken the ethos of people who oppose their points of view if they can "bring them into hatred, unpopularity, or contempt." They can do this by presenting their opponents' actions in a negative light; by showing that they have misused any extrinsic advantages they enjoy, such as "power, political influence, wealth, family connections"; or by revealing their unpreparedness on the issue. A rhetor who opposes hate speech can characterize those who use it as racist or sexist, which is especially serious if they enjoy prestige or power. Or the rhetor can say that people who use hate speech are unfashionable and out of touch with custom.

A rhetor can derive good will from the audience by showing respect for them, or by stating "how eagerly their judgment and opinion are awaited." Using this topic, a rhetor who opposes the regulation of hate speech might urge the audience to examine the arguments, accept them, and join in working against the imposition of such regulations. Last, good will may come from the circumstances themselves "if we praise and exalt our own case, and depreciate our opponent's with contemptuous allusions."

Topics for Making Audiences Attentive

1. Show importance of the issue.
2. Show how the issue affects audience.
3. Show how the issue affects everyone.
4. Show how the issue affects general good of the community.

Topics for Making Audiences Receptive

1. Strengthen your ethos.
2. Weaken the ethos of those who oppose you.
3. Show respect for the audience.
4. Praise an issue or position while denigrating the position of your opponents.

Insinuations

In a difficult case, if audiences are not completely hostile to a rhetor's point of view, the rhetor may risk composing an introduction that introduces them to the issue and her or his position on it; on the other hand, if they are adamantly opposed, either to the rhetor's ethos or position on the issue, the rhetor should compose an insinuation. Cicero wrote that audiences are hostile if "there is something scandalous in the case," or if they are already convinced that a rhetor's point of view is wrong, or if they are weary. If there is something scandalous in the case, rhetors should simply admit that they, too, are scandalized by it, but should add that neither they nor their audience are tainted by the scandal. For example, if rhetors favor the use of hate speech, they might begin as follows:

SAMPLE INSINUATION

Like any other decent person, I am offended by hate speech. Its use is ugly and hurtful. Nonetheless, I support Americans' freedom to say whatever they like, and thus I cannot support regulating the use of hate speech on our campus.

If an audience is hostile for ideological reasons, again, rhetors should simply admit the difference of opinion, and show themselves ready to attack the strongest argument against them or their position.

. SAMPLE INSINUATION

I realize that you and I do not agree about the unfettered use of hate speech on this campus. However, I ask you to read my arguments carefully before you dismiss them out of hand.

If an audience is weary, on the other hand, a rhetor should promise to be brief.

SAMPLE INSINUATION

Since I know that you are tired of hearing about this issue, I will keep my arguments short and to the point.

In sum, there are three available topics for composing an insinuation:

Topics for Insinuations
1. If audience is hostile, admit the difference of opinion.
2. If issue is unsavory, admit this.
3. If audience is tired, promise to be brief.

THE NARRATIVE (STATEMENT OF THE CASE)

In the narrative, a rhetor states the issue as clearly and simply as possible. If the rhetor's argument centers on a conjectural issue, the narrative may be a simple statement of the facts of the case:

SAMPLE NARRATIVES

Hate speech has occurred on our campus.

If hate speech occurs on our campus, it does not occur often.

Hate speech seldom occurs on our campus.

Any statement of the issue should depict a state of affairs in a way that favors the rhetor's position. Quintilian pointed out that statements of the case should be in keeping with the facts we want to establish: "we shall, for instance, represent a person accused of theft as covetous, accused of adultery as lustful, accused of homicide as rash, or attribute the opposite qualities to these persons if we are defending them; further we must do the same with place, time and the like" (IV ii, 52). A rhetor who favors regulation of hate speech, then, might compose a statement of the issue such as this:

SAMPLE NARRATIVE

Ugly and divisive racial epithets are now heard daily on the malls and in the halls of our formerly peaceful and harmonious campus.

A rhetor who opposes regulating hate speech, on the other hand, might compose the statement of the case in this way:

SAMPLE NARRATIVE

While hate speech may be a problem on other campuses, only a few minor incidents have occurred here at Our State University, and these were readily taken care of by existing policy.

Here are some sample narratives for other kinds of cases:

SAMPLE NARRATIVES

definitive: Since hate speech falls under the head of speech that is protected by the First Amendment, it cannot be banned from this campus.

value: The use of hate speech on our campus wrongs those against whom it is used, dishonors those who use it, and creates an atmosphere of fear and distrust.

procedure: Hate speech should be regulated on our campus.

A policy that regulates hate speech will interfere with students' right to free speech on our campus.

According to Cicero, the narrative may be omitted if the audience is familiar with the issue, or if some other rhetor has already mentioned it. He recommended that it not be mentioned at all at the beginning of the discourse if the case were unpopular, or if the audience were hostile to the rhetor's point of view. Quintilian disagreed vociferously on this point, however. To omit the statement of the case, he maintained, was tantamount to saying that it was worthless or dishonorable: "nothing can be more easy, except perhaps to throw up the case altogether" (IV ii, 66). If Quintilian is correct, audiences should be suspicious of discourse whose authors make no statement of their position on the issue at hand.

Ancient authorities agreed that the narrative should be clear, concise, and brief, as it is not meant to be persuasive, and a clear statement of the issue lends credibility to a rhetor. Quintilian admired Cicero's use of seeming simplicity in his defense of Milo. Cicero stated the case as follows: "Milo, on the other hand, having been in the senate all day till the house rose, went home, changed his shoes and clothes, and waited for a short time, while his wife was getting ready" (57). This simple narrative not only indicated Milo's casual behavior on the day he supposedly murdered Claudio; Cicero's use of ordinary, everyday speech lulled the jury into thinking of Milo as an ordinary person, like themselves, going through an ordinary day.

For any number of reasons, a rhetor may not be satisfied with a simple statement of the case. Sometimes it is useful to give an audience some background or history about the issue so that they can understand why it is important to them. Cicero suggested that a narrative could contain an account of the reasons why an issue is being disputed; a digression to attack the opposition, amuse the audience, or to amplify their understanding of the case by comparisons; or a realistic fiction that is analogous to the case, drawn either from history or literature or created by the rhetor. Sometimes it is very important to establish precisely why there is dispute about an issue.

SAMPLE NARRATIVES SHOWING WHY THERE IS DISPUTE

The police have expressed concern that a dark-sky ordinance will interfere with levels of light necessary to protect citizens at night; however, streetlights are not interfering with our astronomical observations, while lighted billboards do.

As many as fifty students have recently complained about the use of offensive remarks in public areas of campus. For this reason, we need to examine whether the university should make a policy regulating the use of hate speech.

Rhetors may also wish to attack the position of those who oppose them in the narrative:

SAMPLE NARRATIVE THAT ATTACKS OPPONENTS

Students have expressed concern that regulation of hate speech will interfere with their right to freedom of speech. Only those who are insensitive to the terrible impact of hate speech on its chosen victims could be opposed to its regulation, which is what I propose for our campus.

A rhetor may also add a vivid historical or fictional example to the narrative. Such examples should be chosen for their relevance to the issue—that is, they should be analogous to the actual facts of the case. Rhetors who oppose hate speech can paint a grim picture of an imaginary campus blighted with the use of racial, religious, or gendered slurs. Or they can resort to a fabulous or historical example of some analogous situation, making vivid allusion to events from history or to novels and films wherein hateful remarks led to persecution of members of some religious or racial group.

THE PARTITION

A **partition** lists the arguments to be used in the order they will appear. In a complex argument, the partition is very helpful to an audience. First, it clarifies for them which issues need to be addressed by any party to the argument. Second, it announces the order in which proofs appear, thus making the discourse easier to follow. These uses of a partition, then, have the ethical effect of making rhetors seem intelligent and considerate of the audience.

Rhetors who have used stasis theory during invention should be quite clear about which issues need to be discussed and which do not. Rhetors who wish to regulate hate speech on their campus, for example, should know whether anyone disputes the fact that hate speech occurs. If there is debate on this point, they are obligated to discuss it, and they may say in a partition that they plan to do so. If all parties agree that incidents of hate speech have occurred, they may move on to a disputed definition; if all agree about a definition of hate speech, they may move to the issues of value that are involved in the discussion; and if all agree on those, they may then discuss procedures that ought to be used (or not) to regulate it. In each case, a partition of the discourse might look like this:

SAMPLE NARRATIVE

Hate speech must (or must not) be regulated on our campus.

SAMPLE PARTITIONS

If there is dispute about conjecture

Hate speech occurs (or does not) occur daily on our campus, and I will demonstrate this fact.

If there is dispute about definition

I define hate speech as any epithet directed at any person that is intended to slur that person's character, ethnic origin, religion, gender, ability, or appearance. (Of course, an opponent of regulation might define hate speech differently, as harmless fun, blowing off steam, or the like.)

If there is dispute about values

Hate speech harms its victims and disrupts campus life. (Again, an opponent of regulation would appeal to different values—perhaps to freedom of speech—if there is dispute about values, as is almost certain in the case of hate speech.)

If there is dispute about procedure

Perhaps hate speech cannot be regulated, but it can be punished if the university adopts a policy regarding it. (Again, an opponent of regulation will recommend a different procedure, such as expelling offenders or ignoring incidents of hate speech.)

As we noted above, a partition may also announce the order in which supporting arguments appear in the discourse to follow. This is a courtesy to listeners and readers. Quintilian argued that this sort of partition "not only makes our arguments clearer by isolating the points from the crowd in which they would otherwise be lost and placing them before the eyes of the judge, but relieves his attention by assigning a definite limit to certain parts of our speech, just as our fatigue upon a journey is relieved by reading the distances on the milestones which we pass" (IV v, 22–23). Ancient authorities agreed that a partition, like a narrative, ought to be clear and brief.

THE ARGUMENTS: CONFIRMATION AND REFUTATION

Once the statement of the case is clear, rhetors present the arguments they have derived by means of invention. Not every argument that is available can or should be used, of course; rhetors should select only those arguments which will be most persuasive to a given audience, and they must keep time or length requirements in mind. Quintilian gave some advice for selecting and ordering arguments. He recommended that the strongest arguments be treated singly and at more length, while the weakest arguments (if they must be used) should all be grouped together. In this way, he wrote, "they may not have the overwhelming force of a thunderbolt, but they will have all the destructive force of hail" (V xii, 5). Or a rhetor can alternate strong and weak arguments. In any case, Quintilian recommended that the weakest arguments not be placed last in the discourse.

Sometimes it is necessary for rhetors to anticipate arguments that might damage their ethos or case if the audience accepts them. Thorough attention to invention should disclose arguments that need to be anticipated and refuted. For instance, if rhetors who approve of regulating hate speech anticipate that liberals will be part of the audience, they must refute their likely assumption that regulation may infringe on individuals' rights to free speech. If they anticipate that conservatives will be in the audience, they need to refute their likely assumption that regulation of hate speech by university policy is too sweeping, and that such speech ought rather to be regulated by community standards, by family upbringing, or by religious values.

THE PERORATION (CONCLUSION)

According to Cicero, rhetors may do three things in a peroration: sum up their arguments, cast anyone who disagrees with them in a negative light, and arouse sympathy for themselves, their clients, or their case.

Composing a Summary

A summary, if included in the discourse, should review all the issues named in the partition, and briefly recall how each was supported. Cicero and Quintilian both recommended that a summary be clear and brief. If rhetors choose to make emotional appeals or to enhance their ethos in the conclusion of their remarks, on the other hand, both rhetoricians recommended that they use all their art and skill on these parts of the discourse, since they constitute the last impression the rhetors leave with an audience. As Quintilian wrote, rhetors who have spoken or written well are "in a position, now that we have emerged from the reefs and shoals, to spread all our canvas" (VI 1, 52).

Composing Appeals to the Emotions

Cicero listed fifteen topics that could be used to appeal to the emotions in a peroration. The first of these was authority, where rhetors call on whatever authorities are most revered in a community to establish the importance or urgency of their position. For Cicero's audiences, authorities were the gods, as well as "ancestors, kings, states, nations, people of supreme wisdom, the senate, the people and authors of laws" (*On Invention* I, 101). In American rhetoric, concluding appeals are often made to the authority of religious texts such as the Bible or to historically important documents such as the Constitution. Rhetors appeal as well as to the authority accorded to respected public figures (usually dead) such as Ben Franklin, Thomas Jefferson, or Martin Luther King, Jr.

The second topic names people who are affected by the state of affairs promoted or deplored by the rhetor, and vividly describes its effects on them. Under this topic the rhetor may comment on the size of the group affected; if it is very large, this is more serious than if it is very small. The third topic inquires what would happen if the state of affairs remains unchanged, or if it is changed in the way recommended by the rhetor. For example, rhetors who support regulation of hate speech could conclude their discourse by suggesting that the ordinarily peaceful atmosphere on campus will deteriorate rapidly if incidents of hate speech go unregulated. He could even paint a vivid picture of what might happen in that case. The fourth topic shows that the issue affects many people in other similar locations, who will apply the outcome of this discussion to their own cases. The fifth topic shows "that in other cases a false decision has been changed when the truth was learned, and the wrong has been righted; but in this case, once the decision has been made it cannot be changed" (102). For example, rhetors who oppose regulation of hate speech might argue that imposition of a policy regulating it will restrain students from speaking freely to one another for fear their words will be construed as hate speech. The sixth topic addresses whether the state of affairs under discussion results from someone's intentions or is unintentional or accidental; Cicero wrote that "misdeeds should not be pardoned, but sometimes inadvertent acts may be forgiven." Certainly, innocent utterances can be mistakenly construed as hate speech, and these should be treated differently than utterances meant to hurt or anger someone. Rhetors opposed to regulation could argue that a regulatory policy won't distinguish between these. The seventh topic aims directly at increasing indignation toward those who oppose a rhetor's position: Cicero recommended showing the audience that "a foul, cruel, nefarious and tyrannical deed has been done by force and violence or by the influence of riches, and that such an act is utterly at variance with law and equity" (102). Using the eighth topic, rhetors may demonstrate the utter outrageousness of the state of affairs they oppose; this is especially effective if they can establish that the state of affairs violates some custom, value, or practice that is important to the community. As Cicero wrote, using this topic, the rhetor shows that the state of affairs is unjust toward "elders, guests, neighbors, friends, against those with whom you have lived, those in whose home you have been reared or by whom you have been educated, against the dead, the wretched or pitiable, against famous people of renown and position, against those who can neither harm another nor defend themselves" (103). The ninth topic compares or contrasts the state of affairs preferred by the rhetor with others, while the tenth creates a vivid picture of the suffering caused by the state of affairs or of the joy that might result if they can be altered according to the rhetor's proposal. The eleventh topic shows that those who oppose the rhetor ought to know better; the thirteenth shows "that insult has been added to injury," thus rousing resentment against haughtiness or arrogance. The fourteenth topic asks the audience "to consider our injuries as their own; if it affects children let them think of their own children . . . if the aged, let them think of their parents" (105). Under the fifteenth topic, the rhetor says "that even foes and enemies are regarded as unworthy of the treatment that we have received."

Enhancing Ethos

Cicero mentioned a third option for the peroration: arguments that arouse the pity of the audience so they will identify with a rhetor or a case. He listed sixteen topics for accomplishing this, all of which are intended to demonstrate to audiences that the state of affairs opposed by the rhetor affects them in some way. We mention only a few of these topics, since most of them reflect Roman customs or laws that perished long ago.

Using the first and second topics, rhetors can show in their perorations that the state of affairs they oppose is much worse than it used to be; that currently things are very bad, or that they will continue to be deplorable in the future. In the third and fifth topics, rhetors mention examples or enumerate a list of things that demonstrate to the audience the specific ways in which they are harmed by the state of affairs they oppose, and they paint vivid pictures of their misery. In the thirteenth topic, rhetors complain that the state of affairs they oppose causes bad treatment of others by those to whom it is least becoming. Here, for example, a rhetor opposed to hate speech can conclude by pointing out that well-educated people, such as college students, should be the last persons to use hateful language against other people.

Topics for Perorations

Summarize

1. Review the issues.
2. Briefly recall how each issue was supported.

Make Emotional Appeals

1. Invoke authority.
2. Point out the effects.

3. Show what happens if a state of affairs remains unchanged.
4. Point out the effects elsewhere.
5. Show that a decision can't be reversed.
6. Show whether the state of affairs is intentional or accidental.
7. Arouse anger at your opponents.
8. Demonstrate that the state of affairs violates community values.
9. Compare/contrast the state of affairs with a similar one.
10. Paint a vivid picture of the effects.
11. Imply ignorance in your opponents.
12. Show how the state of affairs is insulting as well as injurious.
13. Ask the audience to identify with those injured or insulted.
14. Show that the injury or insult would not be applied to enemies.

Enhance Ethos
1. Show how the state of affairs has deteriorated.
2. Show that the state of affairs will continue.
3. Show the audience how they are harmed by the state of affairs.
4. Paint vivid pictures of current misery.
5. Show how the state of affairs causes people to behave badly.

EXERCISES

1. Compose an exordium, a narrative, a partition, and a peroration for some argument you are working on. Carefully consider the rhetorical situation before you begin: Is your audience receptive? Hostile? Indifferent? Does their attitude stem from their relation to the issue or to your ethos? Once you have answered these questions, you can decide whether you need an introduction or an insinuation, and whether you need to make elaborate appeals in the peroration.

2. Examine a few speeches and essays produced by professional rhetors. (Collections of speeches by famous persons are available in most university libraries.) Can you find examples of insinuations, narratives, partitions, perorations? Examine enough pieces of discourse to determine whether modern rhetors feel it necessary to use any or all of these parts of a discourse.

WORK CITED

White, Eric Charles. *Kaironomia*. Ithaca: Cornell UP, 1987.

THE FORMAL TOPICS

ARISTOTLE'S COMPLEX DISCUSSION of the topics in his *Topics* was intended for use in philosophical or logical disputations, and thus is closely tied to his theories of dialectical and scientific demonstration. Nevertheless, some of the topics listed in that treatise found their way into the art of rhetoric. During its distribution by various teachers of logic and rhetoric between the fourth and first centuries BCE, this topical system became detached from Aristotle's logic and took on a life of its own in rhetorical lore. In this truncated form it remained popular for many, many centuries.

The clearest statement of this system is found in Cicero's *Topics*, although Quintilian discusses it at some length in book V, chapter 10 of the *Institutes*. Just as Aristotle had done with proofs in general, Cicero divided topics into two kinds: intrinsic and extrinsic. The former kind, Cicero wrote, "are inherent in the very nature of the subject which is under discussion, and others are brought in from without" (ii, 8). There are four kinds of intrinsic topics: arguments derived from the whole, from consideration of its parts, from its meaning, and from things closely connected with it. Cicero's fourth class—arguments drawn from the circumstances of the inquiry—has many subsets, some of which resemble those listed in Aristotle's *Topics:* conjugation, genus/species, similarity/difference, contraries, adjuncts, antecedents/consequents, contradictions, cause/effect, and comparison with events of greater, less, or equal importance.

These topics differ from Aristotle's common and special topics, since they are structural or formal. That is, these topics depend on certain regular patterns or arrangements of material. Ancient thinkers regularly relied on two formal patterns: whole/part relations and general/specific relations. In whole/part reasoning, whatever is under investigation is treated as a self-sufficient whole that can be divided up into parts. Thinkers using this formal pattern can then examine the relations of the parts to each other, as well as the relations held by any of the parts to the whole. In general/specific reasoning, whatever is under investigation is treated as a class (Latin *genus*); a class is a number of particulars (Latin *species*) grouped together because the particulars bear some likeness to each other. General/specific reasoning differs from whole/part reasoning because items within a class are treated as instances or examples of the class. In whole/part reasoning, the parts may bear other sorts of relations to the whole (such as spatial or temporal relations, for example).

Perhaps the formal quality of these topics accounts for their survival in modern composition textbooks, where they are treated as means of arranging discourse. But Cicero and Quintilian treated them as means of invention, and we try to show here how a few of them can help rhetors to find available means of persuasion.

DEFINITION

Students are sometimes surprised when they read in Cicero that rhetors can compose their own **definitions.** They are surprised because they have been taught that dictionaries are the final authorities about what words mean. The authority of dictionaries is a good thing, of course. But their users should remember that dictionary definitions are written by somebody, and that they change all the time as people change the ways in which they use words. Dictionary publishers do not get their definitions from some Higher Authority. All they do is look at how words are used in contemporary spoken or written discourse; then they try to generalize about these uses and compose a list of definitions for each word that describes its most common uses.

Sometimes rhetors can persuade an audience to accept their arguments if they carefully define crucial terms. In the case of the astronomer who wants her city to pass a dark-sky ordinance, for example, a careful definition of the term "dark-sky" might turn up the fact that the maximum level of light-pollution required for accurate astronomical observation is entirely compatible with the minimum level of light necessary to protect citizens. If she can compose a definition of light-pollution that meets both these limits, and if the police accept the astronomer's definition, the argument is over (unless, of course, some other issue is raised by other interested parties, such as billboard companies).

Definition by Species/Genus

Cicero described the process of defining a term as follows: "when you have taken all the qualities which the thing you wish to define has in common with other things, you should pursue the analysis until you produce its own distinctive quality which can be transferred to no other thing" (*Topics* v, 28). His example of the process was this: an inheritance can be defined as a member of the class "property." But this does not distinguish inheritances from other kinds, or species, of property. So Cicero added the difference "which comes to some one at the death of another" (vi, 29). But, he noted, the property of dead persons can be held without its having been inherited; so more distinctions are needed for a complete definition. Accordingly, he added the word "legally" and the phrase "not bequeathed by will or kept by adverse possession." Now, the word "inheritance" had a satisfactory definition for use in Roman courts of law: "An inheritance is property which has come to one legally at the death of another which was not bequeathed by will or kept by adverse possession."

The process of definition used by Cicero in this example is called **species/genus** definition. This process of definition puts the word to be defined into a class or category. Then it lists any or all differences between the word to be defined and other members of the class. Here is a formula for composing a species/genus definition:

1. Think of the word to be defined as a single instance or as a particular, that is, as a species.
2. Determine a genus, or class of things to which the word belongs.
3. Determine how that word differs from all other members of the selected class, and list these differences.

For example, the word "hammer" can be defined as a member of the class "tools." But hammers differ from all other tools in significant ways. If we select "used for pounding" as its primary difference from other tools we eliminate most members of the class (although we have not eliminated possible exotic members of the class, such as the heels of shoes). We could enumerate more differences as well: hammers have a head for pounding and an elongated tail for pulling nails; they have relatively short handles made of wood or steel, they are generally held in the hand, and so on. The more differences we list, the more kinds of hammers we eliminate—jackhammers, sledgehammers, and so on. Hence our quick and easy definition: "A hammer is a handheld tool used for pounding, which has a flat head and elongated tail for pulling nails as well as a relatively short handle made of steel or wood."

A FORMULA FOR SPECIES/GENUS DEFINITION

To be defined (species) = class + differences

or

To be defined (species) = class to which thing to be defined belongs + ways in which the thing to be defined differs from other members of its designated class

The classic example of a species/genus definition was written by Aristotle: "A human is a featherless biped."

human is featherless biped

species = difference + class

Now this definition is not a perfect equation, since there are other two-footed creatures without feathers, namely primates (which were probably not known to Aristotle). Nor is the definition very useful, since for most purposes we say little about human beings by classifying them according to the number of feet they possess (although this classification is sometimes used for some other animals). In other words, while Aristotle's choice of category yielded a perfectly logical definition, as far as he knew, the category limited the definition's rhetorical usefulness.

Aristotle tried out another example: "Humans are rational animals." This definition did separate humans from all other animate organisms, as far as Aristotle was aware. Later rhetors disagreed with it, though. An eighteenth-century rhetor named Jonathan Swift preferred "humans are animals who are capable of reason." This example illustrates the principle that the choice of a class for a thing to be defined has rhetorical consequences. The class "capable of reason" allowed Swift to imply that even though humans have the ability to reason they don't always behave rationally.

The trick with species/genus definition is to choose a class which limits the scope of the thing to be defined, but which also tells audiences something significant about it. To place a public figure in the class "politician" produces a different effect than putting that figure in the class "honored statesmen" or "fat cats." Of course, each of these classes requires a quite different list of features that distinguish the thing to be defined from other members of the class.

Textbooks and teachers often say that a good definition must list all the differences that exist between a thing to be defined and other members of the designated class. That is, they require that species/genus definitions to be perfect equations. However, this requirement only pertains to contexts where precision and exactness are important, such as logic or some of the natural sciences. In rhetoric, classes should be chosen for their persuasive potential, and rhetors need not give exhaustive lists of differences.

Textbooks also caution students not to use metaphoric language in definitions, arguing that it gets in the way of precision. Cicero agreed with them. He told a story about his friend Aquilius, who, when asked to define "shore" was accustomed to define it as "the place upon which the waves play. This is as if one should choose to define youth as the flower of a person's age or old age as the sunset of life" (vii, 32). This restriction against the use of metaphoric language in definition needs to be tempered a bit, we think. The metaphoric term "fat cat" seems precise enough to do the rhetorical work assigned to it, as in this species/genus definition: "Politicians are fat cats who use elected office for private gain."

Cicero listed three additional ways to compile a definition: by means of **enumeration, analysis,** or **etymology.** With the exception of etymology, these means of definition, like species/genus definitions, can be composed without assistance from reference works.

Enumerative Definition

For some purposes rhetors may find it useful to define something by enumerating the parts into which it can be divided; Cicero's example is "a body has head, shoulders, hands, sides, legs, feet, and so forth" (vi, 30). This approach has the persuasive advantage (noted by Aristotle) of making the whole seem greater than it is. For example, medieval psychologists defined "mind" as having the following constituent parts: reason, intellect, imagination, passions, and will. This definition made mind seem extremely complex, and yet gave the impression that it could be understood if its parts could be understood. "Hate speech" could be usefully defined by enumeration:

> Hate speech includes all speech that slurs someone's abilities, appearance, class, ethnicity, gender, race, religion, or sexual preference.

All the parts of an entity need not be listed in enumeration, since in some cases the parts are infinite (the bodies which make up the universe, for example). An enumerative definition is satisfactory if its list of parts is long enough to suggest the ordinary uses of the word to be defined.

Analytic Definition

Analysis differs from enumeration since the rhetor using analysis must list all the parts that are ordinarily subsumed under the term being treated as a whole. For instance, Aristotle divided rhetoric into three species: *deliberative, epideictic,* and *judicial* (I, 2); Cicero divided jurisprudence into statutes, custom, and equity (vii, 31). Analysis is not a mere listing of parts: In analysis no part may be omitted since the makeup of the whole depends on the presence of all its parts. Analytic definitions are important in the sciences, where precision and completeness are required. Here, for example, is *Webster's* definition of a quark: "any of three hypothetical particles postulated as forming the building blocks of baryons and mesons and accounting in theory for their properties." "Any of three" demonstrates the exhaustiveness of the available categories of quarks.

Etymological Definition

A term may also be defined by its etymology (Greek *etymon,* "original meaning" and *logos,* "study"). The etymology of a word may be determined by breaking it into its parts and learning the older meanings of each part. We have used this device regularly in this book in order to explain the meanings of technical terms, as we did just now with the word "etymology." An etymology may also be established by trying to determine the original, or primitive meaning of a word. For example, *etymos* apparently meant something like "true" or "genuine" in Homeric Greek; later thinkers turned it into a noun, *etymon*. Etymology—the study of words in order to find out their original or true meaning—began with the assumption that the original or primitive meaning of a word was its true meaning. Even though this assumption is faulty, definition by etymology is often illuminating and always interesting. However, its use requires a good historical dictionary, such as the *Oxford English Dictionary* (OED).

Here, for example, is that dictionary's definition of "rhetoric":

rhetoric n.

rhetoric ('rɛtərəɪk), *n.*[1] Forms: 4 [**rethorice,**] **rettorike,** 4–6 **ret(h)orik(e, -yk(e,** 5–7 **rethorick** (4 **-ikke,** 5 **-ykk, -yque, retherique,** 6 **rethoric, -ique, -icke, rhet(h)orike,** 7 **rhet'rique, reth'rick),** 6–7 **rhetorique, -icke, rhethorick, -ique,** 7–8 **rhetorick, rhet'ric,** 7- **rhetoric.**
[a. OF. *rethorique* (mod.F. *rhétorique*), or ad. L. *rhētorica, -icē* (med.L. *reth-*), a. Gr. ῥητορική (sc. τέχνη), fem. of ῥητορικός **RHETORIC** *a.*]
1. a. The art of using language so as to persuade or influence others; the body of rules to be observed by a speaker or writer in order that he may express himself with eloquence.
In the Middle Ages rhetoric was reckoned one of the seven 'liberal arts', being comprised, with grammar and logic, in the 'trivium'.
13.. *Seuyn Sag.* 186 (W.), Geometrie, and arsmetrike, Rettorike, and ek fisike.
1387 TREVISA *Higden* (Rolls) III. 361 Aristotle..tauʒte eloquence..as it is specialliche i-sene..in his Dyalogus of Poetis and in Tretys of Rethorik.
14.. *Bewte will shewe* 69 in *Pol., Rel., & L. Poems,* Was neuer clerk, by retoryk or science, Cowde all hyr verteus reherse to þis day.
1475 *Bk. Noblesse* (Roxb.) 25 The famous clerke of eloquence Tullius seithe in his booke of retherique [etc.].
1481 CAXTON *Myrr.* i. ix. 34 The therde of the vii sciences is called Rethoryque.
1553 T. WILSON *Rhet.* 1 Rhetorique is an art to set furthe by utteraunce of wordes matter at large.
1586 A. DAY *Eng. Secretary* i. (1625) 10 Many excellent Figures and places of Rhetorique.
1656 STANLEY *Hist. Philos.* v. (1687) 176/2 Rhetorick is conversant in singulars, not in universals.
1741 WATTS *Improv. Mind* xx. §33 (1801) 193 Rhetoric in general is the art of persuading.
1836 *Penny Cycl.* V. 280/1 Having lectured successively in grammar, rhetoric,..humanity, and moral philosophy.
1843 MILL *Logic* Introd. §3 The communication of those thoughts to others falls under the consideration of Rhetoric.
b. *fig.* or with personification.
[**c1374** CHAUCER *Boeth.* ii. pr. i. (1868) 30 And wiþ Rethorice com forþe musice a damoisel of oure house.]
1423 JAS. I *Kingis Q.* cxcvii, Gowere and chaucere, that on the steppis satt Of rethorike.

c1430 LYDG. *Min. Poems* (Percy Soc.) 11 And Retoryk had eke in her presence Tulyus, callyd 'Mirrour of Eloquence'.

1530 LYNDESAY *Test. Papyngo* 11 For quhy the bell of Rethorick bene roung Be Chawceir, Goweir, and Lidgate laureate.

1642 FULLER *Holy & Prof. St.* ii. vii. 73 Some condemn Rhetorick as the mother of lies.

1742 POPE *Dunc.* iv. 24 There, stript, fair Rhet'ric languish'd on the ground.

c. A treatise on, or 'body' of, rhetoric.

1565 COOPER *Thesaurus* s.v. *Rhetoricus, In primo Ciceronis rhetorico..*, in the firste booke of Ciceroes rhetorike.

1580 G. HARVEY in *Three Proper Lett.* 32 To bring our Language into Arte, and to frame a Grammer or Rhetorike thereof.

1581 LAMBARDE *Eiren.* i. xi. 63 It is a good Counsell (which Aristotle giueth in his Rhetorikes *ad Theodectem*).

1654 T. BLOUNT (*title*), The Academie of Eloquence, Containing a Compleat English Rhetorique.

1712 ADDISON *Spect.* No. 297 ¶17 Aristotle himself has given it a place in his Rhetorick among the Beauties of that Art.

d. The top class or the second class (from the top) in certain English Roman Catholic schools and colleges. **So † *to make one's rhetoric.***

1599 in Foley *Rec. Eng. Prov. S.J.* (1879) V. 569, I have made my rhetoric in these parts.

c1620 in *Mem. Stonyhurst Coll.* (1881) 8 They go down two by two with their books under their arms, and first those in Rhetoric, into the Refectory.

1908 *Stonyhurst Mag.* in *Tablet* 25 Apr. 646/2 We are informed that any boy from Rhetoric down to Elements may join the class.

e. Literary prose composition, esp. as a school exercise.

1828 R. WHATELY *Elements Rhetoric* 4 Some writers have spoken of Rhetoric as the Art of Composition, universally; or, with the exclusion of Poetry alone, as embracing all Prose-composition.

1944 H. J. C. GRIERSON *Rhetoric & Eng. Composition* p. iii, Of University teaching in English I had enjoyed just fifty lectures at Aberdeen, of which twenty-five were devoted to Rhetoric or, as Rhetoric had come to mean under Dr. Alexander Bain and his successor William Minto, English Composition.

1953 T. S. ELIOT *Amer. Lit. & Amer. Lang.* 5, I am happy to remember that in those days English composition was still called Rhetoric.

1972 *Lebende Sprachen* XVII. 35/2 *US* rhetoric—*BEIUS* literary composition.

2. † a. Elegance or eloquence of language; eloquent speech or writing. *Obs.*

b. Speech or writing expressed in terms calculated to persuade; hence (often in depreciatory sense), language characterized by artificial or ostentatious expression.

c1386 CHAUCER *Clerk's Prol.* 32 Fraunceys Petrak,..whos Rethorik sweete Enlumyned al Ytaille of poetrie.

1426 LYDG. in *Pol. Poems* (Rolls) II. 133 Alle be that I in my translacioun..Of rethoryk have no maner floure.

1562 WINƷET *Cert. Tractates* Wks. (S.T.S.) I. 25 As I persaue rethorik thairof verray small, swa I can espy na thing thairin abhorring fra the truth.

1570 DEE *Math. Pref.* 46 Nor your faire pretense, by such rashe ragged Rhetorike, any whit, well graced.

1615 R. BRATHWAIT *Strappado* (1878) 24 Heere is no substance, but a simple peece Of gaudy Rhetoricke.

1671 MILTON *P.R.* iv. 4 And the perswasive Rhetoric That sleek't his tongue.

1733 SWIFT *Lett.* (1766) II. 189 The one word from you, is of much more weight than my rhetoric.

1784 COWPER *Task* iv. 491 Modern senators..Whose oath is rhet'ric, and who swear for fame!

1825 MACAULAY *Ess., Milton,* The sublime wisdom of the Areopagitica and the nervous rhetoric of the Iconoclast.

1837 LANDOR *Pentameron* 33 Escape from rhetoric by all manner of means.

1880 SWINBURNE *Stud. Shaks.* 269 The limp loquacity of long-winded rhetoric, so natural to men and soldiers in an hour of emergency.

c. *pl.* Elegant expressions; rhetorical flourishes. Also, rhetorical terms.

1426 LYDG. *De Guil. Pilgr.* 19774 That poete, Wyth al hys rethorykes swete.

1543 BALE *Yet a Course* 26 Neuer coude tolwyn throughlye knowe what these rhetoryckes ment, as are denuncyacyon, deteccyon, and presentacyon.

1589 PUTTENHAM *Eng. Poesie* iii. ii. (Arb.) 151 Graue and wise counsellours..do much mislike all scholasticall rhetoricks.

1628 WITHER *Brit. Rememb.* 42 b, Their fantastique Rhetoriques, Who trim their Poesies with schooleboy-tricks.

1942 W. STEVENS *Parts of World* 143 Midsummer love and softest silences, Weather of night creatures, whistling all day, too, And echoing rhetorics more than our own.

1949 KOESTLER *Promise & Fulfilment* ii. v. 274 It was a disappointing speech–emotional rhetorics without a constructive programme.

1976 *Sunday Times* (Lagos) 3 Oct. 10/4 We cannot decide on the fundamental values and goals that will bind the present and future generations on the basis of vague ideas, irrelevant foreign slogans and rhetorics.

d. in ironical or jocular use.

1580 SPENSER in *Three Proper Left.* 14 Like a drunken man, or women (when their Alebench Rhetorick commes vpon them).

1595 W. S. *Locrine* iii. iii, I think you were brought up in the university of Bridewell, you have your rhetoric so ready at your tongue's end.

1613 PURCHAS *Pilgrimage* iii. xiv. (1614) 316 Some of them vpbraiding both him and other Christians with the names of dogs, Ethnickes, vnbeleeuers, and the like zealous Rhetorick.

1742 FIELDING *J. Andrews* i. xviii, The rhetoric of John the hostler, with a new straw hat, and a pint of wine, made a second conquest over her.

c1750 SHENSTONE *Ruin'd Abbey* 10 Fearless he of shouts Or taunts, the rhet'ric of the wat'ry crew.

1849 MACAULAY *Hist. Eng.* iv. I. 450 He [Jeffreys] acquired a boundless command of the rhetoric in which the vulgar express hatred and contempt.

e. *transf.* and *fig.,* said esp.

† **(a)** of the expressive action of the body in speaking;

(b) of the persuasiveness of looks or acts;

(c) of artistic style or technique.

1569 SANFORD tr. *Agrippa's Van. Artes* xxi, This daunsinge or Histrionical Rhetorike in the ende beganne to be lefte of all Oratours.

1587 GREENE *Euphues his Censure* Wks. (Grosart) VI. 252 For he considered with himselfe,..that liberality was the soundest rethoricke.

1588 SHAKES. *L.L.L.* iv. iii. 60 The heauenly Rhetoricke of thine eye.

1597 BRETON *Wit's Trenchmour* Wks. (Grosart) II. 15/1 Silence can best talke with wooden Rethoricke.

1644 J. B. (*title*), Chironomia: Or, The Art of Manuall Rhetorique.

1647 COWLEY *Mistr., Rich Rival* ii, Whilst thy sole Rhetorick shall be *Joynture,* and *Jewels,* and *Our Friends agree.*

1669 STILLINGFL. *Six Serm.* iii. 127 Every part of the Tragedy of his [the Son of God's] life, every wound at his death,..were designed by him as the most prevailing Rhetorick, to perswade men to forsake their sins.

1712 GAY *Trivia* iii. 318 Mov'd by the Rhet'rick of a Silver Fee.

1851 RUSKIN *Stones Venice* I. i. 11 His larger sacred subjects are merely themes for the exhibition of pictorial rhetoric,—composition and colour.

1941 W. H. AUDEN in *Southern Rev.* VI. 729 Around them boomed the rhetoric of time.

1963 R. I. MCDAVID *Mencken's Amer. Lang.* 339 Among the neo-Aristotelian critics *rhetoric* is a current fashionable synonym for technique... The *Rhetoric* of Fiction.

1964 J. SUMMERSON *Classical Lang. Archit.* iv. 33 Well, there are three buildings which, I believe, demonstrate..the 'rhetoric' of the Baroque.

1976 *Howard Jrnl.* XV. i. 52 The rhetoric of treatment will have to be replaced by the reality of treatment.

†**3.** Skill in or faculty of using eloquent and persuasive language. *Obs.*

c1440 *Partonope* 5835 These lordis are chosyn be myn assent. The fyrst ys the kyng of affryke For his grete wytte and his retoryke.

1509 BARCLAY *Shyp of Folys* (1570) 17 Though he be wise and of might meruailous, Endued with Rhethorike and with eloquence.

1634 MILTON *Comus* 790 Enjoy your deer Wit, and gay Rhetorick That hath so well been taught her dazling fence.

1680 H. MORE *Apocal. Apoc.* Pref. 7 The highest Encomium..that the Wit and Rhetorick of men or Angels can invent.

1711 ADDISON *Spect.* No. 171 ¶2 Joseph..endeavoured, with all his Art and Rhetorick, to set out the Excess of Herod's Passion for her.

1750 GRAY *Long Story* 117 But soon his rhetorick forsook him.

4. *attrib.* and *Comb.*

1656 EARL OF MONMOUTH tr. *Boccalini's Advts. from Parnass.* ii. lxxxviii. (1674) 240 To Declaim..publickly in the Rhetorick-School.

1806 H. K. WHITE *Let. to Bro. Neville* 30 July, The Rhetoric Lecturer sent me one of my Latin Essays to copy for the purpose of inspection.

1884 *Punch* 23 Feb. 87 To unmask His rhetoric-shrouded weakness.

The first lines of this entry in the OED show all the grammatical and historical forms in which the word "rhetoric" has ever appeared in English. The second section of the entry tells the history of the word in other languages. In this instance, the English word "rhetoric" apparently came into the language from Old or modern French ("OF," "mod. F"). Apparently it entered French via its earlier use in Latin. It entered Latin from the Greek language, where the noun form was spelled *rhetorike*. The dictionary author then provides a series of definitions of the term as it is presently used: "The art of using language so as to persuade or influence others," and so on. The long list of lines beginning with numbers indicates the dates when the authors of the dictionary were able to find the word used in old books and manuscripts. They reprint instances of its use so that readers can grasp the contexts in which it appeared over time. In this case, ancestors of the contemporary term "rhetoric" appeared in English sometime during the fourteenth century BCE. Within this list of dates and usages, you can also find other historical meanings that have been given the term in English.

DIVISION

Throughout its long history in Western rhetoric and logic, this topic has variously been called division, partition, analysis, enumeration, and classification. (We use the term "division" to avoid confusion with our different uses elsewhere of the other terms in the list.) Division is ordinarily paired with definition; indeed Plato made definition and division basic procedures in his art of rhetoric:

> The first is that in which we bring a dispersed plurality under a single form, seeing it all together—the purpose being to define so-and-so, and thus to make plain whatever may be chosen as the topic for exposition. . . . [The second is] the reverse of the other, whereby we are enabled to divide into forms, following the objective articulation; we are not to hack off parts like a clumsy butcher. (*Phaedrus,* 265d–e)

In other words, for Plato definition and division represented two opposing movements: establishing a whole and then carving it up into its constituent parts.

Division may be defined, then, as a conceptual act wherein the parts of a whole are named and enumerated. As Quintilian sensibly said, the rhetorical force of the topic of division accrues from its elimination of possibilities (V x, 66). If there are only two possible parts of a whole, and if a rhetor can show that only one, or neither, is true, the proof from division is very simple and effective: "To be a citizen, a person must either have been born or made such" (65). The rhetor may continue: "Since the defendant was not born in this country, and since there is no record of her having been made a citizen, we conclude that she is not a citizen." Quintilian liked this twofold sort of division because it gave the opposition a simple choice. This is especially effective when neither possibility is attractive to the opposition. Quintilian gave this example from Cicero: "Was the weapon snatched from his hands when he had attacked Cotta, or when he was trying to commit suicide?" (69). Neither motive—attacking a man or committing suicide—was an attractive one for a Roman citizen to admit.

Division, then, can serve rhetors as both an inventional and an organizational strategy. The process of division can become very elaborate if there are many possibilities under a given class. In this case, a rhetor must either show that "the whole is false" or that "only that which remains after the process of elimination is true" (66). Quintilian gave this example:

> You say that you lent him money. Either you possessed it yourself, received it from another, found it or stole it. If you did not possess it, receive it from another, find or steal it, you did not lend it to him.

Here the rhetor shows that the defendant must be lying by eliminating every possible way in which he could have accrued money he claims to have lent to another. Or, rhetors can eliminate all but one possibility, the one they wish to establish as true: "This slave whom you claim was either born in your house or bought or given you or left you by will or captured from the enemy or belongs to another" (67). This is a fairly exhaustive list of the possibilities for acquiring a slave; the rhetor now can eliminate all but the possibility she or he wishes to establish as true.

A rhetor who wished to compose a discourse about the use of hate speech could use division as follows: "Those who use hate speech do so because they are ignorant, insensitive, or prejudiced." Since this division establishes the terms in which the argument will proceed and yet presents no attractive alternatives, it must be refuted by anyone who disagrees. It also provides the rhetor with a pattern of arrangement if it is used as a means of organizing the argument.

CLASSIFICATION

Classification (also called generalization) is very similar to division. However, a rhetor using classification assumes that whatever is true of the whole is true of all of its parts, and vice versa. In other words, where division relies on whole/part reasoning, classification relies on general/specific reasoning.

In Cicero's example of classification, if a husband's will has left all his silver to his wife, she has, without doubt, claim to his silver coins as well (iii, 13). Here, the class is "silver left by husband to wife"; presumably several items or parts fit under this class—silver plate, silver jewelry, and the like—and so do the husband's silver coins.

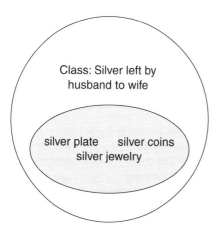

Or, a rhetor can argue from the specifics to the class. Cicero used this example: say that rainwater has done damage to someone's land. There are only two possible ways in which water erodes land (through natural rainfall or through human intervention, as in the case of erosion of topsoil by overgrazing). If someone's land has been damaged by rainwater, she can review the possible events that can create this class of things (damaged land): either some fault exists in the land such as its lying in a flood plain; or the runoff was caused by human intervention, such as the excavation of the land by a city road crew (vii, 38).

Rhetors using this classification can systematically eliminate members of subclasses until the only explanation left is the one they wish to argue.

In a discourse about hate speech, rhetors can use classification to understand the relations of incidents of hate speech to one another. If they have a list of such incidents, they can try to generate a classification that distinguishes, say, among instances where their use was unintentional or careless and those uses of hate speech that were obviously intended to insult or hurt someone.

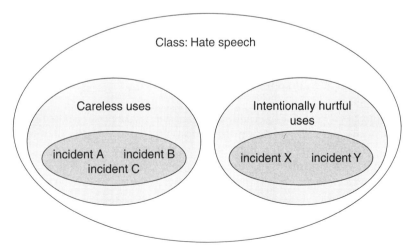

This classification has heuristic value for the rhetor, in that it may clarify some relations between incidents where hate speech was used; it can also be used to structure the rhetor's discourse, if it seems powerful and accurate enough.

SIMILARITY (COMPARISON)

Anything that is similar to something else is nearly but not exactly the same; anything that bears a similarity to something else resembles it or is like it. Apples are similar to oranges insofar as both are fruits; New York and Los Angeles are similar to each other insofar as both are large American cities. When a rhetor discusses similar things, events, or concepts together, he makes a **comparison.** The rhetorical force of comparison lies in the conclusion that is implied whenever two things are compared: whatever is true of one thing must also be true of whatever is like it.

We can argue from **similarity** that since Karen Jones voted for Reagan, Bush, and Dole, she is likely to vote for the next Republican candidate for president. The more differences that exist between the items being compared, the less forceful the comparison; it is more risky to argue from Jones' having voted for Republicans for president that she will vote for a Republican mayor. We can argue from similarity that since the United States government has a long record of intervention in the politics of South American countries such as Chile, Guatemala, and Nicaragua, we can safely assume that it has attempted to intervene in the politics of Panama. It is riskier to argue from these examples that the United States has attempted to intervene in the politics of our northern neighbor, Canada. We can argue that someone who uses hate speech is likely to say or do other things that are offensive; the topic of similarity does not justify the assumption that a user of hate speech will commit violent acts.

The argument from **parallel case** also uses the topic of similarity, and it works in exactly the same way: The orator piles up situations which are similar to the one at hand, and the audience concludes that the case at issue will resolve itself in the same way. A man who has married and divorced four or five times is likely to marry and divorce again. A baseball team that has blown its last nine games in the final inning is likely to do so again. Someone who has used hate speech on several occasions is likely to do so again.

Reasoning from similarity differs from induction in that in comparison audiences are asked only to compare one or more instances against one that is like them; in rhetorical induction, audiences are asked to reason from a group of similar things to a conclusion about an entire class (see the chapter on enthymemes).

Comparisons can also be made in terms of the relations that obtain between the items compared. Quintilian illustrated the effectiveness of comparisons from greater to lesser: "Cities have been overthrown by the violation of the marriage bond. What punishment then will meet this case of adultery?" (V xi, 9). Here is an example that compares a lesser to a greater: "Flute players have been recalled by the state to the city which they had left. How much more then is it just that leading citizens who have rendered good service to their country should be recalled from that exile to which they have been driven?" Here is an example of comparison from lesser to greater, drawn from an argument about the use of hate speech: "Students are prevented by university policy from engaging in fraternity hazing; how much more appropriate that a university policy prevent them from using hate speech?"

Ancient teachers also pointed out that differences exist between similar things. Apples and oranges are both fruits, granted, but they differ in almost every other respect—size, shape, color, taste. New York and Los Angeles are both American cities, but they differ from each other in size, population, architecture, quality of city services, kinds of neighborhoods, and so on. Sometimes, examining the differences between similar things produces interesting rhetorical arguments, although this is difficult to pull off effectively. Here are some ancient examples that use the topic of difference: "It does not follow that if joy is a good thing, pleasure also is a good thing" (Quintilian, *Institutes* V x, 73); "Courage is more remarkable in a woman than in a man. . . . If we wish to urge a man to meet death, the cases of Cato and Scipio will carry less weight than that of Lucretia" (this example of difference, needless to say, betrays ancient sexism) (10).

Rhetors may also compare **contraries**—things that are considered opposites. Rhetors using the topic of contraries divide the universe of discourse into two opposing halves; in essence, they assume that there are only two choices in any system of contraries or opposites, and overlook the possibility that opposites may exist on a spectrum full of distinctions or degrees. We often hear that you can't compare apples and oranges, but the ancients did it anyway. Here are some examples, again from Quintilian: "Frugality is a good thing, since luxury is an evil thing"; "If he who does harm unwittingly deserves pardon, he who does good unwittingly does not deserve a reward" (73–74).

One kind of proof from contraries involves things that belong to the same class but differ absolutely, such as wisdom and folly, slowness and speed, kindness and malice. This topic produces statements such as "She who would shun folly must seek wisdom"; "If one does not bear malice to his neighbors, he certainly should show them kindness." Another proof from contraries applies a specific reference to a general phrase: "If this (specific) is so, that (generality) is not." Hence: "a man who has spent all his money is in no position to lend money to others"; "a person who has used hate speech in the past cannot be trusted to argue against its regulation."

Contraries also appear in words with prefixes like "in-" or "un-": dignity and indignity, humanity and inhumanity. Animal rights activists apparently operate on the assumption that since the treatment of experimental animals cannot be called "humane," it must be inhumane. Unfortunately, arguments over legalized abortion have become almost entirely framed in terms of contraries: pro-choice advocates are pitted against persons who are anti-choice, while use of the term "pro-life" implies that persons who support legalized abortion are anti-life.

EXERCISES

1. Select a word or phrase that is crucial to some argument in which you wish to participate. Say that you are arguing about the regulation of hate speech with your roommate. She asks you to define what you mean by "hate speech." Try to respond to her request without using a dictionary.

   First, define the term by means of species/genus definition. You can begin by listing concepts or events that are associated with hate speech.

Compose this list very fast, either by free association or by brainstorming with someone else. Now, decide in what class of concepts you want to place hate speech. Is it an example of free speech? A violation of good manners? An insult? A prelude to violence? A way of letting off steam? Once you have decided on a class, determine which members of your list fit into the class—these become the differences of the species/genus definition. Now compose a definition. Have you included enough differences to distinguish hate speech from other sorts of speech? If not, try to include differences that will distinguish hate speech from all other sorts of utterances.

Second, define the term by means of enumeration. List all the possible kinds or instances of the term that you can think of. If the term you are trying to define is a technical or scientific term, it can perhaps be defined by analysis as well. If so, try to list all its relevant parts in an analytic definition.

Now you're ready to use a dictionary. Look up your term in any standard dictionary. Does it supply you with meanings of the term that you might have overlooked? Remember that dictionaries give the most common uses of terms, and so their definitions may not be relevant to the specific rhetorical situation for which you are composing a definition. Rhetorical definitions should be persuasive as well as accurate.

Last, find a good historical dictionary such as the *Oxford English Dictionary*. Look up your term. Does its history provide you with any illumination about its uses? If so, add these to your definition.

2. Try to create a division to add to some proposition you are interested in arguing. Take, for example, the following proposition:

Regulating hate speech causes more problems than it solves.

This proposition fairly cries out for a division that distinguishes problems caused by regulation from those solved by it. Such a division can channel the discussion in ways that are useful to a rhetor, and it can also be used to organize arguments.

3. Devise a classification for some argument you are working on. Here, for example, is a classification of persons who use hate speech:

People who use hate speech

Those who use it inadvertently—	Those who use it to hurt others—
unawareness, insensitivity, etc.	sexist, racist, homophobic, etc.

Creating classes and subclasses and listing their members can serve as a heuristic device, turning up items you might have overlooked in a less systematic procedure.

4. Writing very fast, compose a list of items or concepts that bear similarities to an item or concept that interests you. Using this list, try to compose comparisons. Do any of these help you to advance your argument? Now try to think of differences between the item or concept that interests you and one or two of the items or concepts on your list. Try to compare the item or concept that interests you to one or more of its opposites. Does this exercise generate any arguments?

STYLE

Cicero holds that, while invention and arrangement are within the reach of anyone of good sense, eloquence belongs to the rhetor alone. . . . The verb eloqui means the production and communication to the audience of all that the rhetor has conceived . . . and without this power all the preliminary accomplishments of rhetoric are as useless as a sword that is kept permanently concealed within its sheath.

—Quintilian, *Institutes*, VIII, Pr. 14–15

ANCIENT RHETORICIANS DEVOTED an entire canon of their art to the study of unusual uses or arrangements of words. They called this canon "style" (*lexis* or "words," in Greek; *elocutio* or "speaking out" in Latin). Defined as persuasive or extraordinary uses of language, **style** can be distinguished from grammar, which is the study of ordinary uses of language.

No one knows for sure when style emerged as the third canon of rhetoric. From earliest times, of course, poets and singers had used unusual words and patterns in their work. Here, for example, are some lines from the *Iliad*, which is usually dated from the eighth century BCE:

> Ah, Hektor,
> this harshness is no more than just. Remember, though,
> your spirit's like an ax-edge whetted sharp
> that goes through timber, when a good shipwright
> hews out a beam: the tool triples his power.
> That is the way your heart is in your breast. (III, 58–62)

When he compared Hector's heart to an axe used by a strong shipbuilder, the poet employed a figure later called a **simile,** wherein two unlike things are placed together so that the attributes of one are transferred to the other. Notice how the simile adds meaning to the picture of Hector that the poet is painting; we learn from it that, like the strokes of an axe wielded by a strong man, Hector's courage is tireless, regular, and strong. As Quintilian remarked, such uses of language make things even more intelligible than does clarity alone (VIII ii, 11).

Historians of rhetoric usually credit Gorgias with the discovery that extraordinary uses of language were persuasive in prose as well as poetry. Here, for example, is the opening passage of Gorgias' "Encomium to Helen":

> Fairest ornament to a city is a goodly army and to a body beauty and to a soul wisdom and to an action virtue and to speech truth, but their opposites are unbefitting. Man and woman and speech and deed and city and object should be honored with praise if praiseworthy but on the unworthy blame should be laid; for it is equal error and ignorance to blame the praiseworthy and to praise the blameworthy.

The first sentence shows careful attention to **sentence composition** in its use of balanced phrases ("to a body beauty" and so on). Both sentences contain examples of **antithesis,** wherein contrary or contradictory ideas are expressed in phrases that are grammatically alike ("to blame the praiseworthy and to praise the blameworthy," for example).

Even though Aristotle was skeptical about verbal pyrotechnics like these, he was aware of the persuasive power of language. In fact, he was among the first teachers of rhetoric to recognize that extraordinary uses of language like Gorgias' could be systematically studied. In both the *Rhetoric* and the *Poetics,* he drew up rules for language use that exploited its tendencies to excite the emotions as well as its capacity to represent thought clearly. Some historians credit Aristotle's nephew, Theophrastus, with the realization that style could be studied separately from other closely related features of rhetoric, such as ethos or delivery, but other historians place the emergence of style as a separate area of study much later, during the Hellenistic period.

Stylistic ornament is still widely used. In an article on summertime movies written for *Esquire,* David Thomson employed a simile: "the movies are so hot and the air inside the theaters so temptingly cold, it's a recipe like hot fudge on vanilla ice cream" (August 1997, 36). Stylistic play abounds in the music industry. The headline on the July 1997 issue of *Alternative Press,* which read "Punk Gets Ska'd For Life," employed a pun (**paronomasia**) on the word "Ska," a burgeoning branch of alternative rock, and the word "scar," a new **homonym** (especially in the Boston dialect). Also, this particular use of "Ska" constituted **antihimera,** the name for using one part of speech as another; in this case the noun "Ska" is used as a verb. Pop singer Jewel used **zeugma** in her song "You Were Meant for Me": I got my eggs, I got my pancakes too/I got maple syrup, everything but you." The two objects that share a verb, "got," used in slightly different senses, qualify this line as a zeugma (the Greek word for "yoke" or "bind").

Ancient teachers of rhetoric combined Aristotle's philosophical view of language with Gorgias' sophistic view to argue that rhetorical language ought to be clear and that it ought to touch the emotions as well. Teachers helped their students to achieve stylistic excellence by teaching them about as many unusual uses of language as they could isolate and classify, by asking them to imitate famous authors and to practice composing their own examples of various **schemes** or **figures** (Greek *schemata*; Latin *figura,* "shape"). Ancient rhetoricians isolated four qualities of style that permitted them to distinguish a persuasive style from a less effective one. While there was some disagreement about which qualities ought to be included in a list of stylistic excellences, most ancient authors agreed that a good style ought to manifest correctness, clearness, appropriateness, and ornament.

CORRECTNESS

The Greek and Latin words for correctness were *hellenismos* and *latinitas,* respectively. Sometimes translated as "purity," correctness meant that rhetors should use words that were current, and should adhere to the grammatical rules of whatever language they used. In Greek and Latin, meaning depended to a great degree on word endings; nouns had different endings depending on their case, number, and gender, while verb endings indicated such things as tense and mood. Thus, the achievement of correctness in one of those languages was a more complex and interesting task than it is in English, which depends primarily on word order for its meanings.

Ancient rhetoricians ordinarily left instruction in correctness (and sometimes clarity as well) to the elementary school teachers, who were grammarians and students of literature. Cicero wrote in *De Oratore* that "the rules of correct Latin style . . . are imparted by education in childhood and fostered by a more intensive and systematic study of literature, or else by the habit of daily conversation in the family circle, and confirmed by books and by reading the old orators and poets" (III xii, 48). Interestingly enough, Cicero agreed in this with contemporary linguists, who argue that native speakers of any language internalize many of its grammatical rules while they are learning it. Since native speakers of a language have an intuitive grasp of its grammar, the correctness rules that trouble people today usually involve conventional niceties of written language such as spelling, punctuation, and some outdated rules of grammar and usage. Since these features of correctness govern choices that can be made while editing, we discuss a few of them in the chapter on delivery.

CLARITY

Clarity is the English word most often used for the Greek *sapheneia,* although it is sometimes translated "lucidity" (from Latin *lucere,* "to shine"), or "perspicuity" (from Latin *perspicere,* "to see through"). The Latin terms demonstrate that clarity once connoted language that let meanings "shine through" it, like light through a window. As we noted earlier, however, rhetoricians like Gorgias were suspicious about the capacity of language to transfer meaning clearly from rhetors to audiences. For most ancient teachers, clarity simply meant that rhetors should use words in their ordinary or usual everyday senses, unless they had some compelling reason to do otherwise.

According to Quintilian, rhetors could avoid the obligation to be clear only if they were compelled to refer to obscenities, unseemly behavior, or trivial matters. In any of these cases, they could resort to **circumlocution** (Greek *periphrasis,* "speaking around"), a more roundabout means of reference. Terms like "restroom" or "powder room" are circumlocutions for "toilet"; it is a circumlocution to say that "Henry and the company decided to part ways" when Henry was fired. Clarity can also be obscured by the use of obsolete, technical, new, or colloquial words. Obsolete words are those that are no longer in popular use ("motored" for "drove"). Technical language (that is, jargon) is used by specialists in a profession or discipline (for example, "valorize" and "abjection" from current talk among academics). Quintilian also advised against the practice of coining of new words (neologism) since new words are not familiar to those who hear or read them. He told a funny story about a speaker who, in his anxiety to give a formal tone to his talk, used the phrase "Iberian grass" to refer to the plant known as "Spanish broom" (VIII I, 2–3). The problem with "Iberian grass" was that the phrase puzzled everyone who heard it, which is, we must admit, an offense against clarity. Colloquial words are used in a very specific locale or culture. For example, "with it," originally from the beat culture of the 1950s, is colloquial and now obsolete as well. So are the "in" terms from the 1970s—"groovy" and "far out." However, other colloquial terms, such as "hip" and "cool," are amazingly tenacious: "hip" was "cool" in the 1960s, while "cool" was "hip" in the 1950s and the 1970s; both terms are still in popular use today.

Modern composition textbooks tell writers to avoid colloquial or technical language altogether. This is nonsense. As Quintilian said, the best course is to call things by the names people ordinarily use, unless for some reason the name would puzzle an audience or give offense. In other words, rhetors should always use language that is familiar to their audiences, even if this language is colloquial or jargon-ridden. Rhetors who address an audience that uses a dialect should use it if they are comfortable doing so. (Former president Jimmy Carter, who was raised in Georgia, uses a Southern dialect of English. When he campaigned in the South, he told his audiences that they should elect him in order to have someone in the presidency who had no accent.) Likewise, a rhetor who addresses literary critics should use whatever jargon is currently in vogue within that group, because jargon is ordinarily invented as a means of attaining precision—that is, clarity. A rhetor who is addressing teachers or bosses should try to use language that is familiar to those audiences. If this means learning a technical vocabulary, so be it.

APPROPRIATENESS: KAIROS AND STYLE

Once we move past correctness and clarity, we are working in more truly rhetorical realms of style—appropriateness and ornament. Oddly enough, these realms are not often treated in modern composition textbooks, whose authors are more anxious that writers be correct and clear than that they be persuasive.[1]

Appropriateness probably derives from the Greek rhetorical notion to *prepon*, meaning to say or do whatever is fitting in a given situation. Perhaps it is also descended from Gorgias' notion of *kairos*, seizing the right moment to speak, the moment when listeners are ready to hear. Cicero upheld propriety as the most important rule of thumb for effective rhetoric when he wrote that "the universal rule, in oratory as in life, is to consider propriety" (*Orator* xxi, 71). But for Cicero, propriety was not something that can be made into a list of hard and fast rules. Cicero defined propriety as "what is fitting and agreeable to an occasion or person; it is important often in actions as well as in words, in the expression of the face, in gesture and in gait" (xxii, 74). So Cicero favored a situational propriety, one that comes closer to the Greek notion of *kairos*. As we discussed in chapter 2, the mythical figure *Kairos* was often depicted balancing on some object—be it a razorblade or a ball or a wheel. Achieving a balanced, appropriate style is one of the challenges rhetors often face. Cicero was well aware of this challenge as a central concern for rhetoric. He wrote: "When a case presents itself in which the full force of eloquence can be expended, then the orator will display his powers more fully; then we will rule and sway men's minds, and move them as he will, that is as the nature of the case and the exigency of the occasion demand" (xxxv, 125).

Cicero was not the only ancient who expressed a concern for propriety in rhetoric. Even Plato, who was skeptical about the value of rhetoric, emphasized the importance of using an appropriate style. In Plato's *Phaedrus,* the character Socrates tells Phaedrus that when a rhetor supplements an awareness of the audience with "a knowledge of the times for speaking and for keeping silence, and has also distinguished the favorable occasions (*kairous*) for brief speech or pitiful speech or intensity and all the classes of speech which he has learned, then, and not till then, will his art be fully and completely finished" (272). For Plato, then, attention to kairos—the nature of the subject matter, the general attitudes and backgrounds of the audience—helped the rhetor make decisions about an appropriate style. A young aspiring rhetor like Phaedrus, for example, might steer clear of using hyperbole (exaggeration of a case) in front of Socrates, the teacher of reason, for it would be in Phaedrus' best interest to establish himself as a reasonable rhetor. As you can see, concerns about style are linked to the ethical proofs discussed in chapter 5.

Like ethical proof, attention to *kairos* in style requires sensitivity to community standards of behavior, since appropriateness is dictated by the standards of the community in which we live. In our culture, for example, people do not generally pick their noses in public, because the community defines this as inappropriate behavior.

The community dictates the standards of rhetorical appropriateness as well. When ancient teachers of rhetoric counseled their students to use an appropriate style, they generally meant that a style should be suited to subject, occasion, and audience. This meant that rhetors had to understand the standards of behavior required by the occasion for which they composed a piece of discourse. Furthermore, since every occasion for writing or speaking differs from the next, it is very difficult to generate rules to govern appropriateness. Cicero underscored this difficulty in *De Oratore:*

> different styles are required by deliberative speeches, panegyrics, lawsuits and lectures, and for consolation, protest, discussion and historical narrative, respectively. The audience is also important—whether it is the lords or the commons or the bench; a large audience or a small one or a single person, and their personal character; and

consideration must be given to the age, station and office of the speakers themselves, and to the occasion, in peace time or during a war, urgent or allowing plenty of time. (III iv, 211–212)

In other words, the achievement of an appropriate style requires rhetors to pay attention to the conventional rules for verbal behavior in a given context, rules that have been laid down by their culture. If a rhetor has been asked to give a eulogy (a funeral speech), for example, the language should be dignified and subdued, because our culture dictates dignified and subdued behavior on such occasions. If, on the other hand, a rhetor writes lyrics for country music, dignified and subdued won't cut it, since the style of country music is homey and informal.[2]

Ancient teachers distinguished three general levels of style which were appropriate to various rhetorical settings: grand, middle, and plain. According to the author of *ad Herennium*, discourse was composed in the grand style "if to each idea are applied the most ornate words that can be found for it, whether literal or figurative; if impressive thoughts are chosen . . . and if we employ figures of thought and figures of diction which have grandeur" (IV viii, 11). He supplied us with a fine example of the grand style, which we quote in part:

> Who of you, pray, jury members, could devise a punishment drastic enough for him who has plotted to betray the fatherland to our enemies? What offence can compare with this crime, what punishment can be found commensurate with this offence? Upon those who had done violence to a freeborn youth, outraged the mother of a family, wounded, or—basest crime of all—slain a man, our ancestors exhausted the catalogue of extreme punishments; while for this most savage and impious villainy they bequeath no specific penalty. In other wrongs, indeed, injury arising from another's crime extends to one individual, or only to a few; but the participants in this crime are plotting, with one stroke, the most horrible catastrophes for the whole body of citizens. O such men of savage hearts! O such cruel designs! O such human beings bereft of human feeling! (IV viii, 12)

In keeping with our author's definition of the grand style, this passage concerns a lofty issue—treachery—and uses a great deal of ornament. It opens with two **rhetorical questions,** a figure in which rhetors ask questions to which they don't really expect answers. In fact, asking the question actually provides an opportunity to say more damning things about the traitors. The second rhetorical question also contains an *antistrophe* ("turning about"), the repetition of the same or similar words in successive clauses. Rather than referring to Rome by name, the speaker employs an **epithet**—fatherland—which is also a pun that reminds listeners about their dependent relationship on the state ("father" and "patriotism" have the same root, *patria* in Latin). There are several examples of **isocolon** (balanced clauses), and the final passionate outbursts are examples of **apostrophe** ("turning away" to address absent persons or some abstraction— "O such cruel designs").

The middle style does not use ordinary prose, but it is more relaxed than the grand style. Cicero said that "all the ornaments are appropriate" to this style, especially metaphor and its relatives (*Orator* xxvi, 91–96). A rhetor using the middle style develops arguments in leisurely fashion and as fully as possible, and uses as many commonplaces as can be worked into the argument without drawing attention to their presence. The author of *ad Herennium* also provided an example of the middle style:

> men of the jury, you see against whom we are waging war—against allies who have been wont to fight in our defence, and together with us to preserve our empire by their valor and zeal. Not only must they have known themselves, their resources, and their manpower, but their nearness to us and their alliance with us in all affairs enabled them no less to learn and appraise the power of the Roman people in every sphere. When they had resolved to fight against us, on what, I ask you, did they rely in presuming to undertake the war, since they understood that much the greater part of our allies remained faithful to duty, and since they saw that they had at hand no great supply of soldiers, no competent commanders, and no public money—in short, none of the things needful for carrying on the war? (IV ix, 13)

Here the rhetor used ordinary everyday language and loose sentence construction. While there are fewer ornaments than in the grand style, a few do appear: There is a fairly complex isocolon in the second sentence ("their resources, and their manpower, but their nearness to and their alliance with us"). "On what, I ask you" is another example of a rhetorical question.

According to the author of *ad Herennium,* the plain or simple style uses the "most ordinary speech of every day," almost as though it were conversation (IV x, 14). Cicero elaborated on this bare description of the plain style, noting that it is "stripped of ornament" and "to the point, explaining everything and making every point clear rather than impressive" (*Orator* v, 20). Usually the plain style employs straightforward narrative ("this happened and then this") or simple exposition of the facts, and it uses **loose** rather than **periodic** sentences.

Once again, rhetors should choose the level of style that is appropriate to their ethos, their subject matter, their audience and the occasion. The ornate style is certainly appropriate for ceremonial functions like weddings, funerals, and inaugurations. The plain style is appropriate when clarity is the main goal dictated by the occasion, while the middle style is appropriate for almost any discourse that will be published.

ORNAMENT

The last, and most important, of the excellences of style is ornament. Under this heading, ancient rhetoricians discussed uses of language that were unusual or extraordinary. They divided their study of ornament into three broad categories: **figures of speech** (Latin *figurae verborum*), **figures of thought** (*figurae sententiarum*), and **tropes** (Greek *tropi*, "turn"). Ancient grammarians and rhetoricians argued endlessly over the definitions and distinctions among these three sorts of ornament, and modern scholars haven't done much better at making sense out of the categories. As ancient rhetoric matured, the confusion grew. In some scholarly traditions, ornaments like **climax** and **antithesis** were classed under more than one heading (sometimes as figures, sometimes as tropes), while others, like **metaphor** and epithet, were often discussed both as single words (diction) and in terms of their effects in groups of words (composition).

Contemporary rhetors don't need to keep the categories straight, since discussions of figures and tropes no longer have to be memorized as they did in Aristotle's time. However, rhetoricians should be able to distinguish among figures of language, figures of thought, and tropes. So, with Quintilian's help, we try to make this possible.

Generally, a figure is any form of expression where "we give our language a conformation other than the obvious and ordinary" (IX i, 4). Sometimes Quintilian seems to mean the term "figure" literally; a figure is any piece of language that has a remarkable or artful shape. He likened the changes in language or meaning brought about by the use of figures to the changes in the shape of the body that came about "by sitting, lying down on something or looking back" (IX i, 11). That is, use of a figure changes the shape of language, just as a change in posture or position changes the shape of the body. There are two kinds of figures. Figures of thought involve artful changes in ideas, feelings, or conceptions; these figures depart from ordinary patterns of moving an argument along (17). Figures of language involve unusual patternings of language, such as repetition or juxtaposition of similar words or constructions.

A trope, on the other hand, is any substitution of one word or phrase for another. Grammatically speaking, a trope can transfer words or phrases from their proper place to another. This kind of grammatical trope is rare. Winston Churchill used it when he said "this is a kind of impertinence up with which I will not put." Here Churchill substituted an unusual word order for the ordinary pattern in order to make fun of the traditional grammatical rule that says prepositions may not appear at the end of sentences. Rhetorically speaking, a trope transfers the usual signification of a word or phrase to another, as in "My love is like a red, red rose." Here the poet (Robert Burns) transferred the meanings associated with roses (fragile, thorny, blooming briefly) to his love.

We review the ornaments of style in keeping with the ancient spirit of *copia*. Cicero wrote to his friend Trebatius, "as I have a guest with such a ravenous appetite for this feast of learning, I shall provide such an abundance that there may be something left from the banquet, rather than let you go unsatisfied" (*Topics* IV, 25). Rhetors can study and practice using figures and tropes in order to enlarge their linguistic repertoire, and thus to have them at hand whenever their use is appropriate to occasion, subject, audience, and ethos. But there are yet other reasons for their use. Quintilian argued that "ornament, carefully deployed, contributes not a little to the furtherance of our case as well. For when our audience find it a pleasure to listen, their attention and their readiness to believe what they hear are both alike increased, while they are generally filled with delight, and sometimes even transported by admiration" (VIII iii, 5). A carefully chosen metaphor can make an argument clearer and more striking; a nicely balanced antithesis can lend emphasis to a point. Thus ornament enhances persuasion; indeed, it can also aid clarity.

SENTENCE COMPOSITION

We begin with ancient advice about sentence structure, since an understanding of ancient terms for parts of sentences is necessary to an understanding of figurative language. The ancient term for a sentence was **period** (Greek *periodos*, "a way around"). Modern scholars think that the ancient conception of a period as a whole made up of parts, or **members,** may derive from an analogy to the human body, which also has a main part—its trunk—from which the limbs or members branch off. In any case, ancient rhetoricians called any stretch of words that could stand on its own a "period," giving a sense of completeness (this is the source of our use of the term "period" to name a piece of punctuation that marks the end of a sentence). An ancient period is equivalent to a modern punctuated sentence; in other words, a period is any unit of prose that begins with a capital letter and ends with some mark of terminal punctuation (period, question mark, or exclamation point).

In order to grasp ancient thought about periods, it is helpful to think of any period as having a main part on which all the other parts depend—just like a tree or a human body. The main part of a period is meaningful all by itself, but this is usually not true of its members or branches.

> John loves Mary | even though she is a stranger to him.
>   Main Part   Member

The stretches of language on either side of the | are logically different, because the left-hand one makes sense all by itself, while the one on the right is fragmentary.

Some periods consist only of one main part, with no additional members: "John loves Mary." It is also possible to string several main parts into a single period: "John loves Mary; Mary loves Fred; Fred despises everyone." Each section of this period is meaningful by itself. (Traditional grammarians call this a **compound sentence.** The ancients did not use this terminology, however). It is also possible to add several kinds of dependent structures to the main part of any sentence. As the name implies, dependent structures are not meaningful by themselves. (Traditional grammarians call any sentence that has a main part and one or more dependent parts a **complex sentence.**) Ancient rhetoricians recognized two kinds of dependent structures: **colons** and **commas.**

Quintilian defined a colon (Latin *membrum,* "part" or "limb") as any expression that was rhythmically complete but meaningless if detached from the rest of the sentence. The author of *ad Herennium* gave these examples of colons:

> On the one hand you were helping your enemy
> and on the other you were hurting your friend. (IV xix, 26)

Colons not always equivalent to English clauses. Nevertheless, the structure known in English as a dependent or subordinate clause is a colon. Hence our use of the terms "semicolon" and "colon" to refer to punctuation marks that set off internal parts of sentences.

A comma (Latin *articulus*, "part jointed on") referred to any set of words set apart by pauses (whence our term for the mark of punctuation, the comma, which serves that very function in English sentences). Demetrius of Phaleron called a comma a "chip," since it was a piece cut or hacked off from a longer member (*On Style* I i, 9). Quintilian defined it as an expression lacking rhythmical completeness, or a portion of a colon (IX iv, 122). A comma can consist of a single word, as in these examples from the *ad Herennium*:

> By your vigour, voice, looks you have tarried your adversaries.
> You have destroyed your enemies by jealousy, injuries, influence, perfidy.

In the first example, "voice" is a comma; in the second, "injuries" and "influence" are commas. In modern prose, commas are usually set off by punctuation. Since commas are very short, the English word **phrase** is usually a satisfactory translation.

Isocrates was widely regarded throughout antiquity as a master of artful composition. We use a sentence from his "Helen" to illustrate the ancient terms of composition:

> And although the Trojans might have rid themselves of the misfortunes which encompassed them by surrendering Helen, and the Greeks might have lived in peace for all time by being indifferent to her fate, neither so wished; on the contrary, the Trojans allowed their cities to be laid waste and their land to be ravaged, so as to avoid yielding Helen to the Greeks, and the Greeks chose rather, remaining in a foreign land to grow old there and never to see their own again, than, leaving her behind, to return to their fatherland. (50–51)

This is a very long sentence (94 words) even by ancient standards. And yet it is still readable, because Isocrates (and his translator) paid careful attention to rhythm, internal punctuation, and the placement and balance of its parts. We graph the sentence in order to indicate its parts and their relations:

> And although
> the Trojans might have rid themselves of the misfortunes which encompassed them by surrendering Helen (COLON)
> and
> the Greeks might have lived in peace for all time by being indifferent to her fate (COLON)
> neither [the Trojans or Greeks] so wished (FIRST MAIN PART)
> on the contrary (COMMA)
> the Trojans allowed their cities to be laid waste and their land to be ravaged (FIRST HALF SECOND MAIN PART)
> so as to avoid yielding Helen to the Greeks (COLON)
> and
> the Greeks chose (SECOND HALF SECOND MAIN PART)
> remaining in a foreign land to grow old there and never to see their own again rather than
> leaving her behind to return to their fatherland (COLON).

Traditional grammarians would call this a **compound-complex sentence,** since it has two main parts, and each of these has dependent clauses attached. An ancient rhetorician, however, would have noticed the artful placement of the carefully balanced colons, as well as the rhythms built into the entire period. In order to appreciate these, you may have to read the sentence aloud. You can best appreciate the rhetorical effects of the other examples we provide for ancient figures of language if you read them aloud as well, since they are intended to please the ear as well as the eye. Indeed, we recommend that you get into the habit of reading your own prose aloud, to determine its rhythm and shape. Reading aloud also suggests the places where internal punctuation is needed.

Paratactic and Periodic Styles

Ancient rhetoricians distinguished two types of sentences, which they called loose and periodic. Greek terms for a loose sentence can be translated "running" or "strung-on" or "continuous." Aristotle defined a style made up of loose sentences as having "no natural stopping places." This style "comes to a stop only because there is no more to say of that subject" (III ix, 9). He seems to have meant that the parts of a loose sentence are simply tacked onto one another. If we accept Aristotle's definition, a style made up of loose sentences might most accurately be called **paratactic** (Greek *parataxis,* "placed alongside"). A paratactic style gives the impression that the rhetor placed utterances somewhat carelessly side by side, just as they occurred to her or him. (The preceding sentence is an example.)

Later rhetoricians recommended this style for use in conversation and informal letters because of its simplicity and naturalness. They refined their discussions of the paratactic style to suggest that loosely constructed sentences also observe the ordinary or usual word order of the language in which they are written (as this very sentence does, or did, until we added this parenthesis). Paratactic style is frequently used in electronic mail, since this medium is fast, casual, and conducive to "chat" rather than to formal decrees. Since the paratactic style observes the natural word order of a language, its use does not constitute a figure unless a rhetor uses it to achieve some artistic effect, such as an impression of carelessness or breathlessness.

Aristotle thought that the paratactic style was unpleasant to read "because it goes on indefinitely—one always likes to sight a stopping place in front of one. That explains why runners, just when they have reached the goal, lose their breath and strength, whereas before, when the end is in sight, they show no signs of fatigue" (*Rhetoric* III xi, 1409a).

For this reason, Aristotle preferred a style where units of speech were more carefully demarcated and set off from one another. Like the rhetoricians who would later apply his terminology to all sentences, he called a unit of this kind a "period," and he defined it as "a portion of speech that has in itself a beginning and end, being at the same time not too big to be taken in at a glance" (35). Aristotle wrote that periods satisfied readers because they reached definite conclusions, and they were easier to remember, as well. A periodic sentence, then, has an obvious structure; ordinarily its main part does not come at the beginning, as in a loose sentence. Its meaning may be distributed among several of its parts, as it is in the example from Isocrates, where the two main parts of the sentence are sandwiched between two groups of paired colons. Later rhetoricians dictated that rhetors should postpone the sense of the period until readers reached its final member, but this restriction was not usually a part of classical lore. In this example from Gorgias' "Helen," the main part of the period is placed last: "Who it was and why and how he sailed away, taking Helen as his love, I shall not say" (5). Hellenistic rhetoricians also dictated that periods could contain as few as one member or as many as four. Of course it is possible to write sentences that contain an infinite number of members, but ancient rhetoricians generally cautioned against such excess.

A style becomes periodic when readers have the sense that sentences are carefully constructed and satisfactorily "rounded off." Since the periodic style was appropriate to the most dignified and important occasions, most teachers also cautioned their students to use periodic sentences sparingly.

FIGURATIVE LANGUAGE

In general, a paratactic style does not employ many figures of language because it is structurally simple by definition. This is not true of the periodic style, however. Ancient rhetoricians compiled endless lists of variations on the use and arrangements of the basic parts of the period: these variations are the figures of language. Quintilian wrote that this group of figures has "one special merit, that they relieve the tedium of everyday stereotyped speech and save us from commonplace language" (IX iii, 3–4). When they are used sparingly, they serve as a seasoning to any style.

We have divided the figures of language into two broad categories: those that interrupt normal word order, and those that repeat words or structures for effect.

Figures that Interrupt Normal Word Order

Here is a periodic sentence from Gorgias' "Defense of Palamedes": "If then the accuser, Odysseus, made his accusation through good will toward Greece, either clearly knowing that I was betraying Greece to the barbarians or imagining somehow that this was the case, he would be the best of men" (Sprague, 55).

> If then the accuser made his accusation through good will toward Greece
>   either
>   knowing clearly that I was betraying Greece to the barbarians
>   or
>   imagining somehow that this was the case
>   he [Odysseus] would be the best of men.

Notice that Gorgias delayed the sense of the sentence until the very end (Odysseus is the best of men—if his motives are honest). The periodic structure keeps readers in suspense, heightening their curiosity about the author's opinion of Odysseus. Later on, Gorgias used a sentence constructed on similar lines to state another possibility: "But if he has put together this allegation out of envy or conspiracy or knavery, just as in the former case he would be the finest of men, so in this he would be the worst of men."

> But if he has put together this allegation out of envy or conspiracy or knavery
> 　　just as
> in the former case he would be the finest of men
> 　　　so
> in　　this　　　he would be the worst of men.

Again, the author's judgment of Odysseus' motives is postponed to the very end of the sentence. Taken together, the two sentences create an antithesis that works across several sentences.

Here is a periodic sentence from the nineteenth century written by Ralph Waldo Emerson in his essay "Nature": "Crossing a bare common, in snow puddles, at twilight, under a clouded sky, without having in my thoughts any occurrence of special good fortune, I have enjoyed a perfect exhilaration."

> Crossing the common
> 　　　in snow puddles
> 　　　at twilight
> 　　　under a clouded sky
> 　　　without . . . good fortune
> I have enjoyed a perfect exhilaration.

Emerson postponed the point of the sentence (his achievement of perfect exhilaration) until its end, thus keeping readers in suspense and yet giving them the satisfaction of a firm closure when it finally arrives. He also used grammatically balanced commas (each is a prepositional phrase) inside a longish colon ("crossing . . . fortune") to build up suspense.

Here is a third example, a beautiful periodic sentence written by Alice Walker: "Wrapped in his feathered cape, his winged boots, he sent his soul flying to Zede while holding his body, his thought, his attentions on Carlotta, whom he did not cease to love" (*The Temple of My Familiar*, 24).

> Wrapped in his feathered cape
> 　　　　his winged boots
> he sent his soul flying　　to Zede
> 　　while holding
> 　　　　his body
> 　　　　his thought
> 　　　　his attentions on Carlotta, whom he did not cease to love.

Walker used parallel commas to emphasize her character's divided loyalties, which she reveals to readers only at the conclusion of the period.

Periodic sentences often work effectively at the beginning of a discourse, as in the following example from a book review in *The Nation*:

> A funny thing happened in the progressive American academy on the way to the millennium. While we were distracted by rightist political shifts across Europe and the Americas, by the death throes of the Soviet sphere and China's new capitalist road, by the ineluctably connecting piling-up of greater wealth and poverty across the globe and a host of local level wars and disasters, the university gave birth to—Cultural Studies. (17 March 1997, 35)

The effect here is one of contrast: The importance of all the balanced commas in the dependent clause diminishes the political relevance of the new area of study. The effect is enhanced by the use of anticlimax: the writer bounces through almost a century's worth of political history in one sentence before getting to the main point about Cultural Studies.

Rhetors can also interrupt normal word order by inserting a word or phrase inside a colon or period. Quintilian called this figure *interpositio*, but it is still known in English by its Greek name, **parenthesis** ("a statement alongside another"). As the interpolation in the previous sentence demonstrates, a parenthetical statement decreases distance, since it suddenly discloses the author's presence—as though she or he were speaking behind her hand. Parenthetical statements may appear between commas, like this, but they are more often punctuated by dashes—as we have done here—or with parentheses (as illustrated here). The novelist Robert Graves made interesting use of an almost wholly parenthetical style in the opening passage of his novel, *I Claudius*:

> I, Tiberius Claudius Drusus Nero Germanicus This-that-and-the-other (for I shall not trouble you yet with all my titles) who was once, and not so long ago either, known to my friends and relatives and associates as "Claudius the Idiot", or "That Claudius", or "Claudius the Stammerer", or "Clau-Clau-Claudius" or at best as "poor Uncle Claudius", am now about to write this strange history of my life. (1961, 3)

The parenthetical asides nearly swamp the main part of this sentence, inserted as they are between "I" and "am now about to write." Graves used them to suggest an important feature of Claudius' character: even though he wasn't very well organized, he was a stickler for detail.

Rhetors can interrupt normal word order in a number of other ways. The ancients gave such interruptions the generic name of *hyperbaton* (a sudden turn). A rhetor can attach a descriptive comma, as follows: "Mary, though reputed to be in love with John, is actually quite fond of Fred." The interpolated comma is an *appositio* ("putting off from," **apposition** in English), a phrase that interrupts the main part of the period to modify it or to add commentary about it. Or she can use an apostrophe to call on her audience or someone else: "I am, heaven help me, lost." In a very long sentence, it is sometimes helpful to sum up with an interrupter: "Invention, arrangement, style, memory and delivery—these, the five canons of rhetoric—are all that occupy me now." The ancients called this figure *metabasis*, a summarizing transition.

Ancient rhetoricians also identified a pair of figures having to do with the use of connecting words between colons: **asyndeton** (no connectors) and **polysyndeton** (many connectors). Using the first figure, a rhetor eliminates connectors that ordinarily appear between colons or commas, as in this example from Cicero: "I ordered those against whom information was laid, to be summoned, guarded, brought before the senate: they were led into the senate" (quoted by Quintilian IX iii, 50). Cicero eliminated the "ands" that would ordinarily connect coordinate commas, in order to give an impression of haste and vigor. Compare his version to a version that inserts connecting "ands": "I ordered those against whom information was laid to be summoned and guarded and brought before the senate, and they were led into the senate." Gorgias used the opposing figure in the opening passage of his "Helen":

> Fairest ornament to a city is a goodly army and to a body beauty and to a soul wisdom and to an action virtue and to speech truth, but their opposites are unbefitting. Man and woman and speech and deed and city and object should be honored with praise if praiseworthy but on the unworthy blame should be laid; for it is equal error and ignorance to blame the praiseworthy and to praise the blameworthy.

Both sentences contain examples of polysyndeton, where the rhetor employs more conjunctions ("and" in this case) than are required by either grammar or sense. This figure enabled Gorgias to stretch out a series of words or phrases, thus calling attention to each item in the series and giving the whole a leisurely pace. To grasp the rhetorical effect of polysyndeton compared to that of asyndeton, compare Gorgias' version to a revision that substitutes punctuation for "and":

> Fairest ornament to a city is a goodly army; to a body beauty; to a soul wisdom; to an action virtue; to a speech truth. Man, woman, speech, deed, city, object, should be honored.

Figures of Repetition

Modern composition textbooks often tell their readers to avoid repetition. Most likely, their authors worry that students rely on repetition because they do not have a sufficiently large vocabulary. But the advice to avoid repetition, however well-meant, is not necessarily good advice. Since repetition is a means of calling attention to words and ideas that are important, rhetors should not be afraid to repeat words that are central to their arguments.

Artful repetition was available to speakers of Greek and Latin in single words. Rhetors could simply repeat a word in order to call attention to it, as Demosthenes is said to have done when asked what was the most important part of rhetoric. He replied: "Delivery, delivery, delivery." Gertrude Stein used repetition to make fun of poetic metaphors about roses: "A rose is a rose is a rose."

Another means of repeating words is **synomyny** ("the same name"), that is, using words that are similar in meaning as a means of repeating an important point: "call it treason, betrayal, sedition, or villainy—it is one." The author of *ad Herennium* gave these examples: "You have impiously beaten your father; you have criminally laid hands upon your parent" and "You have overturned the republic from its roots; you have demolished the state from its foundations" (IIV xxviii, 38). Use of this figure can be enhanced with the help of a thesaurus, which should not be used, by the way, to find circumlocutions. Similar words (synonyms) are not equivalents, despite their Greek name. No two words mean exactly the same thing, because meaning depends upon context and use. Students who use a thesaurus to avoid repeating key words, or to find words that "sound fancier" than the ones they ordinarily use, are misusing it. As the ancient rhetoricians repeatedly pointed out, repetition is not necessarily a bad thing; artfully used, it constitutes a figure. But synonomy is only a figure if the rhetor is aiming at artful repetition. Avoiding repetition altogether is not a figure, either.

There is another class of figures of language that use artful synonomy and exploit other similarities between words as well. These are now known generically as **puns.** Puns allow rhetors to repeat something in an artful and often funny way: "He told the sexton and the sexton tolled the bell." The punch lines of shaggy dog stories were funny because they played on some sober maxim: "Don't hatchet your counts before they chicken"; "People who live in grass houses shouldn't stow thrones." Ancient puns often do not survive translation, because the pun depends on some similarity in word shape or sound. Quintilian quoted this one from the Roman poet Ovid: "Cur ego non dicam, Furia, te furiam?" ("Furia, why should I not call you a fury?"); and this one, which can survive translation, from *ad Herennium*: "Nam amari iucundum sit, si curetur ne quid insit amari" ("To be dear to you would bring me joy—if only I take care it shall not in anguish cost me dear") (IV xiv, 21; *Institutes* IX iii, 69–70). Quintilian thought that this form of the figure was a "poor trick even when employed in jest."

According to Quintilian, puns belong to the class of figures that "attracts the ear of the audience and excites their attention by some resemblance, equality or contrast or words" (IX iii, 66). The ancient term for pun was *paronomasia*, which the author of *ad Herennium* defined as "the figure in which, by means of a modification of sound, or change of letters, a close resemblance to a given verb or noun is produced, so that similar words express dissimilar things" (IV xxi, 29). Generally, puns exploit accidental resemblances among words. There are many varieties of this figure, but all have to do with using words that are similar to others, either in sound, shape, meaning, or function. In short, puns can exploit almost any accidental resemblance among the shapes, functions, sounds, spellings, or meanings of words. This headline from an article in *Time*—"Hung up on Competition"—about the effects of the 1996 Telecommunications Act, plays on two senses of "hung up"—one which is an act performed with telephones, and the other which means a slight obsession (21 July 1997, 50).

Using *antanaclasis* ("bending back"), the rhetor repeats a word in two different senses: "I would leave this place, should the Senate give me leave" (*ad Herennium* IV xiv, 21). "If we don't hang together, we'll hang separately" (Ben Franklin). Using *homoioteleuton* ("same ending"), the rhetor repeats words having similar endings: "You dare to act dishonorably, you strive to talk despicably; you live hatefully, you sin zealously, you speak offensively" (*ad Herennium* IV xx, 28). This figure had more uses in Greek and Latin than it does in English, where only a few parts of speech, such as the adverbs illustrated here, have similar endings. Still, *Esquire* writer Walt "Clyde" Frasier used *homoioteleuton* to describe basketball player Lisa Leslie as "tenacious, sagacious, and vivacious" (August 1997, 36).

Using zeugma and its relatives, the rhetor ties a number of commas or colons to the same verb. Quintilian quoted this example from Cicero: "Lust conquered shame, boldness fear, madness reason" (*Pro Cluentio* vi, 15; *Institutes* IX iii, 62). Modern rhetoricians like to cite Alexander Pope's use of zeugma in "The Rape of the Lock," whose heroine's confused values are such that she would just as soon "stain her honor, or her new brocade." Here is another zeugma from Pope:

> Here thou, great Anna! whom three realms obey
> Dost sometimes counsel take—and sometimes tea.

Pope's juxtaposition of the heavily political and the slightly domestic is funny (and it was possibly even funnier when "obey" actually rhymed with "tea"). A writer for the *New York Times,* reporting on unrest in South Boston, used zeugma in the following sentence: "Parents hurled stones, and racial epithets, at school buses carrying the outsiders—terrified black school children from Roxbury" (17 August 1997, A 24). The use of the verb "hurled" to apply to material objects as well as words ties the two actions together, implying that words and stones can be equally harmful.

There is another set of figures that depends on repetition of words, but this group requires the composition of periods having two or more members. Rhetors using these figures repeat words that appear in similar positions in each of several members of a period. For example, words can be repeated at the beginning of successive colons expressing either similar or different ideas (*anaphora* or *epanaphora,* literally "carrying back"): "To you must go the credit for this, to you are thanks due, to you will this act of yours bring glory" (*ad Herennium* IV xiii, 19). Or rhetors can repeat the last word in successive phrases (*epiphora*): "It was by the justice of the Roman people that the Carthaginians were conquered, by its force of arms that they were conquered, by its generosity that they were conquered." Or they can combine epanaphora and epiphora to get *symploke* ("tied together"): "One whom the Senate has condemned, one whom the Roman people has condemned, one whom universal public opinion has condemned, would you by your votes acquit such a one?" (xiv, 20). Note also that this example postpones the rhetorical question, which carries the sense of the sentence, until the very end.

Yet another figure of language links colons or commas together by repeating words in each member (*anadiplosis,* "repeating two pieces"). Here is an example from *ad Herennium*: "You now even dare to come into the sight of these citizens, traitor to the fatherland? Traitor, I say, to the fatherland, you dare come into the sight of these citizens?" (IV xxviii, 38). In a more complex use of anadiplosis, the rhetor repeats the last word of one member as the first word of the next. Here is a wonderful example from the journalist Tom Wolfe:

> And there they have it, the color called Landlord's Brown, immune to time, flood, tropic heat, arctic chill, punk rumbles, slops, blood, leprotic bugs, cockroaches the size of mice, mice the size of rats, rats the size of Airedales and lumpenprole tenants.

Just when this very long sentence threatens to lose itself in a chaotic list, Wolfe brings some order to it by employing anadiplosis—he ends one item in the series with the word that begins the next.

When a period has a series of members that become increasingly important, it displays a figure called **climax** (Greek "ladder"). The author of the *ad Herennium* defined climax as "the figure in which the speaker passes to the following word only after advancing by steps to the preceding one" (IV xxiv, 34). He gave this example: "Now what remnant of the hope of liberty survives, if those men may do what they please, if they can do what they may, if they dare do what they can, if they do what they dare, and if you approve what they do?" Here is another example, from Demosthenes' *On the Crown* (179), quoted by the author of the *ad Herennium* and by Quintilian as well: "I did not say this and then fail to make the motion; I did not make the motion and then fail to act as an ambassador; I did not act as an ambassador and then fail to persuade the Thebans" (IV xxv, 34; IX iii, 55–56).

Strictly speaking, climax uses anadiplosis, as all of these examples do. A less strict application of the figure refers to any placement of phrases or clauses in order of their increasing importance. An eighteenth-century rhetorician named George Campbell quoted this example of climax from the "Song of Solomon":

> My beloved spake and said to me, Arise, my love, my fair, and come away; for lo, the winter is past, the rain is over and gone, the flowers appear on the earth, the time of the singing of birds is come, and the voice of the turtle is heard in our land; the fig-tree putteth forth her green figs, and the vines, with the tender grape, perfume the air. Arise, my love, my fair, and come away. (Ch. II, v. 10–13)

Campbell noted that the poet begins with negative phrases indicating that winter has passed, and moves toward positive indications of the coming of spring, arranged in order of their increasing importance (*Philosophy of Rhetoric* III i, 1). Modern rhetoricians sometimes recommend that whole discourses feature the movement of climax, saving their most important or most persuasive point for last.

Commas or colons themselves can have ornamental effects when two or more that are similarly structured are repeated within a single period. This figure is called *isocolon* in Greek and *parallelism* in English. Here is a famous example from Abraham Lincoln's "Gettysburg Address": "The world will little note nor long remember what we say here, but it can never forget what they did here." We graph this sentence in order to illustrate the balanced colons a little more clearly:

> The world will   little note   what we say here,
>   nor long remember
> but   it   can never forget   what they did here.

In parallelism, verbs should be balanced against verbs, prepositional phrases against prepositional phrases, and so on. Some ancient authors claimed that the members of an isocolon should have a similar number of syllables, so that the parallelism between them was nearly perfect. Here is an example from *ad Herennium*:

> The father was meeting death   in   battle;
> the son   was planning marriage at his home. (IV xx, 27)

Here is a modern example of parallelism, written by the nineteenth-century feminist Elizabeth Cady Stanton:

> I should feel exceedingly diffident to appear before you at this time, having never before spoken in public, were I not nerved by a sense of right and duty, did I not feel the time had fully come for the question of woman's wrongs to be laid before the public, did I not believe that woman herself must do this work; for woman alone can understand the height, the depth, the length, and the breadth of her own degradation. (Speech at the Seneca Falls Convention, 1848)

Cady Stanton repeated the phrase "did I not" in successive colons in order to emphasize her urgent reasons for violating the taboo against women speaking in public. She also used asyndeton to yoke the parallel commas in the last colon, thus vigorously and forcefully expressing the seriousness of women's situation.

President Bill Clinton used parallel construction in a speech in which three short sentences were sandwiched in between two others:

> Building one America is our most important mission . . . Money cannot buy it. Power cannot compel it. Technology cannot create it. It can only come from the human spirit. (February 4, 1997)

When the parallel members express logically contrary thoughts, as they do here, the figure is called an **antithesis** ("counter statement"). In classical rhetorical theory, an antithesis occurred when either words or their meanings were opposed to one another. The author of the *ad Alexandrum* differentiated these two kinds of antitheses as follows: "Let the rich and prosperous give to the poor and needy" (opposition in terms only); "I nursed him when he was ill, but he has caused me a very great deal of harm" (opposition in meaning) (26, 1435b). But the author of *ad Herennium* included any use of opposites or contraries under this figure. He illustrated its use with this jingling example:

> When all is calm, you are confused; when all is in confusion, you are calm. In a situation requiring all your coolness, you are on fire; in one requiring all your ardor, you are cool. When there is need for you to be silent, you are uproarious; when you should

> speak, you grow mute. Present, you wish to be absent; absent, you are eager to return. In peace, you demand war; in war, you yearn for peace. In the Assembly, you talk of valor; in battle, you cannot for cowardice endure the trumpet's sound. (IV xv, 21)

All ancient authorities credit Gorgias with the invention of this figure, and its preference for stating balanced contraries is fully consonant with Sophistic thought. In this example, from his "Helen," Gorgias combined antithesis with the figure of thought known as **division**: "For either by will of Fate and decision of the gods and vote of Necessity did she do what she did, or by force reduced or by words seduced or by love possessed" (6). Modern rhetors often use antithesis in order to express a contrast more effectively. John F. Kennedy's is perhaps the most famous: "Ask not what your country can do for you; ask what you can do for your country." Television commentator Tom Brokaw, in a commencement speech at Fairfield University, used antithesis in a memorable line: "It's easy to make a buck but hard to make a difference" (*Time*, 21 June 1997, 90).

An even more complex use of antithesis appears in the figure called *antimetabole* ("thrown over against"). Here the rhetor expresses contrasting ideas in juxtaposed structures. Here are two examples from *ad Herennium*: "A poem ought to be a painting that speaks; a painting ought to be a silent poem"; "If you are a fool, for that reason you should be silent; and yet, although you should be silent, you are not for that reason a fool" (IV xxxviii, 39). The best-known modern example was made popular by John Dean of Watergate fame: "When the going gets tough, the tough get going."

FIGURES OF THOUGHT

In *De Oratore* and *Orator*, Cicero classed virtually all ornament under the head of figures of thought. This seems appropriate, since these figures (*sententia* in Latin) are the most rhetorical of the ornaments of style. By this we mean two things: first of all, the *sententia* are arguments in themselves; that is, they can function as proofs. Second, they can enhance a rhetor's ethos or appeal to an audience's emotions. As Quintilian noted, the figures of thought "lend credibility to our arguments and steal their way secretly into the minds of the judges" (IX i, 19–20). Perhaps because they are so highly rhetorical, so obviously calling attention to themselves as artifice and to rhetoric as performance, the figures of thought are not often discussed by modern rhetoricians. This was not true of ancient authorities, however. Quintilian treated only those figures of thought that "depart from the direct method of statement," and he still managed to discriminate well over a dozen (IX ii, 1). We have divided our discussion of the *sententia* among figures that call attention to the rhetor, figures that stimulate the emotions of an audience, and figures drawn from the argument itself.

Sententia that Enhance Ethos

This group of figures allows rhetors to call attention to the fact that they are manipulating the flow of the discourse. As such, they strengthen the rhetor's ethos;

in most cases, their use decreases distance between the rhetor and an audience as well. Rhetors may use these figures to emphasize a point or to draw attention away from something, to hesitate, apologize, interrupt, attack opponents, make promises.

Rhetors often use questions (Latin *interrogatio*) to draw attention to important points. Quintilian gave the following example: "How long, Cataline, will you abuse our patience?" (IX 11, 7–8). Notice that the effect of this differs from a flat statement: "You have abused our patience a long time, Cataline." Rhetors can also ask a question to which it is impossible or difficult to reply: "How can this be?" Or we may ask questions in order to belittle or besmirch the character of the person to whom they are addressed ("What would you have me do, you who have cut off my options?"), to excite pity ("Where will I go, what can I do?"), or to embarrass an opponent ("Can't you hear the cries of your victims?") (IX ii, 9–10).

Today, the best-known figure of this group is the rhetorical question: "Do you really expect me to respond to such an outrageous accusation?" or "Who can tell the depths to which this treachery has sunk?" Here, of course, the rhetor does not expect a reply; indeed, the audience is expected to fill in the responses for themselves, in the first case with "no," and in the second with the name of the person to be blamed for the treachery. Variations on rhetorical questioning include *hypophora* or *subjectio,* when rhetors ask what can be said in favor of those who oppose them ("Who, indeed, can support those who discriminate against the helpless poor?") or inquire what can possibly be said against their case ("On what grounds, my friends, can you object to so honorable a cause as mine?"). Use of this figure gives rhetors an opportunity to question the opinions or practices of those who oppose them or to anticipate and answer objections that might be made to their positions. Insofar as it allows rhetors to anticipate and answer objections that might be made to their positions, this figure is useful in **refutation** (see the chapter on arrangement).

Asking a question to get information is not a figure; in order for a question to constitute a figure, it must be used to emphasize a point. Rhetors should also guard against using questions to which they don't know the answers. Audiences can usually discern when rhetors are asking questions in order to avoid committing. The only effective rhetorical question, after all, is one to which the answer is so obvious that everyone, including the audience, can supply its answer. This figure depends for its effect on an audience's feeling that it is participating in the construction of the argument.

The author of *ad Herennium* mentions another *sententia* that depends on questioning. He calls it **reasoning by question and answer** (*ratiocinatio,* reasoning) wherein the rhetor inserts a question between successive affirmative statements. We quote a portion of his rather long illustration of this device (the passage also displays several prejudicial commonplaces about women's characters, prejudices that have not entirely disappeared):

> When our ancestors condemned a woman for one crime, they considered that by this single judgement she was convicted of many transgressions. How so? Judged unchaste, she was also deemed guilty of poisoning. Why? Because, having sold her

body to the basest passion, she had to live in fear of many persons. Who are these? Her husband, her parents, and the others involved, as she sees, in the infamy of her dishonor. And what then? Those whom she fears so much she would inevitably wish to destroy. Why inevitably? Because no honorable motive can restrain a woman who is terrified by the enormity of her crime, emboldened by her lawlessness, and made heedless by the nature of her sex. (IV xvi, 23)

The use of *ratiocinatio* allowed the rhetor to repeat his charges. The repetitions hammer home the accusations, thus making them seem tenable whether they are or not. The device also calls attention to the ways in which the successive statements connect to each other, thus heightening the impression that the rhetor is proceeding rationally.

The author of *ad Herennium* pointed out that not all uses of interrogation are impressive or elegant. It is so when the points against the adversaries' cause have been summed up and it reinforces the argument that has just been delivered, as follows: "So when you were doing and saying and managing all this, were you, or were you not, alienating and estranging from the republic the sentiments of our allies? And was it, or was it not, needful to employ some one to thwart these designs of yours and prevent their fulfillment?" (IV xv, 22). Fans of courtroom drama will easily recognize this device, which contemporary attorneys often use in their summations. The "were you or were you not" construction allows the person using it to repeat statements that may or may not be true without having to commit to them.

Anticipation (Greek *prolepsis,* "to take before") is a generic name given to any figure of thought wherein a rhetor foresees and replies to possible objections to his arguments. For example, rhetors may anticipate that some point or points in their argument will seem weak or dishonorable to the audience. If they are defending the right to use hate speech on first amendment grounds, they may confess their distaste for such language, as did the author of this editorial from the *Washington Post:* "Kids should be taught at home and, certainly as soon as they enter school, that derogatory comments about someone else's race, color, religion or physical or mental disability are rude, stupid, mean and unacceptable" (115:169 [May 22 1992] p. A24). Rhetors may also anticipate an audience's negative reaction to their arguments and apologize in advance: "I realize that many Americans are opposed to abortion, but I have good reasons for supporting the continued legal status of the procedure, and I hope that you will be patient enough to read about them."

Rhetors may also state that they will not speak or write about something all the while they are actually doing so (***paralepsis,*** "to take alongside of"). Here is an example: "I will not here list all the negative effects of hate speech: its divisiveness, its disruptiveness, its cruelty, its ugliness." A closely related figure is **hesitation** or indecision (Latin *dubitatio,* "doubt"). Using this figure, a rhetor pretends to be unable to decide "where to begin or end, or to decide what especially requires to be said or not to be said at all" (*Institutes* IX ii, 19). A rhetor may express indecision over a word choice, for example: "Conservatives label prochoice positions as 'anti-family,' but I am not sure that this is the most informative way to characterize those who favor abortion rights." Using *dubatio,* a rhetor may point out that an issue is so vast that it can't be covered satisfactorily in the time or space allotted. Or she may express hesitation or doubt about introducing unpleasant or distasteful matters: "Most people are so sensitive about racism that I hesitate even to discuss it." Quintilian remarked that this figure lends "an impression of truth to our statements." Rhetors who use it can depict themselves as people who are sensitive to nuance and to the feelings of audiences as well.

Another similar figure of thought is **correction,** where a rhetor replaces a word or phrase he had used earlier with a more precise one. The author of *ad Herennium* gave this example of *correctio:* "After the men in question had conquered—or rather had been conquered, for how shall I call that a conquest which has brought more disaster than benefit to the conquerors?" (IV xxvi, 36). The rhetor's reconsideration makes him seem thoughtful and intelligent. In this example, the use of correction also emphasizes the point that the action being discussed can be read in more than one way. Here is another example: "I refer to hate speech. However, things would be clearer if this practice were known by its rightful name—racism."

Sententia that Involve Audience

Quintilian mentioned a set of figures of thought that involve the audience in the argument. He discussed these under the general heading of communication. In these figures, rhetors address the audience, taking them into their confidence: "No reasonable person can doubt the severe consequences of this practice." One form of this figure is **concession,** where the rhetor concedes a disputed point, or leaves a disputed point up to the audience to decide: "Of course I am aware that hate speech hurts those it is aimed against. Nevertheless, the hurt felt by some does not justify the regulation of all." In **suspension,** the rhetor raises expectations that something bad or sensational will be mentioned, and then mentions something much worse. Quintilian gave this example from Cicero: "What think you? Perhaps you expect to hear of some theft or plunder?" (IX ii, 22). Cicero then went on to discuss serious crimes against the state.

The opposite of suspension is **paradox** ("contrary opinion"), where the rhetor raises expectations and then mentions something trivial. The headlines on supermarket tabloids are paradoxes in this sense. In modern rhetoric, paradox has a different but related meaning. A paradox is any statement that seems self-contradictory, but in some sense may be true: "There are none so credulous as unbelievers."

A related figure of thought is **oxymoron,** where contradictory terms are yoked together, usually as adjective and noun: "cold heat," "eloquent silence." A favorite example of oxymoron comes from a professor of philosophy: "This passage in Heidegger is clearly opaque."

The author of *ad Herennium* discussed a figure of thought called **parrhesia** ("frankness of speech"). This figure occurs "when, talking before those to whom we owe reverence or fear, we yet exercise our right to speak out, because we seem justified in reprehending them, or persons dear to them, for some fault"

(IV xxxvi, 48). For example: "The university administration has tolerated hate speech on this campus, and so to some extent they are to blame for its widespread use." An opposing figure is **litotes** (**understatement**), where a rhetor diminishes some feature of the situation that is obvious to all. The author of *ad Herennium* gave this example from the defence of a wealthy person: "his father left him a patrimony that was—I do not wish to exaggerate—not the smallest" (IV xxxviii, 50). Using litotes, the rhetor avoids stating the exact extent of the rich man's holdings, and the audience is led to admire the rhetor's tact as well. Modern rhetoricians define litotes as any statement that denies its contrary statement: "she was not unmindful of my wishes." But the figure occurs in any deliberate understatement of a state of affairs wherein more is understood than is said: "nuclear weapons are dangerous." Sometimes litotes is not deliberate, as when an American president brushed off "the vision thing" as inappropriate to his administration.

Sententia that Arouse Emotion

According to Quintilian, "the figures best adapted for intensifying emotion consist chiefly in simulation" (IX ii, 26). This group of figures requires more inventiveness from a rhetor than any other, since their persuasive quality depends upon skill in creating convincing fictions. As Quintilian remarked,

> such devices make a great demand on our powers of eloquence. For with things which are false and incredible by nature there are but two alternatives: either they will move our hearers with exceptional force because they are beyond the truth, or they will be regarded as empty nothings because they are not the truth. (IX ii, 33)

This group of sententia includes **personification,** *enargeia,* **irony,** and *ethopoeia.*
Personification or impersonation "consists in representing an absent person as present, or in making a mute thing or one lacking form articulate" (*ad Herennium* IV liii, 66). We may represent someone who has died as though she were present: "if my mother were here, she would say . . ." Or we can represent some abstraction as though it had human characteristics. We can represent animals or nature as having human qualities, as the poet John Milton did in this passage from *Paradise Lost:*

> Earth felt the wound, and Nature from her seat
> Sighing through all her Works gave signs of woe. (IX, 529–530)

The advantage of this figure, according to Quintilian, is that we can display the inner thoughts of others as though they were present. He cautioned, however, that people and things must be represented credibly.
In *enargeia* (usually translated "ocular demonstration" or "vivid demonstration"), a rhetor paints a picture of a scene so vividly that it seems to be happening right in front of the audience. This is usually done by appealing to the sense of sight. The cultural historian Frances Fitzgerald composed this wonderful *enargeia* of evangelist Jerry Falwell's church:

> Winter and summer the congregation consists mainly of couples with two or three children, but there are a number of young adults and a number of elderly people. There is something distinctive about its looks, but at first glance that something is difficult to pin down. The men wear double-knit suits and sport gold wedding bands or heavy brass rings stamped with mottoes; the women, their hair neatly coiffed and lacquered, wear demure print dresses and single-diamond engagement rings. The young women and the high-school girls are far more fashionable. Their flowered print dresses fall to midcalf but are cut low on the bodice and worn with ankle-strap high heels. They wear their hair long, loose, and—almost uniformly—flipped and curled in *Charlie's Angels* style. Like the boys with their white shirts, narrow-fitted pants, and close-cropped hair, they look fresh-faced and extraordinarily clean. . . . There are proportionately about the same number of blacks in the congregation as there are in the choir—which is to say, very few. (The television cameras tend to pan in on the two black choir members thus making them more conspicuous to the television audience than they are to the congregation in the church.) What is startling about the congregation—and this is its distinctiveness—is the amount of effort people have put into creating this uniform appearance. (*Cities on a Hill*, 1986, p. 135)

Fitzgerald peppered this description with references to sight: looks, glance, appearance—because she is trying to convey the carefully crafted scene to readers just as it appears on television.

Simply defined, irony occurs when an audience understands the opposite of what is expressed: someone says "Nice day, huh" when it is windy and snowing; another asks "hot enough for you?" when everyone is obviously suffering from the heat. But irony can be extremely complex. As Quintilian put it, in this figure,

> the meaning, and sometimes the whole aspect of our case, conflicts with the language and the tone of voice adopted; nay, a man's whole life may be colored with irony, as was the case with Socrates, who was called an ironist because he assumed the role of an ignorant man lost in wonder at the wisdom of others. (IX ii, 46)

Irony abounds in contemporary political rhetoric: "my opponent is an honorable woman, I am sure"; "the party of moral values is the party that brought us Watergate, the savings-and-loan scandals, and the Iran-Contra affair." Sometimes irony backfires on its users. When a politician labels his opponent a draft-dodger, the situation becomes ironic if the politician himself somehow escaped mandated military service.

Advertisers often use irony in their promotional campaigns, which can be a risky move with a large audience. ABC Television Network's 1997 promotional campaign turned the focus back on itself—television as a medium—and embraced the commonplace that television is harmful to the mind. The one-line ads made ironic claims such as "Don't worry, you've got billions of brain cells" and "Eight hours a day, that's all we ask." Another advertisement advised that "You can talk to your wife anytime," while another asked "It's a beautiful day, what are you doing outside?" The logic of using irony in this instance is that savvy viewers appreciate a sense of humor, and that a bit of self-mockery might appeal to them. Still, the campaign is risky. Some experts think the ads may have had an adverse effect: viewers may take the messages as serious reminders of television's harmful effects, feel guilty, and turn it off. Irony is very difficult to pull off in writing, where the relation of the rhetor to the audience is ordinarily not intimate.

Ethopoeia, or character portrayal, consists in "representing and depicting in words clearly enough for recognition the bodily form of some person" (*ad Herennium* IV xlix, 63). The author gave this example: "the ruddy, short, bent man, with white and rather curly hair, blue-grey eyes, and a huge scar on his chin." But character portrayal may deal with a person's qualities, as well as physical characteristics. The author of *ad Herennium* portrayed a rich man by depicting his habits:

> That person there . . . thinks it admirable that he is called rich. . . . Once he has propped his chin on his left hand he thinks that he dazzles the eyes of all with the gleam of his jewelry and the glitter of his gold. . . . When he turns to his slave boy here, his only one . . . he calls him now by one name, now by another, and now by a third . . . so that unknowing hearers may think he is selecting one slave from among many. (IV xlix, 63)

It is not difficult to update this sketch: simply put a Rolex on the man's arm and substitute a personal secretary or a bodyguard for the slave. We have encountered this kind of *ethopoeia* before, in the character sketches of Theophrastus (see the chapter on ethos). Quintilian treated this figure as a kind of imitation, where the rhetor copies or emulates someone's words or deeds. He recommended the use of *ethopoeia* because of its charm and variety. He also pointed out that depictions of character, since they seem natural and spontaneous, can make an audience more receptive to a rhetor's ethos (IX ii, 59).

Sententia Borrowed from Invention and Arrangement

Quintilian disapproved of the practice of borrowing figures from invention or arrangement, and so he refused to treat them. In Book IX of the *Institutes*, he quipped: "I will pass by those authors who set no limit to their craze for inventing technical terms and even include among figures what really comes under the head of arguments" (iii, 99). Most ancient rhetoricians were not as fastidious as Quintilian, however. For example, the author of the *ad Herennium* treated **reasoning by contraries** (enthymeme or *conclusio*) as a figure of thought. As you can see from the Greek term for this figure, it is borrowed from invention. In the *ad Herennium* reasoning by contraries is a figure when the rhetor uses one of two opposite statements to prove the other, as in the following: "A faithless friend cannot be an honorable enemy"; or "George has never spoken the truth in private, and so he cannot be expected to refrain from lying in public." This figure resembles an enthymeme because it draws a conclusion (George will lie in public) from a statement that is not open to question (George lies to his friends). The author of *ad Herennium* liked it because of its "brief and complete rounding-off," and so he recommended that it be completed in one unbroken period (IV xviii, 26).

Other figures of thought repeat on the sentence level the parts of arrangement suggested for whole discourses. Cicero was particularly fond of these as a means of helping the audience keep track of the progress of the argument. Along with other ancient rhetoricians, he recommended that complex topics be divided into parts and a reason for accepting the parts be attached to each (*divisio*). Here is an example from *ad Herennium:* "if you are an upright man, you have not deserved reproach; if a wicked man, you will be unmoved" (IV xl, 52). In this case, the rhetor divides alternatives into only two (the man is either upright or wicked); this allows the rhetor to select from among many characteristics that might be chosen and thus to control the audience's response to the man. This figure is closely related to **distribution** (*diairesis, distributio*), where the rhetor divides up possibilities and distributes them among different areas. Here is an example from *ad Herennium:* "The Senate's function is to assist the state with counsel; the magistracy's is to execute, by diligent activity, the Senate's will; the people's to choose and support by its votes the best measures and the most suitable men" (IV xxxv, 47). The distribution makes this political arrangement seem fair and equitable.

Accumulation (*frequentatio*) is another figure of thought based on arrangement. Here the rhetor gathers together points that are scattered about and lists them all together. This has the effect of making a shaky conclusion seem more evident or reasonable. Interestingly enough, accumulation is forbidden in courtroom argument. In many cases, prosecutors are not allowed to introduce an accused person's past offenses into their argument on the grounds that a person should be tried only for the crime with which he is currently charged. This practice testifies to the rhetorical power of accumulation: while juries or judges might not be impressed by the evidence assembled to substantiate one instance of a crime, they are more likely to be impressed by evidence that testifies to the commission of a series of like or related crimes. Television uses a combination of images and speech to create the effect of accumulation, as when, for example, a sportscaster calls an NBA game a "dunkfest" while the rolling clips show twelve different slam dunks from the game. The accumulated images reinforce the credibility of the term.

Cicero and the author of *ad Herennium* also treated **transitions** as figures of thought (*Orator* xl, 137; IV xxvi, 35). A transition is any word or phrase that connects pieces of discourse. Cicero recommended that rhetors use transition to announce what is about to be discussed when introducing a topic (*propositio*) and sum up when concluding a topic (*enumeratio*); if both are used together, they constitute a smooth transition between topics. Using transition, a rhetor can briefly recall what has just been said, and briefly announce what will follow.

Now that we have concluded our discussion of figures, we move to an analysis of tropes.

TROPES

Neither ancient nor modern rhetoricians have ever been able to agree about what distinguishes this class of ornament from figures. It is probably safe to say that **tropes** are characterized by the substitution of one word or phrase for another, but even this distinction does not clearly demarcate tropes from some figures of language, such as **synonomy** or puns. However, even though ancient rhetoricians could not agree about the definition of a trope, they pretty much knew one when they saw one. With the notable exception of Aristotle, who was ambivalent about every ornament except metaphor, major rhetoricians used a list of ten tropes that remained more or less standard throughout antiquity. The ten are: *onomatopoeia, antonomasia*, **metonymy**, *periphrasis, hyperbaton,* **hyperbole, synecdoche, catachresis, metaphor,** and **allegory.**

Onomatopoeia

According to the author of the *ad Herennium*, the rhetor who uses *onomatopeia* ("making a new name") assigns a new word to "a thing which either lacks a name or has an inappropriate name" (IV xxx, 42). This trope could be used either for imitative purposes, as illustrated by words like "roar," "bellow," "murmur," "hiss" (*sibulus* in Latin), or for expressiveness. To exemplify this second use of *onomatopeia,* the author coined a Latin word, *fragor,* which his modern translator renders as "hullabaloo": "After this creature attacked the republic, there was a hullabaloo among the first men of the state." (The 1960s gave us another *onomatopeia* for a hullabaloo—"hootenanny.")

Readers who have been paying attention will notice that *onomatopeia* bears a close resemblance to **neologism**—the coining of new words—a practice that was condemned by Quintilian as "scarcely permissible to a Roman." That quintessential Roman, Julius Caesar himself, warned us to "avoid, as you would a rock, an unheard-of and unfamiliar word." Nonetheless, ancient rhetoricians agreed that *onomatopeia* was the means by which language was invented, as their ancestors found names for things by emulating the noises those things characteristically made (*Institutes* VIII vi, 31). Contemporary rhetoricians define *onomatopeia* simply as words or language whose sound emulates or echoes their sense: "the brook babbled and murmured"; "over the cobbles he clattered and clashed" (Alfred Noyes).

Antonomasia

In the trope called *antonomasia* ("another name"; Latin *pronominatio*), a rhetor substitutes a descriptive phrase for someone's proper name (or vice versa). When Quintilian referred to Cicero as "the prince of Roman orators," he used *antonomasia* (VIII vi, 30). The author of *ad Herennium* suggested that, rather than naming the Gracchi, whose reputations were contested, a rhetor could more effectively refer to them as "the grandsons of Africanus," since Africanus' reputation was impeccable (IV xxxi, 42). *Antonomasia* appears frequently in contemporary rhetoric. Elvis is "the King"; athletes and teams or squads acquire nicknames like "The Mailman," "The Manassas Mauler," "the Fearsome Foursome." The contemporary popularity of this trope is not limited to entertainment or sports. In the 1992 presidential campaign, his handlers labeled Bill Clinton "the Comeback Kid" because he seemed to be able to recover from almost any setback. In the same campaign Clinton's Republican opponents labeled the Democratic ticket "Double Bubba," because it had two Southerners on it (Clinton of Arkansas and Al Gore of Tennessee).

The rhetorical effects of this trope are obvious. It not only suggests that someone is so well known that his name needn't be used, thus cementing group loyalty, it also provides rhetors with opportunities to characterize the people they speak or write about in either positive or negative terms.

Metonomy

Metonymy ("altered name") names something with a word or phrase closely associated with it: "the White House" for the President of the United States or "the Kremlin" for the leadership of the former Union of Socialist Soviet Republics. The maxim "the pen is mightier than the sword" is a metonomy where "pen" stands for persuasive language and "sword" for war. We refer to the works of an author by her or his name: "Morrison" or "Leonard" stand in for novels written by Toni Morrison or Elmore Leonard. We use metonymy when we say "I like R.E.M.," meaning that we like their music.

Periphrasis

We have already encountered the figure called *periphrasis* ("circling speech") under its Latin name of circumlocution. Quintilian defined uses of this figure as "whatever might have been expressed with greater brevity, but is expanded for purposes of ornament" (VIII vi, 61). He gave this poetic example from Virgil's *Aeneid*: "Now was the time/When the first sleep to weary mortals comes/Stealing its way, the sweetest boon of heaven" (ii, 268). Virgil did not simply say "night arrived." Rather, he embroidered on this simple observation to achieve the effect of calmness that sleep brings.

Quintilian worried that rhetors would use this figure simply to fill up space, or to impress:

> some rhetors introduce a whole host of useless words; for, in their eagerness to avoid ordinary methods of expression, and allured by false ideals of beauty they wrap up everything in a multitude of words simply and solely because they are unwilling to make a direct and simple statement of the facts. (VIII ii, 17)

A contemporary rhetorician named Richard Lanham argues persuasively that much contemporary American prose is written in what he calls the "Official Style." He gives this example:

> The history of Western psychological thought has long been dominated by philosophical considerations as to the nature of man. These notions have dictated corresponding considerations of the nature of the child within society, the practices by which children were to be raised, and the purposes of studying the child. (1992, 10)

In essence, this passage says that psychologists are interested in human nature and that this interest has led them to investigate childhood and child rearing practices. In other words, users of the official style do exactly what Quintilian warned against—they pile up more words and phrases than are necessary in order to achieve an impressive effect. There is a big difference between using words in order to enhance an effect or to call attention to a point, and simply failing to notice them.

Hyperbaton

Hyperbaton is the transposition of a word to somewhere other than its usual place: "Backward run sentences, until reels the mind" (a parody of the style of *Time* magazine). Strictly speaking, *hyperbaton* is a figure of language, since its effect depends upon a change in normal word order. But, as Quintilian noted, it can be called a trope when "the meaning is not complete until the two words have been put together" (VIII vi, 66). We parody our own writing by imposing a hyperbaton on the first sentence of this paragraph: "Hyperbaton is the transposition, to somewhere other than its usual place, of a word."

Hyperbole

Quintilian defined hyperbole ("thrown above"; "excess") as "an elegant straining of the truth" (VIII vi, 67), and gives this wonderful example from Cicero: "Vetto gives the name of farm to an estate which might easily be hurled from a sling, though it might well fall through the hole in the hollow sling, so small is it" (73). Aristotle gave these examples: speaking of a man with a black eye, "You would have thought him a basket of mulberries"; and of a skinny man, "he has legs like parsley" (*Rhetoric* III xi, 1413a). In other words, hyperbole is exaggeration used for effect. Sportscasters, especially color commentators, often use hyperbole to create excitement. When a basketball player makes a long-range three pointer, for instance, the sportscaster might yell "From the parking lot!" or, engaging in even more exaggerated hyperbole, he might say the shot came "From Downtown!"

Synecdoche

In synecdoche ("to receive together") rhetors substitute the part for the whole (or vice versa) or cause for effect (or vice versa). Quintilian wrote that this figure occurred most commonly with numbers, as in "The Roman won the day," where "the Roman" refers to an entire army. The author of *ad Herennium* gave this example of synecdoche: "Were not those nuptial flutes reminding you of his marriage?" (the flutes stand for the whole ceremony). Like hyperbole, this trope is common in everyday speech. We say "give us our daily bread," where "bread" means something like "enough food to sustain us." We say "give me a hand," where "hand" refers to help or assistance, and we use the phrase "400 head" to refer to 400 animals. We say that "arms were illegally shipped," where "arms" refers to all kinds of weapons.

Catachresis

Catachresis ("to use against") is "the inexact use of a like and kindred word in place of the precise and proper one" (*ad Herennium* IV xxxiii, 45). The author gave these examples: "the power of man is short," "small height," "long wisdom," "mighty speech." In these examples adjectives are misapplied to nouns: we ordinarily speak of human power as limited rather than short; of wisdom as enduring rather than long and so on. Quintilian defined this trope more narrowly as "the practice of adapting the nearest available term to describe something for which no actual term exists" (VIII vi, 34). The Latin name for catachresis is "abuse," and novice rhetors might be wise to avoid it.

Metaphor

A metaphor transfers or substitutes one word for another. Some metaphors are so common in our daily speech that we no longer think about their metaphoric quality: we say that a disappointed lover "struck out" or "never got to first base," borrowing metaphors from baseball. When someone has exhausted all her alternatives, we say that she is "at the end of her rope," borrowing a grisly metaphor from a method of execution. We say that the abortion question presents us with a thicket of difficult issues, borrowing a metaphor from nature. Truly striking metaphors appear in poetry. Here are two examples from a poem by Emily Dickinson:

> There is no frigate like a book
> To take us lands away,
> Nor any coursers like a page
> Of prancing poetry.

Dickinson compared a book to a ship and its pages to horses. In our prose these comparisons don't make much sense, but they work beautifully in Dickinson's poem to evoke images and emotions.

Metaphors abound in news articles. Here, for example, is a metaphorical description from the *New York Times*: "Mr. Clinton, they say, is charting his own moderate course, one that embraces once-Republican ideas like balanced budgets and free trade, yet includes Democratic grace notes like a children's health care program, environmental activism, and tax cuts for higher education." The phrase "charting his own course" invokes images of an independent, courageous captain navigating unfamiliar waters, while the use of "grace note" invokes careful orchestration of musical instruments. Without the metaphors, the description would lose much of its force: "Mr. Clinton, they say, is creating an agenda that embraces once-Republican ideas . . ." Metaphors, then, can help readers think about otherwise mundane activities or objects in different and interesting ways.

Metaphor is often the only trope mentioned in traditional composition textbooks, giving the impression that modern writers should limit their use of ornament to a single trope. Aristotle, like other ancient rhetoricians, was more interested in metaphor than he was in other tropes or figures, and metaphor has received more attention from modern rhetoricians and literary critics than has any other trope or figure. In the *Poetics,* Aristotle defined metaphor as the movement of a name from its own genus or species to another genus or species (XXI 7, 1457b). In the *Rhetoric,* he noted that metaphors borrowed from something greater in the same genus or species were complimentary, while those borrowed from something lesser could be used to denigrate the person or thing to whom it was applied. Thus, pirates can be called "entrepreneurs" or "businesspeople" while someone who has made a mistake can be accused of criminal behavior (III ii, 1405a). Humans often get compared to other species because of some shared characteristic that the rhetor wants to highlight. WNBA guard Theresa Weatherspoon, when asked about her stellar defensive game against the league's leading scorer, said: "She told me I was like a gnat, a pest who wouldn't go away." Here the comparison to a pesky insect conveys the frustration an offensive-minded player feels when guarded closely.

At another point in the *Rhetoric,* Aristotle classed metaphors among those tropes and figures he called witty or urbane sayings, and he developed a theory about why metaphors give us pleasure. They do so, he wrote, "because metaphors help us to learn new things, and learning is naturally pleasurable to humans" (x, 1410b). In other words, since metaphors express ideas in new or unusual ways, they help us to see things in new ways.

Aristotle suggested that metaphors be taken from two sources: those that are beautiful, either in sound or effect, and those that appealed to the senses (ii, 1405b). It would not do, he wrote, to substitute "red-fingered" or even "purple-fingered" for Homer's "rosy-fingered dawn." He told a funny story about Simonides, who at first declined to write a poem for a man who had won a mule race, on the ground that he did not want to celebrate half-asses. When the man paid enough, however, Simonides accepted the commission and wrote "Hail, daughters of storm-footed mares!" Aristotle gave many examples of successful metaphors: citizens are like a ship's captain who is strong but deaf; ungrateful neighbors are like children who accept candy but keep on crying; orators are like babysitters who eat the baby's food and then moisten the baby's lips with their saliva (iv, 1406b, 1407a). Sometimes beautiful metaphors seem exaggerated and take on an ironic force, as in this description of golfers' form written by Lee Eisenburg: "Golf Lit's most familiar genre is the instruction manual, that object of perennial hope and self-delusion whose explicit purpose is to tell a hacker how to move his arms and legs with the unified grace of the Cleveland Symphony" (*New York Times Book Review,* 17 August 1997, 27). Eisenburg's comparison of the ideal golf form to a symphony orchestra humorously speaks to the drive for unattainable perfection harbored by aspiring golfers.

Quintilian distinguished several kinds of metaphor. In one of these, a rhetor substitutes one living thing for another: "he is a lion"; "Scipio was continually barked at by Cato" (VIII vi, 9). In another kind, inanimate things may be substituted for animate, and vice versa. Quintilian thought this was most impressive when an inanimate object is spoken of as though it were alive, as in Cicero's "what was that sword of yours doing, Tubero?", or "the dam decided to collapse at that moment." Aristotle would have classed both of these kinds of metaphor under the head of species-to-species, where a rhetor substitutes the name of one particular for another. Aristotle and Quintilian both named metaphors that substitute a part for a whole, or vice versa, as a separate class, but modern rhetoricians label such metaphors as synecdoches (for example, "Jane Doe" to represent all women).

Aristotle also treated **analogy** as a kind of metaphor. In analogy, rhetors compare a relationship rather than items. Aristotle cited Pericles' saying that the young men killed in a recent war had vanished from Athens as though someone had taken Spring from the year (III x, 1411a). A metaphor becomes an **allegory** when it is sustained throughout a long passage.

In her book *Writing Permitted in Designated Areas Only,* English professor and rhetoric scholar Linda Brodkey uses allegory to compare the marking off of public smoking spaces to the marking off of writing spaces in American universities. We offer two excerpts from her book to illustrate the use of allegory:

> The international sign that bans smoking in public places can also be read as a sign of cultural hegemony, a frequent and forcible reminder that in democratic societies civic regulations commonly inscribe the will of the dominant culture. That there are two versions of the sign suggests that the dominant culture is of at least two minds when it comes to smoking in public places. One version of the sign prohibits smoking altogether, and the other regulates smoking by appending a note that may be more familiar to smokers than to nonsmokers: "Smoking Permitted in Designated Areas Only." This second sign, signaling the temporary segregation of smokers from nonsmokers, is part of the same expansionist public policy as the first, which seems likely to succeed eventually given the rapidly diminishing number and size of public spaces where smokers are still allowed to smoke. In the meantime, however—so long as they remove themselves to those designated areas—smokers constitute a literal and figurative body of evidence that a desire to smoke remains strong enough in some people to withstand the ever increasing pressure of social hostility and medical injunctions. That smokers commonly honor the signs, either by not smoking or by smoking only in designated areas, provides smokers and nonsmokers alike with continual public enactments of civil power, namely, the power of the professional-managerial middle class to enforce the public suppression of a desire it has recently identified and articulated via science as endangering its well being—as a class. (130)

Here Brodkey sets up one end of the allegory, the smoking signs and regulations with which her readers are already familiar. Boldly questioning the assumptions behind such regulation and its subscription to scientific ideology, Brodkey rearticulates the regulations as "cultural hegemony," the imposition of one group's will onto another group or groups. After developing her critique of smoking regulation a bit further, Brodkey moves to the other side of the allegory, the set of practices she wants to cast in a different light by way of the extended metaphor itself and a series of direct argument: American writing instruction. Brodkey writes:

> Composition classrooms are the designated areas of American colleges and universities. Composition courses are middle-class holding pens populated by students from all classes who for one reason or another do not produce fluent, thesis-driven essays of around five hundred words in response to either prompts designed for standardized tests or assignments developed by classroom teachers . . .
>
> It has always seemed to me gratuitous to regulate writing and writers via the contents of prompts and assignments, since a policy of coherence is already being "objectively" executed by assessing student writing on the basis of form and format: the grammar, spelling, diction, and punctuation along with the thesis sentence, body paragraphs, and conclusion. Perhaps both are necessary, however, because while form identifies class interlopers (working-class ethnic and black students) content singles out class malcontents. While it seems to take longer in some cases than in others, composition instruction appears to have succeeded best at establishing in most people a lifelong aversion to writing. They have learned to associate a desire to write with a set of punishing exercises called writing in school: printing, penmanship, spelling, punctuation, and vocabulary in nearly all cases; grammar lessons, thesis sentences, paragraphs, themes, book reports, and library research papers in college preparatory and advanced placement courses. (135–136)

Through subtle language cues, Brodkey sustains the smoking metaphor throughout the passage—and the rest of the chapter (indeed, the metaphor permeates the entire book, thanks to the title). Words like "designated areas" and "regulate" transfer the arguments Brodkey made about regulating smoking to regulating student writing. The allegory enables Brodkey to clarify what annoys her most about prevailing practices in composition classes: writing is reserved for one place, she argues, and that place is tainted by our culture, marked as the "lower" training ground for other university classes. In this schema, untrained writers—like smokers—are seen as potentially dangerous, threatening, or at least irritating to middle- and upper-class standards, hence necessitating strict regulation. The allegory certainly does powerful work for Brodkey and makes her argument all the more compelling, or at least we think so.

EXERCISES

1. Try your hand at composing sentences that contain figures and tropes. Find a passage of your writing and examine it to see whether you unconsciously used any of the figures or tropes discussed in this chapter. Rewrite any of the sentences in the passage, inserting figures or tropes where they are appropriate. Approach this task systematically over a few days or weeks; your eventual goal is to use each kind of figure or trope discussed in this chapter.

2. Revise a passage you've written in the plain style so that it is appropriate for a more formal rhetorical situation. Use complex sentence constructions,

longer words, and lots of figures and tropes. For models of highly ornate prose styles you can turn to the work of composers from earlier periods of history. John Donne's sermons are good examples, as are those composed by American preachers such as Jonathan Edwards or Martin Luther King.

3. Like ancient teachers, we recommend that aspiring rhetors practice imitating sentences and longer passages composed by writers and speakers they admire. We describe a number of ancient exercises in imitation in a later chapter of this book.

4. We also recommend that rhetors be on the lookout for professional speakers' and writers' uses of the various figures discussed in this chapter. When you find figures or tropes that you admire, write them down in a commonplace book. Practice imitating them. A modern handbook of the figures is a very useful aid to composers. We highly recommend Richard Lanham's *A Handlist of Rhetorical Figures.*

NOTES

1. Like ancient rhetoricians, we think that correctness and clarity are not truly rhetorical considerations, and so we don't pay much attention to them in this book. We also think that Americans' obsession with correctness and clarity has kept us from studying and enjoying the more complex uses of language that are addressed here. There are plenty of books available that discuss correctness and clarity. Any good handbook for writers will delineate the rules of traditional grammar. We recommend *The St. Martin's Handbook* by Andrea Lunsford and Robert Connors. Dictionaries of usage are also available; Fowler's *Modern English Usage* is a standard reference work. Writers who are interested in achieving a clearer style can consult Richard Lanham's *Revising Prose* and Joseph Williams' *Ten Lessons in Clarity and Grace.*

2. Writers who are interested in practicing this kind of stylistic appropriateness can consult the ancient treatises written by Hermogenes of Tarsus, usually called *The Ideas of Style* or *The Types of Style,* as well as that by Demetrius of Phaleron, called *On Style.* These treatises give copious advice about how to achieve effects such as solemnity, vehemence, simplicity, force, and so on.

CHAPTER 13

MEMORY

Now let me turn to the treasure-house of the ideas supplied by Invention, to the guardian of all the parts of rhetoric, the Memory.

—*ad Herennium*
III xvi, 28.

A RICH MAN named Scopas once invited Simonides of Ceos, a magician and poet, to write a poem in celebration of a banquet he was hosting. When Simonides read his poem at the banquet he praised the twin gods Castor and Pollux. Scopas was so angry that the poem praised someone other than himself that he paid Simonides only half the fee he had promised. After the banquet began, Simonides was given a message that two young men wished to see him outside the hall. While he searched for them outside, the hall collapsed and everyone inside was killed. When relatives came to collect the remains, Simonides was able to remember the exact place at the table where everyone had been sitting, thus making sure that the right relatives claimed the right bodies. Of course, the two young men who had sent the message were Castor and Pollux. They repaid Simonides' praise by saving him from certain death.

From a rhetorician's perspective, Simonides' prodigious feat of memory is the important part of this story. Ancient authors were so impressed with the powers of memory that they awarded it a place among the rhetorical canons. Obviously, people who speak in public need reliable memories, especially if they are asked to speak without preparation, as politicians often are. Although the role of memory is not as apparent in written composition, writers do have to be able to remember information or to recall where it is located.

It may be hard for us to grasp the importance of memory to premodern thinkers. Until the modern period, memory held a central place within rhetorical theory (and in most other intellectual endeavors, as well). Ancient rhetoricians distinguished between natural memory and artificial memory. An artificial memory is a memory that has been carefully trained to remember things. While every human being relies on natural memory to some extent, it is possible to enhance memory through training and practice. A person who possesses an artificial or trained memory has organized it into a set of orderly memory places through which she or he can locate and retrieve relevant information easily. ("Artificial" in this context simply means created by humans, something not given by nature; for ancient peoples something that was "artificed" was something made or created by human beings. The term did not carry its modern connotations of "fake" or "phony.")

In ancient times even people who could write easily and well relied on their memories, not merely as storage facilities, but as structured heuristic systems. In other words, memory was not only a system of recollection for ancient and medieval peoples; it was a means of invention. In ancient and medieval times, people memorized huge volumes of information, along with keys to its organization, and carried all this in their heads. Whenever the need arose to speak or write, they simply retrieved any relevant topics or commentary from their ordered places within memory, reorganized and expanded on these, and added their own interpretations of the traditional material. People who had trained their memories could do this sort of composing without using writing at all. If they wanted to share their memorial compositions with others, they dictated them to scribes.

Some scholars think that ancient peoples invented memorial composition because writing materials were scarce and expensive. Certainly, literacy was not widespread until the modern period. But this explanation for the ancient interest in memory overlooks the fact that people relied on memory systems long past the time when printed books and libraries became accessible to most educated people. In fact, rhetors continued to use memorial composing strategies right up to the modern period. After all, unlike pen and paper or a even a portable computer, a trained memory is always readily available as a source of invention.

MEMORY IN ANCIENT RHETORICS

We shall probably never know whether artificial memory systems were in use prior to the fifth century BCE. It seems likely that they were, since the ability of the itinerant poets, called rhapsodes, to recall long poems cannot easily be explained in any other way. Perhaps rhapsodes used vivid mental images taken from the Homeric poems as memory aids; a trained memory could easily enough connect a vividly constructed mental image of the "wine-dark sea" either to events associated in the poems with seagoing, or to the words and lines that narrated these events.

The sophists must have played an important role in establishing artificial memory as an important part of rhetorical training. The sophist Hippias was famous for his memory. According to the ancient historian Philostratus, "after hearing fifty names only once [Hippias] could repeat them from memory in the order in which he had heard them"; he could do this "even in his old age" (*Lives of the Sophists* I, 495). After writing came into general use, Hippias and the other sophists could store lists of topics in manuscript as well as in memory. The handbooks mentioned in Aristotle's *Rhetoric* may be manuscripts that gave lists of sophistic topics. The topics in these lists were arranged in contradictory pairs, since the sophists taught their students how to argue both sides of any question. However, this arrangement may also have been a memory aid.

As we have seen, the sophistic *Dissoi Logoi* also contains several lists of commonplaces for use in public argument. The lists give possible variations on topics such as "what is true for one person is true for another." Rhetors could memorize this topic by connecting it to some vivid image and locating its variants in some orderly way. They would then be ready to invent arguments drawn from this topic for use on any occasion simply by combining and expanding on the appropriate variations. A trained memory could house many such topics, along with their associated variations, if these were placed in some orderly manner. Composition, whether written or oral, would then amount to selection, combination, and amplification of appropriate topics and their variations to suit a particular occasion.

Scholars do not know when memory was added to the list of the rhetorical canons. Hellenistic teachers probably included formal instruction in artificial memory in their instruction; we possess a full treatment in the *Rhetorica ad Herennium*, which dates from the second century BCE, and Cicero includes a brief discussion of memory in *De Oratore* (II, 350ff). Cicero's famous contemporary, Julius Caesar, must have practiced an art of memory; Caesar was famous in ancient times for prodigious feats of remembering. The historian Pliny wrote "we are told that he used to write or read and dictate or listen simultaneously, and to dictate to his secretaries four letters at once on his important affairs—or, if otherwise unoccupied, seven letters at once" (*Natural History* VII xxv, 92). Such feats would be impossible without the aid of a trained memory. Later Roman rhetors must have used memory arts as well; Quintilian gives a very full treatment of artificial memory in the *Institutes* (XI, 2), and many rhetors of the Second Sophistic were famous for their memories.

Ancient Memory Systems

Ancient authorities agree that Simonides should be credited with the invention of artificial memory as an art that can be systematically studied and practiced. According to Cicero, Simonides taught

> that persons desiring to train this faculty must select localities and form mental images of the facts they wish to remember and store those images in the localities, with the result that the arrangement of the localities will preserve the order of the facts, and the images of the facts will designate the facts themselves. (*De Oratore* II lxxxvi, 354)

In other words, Simonides concluded that a mental construction, consisting of a series of images connected in an orderly fashion to a series of mental places, would allow people to remember lists of names or items if they simply associated each name or item with a mental place and/or its associated image. A person had only to review each of the places, in order, to remember the images names associated with it; a review of the images called up the information being searched for. (The expression "in the first place" may originate from this memory practice.)

This memory system took the notion of "place" literally. Its teachers recommended that students visualize a street or a house with which they were familiar. They were then to associate points along the street (say, houses or buildings), or rooms inside the house with the items they wished to remember. People who wish to use this memory system should choose some arrangement or ordering of items that is quite familiar and thus easy to walk through in memory. For example, if rhetors want to remember three arguments, they can associate the first of these with the entryways to their home. They then associate the second argument with the next room that they enter in their houses or apartments—say it is the living room—and the third argument with the room that comes next—say, the kitchen. It is easy for rhetors to remember the order in which they enter each room of their houses, since they follow this order each time they go in and out of the house.

Rhetors can use any geographical layout with which they are very familiar as an ordering principle for memory. The main street of a town or city was a favorite organizing device among ancient and medieval practitioners of artificial memory, for instance. It is important, however, that the geographical layout contain memorable features; the hallway of the building where I work, for example, would not be useful as an ordering principle because it contains a series of office doors that all look alike.

The second task in this memory system was to place some striking or memorable item within each of the ordered places. Teachers recommended that the images be vivid and strange enough to be remembered easily, and, if possible, the images should be in some way associated with the items to be remembered. For example, rhetors might place a large red umbrella stand in the imaginary entryways of their houses. If the first argument they wanted to remember had to do with the necessity of stopping acid rain, they might imagine large yellow umbrellas with ragged holes placed in the imaginary red umbrella stands in the imagined entryways to their house.

The *Dissoi Logoi*, the oldest rhetorical treatise we possess, gave instructions for creating a second kind of artificial memory system:

> The greatest and fairest discovery has been found to be memory; it is useful for everything, for wisdom as well as for the conduct of life. This is the first step: if you focus your attention, your mind, making progress by this means, will perceive more. The second step is to practice whatever you hear. If you hear the same things many times and repeat them, what you have learned presents itself to your memory as a connected whole. The third step is: whenever you hear something, connect it with what you know already. For instance, suppose you need to remember the name "Chrysippos," you must connect it with *chrusos* (gold) and *hippos* (horse). Or another example: if you need to remember the name "Pyrilampes" you must connect it with *pyr* (fire) and *lampein* (to shine). These are examples for words. In the case of things, do this: if you want to remember courage, think of Ares and Achilles, or metal working, of Hephaistos, or cowardice, of Epeios. (Sprague 1968, 166–167)

This treatise counseled students of memory, first, to focus on things they wish to remember. Second, things to be remembered should be repeated many times. The third step resembled Simonides' system in part; here students were to associate the material to be lodged in memory with a vivid image that is connected either to words or to things. If he wished to remember the name "Chrysippos," the rhetoric student might imagine a golden horse. Or he might imagine a fiery lamp in order to remember Pyrilampes' name. Both images should be vivid enough to be easily remembered.

If rhetors wish to remember the names of people they meet, using this system, they should listen very carefully to the names when introduced to the people. Then repeat the names aloud. Last, rhetors should mentally associate the names with vivid and familiar images of objects in memory. Say, for example, that the name is Patricia Smith. The rhetors can associate "Patricia" with a vivid image of an aristocratic person (a patrician), and "Smith" with an image of someone crafting metal, as a blacksmith or locksmith does.

Memory for things is achieved by associating whatever is to be remembered—especially if it is an abstraction like courage or cowardice—with some mythological figure who is associated with that quality. So, if our rhetors learn that Patricia Smith is an astronaut, they can remember that by associating her in memory with Icarus, who courageously flew all the way to the sun. (This example works only if mythological images are familiar and meaningful to the rhetors.) Or they can combine memory for words and memory for things: since the English term "astronaut" is formed from two ancient Greek words, *astron* ("star") and *nautes* ("sailor"), they can form a vivid image of a "star sailor" in order to remember Smith's occupation.

In the *Topics*, Aristotle recommended yet a third memory system. He counseled his students to memorize a "good stock of definitions," as well as a stock of premises to use in constructing enthymemes: "for just as in a person with a trained memory, a memory of things themselves is immediately caused by the mere mention of their places, so these habits too will make a man readier in reasoning, because he has his premises classified before his mind's eye, each under its number" (VIII 14, 163b). In other words, Aristotle suggested that rhetors memorize the most frequently used commonplaces that serve as major premises for enthymemes. He also recommended that they group these into categories and give each category to a number, so that premises can easily be recalled by mentally running through the numbered system. To use Aristotle's memory system, rhetors can group commonplaces on similar subjects under one mental category and invent a term to name the category. Then choose a key word from each commonplace, assign it a letter of the alphabet or a number, and organize the commonplaces in each category either alphabetically or numerically.

Modern Versions of Ancient Memory Systems

Today, since many people are literate, they rely on writing to do the kind of work done by artificial memory among ancient peoples. People who use research in their writing, for example, take notes on their reading or make records of experiments while they are performing them; they refer to these notes and records when they begin writing up the results of their work. Thus the role played by memory in modern invention is not immediately obvious. Nevertheless, it is substantial.

When people begin to compose, they necessarily rely on their memories, no matter what composing strategies they use. Even if they take notes on experiments or reading, composers must rely on memory to reconstruct meanings for those notes. They must also remember commonplaces and other argumentative strategies. They must remember how they went about composing other pieces of discourse on other occasions, and they remember what they've been taught about usage and spelling. In other words, people do not begin composing as though nothing has ever happened to them or as though they remember nothing of their past lives.

The ancient notion of communal memory seems quite foreign to modern students because in modern times people tend to think of their memories as narratives of their past lives, rather than as carefully organized depositories of common knowledge. Despite this belief, our memories are stocked with many things besides narratives of our experiences; we remember things we learn from teachers, parents, clergy, relatives and friends, the media and books, just as well as we remember experiences. Certainly we rely on our memories of all these kinds of teachings whenever we compose.

Even more important, perhaps, is the role played by our memories in organizing the things we remember. In an untrained memory, the organization of remembered material may seem chaotic and disjointed, just as it appears to us in dreams. But memories can be trained and organized, just as the ancients said. A little memory work can pay off handsomely if it teaches us how to find things in our memories more quickly.

Some very simple memory systems are available to everyone. The letters of the alphabet are quite useful in this regard. If, for example, you want to remember a list of items to buy at the grocery store, you can organize them in alphabetical order: apples, bananas, cheese, lettuce, pepper, vitamins. It helps to repeat the list aloud a couple of times. When you arrive at the grocery store, simply skim through the alphabet letter by letter, searching your memory for any image you have attached to any letter. Another memory tactic, which resembles ancient geographical memory systems, is to organize your grocery list according to the floor plan of a grocery store in which you frequently shop. The first time you try this, you may need to walk through the store, noting the relation of its aisles to one another, and making a mental place to coincide with each aisle. Then, when you make a grocery list, you can create the appropriate images and stash them on the appropriate aisles—carrots and potatoes on the vegetable aisle, milk at the back of the store, and so on. People who learn to do this don't need to make written grocery lists, and they never have to worry about leaving the grocery list at home.

These simple memory systems also help writers and speakers to remember things that may be needed during composing. Ideas often come to rhetors when they are unable to write them down—while riding a bicycle, for example, or doing dishes, or watching television, or talking to someone. You can imprint such ideas on your memory by associating them with a letter of the alphabet and placing them in memory according to alphabetical order. Say that a rhetor has an idea about memory systems while having coffee with a friend. Rather than rudely interrupting the conversation to write this idea down, the rhetor can simply file the idea under "m" in memory. This works even better if the rhetor mentally ties the idea to some vivid image. If, for example, the rhetor is having coffee with someone named "Michael," his image can be used later to conjure up the idea filed under "m"; better yet, an image can be created that is suitable to the idea. For example, the idea about memory could be associated with a vivid mental image of Simonides standing in front of Scopas' collapsed house.

Since contemporary rhetors tend to associate memory with narratives of their lives, it might be useful for them to use their remembered chronology of their lives as the organizing principle in a memory system. Young persons can use each year of their lives from age seven or so, while older persons might wish to divide the remembered chronology of their lives into five-year periods or decades. Assign each section of the chronology a letter of the alphabet or a number (such as "1979"). Try to characterize each section by associating it with something important that happened to you during that period of your life. Then, when you wish to remember something, mentally stash it in the section of your remembered chronology that is most relevant to it. This system is a variant of the one suggested by Aristotle, and it may work for people who have difficulty with memory systems that use places as organizing principles.

LITERATE MEMORY SYSTEMS

With the spread of literacy, the storage function of human memory was superseded. Public libraries and encyclopedias were developed during the modern period, and to some extent they took the place of artificial memory for things. People no longer needed to remember information or arguments that they could easily look up in print. However, literate storage cannot do something that artificial memory can do: it cannot tell you where to look for the information you need (although electronic storage can do this). Libraries use systems such as the Library of Congress numbers to organize printed materials, and encyclopedias use the alphabet (along with other literate memory systems such as indexes). Books and journals use tables of contents, indexes, and bibliographies to help users determine whether the material they contain is relevant to their needs.

The organizational principles of literate storage systems have to be learned and memorized if they are to be of any help in locating materials. Students should get in the habit of reading the organizational sections of printed materials first, in order to save the time and energy that may be spent in reading irrelevant sources. It is also useful for students to get to know their way around the library they use most.

Books

The front and back matter of any book can help you to locate material within it more quickly. Books usually begin with a **title page** and a page that gives reference information—including its Library of Congress **call number,** its date of publication and its publisher. Nonfiction books include a table of contents, which outlines the main headings of material discussed in the book. Read the table of contents to determine whether the book covers material that interests you. If you decide to use the book as a source, write down its author's name, its full title, its date of publication, and its library call number. You will need this information if you cite the book either in footnotes or a bibliography, and you need the call number in case you have to look something up later. If you plan to quote anything directly from the book, be sure to record the page numbers from which you took the quotation.

Books may optionally contain a **foreword,** sometimes written by someone other than the author, which introduces the book and places it in the context of other related work. Ordinarily, the author includes a **preface** (literally "a speaking before"). In a preface, an author may indicate the purposes in composing the book; outline the methods or indicate the scholarly or intellectual tradition to which the book is indebted; and acknowledge those who helped compose the work. Skimming a preface can tell you much about a book, and prefaces are often fun to read since authors sometimes feel they can be more informal in a preface than in the rest of the text.

At the back of most nonfiction books, you will find a **bibliography** and an **index.** The bibliography lists all of the works mentioned or used in the book, usually listed in alphabetical order by their authors' last names. Sometimes bibliographies will suggest related sources as well, and so you can use its entries to find more information. Indexes list persons' names and specific or technical terms used in the book, along with the page numbers on which these terms appear. Indexes are extremely valuable tools in literate storage systems. We often begin our reading of a book by looking at its index, to see if it lists any terms that we need in our current research, or if it lists the names of persons who are important thinkers in the area we are researching. Sometimes footnotes appear at the back of a book; however they sometimes appear at the bottom of pages or at the ends of chapters. **Glossaries** that explain the meanings of difficult or technical terms, **appendixes,** and other useful materials may also be included at the end of a book.

Periodicals

Librarians use term **periodical** to refer to any literate materials that are published under the same name over a stretch of time. Periodicals include magazines, newspapers, and scholarly journals. Most periodicals include the organizational information found in books: title pages, information pages, and tables of contents. Sometimes all of this information appears on a single page in a magazine or newspaper. Most periodicals have indexes, but these are issued periodically—once a year, or every three years, or the like. Sometimes it is necessary to browse through one to three years' worth of journal issues to find out when they publish their indexes. Periodical indexes are usually organized by author, title, and subject; they list all the materials published in the periodical over the time period covered by the index. The *New York Times,* for example, publishes a yearly index of materials contained in that newspaper. This index is usually kept in the reference rooms of large libraries.

Ordinarily, the publishers of periodicals assign a **volume number** to all the issues published in a given year. For example, Volume 23 of *Rhetors Monthly,* dated 1992, indicates that all issues of this journal published in 1992 will be bound together as volume 23; each will have a separate issue number. The volume number most likely indicates that *Rhetors Monthly* has been published for twenty-three years. Its title indicates that this journal probably appears twelve times a year, so there will be twelve issues in each volume. The May issue, then, should be labeled "Vol. 23, No. 5." Sometimes page numbers are consecutive throughout a volume. The text of issue number one begins with page 1, but the text of the May issue begins with the number that comes after the number on the last page of the April issue.

Libraries

Libraries are to literate information storage what vivid images of city streets were to artificial memory. To be really useful, the literate storage systems used to organize libraries have to be memorized. Students who compose discourse in response to school assignments should study the indexing system used by the nearest library. Find out whether the library uses the Dewey Decimal or the Library of Congress cataloging system. Get a copy of the library handout that explains the system, and memorize as much of it as you can. Get a map of the library, and find the reference room.

A few libraries still catalog their holdings in large cases called **card catalogues.** (Some libraries that have switched to electronic cataloging still retain card catalogues as resources for finding older holdings.) These are ordinarily arranged according to three indexing systems: by author, by title, and by subject. If you know the author or the title of a book you are looking for, you can open the drawer that contains cards listing authors' names or titles that occur in the appropriate section of the alphabet. If you are searching for materials on a given subject, you can use the alphabetical listing of standard subject headings used by the Library of Congress, which is usually available somewhere nearby the card catalogue. Other reference materials, such as the *Readers' Guide to Periodical Literature,* are also organized according to author, title, and subject. If you need help in using these basic reference materials, take a library tour, or ask a reference librarian to explain the basic reference system to you.

If the library you use is a large university library, walk through it in order to find where materials catalogued under each section of the system are stored. Ask a reference librarian to tell you when the library's periodicals began to be stored on microforms. Memorize that date or write it down. This information can save you time otherwise spent walking between the rooms that house printed periodicals and those where microforms can be read.

Most libraries divide their periodical holdings into two categories: bound and current. **Bound periodicals** are older issues of newspapers, magazines, and journals that have either been bound together into a book according to year of publication or volume number, or that have been transferred to microforms for ease of storage. **Current periodicals** are piled on shelves just as they are; most libraries retain current issues of periodicals in their current periodical section for at least several months, depending on how often the periodical is issued. Daily newspapers, for example, are bound more often because they are so bulky. Bound and current periodicals are sometimes housed in different locations in a large library.

The rooms and shelves that hold books are called **stacks.** Most libraries allow everyone to browse the stacks. You can find books in the stacks by continually referring to the indexing system that is ordinarily posted or painted on walls; but library research goes much faster if you memorize at least the sections of the system to which you frequently refer. Once you have memorized the Library of Congress numbers that you use most often, for example, you can use the system heuristically. That is, you know where relevant materials are likely housed, and you can find them by browsing the appropriate shelves in the library. If you know that books on rhetoric are housed under Library of Congress call numbers that begin with PN or PR, for example, you do not have to remember specific titles or authors' names in order to find their work. (This method of searching also saves searchers the frustration of finding that materials cited in a card catalog have been checked out.) Of course, a thorough search of relevant materials requires use of the library's cataloging systems.

ELECTRONIC MEMORY SYSTEMS

Electronic memory represents a vast improvement on both artificial memory and literate storage facilities. Nowadays, computers can remember more information than any single human will ever need. It is no longer necessary for researchers to develop elaborate card systems to help them remember bibliographic information, since this information can be called up from the electronic **databases** of any good library at any time of the day or night and from any location where there are computer terminals. Note-taking can be done wherever research takes place, at the keyboard of a portable computer or with the aid of a portable scanning device. Soon (perhaps by the time you read this), oral composing will be done electronically with the aid of voice-activated word-processing programs that can remember and store every sound uttered by a composer.

Computer programs are now available that serve the heuristic functions of ancient memory—something that literate storage could not do. There are now programs that remember where any file in an electronic system is located, even if their users can't remember the file's name, let alone where they stored it. Dictionaries, encyclopedias, thesauruses, collections of proverbs and quotations—reference materials of all kinds—are now available on disk or CD-ROM. These electronic references have elaborate cross-referencing systems that are larger and far more subtle than human memory; they will search for related information in places where humans would never think to look. Electronic databases have eliminated the need to use literate cataloging systems; a researcher can simply type in a word or name or call number and the database will display all related items held by that library or any others to which it is connected.

Electronic databases contain records of most, if not all, materials published in popular periodicals since the database was compiled. Many libraries subscribe to more specialized databases that are organized by field or subject: business, humanities, sciences. Most such databases are user-friendly, providing users with step-by-step instructions for entering and using them. Libraries usually supply directions on paper, as well, and librarians can always be called on to help with a search of library holdings.

It is an open question whether electronic memory will replace human memory. It is probably more accurate to think of electronic memory as a supplement to, or expression of, human memory. The sci-fi image of the cyborg—part human, part machine—need no longer be limited to movie creations like the Terminator. Imagine Simonides seated before a fast computer equipped with plenty of RAM, efficient word-processing and telecommunications facilities, a CD-ROM drive, a scanner, access to the Web and many megabytes of information stored on disk. We suspect that he would program his machine with one or several of the electronic memory systems that are now available, but he could program and install a version of the artificial memory system he created in the fifth century BCE. Would he then quit using his mental memory system to remember things and their relations, relying instead only on his computer whenever he needed to remember something? We think not. We think he would continue to use both. In fact, interaction with his machine might stimulate Simonides to achieve even more dazzling feats of memory than those he displayed during the fifth century BCE.

CHAPTER 14

DELIVERY

What a great difference there is in persuasiveness between discourses which are spoken and those which are to be read . . . the former are delivered on subjects which are important and urgent, while the latter are composed for display and gain . . . when a discourse is robbed of the prestige of the speaker, the tones of his voice, the variations which are made in the delivery, and, besides, of the advantages of timeliness and keen interest in the subject matter . . . when it has not a single accessory to support its contention and enforce its plea . . . in these circumstances it is natural, I think, that it should make an indifferent impression upon its hearers.

—Isocrates, "To Philip," 25–27.

FOR ANCIENT RHETORS and rhetoricians, spoken discourse was infinitely more powerful and persuasive than was written composition. Most discourses were composed in order to be performed, and, as ancient lore about memory makes clear, composition could be accomplished without the aid of writing.

The ability to write was not widespread in ancient cultures. While most members of classical Greek aristocracy could read, it was not fashionable to do one's own writing, and so those who did compose dictated their work to a scribe. Those who could write probably edited the scribe's work, especially if they planned to publish a written version of a composition. Nonetheless, they may have done this orally as well, by asking the scribe to read his copy aloud. These practices remained in vogue within Roman culture even among people who wrote easily, like Cicero.

But the relative importance of spoken discourse was not only related to the scarcity of writing ability. Rhetoric was invented for use within very small cultures, where citizens knew one another by sight, if not personally. The agora and the forum were not large by the modern standards set by arenas such as the Astrodome in Houston or Madison Square Garden in New York City. Of course, the ancients had few ways to amplify their voices, as is done electronically today, and so the sites of public gatherings were necessarily small.

Ancient rhetoricians would be very surprised by the modern association of intelligence and education with literacy—the ability to read and write. For them, writing was an accessory technology, a support for memory as a way of storing information (*Institutes* XI 11, 10). Throughout antiquity, discourse was primarily composed to be spoken. Because of this, the ancients were very concerned about how speeches ought to be delivered: the proper management of the voice, bodily movement, and gestures. Because of this concern, they made delivery the fifth canon of rhetoric. In our own time, these features of rhetoric are becoming important once again, since we appear to be moving away from our primary dependence on the printed word and into dependence on electronic storage and transfer of information and cultural productions.

However, the delivery of written discourse is not without interest and usefulness. Much of our communication is still carried on through printed media, and some of the conventions of print have been transferred into electronic discourse—as in faxing and e-mail, for example. These media are creating their own conventions, which differ from the conventions that govern page literacy. Nonetheless, it may be useful for students of rhetoric to review some of the conventions developed for printed media, and we do so later in this chapter.

ANCIENT COMMENTARY ON DELIVERY

The Greek word for delivery was *hypokrisis,* and yes, the English word "hypocrisy" is a direct descendant. The term comes from a verb (*hypokrinesthai*) used to describe the work of the actor who responded to the chorus in Greek tragedy. Later, the term *hypokrites* meant simply "actor." There are many stories about ancient orators learning the craft of delivery from famous actors. Plutarch recounted this one about Demosthenes:

> when the assembly had refused to hear him, and he was going home with his head muffled up, taking it very heavily, they relate that Satyrus, the actor, followed him, and being his familiar acquaintance, entered into conversation with him. To whom, when Demosthenes bemoaned himself, that having been the most industrious of all the pleaders, and having almost spent the whole strength and vigor of his body in that employment, he could not yet find any acceptance with the people, that drunken sots, mariners, and illiterate fellows were heard, and had the hustings for their own, while he himself was despised, "You say true, Demosthenes," replied Satyrus, "but I will quickly remedy the cause of all this, if you will repeat to me some passage out of Euripides or Sophocles." Which when Demosthenes had pronounced, Satyrus presently taking it up after him, gave the same passage, in his rendering of it, such a new form, by accompanying it with the proper mien and gesture, that to Demosthenes it seemed quite another thing. By this, being convinced how much grace and ornament language acquires from action, he began to esteem it a small matter, and as good as nothing for a man to exercise himself in declaiming, if he neglected enunciation and delivery. Hereupon he built himself a place to study in under ground (which was still remaining in our time), and hither he would come constantly every day to form his action and to exercise his voice; and here he would continue, often times without intermission, two or three months together, shaving one half of his head, that so for shame he might not go abroad, though he desire it ever so much. (1025–1026)

However much rhetors could learn from actors, there was still a difference between their arts. As Cicero pointed out, orators act in real life, while actors mimic reality (*De Oratore* III lvi, 214–215).

Modern scholars are not sure when delivery began to be included among the rhetorical canons. The fourth-century *ad Alexandrum* included only invention, arrangement, and style. Aristotle briefly discussed delivery, however (*Rhetoric* III i, 1402b–1404a). In a very interesting aside, he noted that no systematic treatment of delivery had yet been composed, and he speculated that this was the case because "originally, the poets themselves acted their tragedies." What this means is that by the time Aristotle composed the *Rhetoric* (ca. 330 BCE), professional actors had replaced poets as reciters of tragedies. These actors must have learned to recite tragedies in one of two ways: either by memorizing them while the poets recited, or by memorizing written copies produced by scribes. In other words, by this time performance could be separated from composition; the person who composed the play did not need to be the same person who delivered it. Now the actor was copying the words composed by the poet, but he did not have to copy the poet's performance into the bargain. Likely, actors imbued their performances with their own interpretations, and this mimicry is what set Aristotle's teeth on edge.

This state of affairs lends another level of meaning to the term *hypokrites:* An actor is someone who pretends to be somebody else. It also means that acting and delivery could now become arts, with principles that could be learned and transmitted to others. Once these arts were written down, they could be learned without the example of a teacher, although in the case of delivery a teacher's example is always helpful.

In his comments on delivery in the *Rhetoric,* Aristotle remarked in passing that performers who give careful attention to delivery "are generally the ones who win poetic contests; and just as actors are more important than poets now in the poetic contests, so it is in political contests because of the sad state of governments." This analogy—actors are to poets as orators are to statesmen—indicates a quite conservative attitude toward Athenian democracy on Aristotle's part. Just as poets are somehow the "real" owners and creators of their compositions, aristocrats are the "real" owners and creators of government. With the establishment of acting and rhetoric as arts that anyone could learn, poetic compositions, like political decision making, were available to anyone, and not just to those who fancied they had some natural talent or hereditary claim to them. This state of affairs apparently disgruntled Aristotle.

Even though he thought delivery was a "vulgar matter," Aristotle paid it some attention. He wrote that delivery "was a matter of how the voice should be used in expressing each emotion." The expression of emotion could be altered by variations in volume, pitch, and rhythm. He also distinguished between oral and written delivery, noting that "where there is most need of performance, the least exactness is present" (III 12, 1414a). In other words, written discourse must be more precise than spoken discourse.

Aristotle's student, Theophrastus, was widely credited throughout antiquity with having written a treatise on delivery. But this treatise, if it ever existed, has been lost. While Hellenistic rhetoricians regularly remarked that delivery was the most important of the canons, they didn't have much to say about it. Indeed, the author of *ad Herennium* stated flatly that no consistent treatment of delivery had ever been composed, and that text provided us with the oldest account that we possess.

Discussions of delivery do appear in all of Cicero's theoretical works on rhetoric and in Quintilian's *Institutes* as well. Both authors associate delivery with the stylistic excellence of appropriateness. Use of the voice and gestures should be appropriate to the rhetorical situation—delivery should be subdued on formal occasions but animated in the courtroom or legislature, especially when vigorous debate is in progress. The importance of appropriate delivery is underscored if we consider the standards of decorous delivery that governed Roman rhetoric. Apparently it was appropriate (and expected) that Roman orators would strike their brows, stamp their feet, tear their clothing, and slap their thighs. (This last gesture served to keep the crowd awake as well.) Such antics would excite only laughter or anxiety in modern audiences, who expect restrained delivery from orators. The convention of restrained delivery applies even to actors today; the only performers we exempt from this rule are stand-up comedians.

Cicero and Quintilian both argue that the proper delivery can excite the emotions. As Cicero asserted in *De Oratore*, "nature has assigned to every emotion a particular look and tone of voice and bearing of its own; and the whole of a person's frame and every look on his face and utterance of his voice are like the strings of a harp, and sound according as they are struck by each successive emotion" (III lvii, 216). People who have watched great actors at work know that emotions can be powerfully conveyed by facial gestures and tone of voice.

DELIVERY OF ORAL DISCOURSE

Ancient authorities divided their approach to oral delivery between the uses of voice and gesture. As Quintilian remarked, these two features of spoken discourse appeal to the ear and the eye, "the two senses by which all emotion reaches the soul" (XI iii, 14).

In general, the ancients recommended that speakers use a modulated tone and speak slowly and clearly. They gave a great deal of attention to the use of tone and pitch to convey emotions; but since contemporary audiences prefer that a speaker's tone and pitch reflect those that occur in conversational speech, today speakers needn't worry about such matters. Ancient rhetoricians also recommended that speakers vary the volume of their voices throughout the speech, using a louder voice to emphasize important words.

The appropriate volume to use is determined to some extent by the size of the room and the audience. People who are asked to speak in a room that does not have electronic amplification should check it out ahead of time. Ask an acquaintance to sit in the back row, and deliver a few lines of your speech from the front in order to determine whether you can be heard throughout the room. If you are using a microphone, try to maintain the same distance from it throughout your talk, so that your voice does not fade in and out.

Wise rhetoric teachers insist that anyone who speaks in public should rehearse their remarks out loud. This is good advice, and we follow it whenever we are asked to speak in a formal setting. Rehearsal is important for several reasons. First of all, practice allows you to time your remarks. Adhering to set time limit is professional and courteous when others are speaking after you, and it is a necessity for those who speak in broadcasting. Second, rehearsal helps you decide where to pause, and where you can look up at your audience in order to establish contact with them. Third, reading aloud helps you to hear the rhythms of the sentences you have written. We often read our work aloud while we are revising it. Sometimes this practice tells us where a sentence construction has gone wrong, but more often it helps us to determine which sentences are too long to read or hear easily. Sentences composed for oral delivery should never be so long that they cannot be uttered in a single breath, unless they are carefully punctuated. Long sentences are elegant if their internal punctuation, balance, and rhythm signal the relations of their parts to readers and listeners. Where this is not the case, long sentences can confuse and ultimately tire an audience.

The ancients gave elaborate advice about facial and bodily gestures. Since a speaker's face and movement could not be electronically amplified in ancient settings, gestures were very important means of amplifying the speaker's mood and conveying it to distant members of an audience. However, since modern audiences do not care for elaborate facial and bodily gestures, a very limited repertoire of these will suffice in most settings. The most important consideration is use of the eyes. As Cicero wrote, "by action the body talks . . . nature has given us eyes, as she has given the horse and the lion their mane and tail and ears, to indicate the feelings of the mind" (*De Oratore* III lix, 222–223). If you are speaking to a live audience, look at them as frequently as you can. If you are speaking before a camera, be sure to look directly into it whenever possible. Today, gestures should be as natural and spontaneous as possible. Live audiences respond surprisingly well to a few hand gestures, such as pointing the index finger to underscore an important remark, or slicing the hand downward to indicate a conclusion. But modern audiences do not expect rhetors to do much of this.

If you are interested in improving your oral delivery, you can do no better than to take Quintilian's advice to memorize a few passages of written discourse and practice reciting them aloud whenever you can. Or watch carefully speakers you admire, and try to imitate their facial gestures and vocal control. The anchors on national network news are very good speakers worthy of imitation. If you want to imitate more flamboyant deliveries, watch effective politicians, attorneys, and clergy.

DELIVERY OF WRITTEN DISCOURSE

In written discourse, delivery has to do with editing a discourse so that it is accessible and pleasant to read. Editing is the very last stage in the composing process. Writers should not attempt it until they are 95% sure that they have finished working through the other canons. Nothing stifles composing quite so quickly as trying to edit too soon. Three issues face modern rhetors during the editing process: **correctness rules, format,** and **presentation.**

Correctness Rules I: Spelling and Punctuation

Obviously, spelling and punctuation present no problems to speakers, but they can be troublesome for writers. People who are chronically bad spellers often think of themselves as bad writers. However, there is *no connection* between one's ability to spell and one's ability to write. Furthermore, if you are a bad speller, this does not (and should not) reflect negatively on your character.

People have trouble spelling English words because English spelling is irregular and erratic; it is irregular and erratic because it reflects accidents of linguistic history. For example, the "gh" in words like "light" and "bright" is there because it used to be pronounced. The written forms of these words are slowly conforming to their current pronunciation: "lite," "brite." Soon, everyone but traditional grammarians will have forgotten that they were ever spelled differently.

Happily, inability to spell is no longer a problem (for people who can afford the technology), since portable spell-checkers and electronic dictionaries are now available, and most word-processing programs have spell-checkers and dictionaries built into their files. If you can't afford to get electronic help, read as much as you can. When you come across words that are difficult for you to spell, write them down. Once a week, organize the words in alphabetical order and memorize your list (see the chapter on memory). Use the words as often as you can when you write. This method won't turn you into a champion speller overnight, but it works for most people.

Traditional grammar books contain lists of rules governing the use of punctuation. Some of these are necessary and some are not. Most are simply confusing. There are four kinds of punctuation in written discourse. The first indicates where pauses would occur if the discourse were spoken (for example, commas and periods). A second group of punctuation marks indicates the logical relations of parts of sentences to one another (semicolons and colons, parentheses and dashes). The third indicates the graphic or logical relations of larger parts of discourse (paragraphs, headers). The fourth indicates insertions or omissions.

The best advice we can give about the first and second classes of punctuation is this: read your writing aloud, and mark the places where you pause. Then put punctuation in these places. Better yet, ask someone else to read your writing aloud while you follow along on another copy. Mark the places where your reader pauses, and put punctuation there when you revise. If your reader falters, mark the passage. Usually, readers falter when writers haven't punctuated clearly enough. Wait to put in larger marks of punctuation, like paragraphs and headers, until you've drafted the entire discourse at least once. Then outline it, and use indentations and headers to mark the divisions of the discourse.

If the "play it by ear" method isn't sufficient, try memorizing or referring to the following list.

Punctuation that Marks Internal Pauses

These marks can appear within sentences.

1. Comma (,) marks a relatively weak internal pause. Used to set off short phrases (ancient commas) that would interfere with readers' understanding of the sentence, like this, if not so marked.

2. Semicolon (;) marks a stronger internal pause; like this. Used to set off clauses (ancient members or colons) from one another.

3. Colon (:) marks the strongest available internal pause: like this. Generally used to set off longer colons from the main part of a sentence; if so used, sticklers for correctness will look for semicolons at the end of each member; can also be used alone to indicate a very strong internal pause. (Sticklers don't like this use of the colon; you may have noticed that we use it a lot.)

4. One dash (—) can be used to set off some loosely connected comma from the main part of a sentence—as though it were an afterthought. Paired dashes—used to set off any *interruptio*—are appearing more frequently in modern prose (see the chapter on style for discussion of the figure known as *interruptio*). Parentheses (like these) serve essentially the same function as paired dashes (that is, they interrupt or comment on the main point of the sentence).

External Punctuation Marks

These pieces of punctuation are used to mark the beginnings and ends of sentences.

1. In modern written English, a capital letter (Latin *caput*, "head" or "chief") ordinarily marks the beginning of sentences. But a capital letter can also mark the beginning of a fragment. Like this. (In Early Modern Written English, Things were Easier, because Capitals were Used to Mark most of the Important Words. Written German still Employs this Convention.)

2. Period (.) marks the end of any punctuated sentence that makes a statement. It is also used to mark fragments that are statements. Such as this.

3. Question mark (?) marks the end of any punctuated sentence that asks a question. It also marks fragments that are questions. Got it?

4. Exclamation point (!) marks the end of any punctuated sentence that expresses some strong emotion. It also marks fragments that express strong emotion. Exclamation points are seldom used in formal discourse because they express too much emotion, thus closing the distance between rhetor and audience!

5. Indentation (the writing begins five or six spaces from the left margin). Indentation is used to mark the beginning of a new section of discourse. During the Middle Ages, when people wrote everything by hand, and when paper was scarce and expensive, it became necessary to mark off sections of longer discourses in some way so that handwritten texts would be

intelligible. Medieval scribes invented a mark for such sections, and they called it a paragraph (Greek "written separately"). Eventually the name for the mark got transferred to the section of discourse itself. Paragraphs are a necessity only in written texts, and they are a product of page literacy. Forget all that stuff about the "logic" of paragraphs and topic sentences and methods of development. Those rules about paragraphs were invented by a nineteenth-century logician named Alexander Bain, who thought that every paragraph should represent a single idea (whatever that is). (He also thought that if everyone were to write like logicians, rhetoric would disappear from the face of the earth. Bain wasn't any Cicero.)

Headers serve exactly the same function as paragraphs except that they mark larger pieces of text. We used them in this book to indicate the relations of one part of a chapter to another. But to some extent, we must confess, the choice of where to put headers is arbitrary, having as much to do with their relative length as with any internal logic of the discourse. The larger divisions of a discourse do not become clear to us until very late in the composing process.

Punctuation that Marks Omissions and Insertions

1. The mark of punctuation called an **apostrophe** (') should not be confused with the figure of the same name (see the chapter on style). Apostrophes appear only in written English, and they are there to prevent confusion. In modern English, apostrophes have three uses. First, they indicate that someone or something possesses something else, as in "Colleen's cat" or "the audience's response." If the apostrophe did not appear, readers might take the words to be plurals. In this use, apostrophes can cause their own brand of confusion if the word in which they appear ends with an "s" or an "x." At the moment, there is considerable debate about how to mark this occurrence in written English. Should one write "Socrates' belief" or "Socrates's belief"? We prefer the former, but many authors like the latter. Second, apostrophes substitute for an omitted letter. This occurs most frequently in contractions, such as "isn't" for "is not," or "don't" for "do not." They are also used, mostly in poetry, to mark the figure called *ellipsis,* where a letter has been omitted to make the meter come out right ("e'en for "even"). Third, apostrophes are used to form the plural of numbers, symbols, letters, and abbreviations: "Ph.D's"; "There were three e's in the word"; "I counted eight occurrences of 8's."

2. Quotation marks (") are used chiefly to indicate material that has been borrowed from some other text, or to show that the words they enclose are being referred to, "as in this example." When you quote or emphasize something that is already within quotation marks, use single quotation marks (that is, apostrophes) to indicate the quote-within-a-quote: "We don't 'cash' checks."

3. Ellipses (. . .) are used to mark places in quoted material where text has been omitted. Use three dots if no period occurred in the omitted text; use four if a period did appear.

If this list doesn't work for you, get hold of a writers' handbook and read the chapters on punctuation. Memorize as much as you can. If necessary, refer to these chapters when you edit your writing (but not before—trying to edit while you are inventing is the surest way we know to bring both processes to a dead halt). Or hire or beg somebody to edit your work for you.

Correctness Rules II: Traditional Grammar and Usage

Grammar becomes a problem for writers if they try to adhere to the rules laid down in traditional grammar, which is an artificial grammar imposed on English during the eighteenth century, and which observes grammatical rules borrowed from Latin. The rules of traditional grammar include this one: infinitive verbs should not be split (write "to speak carefully" rather than "to carefully speak"). In Latin, infinitive verbs could not be split, because they were a single word (*dicere,* "to speak"; *scribere,* "to write"). In English, of course, infinitives are composed of two words, which allows rhetors to insert words in between them if they wish. But this important difference doesn't stop traditional grammarians from imposing an archaic rule on writers.

Our advice concerning such traditional niceties is this: Rely on your intuitive grammatical sense about your native language when you write, and on your ear when you read your work aloud. This is good advice unless, of course, your teacher or boss is a traditional grammarian. In that case, find a writers' handbook that lists traditional rules about grammar, and use it when you edit your work, or hire someone to edit it for you, if you can afford to. If you are not a native speaker of English, continue to do what your teachers told you to do: Read and listen to the English used by native speakers whenever you can. Non-native speakers of English, and people who use dialects such as Black English, have an advantage over the many Americans who are monolingual or monodialectical because they can use the ancient exercise of **translation** to improve their grasp of both languages or dialects. Ancient rhetoricians recommended translation from one language to another as a useful means of understanding the grammar of a second language, as well as its rhythmic patterns (see the chapter on imitation).

Usage is another matter altogether. Usage can be defined neutrally as the customary ways in which things are done in written discourse. A more biased and yet more accurate definition is this: usage rules are the conventions of written English that allow Americans to discriminate against one another. Questions of usage are tied to social attitudes about who is intelligent and well-educated, and who is not. People who say "I ain't got no idea" obviously learned to say this somewhere, probably in their native community. If they were to say this in other settings or to write it, they risk being marked as illiterate, uneducated, and possibly stupid in the bargain. This is manifestly unfair, since their usage is perfectly appropriate in their native community. Despite their manifest unfairness, however, usage rules do exist; they are enforced by people with power (such as our copyeditor); and so they must be observed in situations where they have been deemed important.

Because of its social aspect, usage differs from grammar, which describes the rules people use to form utterances in their native languages. Many of the rules of usage are drawn from traditional grammar, which is not a natural grammar because it does not describe language as it is actually used. Its rules represent an attempt to freeze the language in time, to create a standard for "good English" that allows people who care to do so to mark deviations from it. Utterances that are deemed bad usage in terms of traditional grammar may be perfectly grammatical (and appropriate) in the language or dialect from which they are drawn.

The usages that raise the hackles of traditional grammarians involve perceived misuses of verb forms, pronouns, and adverbs. Writers should try to avoid using verb forms that are perceived as incorrect ("She blowed into town" rather than the standard "She blew into town"). They should insure that the number (plural or singular) of the main verb in any sentence agrees with the number of the main noun. ("She blow into town," rather than "She blows into town" violates standard usage. The first construction is perfectly appropriate in some dialects of English, but people who use usage rules to discriminate disapprove of its use in writing.)

Writers should also try not to use objective-case pronouns in subject positions ("Her and him blew into town"). This archaic rule really irritates us, because case endings are not necessary to preserve meaning in English, as they were in Latin, and so they are not often observed in spoken English. People answering a phone don't often say "It is I" or "this is she"; they say "It's me" and "this is her" and are perfectly understood. But the usage police disapprove of case-switching, and we are obliged to report this to you.

Another traditional rule of usage cautions writers to avoid double or triple negatives ("I *ain't* got *no* idea," "It *don't* make me *no never* mind"). Of course, absolute observance of this rule would make it impossible to use the ancient figure called *litotes* ("this is *not un*expected"). Standard usage doesn't let you double up on comparative adverbs, either ("She blew into town acting *more crazier* than ever"). It also dictates that writers avoid substituting adjectives for adverbs, especially with the pair "good" (adjective) and "well" (adverb). "She blew into town real good" is not acceptable in standard usage, because "good" modifies "blew" which is a verb, and, as every good usage police officer knows, only adverbs can modify verbs, and only adjectives (and pronouns) can modify nouns.

Those are the usage rules that bother everyone who sets themselves up as arbiters of right and wrong uses of the written language. There are a few others that bother the real strict usage police (we committed a usage error in that sentence—can you spot it?). One of these is sentence fragments. Some people don't like other people to write sentences that don't have subjects or verbs: "So there"; "Even though she reads Milton." This nonsense derives from an eighteenth-century superstition about sentences, which supposed that every sentence represents a complete thought. Whatever that is.

Usually, reading your writing aloud will tell you when you have committed a fragment. You need to answer two questions about any fragment that appears in your writing: Did you commit it intentionally? Will your audience love and appreciate it as much as you do? If the answers to both questions are "no," attach the fragment to some nearby sentence by means of internal punctuation.

An opposite breach of usage rules occurs when a sentence has two members, or an internal comma, that have not been marked off by internal punctuation. This is often called a "run-on" or "fused" sentence. This can be cured by reading aloud and paying careful attention to the places where pauses occur. Mark them with internal punctuation.

If you have difficulty understanding why these problems are problems, or how to correct them, find a writers' handbook that devotes sections to traditional grammar and usage. Read the explanations. Do the exercises. Consult them when you edit. If you don't commit any of these breaches of usage, throw a party and forget about them.

Documentation Conventions

Most professional groups have produced lists of rules for formatting any texts used in their field. These are usually (and misleadingly) called "style sheets," but they would be more correctly named "lists of editing conventions." They review the accepted conventions adopted by a specific group of writers regarding headers, footnotes, spacing, documentation, and the like. Many also include discussions of the grammar ticks that irritate people who work in a particular profession.

Journalists use a style sheet compiled by the Associated Press (AP), humanists use a style book produced by the Modern Language Association (MLA) and most people who work in the social sciences subscribe to the conventions set down in the style book produced by the American Psychological Association (APA). There are also style sheets for general use, such as those by Turabian and Campbell. Anyone who works in a discipline should find out which formatting rules are preferred by its members, and use these. If you are a student, ask your professors which format they prefer, and use it. Most style sheets are available in the reference sections of bookstores and libraries.

Textual Presentation

The last part of written delivery concerns the physical appearance of the manuscript itself. Capable rhetors make things easy for their audiences, and the features of presentation that we survey here are designed to do just that for readers.

When it comes to physical presentation of the written text, contemporary rhetors are faced with a variety of choices; indeed, textual features and page layouts are an "available means of persuasion," to employ Aristotle's definition of rhetoric. Standard word-processing programs offer several kinds of fonts and various styles (italic, bold, underline, shadow), thus necessitating an attention to the effects of different typographical choices. Typographical choices divide into three basic categories: design, size, and style (Dragga and Gong, 142).

In design discourse, fonts are categorized as either *serif* or *sans serif*. Serif type features a fine line that finishes off the main strokes of a letter, as in the font used in this book. The term "sans serif" means "without serifs," and looks like this. Generally, serif type is thought to be more reader friendly, since the enhanced edges of each letter help the eyes move more easily through the words; serif type is also considered to be more traditional and formal while sans serif looks more contemporary. Design experts also claim that serif and sans serif designs put forth a particular character; specialists Sam Dragga and Gwendolyn Gong, for instance, claim that "serif type seems artistic, designed with grace and flourish; sans serif type looks clean, objective, direct" (143). In short, fonts present a particular ethos.

Further, typefaces are available in different sizes and styles. The measuring unit for a typeface is points; there are 72 points in an inch, so a capital letter "M" in a 72 point font will be about an inch wide. A readable type size is 10 to 12 point type; smaller than 8 point type may strain the readers' eyes. Many writers, especially journalists, use large fonts as a way of drawing the readers' eyes to important material. The more urgent the news headline, the larger the typesize of the headline, and readers' eyes are trained to recognize this correlation between size and importance.

Typestyles are another way to assist readers by adding emphasis. Some basic type style choices include plain, bold, italic, outline, and shadow. Plain, bold, and italic are the most commonly used typestyles. The bold style usually indicates emphasis of importance; for example, we use boldface type to draw attention to the key terms in this text. Italic type also indicates emphasis, sometimes imparting a particularly forceful tone to the italicized word or words. The main thing for rhetors to remember when experimenting with typeface and style is consistency; if bold is used for headings and italics for subheadings, then this should be a constant textual feature. Inconsistent or arbitrary changes in typestyle can be distracting for readers.

Another key element of textual presentation is page layout. The most common page size is 8½" × 11", and once rhetors allow room for at least 1" margins all around, the area of the page becomes 6½" × 9". The major layout issues deal with general organization of information and page format, but they also extend to the use of visual aids (photographs, charts, tables). We believe that good page layout works together with typeface to guide the reader's eye across and down the page, providing textual cues to indicate important information. Moreover, a well designed page is one that achieves visual balance, that is, the text works together with the white space and other layout elements such as visuals to focus readers' attention.

White space can be an effective rhetorical tool; room left in the margins and spaces between the typed lines make the page look more inviting to read, and many readers (especially teachers and supervisors) like to have space in which to write responses. While too little white space can make a text seem crowded and intimidating, too much white space can cause the text to get lost on a page or send certain signals to readers. If the bottom margin, for example, is larger than the top margin, then the reader may think she has reached the end of the discourse and might not turn the page. Headers and subheaders are useful in longer arguments to "chunk" texts and allow extra space for readers to pause and consider important shifts in arguments.

Balance with the written text is also important when using visuals. Consider, for example, the opening page to each chapter in this book. In Western cultures, the reading eye moves from left to right and top to bottom. Note how the opening page to each chapter offers a graphic—the top of a classical column—at the upper left corner of the page. This column draws in the reader's eye and directs it to the epigraph, written in italics, underneath the column. Then, next to the column, in a larger typesize and bold style is the chapter title. The title is followed by significant amount of white space in order to let the readers pause momentarily before diving into the introductory portion of the chapter. Because the page layout seems fairly complicated, featuring a graphic, three different type styles, and two columns of text, we provided ample white space to allow a "break" from the written text, thus guiding readers' eyes slowly down the page.

With recent advances in desktop publishing systems, design options that were formerly available only to professional publishers are now widely available. We encourage you to experiment with various options, but remember to consider the effects on your reader if the pages are cluttered or design choices seem arbitrary and inconsistent. Rhetors interested in issues of graphic design might consult the list of sources at the end of this chapter, or, for the most up-to-date material, we recommend checking out the graphic design section at the local bookstore.

CYBERRHETORS

Until now, we have focused on design issues for the printed page. But these issues also extend—in a much different way—to writing in cyberspace. Those who have surfed on the World Wide Web have probably realized what an expansive, versatile, and convenient medium it is. The design choices available for delivering information on the internet are virtually limitless. In addition to the typographical choices available for the printed page, rhetors may choose background patterns and colors, and they have easy access to all kinds of dynamite graphics—blinking icons, moving pictures, fun sounds—that can enhance the design of hypertext.

Cyberdelivery brings with it new vocabularies as well. For instance, in addition to "points" as a measurement for fonts is the term *pixel*, which refers to the dots that comprise an image or character on a computer monitor or TV screen—resolution increases with the number of pixels. Since there is already a flood of information available on Web design, at the end of this chapter we offer a guide to available resources for rhetors interested in spinning their rhetorical abilities onto the Web.

EXERCISES

1. Choose a punctuation mark—the dash, the comma, the semicolon, or any mark discussed in this chapter—and do a little research on how it is used. Consult a variety of textual sources: magazines, newspaper articles, textbooks, ads in buses and trains, instructions on the back of a shampoo bottle. Note the instances in which writers use that particular punctuation mark. From the usages you observe, write a one page analysis of the various

functions of the mark. Did different writers use the same mark in contradictory ways? What rhetorical effects did the various usages have on you?

2. Tape record a conversation with a group of friends and transcribe it, using only periods to punctuate. Then go back through the transcription while replaying the tape, and place the various punctuation mark where you hear distinctive pauses. Write a brief analysis of the editorial choices you made: How did you decide to use a semicolon? Did you use any dashes? If so why?

3. Explore the relationship between design choices and ethos by examining a few different magazines, focusing on the typography, page layout, and spacing. What effects do the design choices have on you as a reader? Is there a connection between the ideology of the publication and the font choices?

4. Log on to the internet and examine the design of several different websites. Click on a few links that look interesting, then return to the home page. What kind of ethos does the website foster? That is, what pictures do you have of the website creator or the organization that it represents? What is the apparent purpose of the website (education/self-promotion/resource hub?) Now, look at the design features. What background colors and patterns are conducive to reader/text interaction? What font colors work well? How do pictures help facilitate communication? Is spacing used efficiently? Which sites look "cluttered" and why? What are some rhetorical effects of cluttering?

RESOURCES FOR PRINT DESIGN

Dragga, Sam and Gwendolyn Gong. *Editing: The Design of Rhetoric.* Amityville: Baywood, 1989.

Hale, Constance, ed. *Wired Style: Principles of English Usage in the Digital Age.* San Francisco: HardWired, 1996.

Mason, Lisa D. "Design Issues for Producing Effective Multimedia Presentations." *Technical Communication,* First Quarter, 1997: 65–71.

Parker, Roger C. *Looking Good in Print: A Guide to Basic Design for Desktop Publishing.* 3rd ed. Chapel Hill: Ventana Communications, 1993.

Ver Hague, James C. "Graphic Design for Desktop Publishing, Part 1: Typography." *Journal of Biological Photography* 59 (July 1991): 117–123.

_____. "Graphic Design for Desktop Publishing, Part 2: Layouts." *Journal of Biological Photography* 60 (January 1992): 25–31.

RESOURCES FOR WEB DESIGN

DiNucci, Darcy. *Elements of Web Design.* Berkeley: Peachpit Press, 1997.

Fraterdeus, Peter. *Killer Web Design: Typography.* Indianapolis: Hayden, 1997.

Horton, William K. *The Web Page Design Cookbook, All the Ingredients You Need to Create 5-Star Web Pages.* New York: Wiley, 1995.

McCoy, John. *Mastering Web Design.* San Francisco: Sybex, 1996.

Morris, Mary E. S. *Web Page Design: A Different Multimedia.* Mountain View, SunSoft Press, 1996.

Siegel, David. *Creating Killer Websites: The Art of Third-Generation Site Design.* Indianapolis: Hayden, 1996.

Waters, Crystal. *Web Concept and Design.* 2nd ed. Indianapolis: New Riders, 1997.

Wilson, Stephen. *World Wide Web Design Guide.* Indianapolis: Hayden, 1995.

WORK CITED

Dragga, Sam and Gwendolyn Gong. *Editing: The Design of Rhetoric.* Amityville: Baywood, 1989.

IMITATION:
ACHIEVING
COPIOUSNESS

*In the art of rhetoric,
credit is won not by gifts
of fortune, but by efforts
of study. For those who
have been gifted with
eloquence by nature and
by fortune, are governed
in what they say by
chance, and not by any
standard of what is best,
whereas those who have
gained this power by
study and by the
exercise of language
never speak without
weighing their words,
and so are less often in
error as to a course of
action.*

—Isocrates,
Antidosis, 292

CONTEMPORARY RHETORS SOMETIMES assume that great writers are born with an inherent creative ability that is denied to the rest of us. This myth about writing is so powerful in our culture that it sometimes discourages people from even trying to learn how to write better. But the myth isn't true. Ancient teachers recognized that the ability to compose fluently and efficiently resulted from a lifetime of study and practice. Moreover, as Isocrates observed, study and practice are in some ways superior to talent. A writer who is only gifted may produce good work on occasion. Study and practice, on the other hand, guarantee the production of good work on every occasion.

Ancient orators and teachers of rhetoric everywhere extolled the virtues of study and practice. Demosthenes, the greatest ancient Greek rhetor, shaved half his head so that he would be too ashamed to go out of the house and leave his studies. Cicero, the greatest Roman rhetor, wrote that skill in rhetoric derived from "painstaking," which included "carefulness, mental concentration, reflection, watchfulness, persistence and hard work" (*De Oratore* II, 35).

Students can learn an art by imitating the example of people who are good at it. Watching Michael Jordan or Lisa Leslie play basketball is an exhilarating experience, and we can learn some beautiful basketball moves by watching them work the court. But the examples set by outstanding models can be made clearer if we study with a coach or teacher. A coach can explain the rules of basketball, show us how each member of a team relates to the other, and develop game plans and strategies that may make up for lack of individual ability.

Another way to learn any art is to study its principles. A cookbook enhances and reinforces what we learn by watching Julia Child put together an exotic dessert, because the cookbook provides us with basic principles that Child never bothers to mention: weights and measures, the effect of temperature on various foods, and so forth. In fact, study of principles has an advantage over learning from either models or teachers: principles can be studied anytime, anywhere. In the other modes of learning, students need a highly skilled or trained person to work with. If a model or a teacher is not available, students who have access to principles can continue their studies on their own.

But practice is important too. The ancients believed that regular practice put people in the habit of composing, so that they could begin easily and work without stopping. Quintilian borrowed a Greek term, *hexis* or "habit," to describe the "assured facility" with which capable writers use the strategies and knowledge they possess (X i, 1). The Latin term for this supply of arguments was *copia*, "abundance." In his autobiography, Cicero remarked that he did rhetorical exercises every day while he was studying philosophy (*Brutus,* 310). He continued to compose rhetorical exercises throughout his lifetime, even after he had become an acclaimed public speaker. Ancient teachers also thought that daily practice in speaking or composing was crucial for the attainment and maintenance of *hexis* and *copia;* as Quintilian remarked, "facility is mainly the result of habit and exercise" (X vii, 8). He compared the orator who had completed his course of study to an athlete "who has learned all the technique of his art from his trainer," and who then "is to be prepared by actual practice for the contests in which he will have to engage" (i, 4).

ANCIENT RHETORICAL EXERCISES

Ancient students practiced a number of oral and written exercises intended to enhance their skills and their stocks of rhetorical resources. These included a variety of exercises in imitation, translation, and paraphrase, as well as elementary exercises in amplification of **fables, tales, maxims,** and **commonplaces.** More difficult advanced exercises, such as the composition of **characters,** were practiced by mature rhetors throughout their careers.

All of these exercises required students to copy the work of some admired author or to elaborate on a set theme. Ancient dependence upon material composed by others may seem strange to modern students, who have been taught that their work should be original. But ancient teachers and students would have found the notion of originality quite strange; they assumed that real skill lay in being able to imitate or to improve on something written by others. Isocrates described ancient attitudes about original composition in a passage from *Panegyricus:*

> since language is of such a nature that it is possible to discourse on the same subject matter in many different ways—to represent the great as lowly or invest the little

> with grandeur, to recount the things of old in a new manner or set forth events of re-cent date in an old fashion—it follows that one must not shun the subjects upon which others have composed before, but must try to compose better than they. For the deeds of the past are, indeed, an inheritance common to us all; but the ability to make proper use of them at the appropriate time, to conceive the right sentiments about them in each instance, and to set them forth in finished phrase, is the peculiar gift of the wise. . . . We should honor . . . not those who seek to discourse on subjects on which no one has discoursed before, but those who know how to use discourse as no one else could. (8–10)

Ancient teachers were not in the business of developing individual personalities or teaching self-expression. They knew that cultures were held together by im-portant themes, and that these themes are reproduced in speeches and writing on many different occasions. Thus they encouraged students of rhetoric to re-work important themes and to imitate revered pieces of discourse as prepara-tion for their roles as citizens. The rhetorical exercises that imitated or elaborated on the work of well-known authors had the double effect of ac-quainting students with the best products of their culture at the same time as they increased their stock of available arguments.

The rhetorical exercises are meant to be written, even though the discourses which result from them eventually may be delivered orally. Cicero and Quintil-ian were both great fans of writing practice as a means of attaining copia. In *De Oratore,* Cicero's spokesman, Crassus, recommended that aspiring rhetors "write as much as possible. The pen is the best and most eminent author and teacher of eloquence" (I xxxii, 150). Quintilian quoted this passage and added his own praise for writing practice: "We must therefore write as much as possi-ble and with the utmost care. For as deep plowing makes the soil more fertile for the production and support of crops, so, if we improve our minds by something more than mere superficial study, we shall produce a richer growth of knowl-edge and shall retain it with greater accuracy" (X iii, 2).

At first, these exercises may seem strange and uncomfortable to modern students, since, as we have said elsewhere, it is the modern custom to aim at clarity and economy rather than at copiousness. The exercises become less strange and uncomfortable with practice, however. And the practice pays off: if you do a bit of composing every day, you should soon see a dramatic improve-ment in your powers of invention and arrangement, and in your stylistic flu-ency as well.

Historians do not know exactly when ancient rhetoric teachers began to in-clude formal exercises in their instruction. The use of imitation as a means of learning, at least, must be very old. According to Quintilian, the desire to imi-tate is universal among humans, if not entirely natural:

> It is a universal rule of life that we should wish to copy what we approve in others. It is for this reason that children copy the shapes of letters that they may learn to write, and that musicians take the voices of their teachers, painters the works of their predecessors, and farmers the principles of agriculture which have been proved in practice, as models for their imitation. In fact, we may note that the elementary

study of every branch of learning is directed by reference to some definite standard that is placed before the learner. (*Institutes* X ii, 1)

Before the advent of writing, rhapsodes and actors must have learned their arts, in part, by studying and imitating their teachers.

Most likely, imitation was introduced into the formal curriculum of rhetorical instruction by the Older Sophists, who taught by example rather than precept. That is, they composed and delivered sample speeches, and their students attempted to imitate both the master's compositions and his delivery. According to Cicero, Gorgias and Protagoras composed lists of commonplaces; if so, students might have imitated these as well (*Brutus,* 46–47). And surely the *Dissoi Logoi* and Antiphon's *Tetralogies,* both of which date from the fifth century BCE, are rhetorical exercises meant for imitation by students, since neither refers to any specific circumstances (as would be the case with speeches composed for actual use).

The sophistic practice of imitation remained popular throughout ancient times. Greek and Roman teachers of rhetoric developed a variety of exercises in which students copied, or imitated, the work of admired authors; these included reading aloud, **copying, imitation, translation,** and **paraphrase.**

Reading Aloud and Copying

Silent reading is a modern practice. Throughout most of Western history, people read aloud, even when they were alone. Reading aloud develops an ear for sentence rhythm, and it strengthens reading skills, as well. Reading aloud from the work of others may also enable you to absorb some habits of style that are not currently in your repertoire. Quintilian thought that it improved delivery, as well (*Institutes* II v, 7). Try reading aloud from the work of writers you admire. Read aloud to yourself or to others. You can practice with any of the passages quoted in this chapter, or you may begin by reading your own work aloud. In fact, you should get in the habit of reading your own writing aloud; this will help you to spot places where punctuation is needed (or not), and to determine whether the rhythm of the sentence is pleasing to the ear.

Since ancient times, people have copied out passages from their reading that they wished to remember or to consult later. Malcolm X, who became one of the twentieth century's most compelling orators, used the ancient technique of copying as a means of learning:

> I saw that the best thing I could do was get hold of a dictionary—to study, to learn some words. I was lucky enough to reason also that I should try to improve my penmanship. It was sad. I couldn't even write in a straight line. It was both ideas together that moved me to request a dictionary along with some tablets and pencils from the Norfolk Prison Colony school.
>
> I spent two days just riffling uncertainly through the dictionary's pages. I'd never realized so many words existed! I didn't know *which* words I needed to learn. Finally, just to start some kind of action, I began copying.

In my slow, painstaking, ragged handwriting, I copied into my tablet everything printed on that first page, down to the punctuation marks.

I believe it took me a day. Then, aloud, I read back, to myself, everything I'd written on the tablet. Over and over, aloud, to myself, I read my own handwriting.

I woke up the next morning, thinking about those words—immensely proud to realize that not only had I written so much at one time, but I'd written words that I never knew were in the world. Moreover, with a little effort, I also could remember what many of these words meant. I reviewed the words whose meanings I didn't remember. Funny thing, from the dictionary first page right now, that "aardvark" springs to my mind. The dictionary had a picture of it, a long-tailed, long-eared, burrowing African mammal, which lives off termites caught by sticking out its tongue as an anteater does for ants.

I was so fascinated that I went on—I copied the dictionary's next page. And the same experience came when I studied that. With every succeeding page, I also learned of people and places and events from history. Actually the dictionary is like a miniature encyclopedia. Finally the dictionary's A section had filled a whole tablet—and I went on to the B's. That was the way I started copying what eventually became the entire dictionary. It went a lot faster after so much practice helped me to pick up handwriting speed. Between what I wrote in my tablet, and writing letters, during the rest of my time in prison I would guess I wrote a million words. (172)

As Malcolm X points out, copying also enhances copia, and is an aid to memory as well.

Even though we live in the age of electronic composing, the time-honored practice of copying by hand is still useful. If you want to use copying to enhance copia, you should get in the habit of doing a little copying every day. Handwriting works better than typing, because writing by hand slows you down and helps you to focus on the passage being copied. Copy passages you admire into a notebook, word for word. Since the aim of this exercise is the achievement of copia, try to copy short passages from many different authors. As Quintilian wrote, no single author displays the best wisdom or eloquence in every passage, and so "we shall do well to keep a number of different excellences before our eyes, so that different qualities from different authors may impress themselves on our minds, to be adopted for use in the place that becomes them best" (X ii, 26). Ancient teachers helped their students with this exercise by analyzing selected passages before the students began to copy, but you can do this work for yourself. Read the whole passage carefully before you begin to copy, noting words that you may not know or structures that seem especially elegant or pleasing. Read each sentence before you begin to copy it. Above all, take your time and enjoy yourself.

A collection of copied passages is also useful, by the way, as a source of quotations and commonplaces that can be used in compositions. In premodern times, most rhetors kept written collections of copied passages; these were called *florilegia* (flowers of reading) in medieval times, and **commonplace books** during the Renaissance and into the eighteenth century. People often organized their commonplace books in the same way that ancient rhetors organized their trained memories. Erasmus, writing in the sixteenth century, recommended that students who wished to become educated begin by making a "full list of subjects" that they might read or write about (*De Copia*, 636). He suggested, for example, that the list "consist partly of the main types and subdivisions of vice and virtue, partly of the things of most prominence in human affairs which frequently occur when we have a case to put forward, and they should be arranged according to similars and opposites." The first division might be "reverence" and "irreverence." Under the section of the commonplace book devoted to reverence, Erasmus suggested, writers could copy any items they ran across that had to do with patriotism, love for children, or respect for parents and teachers.

Apparently this advice about organizing commonplace books was, well, common. The poet John Milton kept commonplace books, one each devoted to theology and law. He organized another under the headings of ethics, economy, and politics. He divided each of these main headings into smaller subsections; under ethics he copied passages dealing with virtue, chastity, and courage, along with entries on lust, drunkenness, and gluttony. A modern writer who wished to adopt this scheme might not be so interested in virtue and vice as people were in the sixteenth and seventeenth centuries. No matter. Whatever subjects or issues are of interest to a writer—business or politics or engineering or anything at all—can be listed and divided into their respective parts or into important issues. Whenever writers hear or read something that they wish to remember or use later on in their own work, they can copy it down under the appropriate heading in the commonplace book.

But a commonplace book need not feature such elaborate arrangements. Writers' commonplace books can be organized in any way that suits their working habits. If you want to look at examples of commonplace books to see how others organize them, you can find copies of the commonplace books kept by well-known people, such as Ben Jonson or Thomas Jefferson, in many libraries.

Professional writers still carry notebooks that resemble commonplace books. In keeping with this practice, we suggest that aspiring rhetors carry a notebook with them so that they can write down ideas that occur to them while they are doing other things. And when you are reading, or talking, or listening to others, you can use the notebook as a commonplace book, writing down comments or passages that you want to remember, copy, or imitate.

Imitation

In addition to reading aloud and copying, ancient rhetoricians encouraged their students to imitate the work of authors they admired. Imitation differs from simple copying; imitators may borrow the structures used in the imitated sentence, supplying their own material, or they may try to render the gist of the original passage in other words. The latter exercise is more aptly referred to as paraphrase.

Most authorities agree that the proper procedure for imitation involved copying the model, studying it carefully, and imitating its structures. Here are some sample sentences, all taken from the work of professional writers. Our imitations of the samples are fairly close in that they borrow the grammatical structures of the originals. The samples are arranged in order of increasing grammatical complexity.

A simple sentence has only one colon. Simple sentences can be expanded in all sorts of ways: for example, by the insertion of commas set off by punctuation (as is done by James and Marquez in the samples given below), or by the addition of prepositional phrases (as in the sample from Tuchman).

Simple Sentence

John loves Mary.

Sample 1

London was hideous, vicious, cruel, and above all overwhelming.

—Henry James

Imitation

Ourtown was ugly, empty, cold, and above all forbidding.

Analysis

James inserted two one-word commas into this simple sentence. The commas, separated by punctuation marks, slow readers down and help them to feel London's overwhelming atmosphere.

Sample 2

He remembered much of his stay in the womb. While there, he began to be aware of sounds and tastes. . . . Yet he was not afraid. The changes were right. It was time for them. His body was ready.

—Octavia Butler, *Adulthood Rites*

Imitation

She planned most of her day in the morning. At home, she recognized familiar sounds and smells. Yet she was not at home. The feeling was all wrong. The time was not ripe. She was not ready.

Analysis

Butler composed a string of plain simple sentences to convey the impressions felt by a sensitive young child. Strings of simple sentences can also convey other ethical effects, such as intense concentration.

Some Simple Sentences to Imitate

A phenomenon noticeable throughout history regardless of place or period is the pursuit by governments of policies contrary to their own interests.

—Barbara Tuchman, *The March of Folly*

The Antillean refugee Jeremiah de Saint-Amour, disabled war veteran, photographer of children, and his most sympathetic opponent in chess, had escaped the torments of memory with the aromatic fumes of gold cyanide.

—Gabriel Garcia Marquez, *Love in the Time of Cholera*

Early in the sixteenth century, Francis Bacon proposed that science consisted in the elevation of the authority of experiment and observation over that of reason, intuition, and convention.

—Marvin Harris, *Cultural Materialism*

Out of the back of the truck the city of San Francisco is bouncing down the hill, all those endless staggers of bay windows, slums with a view, bouncing and streaming down the hill.

—Tom Wolfe, "Black Shiny FBI Shoes"

Complex Sentence

John loves Mary even though she reads Milton.

In a complex sentence, one or more dependent colons are attached to one or more independent colons. A colon is dependent if it doesn't make sense by itself; it depends on another colon to make it complete.

Sample 1

Writing, reading, thinking, imagining, speculating. These are luxury activities, so I am reminded, permitted to a privileged few, whose idle hours of the day can be viewed otherwise than as a bowl of rice or a loaf of bread less to share with the family.

—Trinh T. Minh-ha, "Commitment from the Mirror-Writing Box"

Imitation

Aspen, sycamore, ponderosa, oak, laurel. These are the hardy trees, so I understand, classed among the privileged few, whose growth patterns in every season cannot be viewed otherwise than as a mere creeping along, a finely tuned adjustment to their surroundings.

Analysis

In this passage Minh-ha punctuated the first string of words as a sentence, even though a grammatical purist would deny them that status. In the second sentence, she interrupted the independent colon with a another, brief independent colon ("so I am reminded"), and attached a dependent colon at the end.

Sample 2

As cars slowed to a crawl and stopped, students sprang out and raced to the rear doors to begin removing the objects inside; the stereo sets, radios, personal computers; small refrigerators and table ranges; the cartons of phonograph records and cassettes; the hairdryers and styling irons; the tennis rackets, soccer balls, hockey and lacrosse sticks, bows and arrows; the controlled substances, the birth control pills and devices; the junk food still in shopping bags—onion-and-garlic chips, nacho thins, peanut creme patties, Waffelos and Kabooms, fruit chews and toffee popcorn; the Dum-Dum pops, the Mystic mints.

—Don DeLillo, *White Noise*

Analysis

This very long utterance is, nevertheless, a single complex sentence. The main colon is "students sprang out and raced to the rear doors to begin removing the objects inside." The dependent colon begins the sentence, and the rest of the sentence is filled out with noun phrases.

Some Complex Sentences to Imitate

His name was Domenico Scandella, but he was called Menocchio. He was born in 1532 (at his first trial he claimed he was fifty-two years old) in Montereale, a small hill town of the Friuli twenty-five kilometers north of Pordenone at the foot of the mountains. Here he had always lived, except for two years when he was banished following a brawl (1564–1565).

—Carlo Ginzburg, *The Cheese and the Worms*

The effect was exactly what one expects that many simultaneous crashes to produce: the unmistakable tympany of automobiles colliding and cheap-gauge sheet metal buckling, front ends folding together at the same cockeyed angles police photographs of night-time wreck scenes capture so well on grainy paper; smoke pouring from under the hoods and hanging over the infield like a howitzer cloud; a few of the surviving cars lurching eccentrically on bent axles.

—Tom Wolfe, "Clean Fun at Riverhead"

A compound sentence has two or more colons that are independent of one another. That is, each could stand alone as a simple sentence. Usually, the colons in a compound sentence are linked together by "and," "but," or "or." In order to produce a different effect, however, writers can omit the words that ordinarily connect colons in a compound sentence and substitute punctuation instead (thus producing the figure **asyndeton**).

Compound Sentences

John loves Mary but Mary despises John.

Sample 1

She was traveling alone and was too short to wield her roll easily. She tried once, and she tried twice, and finally I got up and helped her. The plane was packed: I'd never seen a plane quite so crowded before.

—Audre Lord, "Notes from a Trip to Russia"

Imitation

Mary was working hard and was too tired to deal with John well. She put it off, and put it off again, and finally she gave in and called him. The conversation was trying: she'd never known how to do this sort of thing.

Analysis

In the first sentence in this passage, Lord connected the two colons in the standard way, with "and." In the second, however, she used both punctuation and a connecting word, thus creating the figure **polysyndeton.** In the third sentence in the passage, she used a punctuation mark to connect the compound colons. Compound sentences can be used to pile up images or assertions; this piling up yields a variety of effects.

Sample 2

And I never cease to be amazed at the extent to which our reality is predicated on the premises with which we begin; or the extent to which measurement is in the eye of the beholder—or the ear of the listener.

—Dale Spender, *The Writing or the Sex?*

Analysis

Here Spender ignored the traditional advice that sentences should never begin with "and." Furthermore, she broke up her sentence at unusual and interesting points; another writer might not have employed dashes as an *interruptio* between references to "eye" and "ear," which are commonly paired.

Some Compound Sentences to Imitate

The late eighteenth century abounded in schemes of social goodness thrown off by its burgeoning sense of revolution. But here, the process was to be reversed: not Utopia, but Dystopia; not Rousseau's natural man moving in moral grace amid free social contracts, but man coerced, exiled, deracinated, in chains.

—Robert Hughes, *The Fatal Shore*

Orlando's fathers had ridden in fields of asphodel, and stony fields, and fields watered by strange rivers, and they had struck many heads of many colours off many shoulders, and brought them back to hang from the rafters.

—Virginia Woolf, *Orlando*

We called the waiter, paid, and started to walk through the town. I started off walking with Brett, but Robert Cohn came up and joined her on the other side. . . . There were many people walking to go and see the bulls, and carriages drove down the hill and across the bridge, the drivers, the horses, and the whips rising above the walking people in the street.

—Ernest Hemingway, *The Sun Also Rises*

A compound-complex sentence contains at least two independent colons and at least one dependent colon.

Compound-Complex Sentence

John loves Mary and remains faithful to her even though he reads Milton.

Sample 1

This work came together in a slow way. Always something would get in the way—relationships ending, exile, loneliness, some recently discovered pain—and I had to hurt again, hurt myself all the way away from writing, re-writing, putting the book together.

—bell hooks, *Talking Back*

Imitation

We traveled very slowly. Always events would block our progress—equipment failing, travel, illness, some newly discovered glitch—and we had to think again, re-think our work all the way back to the beginning, tinkering, improvising, putting our plans aside.

Analysis

The first sentence in this passage is, of course, a simple sentence. In the compound-complex sentence that follows, hooks inserts a comma between the two independent colons, punctuating it with dashes. She then repeats the verb of the second independent colon ("hurt") to create a dependent colon that concludes with three participial phrases (writing, re-writing, putting), thus creating the small parallelism that brings the sentence to a close.

Sample 2

In the nineteenth century, Parkinsonism was almost never seen before the age of fifty, and was usually considered to be a reflection of a degenerative process or defect of nutrition in certain "weak" or vulnerable cells; since this degeneration could not actually be demonstrated at the time, and since its cause was unknown, Parkinson's disease was termed an idiosyncrasy or "ideopathy."

—Oliver Sacks, *Awakenings*

Analysis

The first half of this sentence (before the semicolon) is a compound sentence. The second half begins with paired dependent colons, both beginning with "since"; these colons are attached to the independent colon that concludes the sentence.

Some Compound-Complex Sentences to Imitate

We all begin well, for in our youth there is nothing we are more intolerant of than our own sins writ large in others and we fight them fiercely in ourselves; but we grow old and we see that these our sins are of all sins the really harmless ones to own, nay that they give a charm to any character, and so our struggle with them dies away.

—Gertrude Stein, *The Making of Americans*

There was a man and a dog too this time. Two beasts, counting Old Ben, the bear, and two men, counting Boon Hogganbeck, in whom some of the same blood ran which ran in Sam Fathers, even though Boon's was a plebeian strain of it and only Sam and Old Ben and the mongrel Lion were taintless and incorruptible.

—William Faulkner, "The Bear"

Of course, imitation need not be limited only to sentences. Actually, imitation works best with short passages, because you can study the techniques writers use to move from sentence to sentence. Here, for example, is an interesting passage from Toni Morrison's *Song of Solomon*:

At that time of day, during the middle of the week, word-of-mouth news just lumbered along. Children were in school; men were at work; and most of the women were fastening their corsets and getting ready to go see what tails or entrails the butcher might be giving away. Only the unemployed, the self-employed, and the very young were available—deliberately available because they'd heard about it, or accidentally available because they happened to be walking at that exact moment in the shore end of Not Doctor Street, a name the post office did not recognize. (1977, 3)

Imitation

At that time of year, during the middle of winter, four-wheel drives just crept along. Cars with chains were sometimes seen; cars without were left at home; and most residents were putting on their warmest clothes and getting set to go out and see the drifts that rifted across their doorways. Only the old, the bold, and the quick-tongued were excepted—deliberately excepted because of infirmity, or grudgingly excepted because they were good at finding reasons why they should not shovel the snow piling ever higher outside, a place that at the moment they did not recognize as relevant to their lives.

Analysis

When we copied this passage, we noticed several interesting things in it. The first sentence is periodic. The second sentence begins with two balanced colons. These are connected to a third, much longer colon that itself contains two balanced pairs (the verbs "fastening" and "getting"; and the rhyming "tails or entrails"). The faint rhyming echo of "tails" and "entrails" is picked up again in the third sentence with "unemployed" and "self-employed" and the repetition, with variation, of "available." The third sentence ends with a final colon that seems like an irrelevance or a digression (in fact, the rest of the passage elaborates on it). This carrying of reference across sentences is unusual (it may be one distinguishing mark of Morrison's style); most writers would begin a new sentence to discuss the post office's failure to recognize Not Doctor Street.

As you can see, imitation does not necessarily produce great writing. It does, however, enable rhetors to recognize and use patterns that they might not otherwise notice. If you use these patterns regularly in your own writing, they rapidly become second nature.

Some Passages to Imitate

Well, children, where there is so much racket there must be something out of kilter. I think that betwixt the Negroes of the South and the women of the North all talking about rights, the white men will be in a fix pretty soon.

But what's all this here talking about? That man over there says that women need to be helped into carriages, and lifted over ditches, and to have the best place everywhere. Nobody ever helps me into carriages, or over mud puddles or gives me any best place. And ain't I a woman? Look at me! Look at my arm! I have plowed, and planted, and gathered into barns, and no man could head me. And ain't I a woman? I could work as much and eat as much as a man (when I could get it), and bear the lash as well. And ain't I a woman? I have borne thirteen children and seen them almost all sold off into slavery, and when I cried out with a mother's grief, none but Jesus heard. And ain't I a woman?

—Sojourner Truth, "Ain't I a Woman?"

Fourscore and seven years ago our fathers brought forth on this continent a new nation, conceived in liberty and dedicated to the proposition that all men are created equal.

Now we are engaged in a great civil war, testing whether that nation, or any nation so conceived and so dedicated, can long endure. We are met on a great battlefield of that war. We have come to dedicate a portion of that field as a final resting place for those who here gave their lives that that nation might live. It is altogether fitting and proper that we should do this.

But, in a larger sense, we cannot dedicate—we cannot consecrate—we cannot hallow—this ground. The brave men, living and dead, who struggled here, have consecrated it far above our poor power to add or detract. The world will little note nor long remember what we say here, but it can never forget what they did here. It is for us, the living, rather, to be dedicated here to the unfinished work which they who fought here have thus far so nobly advanced. It is rather for us to be here dedicated to the great task remaining before us—that from these honored dead we take increased devotion to that cause for which they gave the last full measure of devotion; that we here highly resolve that these dead shall not have died in vain; that this nation, under God, shall have a new birth of freedom; and that government of the people, by the people, for the people, shall not perish from the Earth.

—Abraham Lincoln, "The Gettysburg Address"

We dare not forget today that we are the heirs of that first revolution. Let the word go forth from this time and place, to friend and foe alike, that the torch has been passed to a new generation of Americans, born in this century, tempered by war, disciplined by a hard and bitter peace, proud of our ancient heritage, and unwilling to witness or permit the slow undoing of those human rights to which this nation has always been committed, and to which we are committed today at home and around the world. Let every nation know, whether it wishes us well or ill, that we shall pay any price, bear any burden, meet any hardship, support any friend, oppose any foe to assure the survival and success of liberty.

—John F. Kennedy, "First Inaugural Address"

Translation

Roman teachers regularly advised their students to translate passages from Greek into Latin and Latin into Greek. They argued that this exercise improved their students' understandings of both languages. Obviously, translation also improves one's grasp of the idioms used in a foreign language, something that is difficult to learn by studying its grammar. Translation, like imitation, also improves reading skills and enhances appreciation of good writing in any language.

Of course, translation is useful only for students who are bilingual or multilingual, or for students who are trying to learn a second or third language. But translation can also work within a single language, when students translate passages into dialects or across levels of usage. If you are lucky enough to use more than one variant of English, you may profit by translating your writing, as well as that of professional writers, into and out of both variants.

Paraphrase

In *De Oratore,* Crassus described his favorite rhetorical exercise: "this was to set myself some poetry, the most impressive to be found, or to read as much of some speech as I could keep in my memory, and then to declaim upon the actual subject matter of my reading, choosing as far as possible different words" (I xxxiv, 154). Here Crassus referred to the ancient exercise called paraphrase, which literally means "to express in other words."

Paraphrase is a very old exercise. A sophist named Theon, writing in the first century CE, provided us with some truly ancient examples of paraphrase:

> Paraphrasing Homer, when he says,
>
> > For such is the mind of men who dwell on earth
> > As the father of men and gods may bring for a day. [*Odyssey* 18.136–137]
>
> Archilochus says,
>
> > Glaucus, son of Leptines, such a spirit for mortal
> > Men is born as Zeus brings for a day.
>
> And again, Homer has spoken of a city's capture in this manner,
>
> > They kill the men, and fire levels the city,
> > But others lead away the children and deep-belted women. [*Iliad* 9.593–594]
>
> And Demosthens, thus:
>
> > Now when we were on our way in Delphi, it was of necessity to see all these things, houses razed to the ground, walls taken away, a land in the prime of life, but a few women and little children and pitiable old men. [19.361]
>
> And Aeschines, thus:
>
> > But look away in your thoughts to their misfortunes and imagine that you see the city being taken, destruction of walls, burning of houses, temples being pillaged, women and children being led into slavery, old men, old women, too late unlearning their freedom. [3.157] (Matsen, Rollinson, & Sousa, 246)

These examples, all composed during or before the fourth century BCE, indicate that paraphrase is a very old rhetorical exercise indeed.

Throughout antiquity, rhetoric teachers believed that there were many ways in which to express any meaning. As Quintilian pointed out, the variety of expression available in language can never be used up:

> if there were only one way in which anything could be satisfactorily expressed, we should be justified in thinking that the path to success had been sealed to us by our predecessors. But, as a matter of fact, the methods of expression still left us are innumerable, and many roads lead us to the same goal. (X v, 7–8)

This attitude toward the possibilities of paraphrase prevailed throughout the European Middle Ages and into the Renaissance. In his sixteenth century textbook on copia, Erasmus demonstrated that there are over 200 ways to write "Your letter pleased me mightily." He changed the word order: "your letter mightily pleased me; to a wonderful degree did your letter please me; me exceedingly did your letter please" (the last version works better in Latin than it does in English). Then he added **hyperbole** (overstatement): "Your epistle exhilarated me intensely; I was intensely exhilarated by your epistle; your brief note refreshed my spirits in no small measure; I was in no small measure refreshed in spirit by your grace's hand; from your affectionate letter I received unbelievable pleasure; your affectionate letter brought me unbelievable pleasure" (349). If you wish to see how far Erasmus was able to extend these variations on a theme, find a copy of his *De Copia* and see for yourself. You might want to try this exercise on another sentence, just to see how many variations are possible; better yet, compete with someone else to see who can write the most, or the best, paraphrases of a single sentence.

Paraphrase was still in use in modern times as a means of improving writing skill. In a famous passage of his *Autobiography,* Benjamin Franklin described the paraphrasing exercises he did as a young man:

> About this time I met with an odd volume of the *Spectator.* It was the third. I had never before seen any of them. I bought it, read it over and over, and was much delighted with it. I thought the writing excellent, and wished, if possible, to imitate it. With that view I took some of the papers, and, making short hints of the sentiment in each sentence, laid them by a few days, and then, without looking at the book, tried to complete the papers again by expressing each hinted sentiment at length, and as fully as it had been expressed before, in any suitable words that should come to hand. Then I compared my *Spectator* with the original, discovered some of my faults, and corrected them. But I found I wanted a stock of words, or a readiness in recollecting and using them, which I thought I should have acquired before that time if I had gone on making verses; since the continual occasion for words of the same import, but of different length to suit the measure, or of different sound for the rhyme, would have laid me under a constant necessity of searching for variety and also have tended to fix that variety in my mind and make me master of it. Therefore, I took some of the tales and turned them into verse; and, after a time, when I had pretty well forgotten the prose, turned then back again. I also sometimes jumbled my collections of hints into confusion, and after some weeks endeavored to reduce them into the best order, before I began to form the

full sentences and complete the paper. This was to teach me method in the arrangement of thoughts. By comparing my work afterwards with the original, I discovered many faults and amended them; but I sometimes had the pleasure of fancying that in certain particulars of small import I had been lucky enough to improve the method or the language, and this encouraged me to think I might possibly in time come to be a tolerable English writer, of which I was extremely ambitious.

Franklin knew the importance of copia—a "stock of words"—to anyone who wishes to become "a tolerable English writer." His method was similar to Crassus', except that Franklin took notes on the material he read rather than retaining it in memory.

In order to demonstrate how paraphrase works, we performed one of the exercises recommended by Franklin. The *Spectator* was a popular newspaper published in London between 1711 and 1714. It contained essays about morals, current events, education, and good taste, among other things. Essay number 157, written by Joseph Steele, was a meditation on the use of corporal punishment in British elementary schools. At the time Steele wrote this essay, such punishment was frequently used with students who failed to memorize or recite their lessons correctly. Here is the text of his essay:

> I am very much at a Loss to express by any Word that occurs to me in our Language that which is understood by *Indoles* in Latin. The natural Disposition to any particular Art, Science, Profession, or Trade, is very much to be consulted in the Care of Youth, and studied by Men for their own Conduct when they form to themselves any Scheme of Life. It is wonderfully hard indeed for a Man to judge of his own Capacity impartially; that may look great to me which may appear little to another, and I may be carried by Fondness towards my self so far, as to attempt things too high for my Talents and Accomplishments: But it is not methinks so very difficult a Matter to make a Judgment of the Abilities of others, especially of those who are in their Infancy. My common-place Book directs me on this Occasion to mention the Dawning of Greatness in *Alexander,* who being asked in his Youth to contend for a Prize in the Olympick Games, answered he would if he had Kings to run against him. *Cassius,* who was one of the Conspirators against *Caesar,* gave as great a Proof of his Temper, when in his Childhood he struck a Play-fellow, the Son of *Sylla,* for saying his Father was Master of the *Roman* People. *Scipio* is reported to have answered (when some Flatterers at Supper were asking him what the *Romans* should do for a General after his Death), Take *Marius. Marius* was then a very Boy, and had given no Instances of his Valour; but it was visible to *Scipio* from the Manners of the Youth, that he had a Soul formed for the Attempt and Execution of great Undertakings. I must confess I have very often with much Sorrow bewailed the Misfortune of the Children of *Great Britain,* when I consider the Ignorance and Undiscerning of the Generality of School-masters. The boasted Liberty we talk of is but a mean Reward for the long Servitude, the many Heart Aches and Terrours, to which our Childhood is exposed in going through a Grammer-School: Many of these stupid Tyrants exercise their Cruelty without any Manner of Distinction of the Capabilities of Children, or the Intention of Parents in their Behalf. There are many excellent Tempers which

are worthy to be nourished and cultivated with all possible Diligence and Care, that were never designed to be acquainted with *Aristotle, Tully,* or *Virgil;* and there are as many who have Capacities for understanding every Word those great Persons have writ, and yet were not born to have any Relish of their Writings. For want of this common and obvious discerning in those who have the Care of Youth, we have so many Hundred unaccountable Creatures every Age whipped up into great Scholars, that are for ever near a right Understanding, and will never arrive at it. These are the Scandal of Letters, and these are generally the Men who are to teach others. The Sense of Shame and Honour is enough to keep the World it self in Order without Corporal Punishment, much more to train the Minds of uncorrupted and innocent Children. It happens, I doubt not, more than once in a Year, that a Lad is chastised for a Blockhead, when it is good Apprehension that makes him incapable of knowing what his Teacher means: A brisk Imagination very often may suggest an Errour, which a Lad could not have fallen into if he had been as heavy in conjecturing as his Master in explaining: But there is no Mercy even towards a wrong Interpretation of his Meaning; the Sufferings of the Scholar's Body are to rectify the Mistakes of his Mind.

I am confident that no Boy who will not be allured to Letters without Blows, will ever be brought to any thing with them. A great or good Mind must necessarily be the worse for such Indignities: and it is a sad Change to lose of its Virtue for the Improvement of its Knowledge. No one who has gone through what they call a great School, but must remember to have seen Children of excellent and ingenuous Natures, (as has afterwards appeared in their Manhood;) I say no Man has passed through this Way of Education, but must have seen an ingenuous Creature expiring with Shame, with pale Looks, beseeching Sorrow, and silent Tears, throw up its honest Eyes, and kneel on its tender Knees to an inexorable Blockhead, to be forgiven the false Quantity of a Word in making a Latin Verse: The Child is punished, and the next Day he commits a like Crime, and so a third with the same Consequence. I would fain ask any reasonable Man whether this Lad, in the Simplicity of his native Innocence, full of Shame, and capable of any Impression from that Grace of Soul, was not fitter for any Purpose in this Life, than after that Spark of Virtue is extinguished in him, tho' he is able to write twenty Verses in an Evening?

Seneca says, after his exalted Way of talking, *As the immortal Gods never learnt any Virtue, tho' they are endued with all that is good; so there are some Men who have so natural a Propensity to what they should follow, that they learn it almost as soon as they hear it.* Plants and Vegetables are cultivated into the Production of finer Fruit than they would yield without that Care; and yet we cannot entertain Hopes of producing a tender conscious Spirit into Acts of Virtue, without the same Methods as is used to cut Timber, or give new Shape to a Piece of Stone.

It is wholly to this dreadful Practice that we may attribute a certain Hardness and Ferocity which some Men, tho' liberally educated, carry about them in all their Behaviour. To be bred like a Gentleman, and punished like a Malefactor, must, as we see it does, produce that illiberal Sauciness which we see sometimes in Men of Letters.

The *Spartan* Boy who suffered the Fox (which he had stolen and hid under his Coat) to eat into his Bowels, I dare say had not half the Wit or Petulance which we learn at great Schools among us: But the glorious Sense of Honour, or rather Fear of Shame, which he demonstrated in that Action, was worth all the Learning in the World without it.

It is methinks a very melancholy Consideration, that a little Negligence can spoil us, but great Industry is necessary to improve us; the most excellent Natures are soon depreciated, but evil Tempers are long before they are exalted into good Habits. To help this by Punishments, is the same thing as killing a Man to cure him of a Distemper; when he comes to suffer Punishment in that one Circumstance, he is brought below the Existence of a rational Creature, and is in the State of a Brute that moves only by the Admonition of Stripes. But since this Custom of educating by the Lash is suffered by the Gentry of *Great Britain*, I would prevail only that honest heavy Lads may be dismissed from slavery sooner than they are at present, and not whipped on to their fourteenth or fifteenth Year, whether they expect any Progress from them or not. Let the Child's Capacity be forthwith examined, and he sent to some Mechanick Way of Life, without Respect to his Birth, if Nature design'd him for nothing higher; let him go before he has innocently suffered, and is debased into a Dereliction of Mind for being what it is no Guilt to be, a plain Man. I would not here be supposed to have said, that our learned Men of either Robe who have been whipped at School, are not still Men of noble and liberal Minds; but I am sure they had been much more so than they are, had they never suffered that Infamy. (157–161)

We read Steele's essay carefully, and one of us copied it out by hand. Then we made notes about important points. The next day we wrote the following paraphrase:

No word in English is a satisfactory translation of the Latin term *indoles.* Perhaps "nature" or "natural disposition" come closest. A person's natural disposition, if there is such a thing, needs to be taken into account in her or his education and in her or his choice of a profession. It is difficult for anyone to know what her or his own natural aptitudes are, although others can sometimes determine these with ease.

History abounds with examples of persons whose early activities hinted at their later greatness. George Washington's honesty about the cherry tree presaged his later courage in the face of difficulties. Abraham Lincoln demonstrated his persistence and ambition as a young man, when he worked long hours and walked many miles to study law.

But bright lights like these can easily be extinguished by ignorant and brutal teachers. It is difficult to believe that the freedom we prize so highly is often purchased at the expense of long years of terror and heartache in school. Ignorant teachers do not distinguish between the able and the less able, but punish all alike for failure to perform correctly. The truth is that many people are not suited for the study of letters. Despite this lack of natural inclination, such persons are beaten into diligence. Often it is these persons who become teachers themselves.

Students' combined senses of honor and shame should suffice to drive them to study. Punishment for failure to give the correct answers does not serve the aim intended for it. Because of their active imaginations, students sometimes give answers that are correct, but are not the answers that teachers were looking for. Students who do this are punished nonetheless. As a result, punishment often extinguishes the scholarly virtue of imagination, while it reinforces the belief that scholarship amounts to absorbing and parroting back trivial bits of information.

Quintilian remarked that "study depends on the good will of the student, a quality that cannot be secured by compulsion" (I iii, 8). We do not recklessly prune fruits or vegetables while we are encouraging them to grow; rather we care for them, making sure they have enough water and sunlight. Teachers should shape young minds with the same care and attention that sculptors use to shape pieces of marble into works of art.

Punishment breeds a certain brutishness in even the best-educated persons. Using punishment to force people to learn is like killing someone to cure him of a cold. This method turns people into brutes who only work when they are forced to. Punishment extinguishes rational behavior, rather than encouraging it.

Given these considerations, it makes sense that children who are not cut out to be scholars should be allowed to quit school when they have learned all they can. Those whose natural dispositions incline them away from learning should be encouraged to follow other career paths. I am not saying that our current crop of intellectuals, who were educated in this way, are not fine and upright people. However, I am sure they would have been persons of even more liberal and noble character, had they been better treated while they were in school.

This paraphrase is fairly accurate; it condenses Steele's essay and renders it in more modern English. Since we do not agree with much of what Steele wrote in this issue of the *Spectator*, this exercise was difficult. However, writing it did stimulate us to think about the issues it raises—more so than simply reading the essay would have done—and so it may be that paraphrase can occasionally jump-start invention.

We recommend that writers paraphrase anyone whose work they admire. A paraphrase can be longer or shorter than the original; it can use a different voice or arrangement; it can have more figures or fewer; it can develop fuller characterizations and add more detail, or it can be as spare as possible—in which case it is more accurately called a summary or precis. All choices like these are up to the paraphraser.

Here is a method for paraphrasing: Read a passage carefully. Copy it into a commonplace book, wait awhile, and then try to compose another passage that captures the sense of the original, without looking at the original again. Or, you can make notes on the original passage, and use these to compose a paraphrase.

The ancients had good reasons for recommending paraphrase to their students. Paraphrase encourages us to look for words and structures that do not appear in the original, thus increasing our stocks of both. Because it requires us to rely on our own linguistic resources, paraphrase is more challenging than imitation. Indeed, Quintilian recommended it precisely because of its difficulty (8).

Paraphrasing Poetry

In the passage quoted above, Benjamin Franklin mentioned another exercise in paraphrase that was also recommended by Quintilian: turning poetry into prose. According to Quintilian, this exercise is useful because "the lofty inspiration of verse serves to elevate the rhetor's style" (X v, 4). In other words, writers of prose may find unusual uses of language in poetry that they can borrow. But paraphrase of poetry into prose may also teach us something about arrangement, as well. Certainly it helps us to read poetry more carefully.

Here is Aesop's fable of the stag and the horse, as told in prose by Aristotle:

A horse had a meadow to himself. When a stag came and quite damaged the pasture, the horse, wanting to avenge himself on the stag, asked a man if he could help him get vengeance on the stag. The man said he could, if the horse were to take a bridle and he himself were to mount on him holding javelins. When the horse agreed and the man mounted, instead of getting vengeance the horse found himself a slave to the man. (*Rhetoric* II 20, 1393b)

Now here is the same fable, told in poetry by a seventeenth-century poet named John Ogilby (we have modernized Ogilby's English):

Long was the war between the hart and horse
Fought with like courage, chance, and equal force;
  Until a fatal day
Gave signal victory to the hart; the steed
Must now no more in pleasant valleys feed,
  Nor verdant commons sway,
The hart who now o'er all did domineer,
  This conquering stag,
  Slights like a nag,
The vanquished horse, which did no more appear.

In want, exiled, driven from native shores,
The horse in cities human aid implores,
  To get his realms again.
Let man now manage him and his affair,
Since he not knows what his own forces are.
  Thus sues he for the rein;
For sweet revenge he will endure the bit,
  Let him o'erthrow
  His cruel foe,
And let his haughty rider heavy fit.

He takes the bridle o'er his yielding head.
With man and arms the horse is furnished,
  And for the battle neighs.
But when the hart two hostile faces saw
And such a centaur to encounter draw,
  He stood awhile at gaze.
At last known valor up he roused again,
  More hopes by fight
  There was, than flight;
What's won by arms, by force he must maintain.

Then to the battle did the hart advance;
The horse a man brings, with a mighty lance
  Longer than the other's crest;
The manner of the fight is changed, he feels

No more the horse's hoof, and ill-aimed heels;
    They charge now breast to breast.
Two to one odds'gainst Hercules; the hart,
      Though strong and stout,
      Could not hold out,
But flies, and must from conquered realms depart.

Nor longer could the horse his joy contain,
But with loud neighs, and erected mane,
      Triumphs after fight;
When to the soldier mounted on his back,
Feeling him heavy now, the beast thus spake;
      Be pleased good sir to light.
Since you restored to me by father's seat,
      And got the day,
      Receive your pay,
And to your city joyfully retreat.

Then said the man; This saddle which you wear
Cost more than all the lands we conquered here,
      Beside this burnished bit,
Your self, and all you have, too little are
To clear my engagements in this mighty war;
      Till that's paid, here I'll sit:
And since against your foe I aided you,
      Can you deny
      Me like supply?
Come, and with me my enemy subdue.

Then sighed the horse, and to the man replied;
I feel thy cruel rowels gall my side,
      And now I am thy slave;
But thank thy self for this, thou foolish beast,
That for revenge to foreign interest
      Thy self and Kingdom gave.
Amongst rocky mountains I had better dwelled,
      And fed on thorns,
      Gored by the hart's horns,
Than wicked man's hard servitude have felt. (1688)

As you can see, Ogilby elaborated the basic story a good deal in his paraphrase, providing more plot detail and giving the horse and stag more character than Aristotle cared to (after all, Aristotle was interested in the moral of the story, while Ogilby wished to entertain his readers). But a prose paraphrase does not need to be as spare as Aristotle's version; a faithful prose paraphrase of Ogilby's poem would be at least twice as long as Aristotle's rendering of the fable. As Quintilian remarked, the duty of a paraphrase is not to replicate an original exactly, but rather "to rival and vie with the original in the expression of the same thoughts" (X v, 5).

Here are modern poetic renderings of two more of Aesop's fables, suitable for paraphrasing into prose:

THE NORTH WIND AND THE SUN

Between the North Wind and the Sun
A quarrel rose as to which one
Could strip the mantle from a man
Walking the road. The wind began,
And blew, for in his Thracian way
He thought that he would quickly lay
The wearer bare by force. But still
The man, shivering with the chill,
Held fast his cloak, nor let it go
The more the North Wind tried to blow,
But drew the edges close around,
Sat himself down upon the ground,
And leaned his back against a stone.
And then the Sun peeped out, and shone,
Pleasant at first, and set him free
From the cold blowing bitterly,
And next applied a little heat.
Then suddenly, from head to feet,
By burning fire the man was gripped,
Cast off his cloak himself, and stripped.

THE TWO PACKS

Among the gods when time began
Prometheus lived. He made a man
All molded out of earth and plaster,
And thus produced for beasts a master.
He hung on him two packs to wear,
Filled with the woes that men must bear,
With strangers' woes the one before,
But that in back, which carried more,
Was filled with evils all his own.
Hence many men, I think, are prone
To see the ills some other bears
But still be ignorant of theirs.

—*Dennison B. Hull, 1960*

Try paraphrasing these fables into prose. If you wish, you can compare your prose version to any of the hundreds of modern translations of Aesop's fables. For further practice, you can turn your prose paraphrase back into poetry, or you can try to write a poetic version in imitation of Ogilby's seventeenth-century style. Once again, this exercise is useful because it demands that writers find new words and structures to express something already written by someone else.

If you find paraphrase to be fun and useful, we recommend that you practice paraphrasing your favorite poetry into prose. We are aware that this exercise may offend the sensibilities of persons who think that great poets have found the best and only way to express anything. This is a quite modern notion, having to do with Romantic attitudes toward originality and the uniqueness of creative ability. The ancients viewed creativity in a far different light: they thought that craft played a large role in the production of fine writing, and that craft could be learned through practice. Nor did they believe that any poem or piece of prose was so good that it couldn't be improved upon. As Quintilian remarked, a paraphrase may "add the vigor of oratory to the thoughts expressed by the poet, make good his omissions, and prune his diffuseness" (X v, 4–5).

Writers need not imitate or paraphrase only the work of others, however. Quintilian recommended that writers get in the habit of paraphrasing their own work: "for instance, we may specially select certain thoughts and recast them in the greatest variety of forms, just as a sculptor will fashion a number of different images from the same piece of wax" (X v, 9–10). In fact, self-paraphrase can become a method of composition. It works like this: after you have written a draft of a composition, set it aside for awhile. Then read it over, and quickly write a second draft. Compare the two drafts, take what you like from each, and compose a third. Continue with this process until you achieve a draft that satisfies you.

The reasons for using paraphrase are many: it promotes copia and it may stimulate invention. Paraphrase also turns people into more careful readers, and it may make reading more enjoyable, too (X v, 8). Plus there's always the chance that a paraphrase will turn out better than the original. In that case, paraphrase provides writers with a rare chance to congratulate themselves.

Examples of Paraphrase

During the seventeenth and eighteenth centuries CE, accomplished poets practiced their art by imitating, translating, or paraphrasing poetry composed by ancient and medieval poets. We conclude this chapter with some examples of their art, suitable for imitation or paraphrase.

At the age of fifteen, John Milton paraphrased Psalm 114 in English, probably as a school exercise. Here is a modern English version of Psalm 114 that purports to be a literal translation of the Hebrew original:

> After Israel went out of Egypt,
> the house of Jacob from a barbaric people,
>   Judah became his sanctuary,
> Israel his dominion.
>   When the sea saw him, it fled,
> the Jordan turned back.
>   The mountains leaped like rams,
> the hills like lambs of the flock.
>   What ailed you, O sea, that you fled?
> O Jordan, that you turned back?
>   O mountains, that you leaped like rams?
> O hills like lambs of the flock?

> In the presence of the Lord writhe, O land,
> in the presence of Jacob's God.
>   Who turned rock into a pool of water,
> flint into a flowing spring.

Here is Milton's paraphrase:

> When the blest seed of Terah's faithful Son,
> After long toil their liberty had won,
> And past from Pharian Fields to Canaan Land,
> Led by the strength of the Almighties hand,
> Jehovah's wonders were in Israel shown,
> His praise and glory was in Israel known.
> That saw the troubled Sea, and shivering fled,
> And sought to hide his froth becurled head
> Low in the earth, Jordan's clear streams recoil,
> As a faint Host that hath receiv'd the foil.
> The high, huge-bellied Mountains skip like Rams
> Amongst their Ewes, the little Hills like Lambs.
> Why fled the Ocean? And why skipt the Mountains?
> Why turned Jordan toward his Chrystal Fountains?
> Shake earth, and at the presence be agast
> Of him that ever was, and ay shall last,
> That glassy floods from rugged rocks can crush,
> And make soft rills from fiery flint-stones gush.
>
> —*John Milton, "A Paraphrase on Psalm 114," 1623*

Try paraphrasing both poems in prose. Or tell the story of the Israelites' escape in more detail.

The playwright Ben Jonson imitated this wonderful love poem by the ancient Greek poet, Sappho:

> As equal to the gods, he seems to me,
> the man who, with his face toward yours,
> sits close and listens to the whispers of
> your sweet voice and enticing laugh.
> To watch has made my heart a pounding hammer in my breast.
> For as I look at you, if only for an instant,
> my voice no longer comes to me.
> My silent tongue is broken,
> and a quick and subtle flame
> runs up beneath my skin.
> I lose my sense of sight, hear only drumming in my ears.
> I drip cold sweat,
> and a trembling chases all through me.
> I am greener than the pale grass
> and it seems to me that I am close to death. (10)

Here is Jonson's imitation:

> Thou dost not know my sufferings, what I feel,
> My fires and fears are met; I burn and freeze,
> My liver's one great coal, my heart shrunk up
> With all the fibres, and the mass of blood
> Within me is a standing lake of fire,
> Curled with the cold wind of my gelid sighs,
> That drive a drift of sleet through all my body,
> And shoot a February through all my veins.
> Until I see him I am drunk with thirst,
> And surfeited with hunger of his presence.
> I know not where I am, or no, or speak,
> Or whether thou dost hear me.
>
> —*"The New Inn" V ii, 45–56*

Try paraphrasing Jonson's poem into modern English. Or compose a paraphrase in prose.

The Roman poet Horace was a great favorite for imitation among English poets. Here is a prose version, in English, of one of his odes:

> To Pyrrha,
>
> What dainty youth, bedewed with liquid perfumes caresses you, Pyrrha, beneath the pleasant grot, amid a profusion of roses? For whom do you bind your golden hair, plain in your neatness? Alas! how often shall he deplore your perfidy, and the altered gods; and through inexperience be amazed at the seas, rough with blackening storms, who now credulous enjoys you all precious, and, ignorant of the faithless gale, hopes you will be always disengaged, always amiable! Wretched are those, to whom thou untried seemest fair! The sacred wall [of Neptune's temple] demonstrates, by a votive tablet, that I have consecrated my dropping garments to the powerful god of the sea. (Horace, Fifth Ode, Book I)

Here is John Milton's translation/paraphrase of Horace's poem:

> What slender Youth bedew'd with liquid odors
> Courts thee on Roses in some pleasant Cave,
>   Pyrrha for whom bindst thou
>   In wreaths thy golden Hair,
> Plain in thy neatness; O how oft shall he
> On faith and changed Gods complain: and Seas
>   Rough with black winds and storms
>   Unwonted shall admire:
> Who now enjoys thee credulous, all Gold,
> Who always vacant always amiable
>   Hopes thee; of flattering gales
>   Unmindful. Hapless they
> To whom thou untried seem'st fair. Me in my vow'd

Picture the sacred wall declares t' have hung
    My dank and dropping weeds
    To the stern God of Sea.

—*"Fifth Ode of Horace"*

Whose version do you prefer? Again, you can paraphrase Milton's version into modern English, or you can paraphrase either version into prose.

    We now quote the opening lines, in Latin, of Horace's Sixth Satire, Book II, in order to demonstrate the freedom with which poetry may be paraphrased.

Hoc erat in votis; modus agri non ita magnus,
Hortus ubi, et tecto vicinus jugis aquae fons,
Et paulum sylvae super his foret: auctius atque
Dii melius fecere: bene est: nil amplius oro,
Maia nate, nisi ut propria haec mihi muner faxis.

Here is a nineteenth century prose translation of these lines:

This was ever among the number of my wishes: a portion of ground not over-large, in which was a garden, and a fountain with a continual stream close to my house, and a little woodland besides. The gods have done more abundantly, and better, for me than this. It is well: O son of Maia, I ask nothing more save that you would render these donations lasting to me.

Here is Alexander Pope's paraphrase of the opening of Horace's satire, composed in 1737. Pope's version is almost twice as long as Horace's original, because he adds an observation about his own situation under English law at the time:

    I've often wish'd that I had clear
For life, six hundred pounds a year,
A handsome House to lodge a Friend,
A River at my garden's end,
A Terras-walk, and half a Rood
Of Land, wet out to plant a Wood.
    Well, now I have all this and more,
I ask not to increase my store;
But here a Grievance seems to lie,
All this is mine but till I die;
I can't but think 'twould sound more clever,
To me and to my Heirs for ever.

—*"The Sixth Satire of the Second Book of Horace Imitated,"* 1714

Try composing a loose paraphrase of these lines that indicates your hopes for your retirement.

    A Roman poet named Ovid, who lived during the first century BCE, was also a great favorite among seventeenth- and eighteenth-century poets. Here is a modern translation of two passages from the eighth book of his *Metamorphoses.* In these passages, Ovid describes a meal served to two gods who are in disguise, and who have sought shelter from a poor couple named Baucis and Philemon:

> Then the old man, raising a forked stick,
> Fetched down a side of bacon from black rafters
> And cut small parings of the precious fat
> To toss them where they steamed in boiling water. . . .
> Then food was served; first came Minerva's fruit,
> The ripe brown olive and September cherries
> Spiced with a measure of sweet wine, new lettuce,
> Creamed cottage cheese, pink radishes, and eggs
> Baked to a turn; and all were handed round
> On plates of country-fashioned earthenware—
> And of the same make came a large bowl, then
> Small wooden cups, all lined with amber wax,
> The service for the soup poured at the hearth;
> Then came the table wine and the next course.
> Set to one side, nuts, figs, and dates, sweet-smelling
> Apples in a flat basket, grapes just off the vine,
> The centerpiece a white comb of clear honey.
> But happier than the simple meal itself,
> A halo of high spirits charmed the table.
>   When the huge bowl drained dry, it filled itself,
> And empty flasks still spouted running wine.

—Horace Gregory, 1958

In these passages, Ovid gave us an example of the ancient exercise known as *ekphrasis,* or description (see the next chapter). Here is John Dryden's translation and paraphrase of the same passages:

> High o'er the Hearth a Chine of Bacon hung;
> Good old Philemon seiz'd it with a Prong,
> And from the sooty Rafter drew it down,
> Then Cut a Slice, but scarce enough for one;
> Yet a large Portion of a little Store,
> Which for their Sakes alone he wish'd were more.
> This in the Pot he plung'd without delay,
> To tame the Flesh, and drain the Salt away. . . .
>   Pallas began the feast, where first was seen
> The party-color'd Olive, Black, and Green:
> Autumnal Cornels next in order serv'd,
> In Lees of Wine well pickl'd, and preserv'd.
> A Garden-Salad was the third Supply,
> Of Endive, Radishes, and Succory:
> Then Curds and Cream, the Flow'r of Country-Fare,
> And new-laid Eggs, which Baucis' busy Care

Turn'd by a gentle Fire, and roasted rare.
All these in Earthen Ware were serve'd to Board;
And next in place, an Earthen Pitcher stor'd
With Liquor of the best the Cottage cou'd afford.
This was the Tables' Ornament, and Pride,
With Figures wrought: Like Pages at his Side
Stood Beechen Bowls; and these were shining clean,
Varnish'd with Wax without, and lin'd within.
By this the boiling Kettle had prepar'd,
And to the Table sent the smoking Lard;
On which with eager Appetite they dine,
A sav'ry Bit, that serv'd to relish Wine:
The Wine itself was suiting to the rest,
Still working in the Must, and lately press'd.
The Second Course succeeds like that before,
Plums, Apples, Nuts, and of their Wintry Store,
Dry Figs, and Grapes, and wrinkl'd Dates were set
In Canisters, t' enlarge the little Treat:
All these a Milk-white Honey-comb surround,
Which in the midst the Country-Banquet crown'd:
But the kind Hosts their Entertainment grace
With hearty Welcome, and an open Face:
In all they did, you might discern with ease,
A willing Mind, and a Desire to please.
   Meantime the Beechen Bowls went round, and still
Though often empty'd, were observ'd to fill;
Fill'd without Hands, and of their own accord
Ran without Feet, and danc'd about the Board.

—John Dryden, 1700

Obviously, Dryden was fascinated with the possibilities of artful description, and he amplified Ovid's description of the feast into a passage that is almost twice as long as the original. When Jonathan Swift imitated this story from Ovid, on the other hand, he omitted the long description of the feast. Rather, he concentrated on the gods' miraculous response to the old couple's generosity:

While he from out the chimney took
A flitch of bacon off the hook;
And freely from the fattest side,
Cut out large slices to be fried.
Then stepped aside to fetch them drink,
Filled a large jug up to the brink;
And saw it fairly twice go round;
Yet (what was wonderful) they found
'Twas still replenished to the top,
As if they ne'er had touched a drop.

—Jonathan Swift, "Baucis and Philemon"

Try telling this story in prose. If you enjoy writing poetry, try paraphrasing any of the three versions into free verse.

Finally, here are two translations and imitations of the Middle English poet Geoffrey Chaucer. As you can see, Chaucer's fourteenth-century English is very hard to read. This was true even for eighteenth-century readers. Written English had changed so much by their day that Dryden and Pope undertook the task of translating Chaucer's English into language that was more familiar to their readers.

FROM "THE WIFE OF BATH'S PROLOGUE"

"Experience, though noon auctoritee
Were in this world, is right ynogh for me
To speke of wo that is in mariage;
For, lordynges, sith I twelve yeer was of age,
Thonked be God that is eterne on lyve,
Housbondes at chirche dore I have had fyve,—
If I so ofte myghte have ywedded bee,—
And alle were worthy men in hir degree.
But me was toold, certeyn, nat longe agoon is,
That sith that Crist ne wente neverer but onis
To weddyng, in the Cane of Galilee,
That by the same ensample taught he me
That I ne sholde wedde be but ones. . . .
Men may devyne and glosen, up and doun,
But wel I woot, express, without lye,
God bad us for to wexe and multiplye;
That gentil text kan I wel understonde.

—*Geoffrey Chaucer (late fourteenth century* CE)

Behold the Woes of Matrimonial Life,
And hear with Rev'rence an experienc'd Wife!
To dear-bought Wisdom give the Credit due,
And think, for once, a Woman tells you true.
In all these Trials I have born a Part;
I was my self the Scourge that caus'd the Smart;
For, since Fifteen, in Triumph have I led
Five Captive Husbands from the Church to Bed.
   Christ saw a Wedding once, the Scripture says,
And saw but one, 'tis thought, in all his Days;
Whence some infer, whose Conscience is too nice,
No pious Christian ought to marry twice. . . .
Encrease and multiply was Heav'ns' Command,
   And that's a Text I clearly understand.

—*Alexander Pope, 1704*

FROM "THE WIFE OF BATH'S TALE"

In th'olde dayes of the Kyng Arthour,
Of which that Britons speken greet honour,
Al was this land fulfild of fayerye.
The elf-queene, with hir joly compaignye,
Daunced ful ofte in many a grene mede.
This was the olde opinion, as I rede;
I speke of manye hundred yeares ago.
But now kan no man se none elves mo,
For now the grete charitee and prayeres
Of lymytours and othere hooly freres,
That serchen every lond and every streem,
As thikke as motes in the soone-beem,
Blessynge halles, chambres, kichenes, boures,
Citees, burghes, castels, hy toures,
Thropes, bernes, shipnes, dayeryes—
This maketh that there ben no fayeryes.

—*Geoffrey Chaucer*

In Days of Old when Arthur fill'd the Throne,
Whose Acts and Fame to Foreign Lands were blown;
The King of Elfs and little Fairy Queen
Gamboll'd on Heaths, and danc'd on ev'ry Green.
And where the jolly Troop had led the round
The Grass unbidden rose, and mark'ed the Ground:
Nor darkling did they dance, the Silver Light
Of Phoebe serv'd to guide their Steps aright,
And, with their Tripping pleas'd, prolong'd the Night.
Her Beams they follow'd, where at full she plaid,
Nor longer than she shed her Horns they staid,
Above the rest our Britain held they dear,
More solemnly they kept their Sabbaths here,
And made more spacious Rings, and revell'd half the Year.
    I speak of ancient Times, for now the Swain
Returning late may pass the Woods in vain,
And never hope to see the nightly Train:
In vain the Dairy now with Mints is dress'd,
The Dairy-Maid expects no Fairy Guest,
To skim the Bowls and after pay the Feast.
She sighs and shakes her empty Shoes in vain,
No silver Penny to reward her Pain:
For Priests with Pray'rs, and other godly Geer,
Have made the merry Goblins disappear . . .

—*John Dryden, 1700*

THE
PROGYMNASMATA

*It is quite evident that
these exercises are
altogether beneficial to
those who take up the
art of rhetoric. For those
who have recited a
narration and a fable
well and with versatility
will also compose a
history well. . . .
Training through the
chreia not only produces
a certain power of
discourse but also a good
and useful character
since we are being
trained in the aphorisms
of wise persons. Both the
so-called commonplace
and description have
benefit that is
conspicuous since the
ancients have used them
everywhere.*

—Aelius Theon,
Progymnasmata
Preface 1

RHETORIC TEACHERS USED the set of exercises called *progymnasmata* (elementary exercises) over a very long stretch of time. The term first appears in the sophistic *Rhetoric to Alexander,* written during the fourth century BCE (unless this is a later insertion in the manuscripts). The author furnished a relatively long list of rhetorical tactics, and suggested that "if we habituate and train ourselves to repeat them on the lines of our preparatory exercises, they will supply us with plenty of matter both in writing and in speaking" (1436a, 25). His casual reference suggests that exercises were routinely used in the rhetorical schools of the time. In fact, Cicero testifies that Aristotle used an exercise called thesis to train his rhetoric students "so that they might be able to uphold either side of the question in copious and elegant language" (*Orator* xiv, 46). If Cicero's information is correct, thesis was used even in schools of philosophy during the fourth century BCE. It was still being practiced in Rome some five centuries later, as Quintilian testifies in the second book of the *Institutes,* and it was still in use in some European schools at least as late as the sixteenth century CE.

Aside from brief accounts that appear in global accounts of ancient rhetorics, such as Quintilian's *Institutes,* four ancient manuscripts devoted solely to the *progymnasmata* have survived. The oldest of these is attributed to Aelius Theon, a sophist who lived in Egyptian Alexandria during the first century CE. Hermogenes of Tarsus wrote another, probably during the second century CE; this treatise, as translated into Latin by the grammarian Priscian, was very popular during the European Middle Ages. A

Byzantine sophist named Nicolaus produced another Greek *progymnasmata* during the fifth century CE. However, the most complete list of elementary exercises we possess is the one put together by Aphthonius, who taught rhetoric in Antioch around the fifth century CE. Translated into Latin, this treatise was enormously popular in Europe during the Renaissance.

In ancient Greece and Rome, when boys became old enough to go to school, their parents placed them with a teacher who was a grammarian. (This ancient association of elementary study with grammar explains why American elementary schools are still sometimes called "grammar schools.") While they studied with a grammarian, young students practiced imitating and elaborating on **fables, tales,** *chreia*, and **proverbs.** When they graduated to higher education in rhetoric, they composed sample parts of orations such as **confirmations** or **refutations,** sometimes imitating famous speeches and sometimes following a standard arrangement of parts. They also composed **commonplaces, descriptions** (*ekphrasis*), **characters** (*ethopoeia*), **comparisons** (*synkresis*), and speeches of **praise** (*encomia*) and blame (*psogos,* **invective**). When students matured, they were set to composing more difficult exercises in deliberative and forensic rhetoric, called thesis and introduction of laws.

The *progymnasmata* remained popular for so long because they are carefully sequenced: they begin with simple paraphrases and end with sophisticated exercises in deliberative and forensic rhetoric. Each successive exercise uses a skill practiced in the preceding one, but each adds some new and more difficult composing task. Ancient teachers were fond of comparing the graded difficulty of the *progymnasmata* to the exercise used by Milo of Croton to gradually increase his strength: Milo lifted a calf each day. Each day the calf grew heavier, and each day his strength grew. He continued to lift the calf until it became a bull (*Institutes* I ix, 5).

Like the exercises in imitation discussed in the previous chapter, the *progymnasmata* may look and feel artificial or formulaic to contemporary writers. However, the directions for amplification that accompany some of them are meant to be freely interpreted; for example, not every encomium must have the same number of parts, and the parts need not always appear in the same order. This freedom of interpretation and arrangement is what distinguishes classical exercises from the prescriptive formulas laid down in modern school rhetoric.

If you choose to practice any or all of the exercises reviewed here, we suggest that you adapt them to contemporary themes or issues that interest you. We give a few suggestions for doing this along the way. The object of these exercises is, of course, the achievement of copia.

FABLE

Fables are fictitious stories meant to teach moral lessons. In the eighteenth century, a scholar and critic named Samuel Johnson defined a fable as "a narrative in which beings irrational, and sometimes inanimate, are, for the purpose of moral instruction, feigned to act and speak with human interests and passions"

("Life of Gay"). The great French fabulist, Jean de la Fontaine, composed a more poetic definition:

> Fables in sooth are not what they appear;
> Our moralists are mice, and such small deer.
> We yawn at sermons, but we gladly turn
> To moral tales, and so amused we learn.

A sixteenth-century teacher named Erasmus praised fables in this way: "their attraction is due to their witty imitation of the way people behave, and the hearers give their assent because the truth is set out vividly before their very eyes" (631).

All cultures produce fables, little stories used to teach moral behavior to children. Aesop's tale of the country mouse and the city mouse, written thousands of years ago, is still part of childhood lore. Native American cultures have produced especially rich traditions of fables that display a fascinating range of human and animal characters such as the trickster coyote and the sturdy turtle.

The rhetoric teacher Aphthonius divided fables into two kinds: those that use human characters and those that use animal characters. The comic strips "Doonesbury," "Pogo," and "Outland" are running fables that comment on current affairs; Doonesbury uses human characters, while "Pogo" is an animal fable, and "Outland" uses both humans and animals. Fabulous uses of animals sometimes appear in political cartoons, as well, as in Figures 16.1 and 16.2. In one of these cartoons, fish are used to represent an abstraction—banking—as

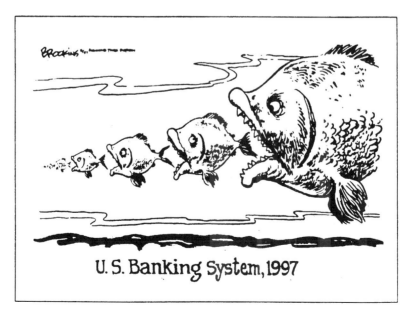

FIGURE 16.1
Political cartoon
Source: Brookins, Gary, "U.S. Banking System, 1997."

FIGURE 16.2
Political cartoon
Source: *Signe*, Philadelphia Daily News, *Cartoonists & Writers Syndicate.*

an entity that is engaged in consuming its young. In the other, endangered animals represent themselves, although the joke is an analogy to another issue altogether—workfare.

Fables are popular with children, of course, and that's why the list of elementary *progymnasmata* begins with them. Ancient teachers asked their very young students to imitate the fables of Aesop. However, older students may enjoy paraphrasing extant fables or even creating their own stories that make some moral or political point.

Here is an ancient fable as told by Xenophon in his *Memorabilia.* Xenophon used this fable to justify Athenian attitudes about the proper relations that ought to obtain between women and men:

> It is said that when beasts could talk, a sheep said to her master: "It is strange that you give us sheep nothing but what we get from the land, though we supply you with wool and lambs and cheese, and yet you share your own food with your dog, who supplies you with none of these things." The dog heard this, and said: "Of course he does. Do not I keep you from being stolen by thieves, and carried off by wolves? Why, but for my protection you couldn't even feed for fear of being killed." And so, they say, the sheep admitted the dog's claim to preference. (II vii, 13–14)

This fable, or any fable, can be used in several rhetorical exercises. You can imitate or paraphrase it, perhaps using human characters. You can compose a moral for it, or write a different interpretation than that implied by Xenophon. Could the sheep and the dog also represent the people of a nation and its standing army, for example?

If you want to stretch your creative abilities, compose a fable that is analogous to some current event or state of affairs about which you are concerned. For example, you can compose a version of Xenophon's fable that justifies a less patriarchal view of the proper relations between men and women. In that case, you might want to use different animals than sheep and a dog. Hermogenes recommended that beast fables employ animals whose actions can be plausibly compared to human activities: "if the contention be about beauty, let this be posed as a peacock; if some one is to be represented as wise, there let us pose a fox; if imitators of the actions of men, monkeys" (24).

We composed a fable about hate speech. In keeping with Hermogenes' advice, we chose a crowing rooster to represent people who are careless about the effects of their actions on others:

> There was once a rooster who was very proud of himself, particularly of his gorgeous feathers and his raucous voice. Every morning he paraded among the chickens, preening his beautiful feathers and crowing as loud as he could. One day he noticed a small group of sparrows foraging near his pen. He strutted as close to the fence as he could get, and crowed very loudly. The sparrows were startled, but they did not fly away in fear, as he had hoped. As days passed, the rooster became more and more frantic about the sparrows who were foraging so close by, and who seemed not to know how important he was among the chickens. He stayed close to the fence, fretting and preening, preening and crowing, until the farmer became irritated by the constant noise. He threw the rooster off the place, and so the rooster lost his good home with plenty of food, as well as his captive audience.

Fables are usually quite brief; the composer simply presents a bare narrative. If you wish to expand a fable, add descriptions of the setting or compose dialogue for the characters. Of course, any fable you compose can be used for purposes of illustration or analogy in a larger composition.

TALE

The second elementary exercise involved students in retelling stories from history and poetry. Since narrative plays an important role in persuasive discourse, it is important that rhetors know how to compose skillful stories, whether these are historical or fictional (see the chapter on arrangement).

The composition of narrative is not simple or artless. Ancient teachers distinguished between longer narratives that recounted a series of events—like Thucydides' history of the Peloponnesian war or Homer's *Iliad*—from shorter narratives that told about one event. Of course, very young students were asked to imitate or paraphrase only the very short narratives that they found in their reading. Here is Aphthonius' example of a short tale:

> Let anyone marveling at the beauty of the rose consider the misfortune of Aphrodite. For the goddess was in love with Adonis but Ares, in turn, was in love with her; in other words, the goddess had the same regard for Adonis that Ares had for Aphrodite. God loved goddess and goddess was pursuing mortal; the longing was

the same, even though the species was different. The jealous Ares, however, wanted to do away with Adonis in the belief that the death of Adonis would bring about a release of his love. Consequently, Ares attacked his rival but the goddess, learning of his action, was hurrying to the rescue. As she stumbled into the rosebush because of her haste, she fell among the thorns and the flat of her foot was pierced. Flowing from the wound, the blood changed the color of the rose to its familiar appearance and the rose, though white in its origin, came to be as it now appears. (translated by Ray Nadeau)

Writers can imitate or paraphrase this short tale. But Quintilian also suggested that students change the order of events in such stories, telling them backwards or starting in the middle, in order to improve their memories (*Institutes* II iv, 15).

Quintilian's exercise is useful for improving writers' skill at arrangement, as well. What happens when events are given in a different order than that chosen by Aphthonius? What if the teller were to narrate the story about the rose before providing the information about the love triangle?

One day, as the goddess Aphrodite was hurrying through the woods, she stumbled into a rosebush because of her haste. She fell among the thorns and the flat of her foot was pierced. Flowing from the wound, the blood changed the color of the rose to its familiar appearance and the rose, though white in its origin, came to be as it now appears.

Aphrodite was hurrying because the god Ares, who loved her, was attacking the mortal man she loved, Adonis. Ares thought that if he could kill Adonis, Aphrodite would forget her mortal lover.

We reordered the events of the story and removed the embellishments given it by Aphthonius. This arrangement presents an entirely different impression of Aphrodite, we think. Which version do you prefer?

Aphthonius' version of the tale omitted the fate of Adonis. According to ancient myth, Aphrodite warned her mortal lover to be careful while hunting, but he ignored her warning and was gored to death by a boar. That part of the story can easily be told in one sentence, as we have just done. Compare our spare version to Ovid's lovely narrative:

Since she believed her warning had been heard,
The goddess yoked her swans and flew toward heaven—
Yet the boy's pride and manliness ignored it.
His hunting dogs took a clear path before them
And in the forest waked a sleeping boar;
As he broke through his lair within a covert,
Adonis pricked him with a swift-turned spear.
The fiery boar tore out the slender splinter
And rushed the boy, who saw his death heave toward him.
With one great thrust he pierced the boy's white loins
And left him dying where one saw his blood
Flow into rivulets on golden sands.

—*Metamorphoses* X

Ovid added touches of description and characterization. Do these additions change the effect of the tale? Can you tell it differently? Can you tell it better? You can find the whole story of Aphrodite and Adonis in any collection of ancient Greek or Roman myths (the goddess is called "Venus" in Roman mythology) or in Shakespeare's poetic retelling entitled "Venus and Adonis."

You needn't go to ancient literature to find short tales to imitate or paraphrase; they abound in our culture. While we prefer telling jokes to writing them down, composing different versions of jokes can be a useful exercise. We can also write and revise or reorder tales about events from our own lives. Often we tell these to friends for their amusement; why not try writing them? There are also fairy tales. Walt Disney Studios has a long history of amplifying these little stories into two-hour animated films, complete with well-developed characters and more complex plot lines than are featured in the originals. Compare the versions of well-known fairy tales found in Grimm or Hans Christian Andersen to those told by Disney, whose versions are ordinarily less gruesome than the originals. Why is this so, do you think? For practice in narrative composition, write a version of a fairy tale that uses bits of Disney along with bits of earlier versions. Or compose your own version of a well-known fairy tale. Update the story of Little Red Riding Hood or the Little Mermaid. Find a copy of the ancient story of Hercules, and compare it to Disney's recent movie.

Writers of contemporary nonfiction conventionally employ small narratives in the beginnings of books or chapters. Here, for example, is the opening of a chapter of *In Our Defense,* a discussion of the Bill of Rights written by Ellen Alderman and Caroline Kennedy:

> On a hot summer night, August 11, 1967, in Pike County, Kentucky, in an old farmhouse in the foothills of the Appalachian Mountains, two young civil rights workers, Alan and Margaret McSurely, were settling in for the evening. Alan was in a spare room writing at a makeshift desk and Margaret was in the kitchen cooking some squash for dinner. From the kitchen window Margaret spotted a dozen or so armed men making their way through the tall grass behind their house. Fearing that the men were looking for an escaped convict, Margaret called out to her husband. He was already up out of his chair and on his way to the front of the house.
>
> "I walked up to the door and reached my hand out to open the door, [it] opened in on me and about five guys came running right by me up into the living room and the first guy said, 'Where is Alan McSurely?' They had gone right by me, I was back by the door. I said, 'I'm right here.' "
>
> The sheriff announced to Alan that he was under arrest for sedition against the Commonwealth of Kentucky and read aloud an arrest warrant and search warrant. "As soon as [the sheriff] finished reading these to me there was a moment when it was clear nobody knew what to do . . . [then] some more guys come walking in the front door . . . in their uniforms with their guns drawn, and there was this guy with a business suit on and a tie. I recognized him as Thomas Ratliff."
>
> The McSurelys and Thomas Ratliff had never met before that night, but what happened next in the McSurely home would lock them into a seventeen-year battle involving a powerful U.S. senator, his feud with a celebrated columnist, and more than eleven trips to five different courts.

Alderman and Kennedy used this narrative to stimulate their readers' interest in the abstract subject of the chapter—the fourth amendment to the constitution, which prohibits unreasonable search and seizure. Compare the impact of their opening narrative to the section of the chapter that begins their discussion of the fourth amendment: "At the heart of the Fourth Amendment is the phrase 'unreasonable search.' To be brought within the amendment, an act by a government official must first be deemed a 'search.' Advances in law enforcement and technology have made this determination far more difficult than the Framers could ever have envisioned" (136). Had the chapter begun with this material, fewer readers would finish it. Obviously Alderman and Kennedy, like many writers of nonfiction, are aware of the power of narrative to entice and hold readers.

Aspiring rhetors can learn much from reading the skillful historical narratives composed by writers such as Taylor Branch, Antonia Frazer, or Barbara Tuchman. Historical novels are currently very popular, as well: Charles Johnson, Colleen McCullough, James Michener, and Sharon Kay Penman are four of the many skilled historical novelists whose work frequently makes the bestseller lists. Try to condense the narrative of a history or novel into a short tale as a useful exercise in summary paraphrase. Reorder the events of a history or novel. Compare the narrative thread of a film version to the book it is based on. What did the filmmakers include and what did they leave out? Did they add anything? Or try your hand at telling the story of some contemporary event: a concert, a snowstorm or tornado, a politician's visit to another country, an athletic event, an accident.

CHREIA

Chreia is an exercise in which students amplify a short narrative, usually taken from history, that points up a moral or teaches a lesson (*Institutes* I ix, 4–6). Sometimes chreia were developed around famous sayings, rather than narratives, however. Hermogenes defined *chreia* as "a concise exposition of some memorable saying or deed, generally for good counsel" (26). Ancient teachers regularly cited the following example of a famous deed, attributed variously to Diogenes or Crates: this man, on seeing a young boy misbehave, struck the boy's teacher. The moral, of course, is that teachers are ultimately responsible for the behavior of their students. Here is another ancient example, from Plato's *Republic:* "I remember hearing Sophocles the poet greeted by a fellow who asked, How about your service of Aphrodite, Sophocles—is your natural force still unabated? And he replied, Hush, man, most gladly have I escaped this thing you talk of, as if I had run away from a raging and savage beast of a master" (329b). To figure out the moral of this little story, you need to know that Aphrodite was the goddess of sexual love.

In *chreia,* ancient students moved from composing narratives to amplifying them, sometimes by fleshing out the bare narrative, but more often by adding commentary on famous deeds or utterances. The ability to amplify on a theme was much prized in antiquity and throughout the premodern period, because it demonstrated the fruits of a rhetor's long study and well-trained memory. In his sixteenth-century text on copia, Erasmus wrote that amplification was "just like displaying some object for sale first of all through a grill or inside a wrapping, and then unwrapping it and opening it out and displaying it fully to the gaze" (572). Ancient rhetors could amplify any theme in order to meet situational constraints, such as resistant audiences who needed a good deal of convincing. They could also shorten their compositions if time limits were imposed on them.

Amplification evolved into something of an art form in Roman rhetoric. Seneca the Elder told a story about a rhetor named Albucius, who could amplify a single theme so fully that he could speak through three soundings of the trumpet (the trumpet blew at the end of each three-hour watch during the night). Seneca reported that Albucius wished "to say not what ought to be said but what is capable of being said. He argued laboriously rather than subtly; he used argument to prove arguments, and as though there were no firm ground anywhere confirmed all his proofs with further proofs" (*Controversiae* 7, pref. 1).

Because of the importance of amplification, Hermogenes and Aphthonius both supplied a list of instructions for amplifying on a simple account of a historical event or speech. The fully amplified *chreia* was to begin with praise of a famous speaker or doer of deeds; then there was to be an explanation or paraphrase of the famous saying or action; composers next supplied a reason for the saying or doing; then they compared and contrasted the famous saying or doing to some other speech or event; next, they added an example and supported the saying or doing with testimony; last, they concluded with a brief epilogue.

Aphthonius supplied the following example of a fully developed *chreia*. The famous saying, taken from the work of Isocrates, is "The root of education is bitter, but sweet are its fruits."

Praise for the Author, or Encomium

It is fitting that Isocrates should be admired for his art, which gained for him an illustrious reputation. Just what it was, he demonstrated by practice and he made the art famous; he was not made famous by it. It would take too long a time to go into all the ways in which he benefitted humanity, whether he was phrasing laws for rulers on the one hand or advising individuals on the other, but we may examine his wise remark on education.

Paraphrase of the Saying

The lover of learning, he says, is beset with difficulties at the beginning, but these eventually end as advantages. That is what he so wisely said, and we shall wonder at it as follows.

Causes or Reasons for the Saying

The lovers of learning search out the leaders in education, to approach whom is fearful and to desert whom is folly. Fear waits upon the boys, both in the present and in the future. After the teachers come the attendants, fearful to look at and dreadful when angered. Further, the fear is as swift as the misdeed and, after fear, comes the punishment. Indeed, they punish the faults of the boys, but they consider the good qualities only fit and proper. The fathers are even more harsh than the attendants in choosing the streets, enjoining the boys to go straight along them, and being suspicious of the marketplace. If there has been need of punishment, however, they do not understand the true nature of it, but the youth approaching manhood is invested with good character through these trials.

A Contrast

If anyone, on the other hand, should flee from the teachers out of fear of these things, or if he should run away from his parents, or if he should turn away from the attendants, he has completely deprived himself of their teaching and he has lost an education along with the fear. All these considerations influence the saying of Isocrates that the root of learning is bitter.

A Comparison

For just as the tillers of the soil throw down the seeds to the earth with hardship and then gather in a greater harvest, in like manner those seeking after an education finally win by toil the subsequent reknown.

An Example

Let me call to mind the life of Demosthenes; in one respect, it was more beset with hardships than that of any other rhetor but, from another point of view, his life came to be more glorious than any other. For he was so preeminent in his zeal that the adornment was often taken from his head, since the best adornment stems from virtue. Moreover, he devoted to his labors those energies that others squander on pleasures.

Testimony

Consequently, there is reason to marvel at Hesiod's saying that the road to virtue is hard, but easy it is to traverse the heights. For that which Hesiod terms a road, Isocrates calls a root; in different terms, both are conveying the same idea.

Epilogue

In regard to these things, there is reason for those looking back on Isocrates to marvel at him for having expressed himself so beautifully on the subject of education.

We encourage our readers to imitate or paraphrase this *chreia;* surely it is possible to write a better theme on Isocrates' observation about education. Copy the saying, and then follow Aphthonius' instructions.

A more interesting challenge is to amplify the saying about Sophocles' service of Aphrodite, or some other short account of a famous saying or deed. Try amplifying on George Washington's act of cutting down the cherry tree or Benjamin Franklin's flying his famous kite. Or amplify John F. Kennedy's "Ask not what your country can do for you" or Sojourner Truth's "Ain't I a Woman?" (these are quoted in full in the preceding chapter). It is not necessary to use every kind of amplification suggested by the ancient teachers, but each of them does provide practice in important subskills of composing.

Chreia need not be developed only from the sayings or deeds of famous people. You may wish to elaborate on some favorite saying, or some habit, of a relative or a friend; or you can use sayings from editorials in newspapers or magazines; or you can develop a *chreia* of action from a news story. Quintilian suggested yet another kind of exercise with *chreia:* try to determine the causes of some well-known symbolic relationships (II iv, 26). His examples were these: "Why in Sparta is Venus represented as wearing armor"? or "Why is Cupid believed to be a winged boy armed with arrows and a torch?" Here are a couple of modern examples of this sort of question, around which a *chreia* could be developed: Why is justice represented as blind? Why does the Statue of Liberty bear a lighted torch? Find out the answers to these questions, and compose a *chreia* that amplifies on the justness of these decisions. Remember the *chreia* differs from the tale because the story taken from history is supposed to point up a lesson or moral.

PROVERB

Proverbs are common sayings that every member of a culture knows: "a stitch in time saves nine," "haste makes waste," and the like. (Aristotle called proverbs "maxims," and he regarded them as a means of proof—see the chapter on rhetorical reasoning.) Hermogenes defined a proverb as "a summary saying, in a statement of general application, dissuading from something or persuading toward something, or showing what is the nature of each" (27). That is, proverbs are either persuasive or expository. Examples of contemporary proverbs that persuade people to action are: "the squeaky wheel gets the grease," "wake up and smell the roses," and "the early bird gets the worm." Proverbs that dissuade people from doing things are "If you drive, don't drink" and "don't count your chickens before they hatch." Explanatory proverbs include "rolling stones gather no moss" and "the spirit is willing, but the flesh is weak."

Any of these proverbs can be amplified according to the ancient directions: begin by praising either the wisdom of the proverb or its author (if the author is known); paraphrase or explain the proverb's meaning; give proof of the proverb's truth or accuracy; give comparative and contrasting examples; supply testimony from another author; compose an epilogue.

Here is an example of this exercise composed by the seventeenth-century poet John Milton, who elaborated on the proverb "In the morning rise up early."

Encomium

Tis a proverb worn with age, "it is most healthy to rise at break of day." Nor indeed is the saying less true than old, for if I shall try to recount in order the several advantages of this, I shall seem to undertake a task of heavy labor.

Paraphrase

Rise, then, rise, thou lazy fellow, let not the soft couch hold thee forever.

Cause

You know not how many pleasures the dawn brings. Would you delight your eyes? Look at the sun rising in ruddy vigor, the pure and healthful sky, the flourishing green of the fields, the variety of all the flowers. Would you delight your ears? Listen to the clear concert of the birds and the light humming of the bees. Would you please your nostrils? You cannot have enough of the sweetness of the scents that breathe from the flowers.

Another Cause

But if this please you not, I beg you to consider a little the argument of your health; for to rise from bed at early morn is in no light degree conducive to a strong constitution; it is in fact best for study, for then you have wit in readiness.

Comparison

Besides, it is the part of a good king not to pamper his body with too much sleep, and live a life all holidays and free from toil, but to plan for the commonwealth night and day.

Ancient Testimony

As Theocritus wisely urges "It is not well to sleep deep." And in Homer the Dream thus speaks to Agamemnon "Sleepest thou, son of a wise-minded, horse-taming Atreus? 'Tis not well for a man of counsel to sleep all night through."

Example

Why do the poets fable Tithonus and Cephalus to have loved Dawn? Surely because they were sparing of sleep; and, leaving their beds, were wont to roam the fields, decked and clad with many-colored flowers.

Contrary

But to extirpate somnolence utterly, to leave no trace of it, I shall attempt to lay bare the numberless inconveniences that flow to all from it. It blunts and dulls keen talent, and greatly injures memory. Can anything be baser than to snore far into the day, and to consecrate, as it were, the chief part of your life to death?

Conclusion

But you who bear rule, you especially should be wide awake, and utterly rout gripping sleep as it creeps upon you. For many, coming upon enemies, whelmed by heavy sleep, and as it were, buried therein, have smitten them with slaughter, and wrought such havoc as it is pitiful to see or hear of. A thousand examples of this kind occur to me which I could tell with an inexhaustible pen. But if I imitate such Asiatic exuberance, I fear lest I shall murder my wretched listeners with boredom. (Quoted by D. C. Clark, 1948, 235–246)

A dictionary of proverbs or quotations will supply you with lots of famous sayings to use for this exercise. For example, we found the following quotations listed under the heading of "greatness" in *The Pocket Book of Quotations:*

> How dreary to be somebody!
> How public, like a frog
> To tell your name the livelong day
> To an admiring bog!
>
> —*Emily Dickinson,* Poems, *I*

> The great are only great because we are on our knees. Let us rise!
>
> —P. J. Proudhon, *Revolutions of Paris*

> But be not afraid of greatness: some are born great, some achieve greatness and some have greatness thrust upon 'em.
>
> —William Shakespeare, *Twelfth Night* II, 5

Very different themes could be amplified from these three very different attitudes toward greatness.

Proverb, *chreia*, tale, and fable were the exercises used by grammarians to help younger students master the basic composing skills. When students matured, they moved on to study with a teacher of rhetoric, who saw to it that they practiced exercises in the achievement of copia that were directly related to composing skills they would need as rhetors.

CONFIRMATION AND REFUTATION

The first of the strictly rhetorical exercises engaged students in composing the main parts of arguments: confirmation and refutation. Confirmation is the section of a composition that lays out the composer's arguments and support for them. The section called refutation answers the anticipated arguments of those who oppose the rhetor's point of view. Matters of fact are not suitable for this exercise since they need not be confirmed, nor can they be refuted. Discourses that are obviously fictional are not suitable for confirmation or refutation either.

Quintilian suggested that students compose confirmations and refutations using the same historical materials they worked with in the elementary exercises before they graduated to the composition of confirmations and refutations for use in actual rhetorical situations (II iv, 18–19). For example, he suggested that students write compositions confirming or refuting the legend that "a raven settled on the head of Valerius in the midst of a combat and with its wings and beak struck the eyes of the Gaul who was his adversary."

Aphthonius taught that a rhetor's first duty in refutation was to state the "false assertion of the opposition," and then to write a brief exposition of the situation. Hermogenes suggested several topics that could be used to find arguments for refutation: "You can refute an argument from the standpoint of its uncertainty, its incredibility, its impossibility, its lack of consistency, its impropriety, its inconvenience" (Miller, 58).

The opposites of these topics (that is, certainty, credibility, possibility, consistency, propriety, and convenience) can be used in confirmation. A confirmation begins with an account of the good reputation enjoyed by the doer of the deed, presents an exposition of the situation, and employs the opposite topics used in refutation: certainty, believability, possibility, consistency, propriety, convenience.

Following Aphthonius' instructions, we composed a sample refutation and confirmation about a contemporary event. In late 1992, President George Bush pardoned several persons who had been convicted or who were under investigation for their roles in the Iran-Contra affair. Here is our refutation of his action:

False Assertion to Be Refuted

President Bush was right to pardon several persons who are connected with the Iran-Contra affair.

Exposition of the Situation

On December 24, 1992, outgoing President George Bush pardoned several people who were under investigation for their suspected roles in the Iran-Contra affair. Bush said the men were victims of a "political witch hunt" conducted by a special prosecutor appointed to investigate the affair. He called the men "patriots," noting that none of them had acted for personal gain.

Arguments Drawn from Topics Relevant to Refutation

Uncertainty

Since some of the people pardoned had not yet been tried, it is uncertain whether they broke the law.

Incredibility

It is hard to believe that all the people pardoned are innocent, since some had been convicted already, while others were either under investigation or were suspected of involvement in the affair.

Impossibility

Since they have been pardoned, it is impossible that any of these persons will be brought to trial in the future, and so the guilty among them, if there are any, will go unpunished.

Lack of Consistency

The pardon is inconsistent with American principles of justice, which demand that persons be considered innocent until proven guilty. To declare them innocent before proof is ascertained is inconsistent with this principle.

Impropriety

Since the President himself may come under investigation, he had a personal stake in granting pardons to others. Thus his action is improper.

Inconvenience

Since the special prosecutor in the case was about to indict some of the people pardoned, the pardon was inconvenient, considering the enormous amounts of money, time, and energy that were spent in pursuing the investigation and securing indictments.

Here is a confirmation of President Bush's action:

Encomium

President George Bush is an honorable and sensitive person.

Exposition of the Situation

On December 24, 1992, outgoing President George Bush pardoned several people who were under investigation for their suspected roles in the Iran-Contra affair. Bush said the men were victims of a "political witch hunt" conducted by a special prosecutor appointed to investigate the affair. He called the men "patriots," noting that none of them had acted for personal gain.

Certainty

Whether those pardoned were guilty or not, it is certain that they did not act in their own interests. Rather, they were behaving as patriots.

Credibility

Since the special prosecutor has been working on the case for a long time, and has secured only a few guilty pleas and convictions of minor officials, it is hard to believe that any far-reaching scandal occurred.

Possibility

It is quite possible that the people pardoned were innocent. Thus Mr. Bush's action saved a good deal of money and time that would have otherwise been spent unnecessarily.

Consistency

Mr. Bush's action was consistent with a tradition in which presidents and governors may pardon anyone they please at year's end.

Propriety

His granting of the pardons on Christmas Eve was perfectly appropriate, since we should be generous to others during the holiday season.

Convenience

The pardon was convenient, since it saved those pardoned from further expense and anxiety.

Remarkably, our systematic use of the ancients' suggested topics produced most of the arguments that were made in the press and elsewhere in regard to this event. This exercise is yet another example of a reality that appears again in again in ancient rhetorics: good arguments can be found to support almost any position on a given issue.

We suggest that rhetors practice composing sample confirmations and refutations about any event drawn from contemporary events. Debatable questions from history are suitable too: should the United States have entered the Vietnam War? Should President Truman have used atomic weapons to end World War II? Was Christopher Columbus' arrival on American shores a good thing?

COMMONPLACE

This exercise should not be confused with the commonplaces of invention. In the context of the *progymnasmata,* a commonplace was an exercise in which students amplified or elaborated on some commonly held belief. When practicing commonplace, students can use the argumentative skills they acquired in the previous exercise, but here they do not argue the facts of an actual case. Rather, they argue against some vice or moral fault such as treachery or theft or greed, or they argue for virtues such as honor or justice. The facts of any case used in this exercise are assumed; the object is rather to elaborate on the moral qualities of a virtue or vice. This is why the exercise was called "common": it addressed general topics rather than specific cases that named individual persons or events. Ancient teachers used this exercise to give their students practice in writing perorations, the last and most emotional part of persuasive discourses.

Erasmus supplied this list of commonplaces:

1. It matters what company you keep.
2. Offence is easy, reconciliation hard.
3. The safest course is to believe no one.
4. Love as one soon to hate, hate as one soon to love.
5. The friendship of princes is perilous.
6. War is pleasant to those who have not experienced it.
7. The best provision for old age is learning.

He pointed out that commonplaces also include stock comparisons such as "Is the married or unmarried state happier? Private or public life? Is monarchy preferable to democracy? Is the life of the student better than that of the uneducated?" (637).

Aphthonius suggested that the composition of a commonplace begin with a prologue. Then the composer should provide a contrary, then an exposition that interests the listener and a comparison that attaches blame to the accused. This was to be followed by an attack on the doer's motives and a digression that castigated the doer's past life. Finally, the composer rejected any feeling of pity for the doer, and reminded the audience of the standard topics that were relevant to the commonplace being amplified: legality, justice, expediency, practicability, honor, or result.

Aphthonius gave an example of a fully elaborated commonplace. Its composer argued against an imaginary ruler who has broken laws and who has been hauled into court. The composer pretended to represent the people against this would-be despot. Here is our paraphrase of Aphthonius' example:

First Prologue

Inasmuch as laws are established among us and courts of justice are part of our political structure, that person who breaks the laws must pay a penalty to law. It is not likely that one who breaks laws will become more moderate if he is let off the hook once; on the contrary, he will be more prone to break the law if he goes unpunished. Thus, leniency in a first case will bring about even more despotic rule.

Second Prologue

Ordinarily, judges are not harmed if they acquit someone who has been brought to trial. In the case of a leader, however, this is not true, since acquittal of a despot will inflict harm upon the judges, for judging is no longer allowed when a despot gains control.

Contrary

Our forefathers, as if with good intent toward us, planned a state free of domination—and with every good reason. Since at different times different fortunes befall humankind, and since these different developments alter people's opinions about what is right and wrong, our constitution balances the chance events of history against the uniformity of laws. Thus our forefathers devised norms of conduct from which they worked out one standard of judgement for all. So it was that law came into being as the rectifier of evils caused by chance or misfortune.

Exposition

However, our ruler has conceived a very evil purpose, that of altering the constitution. Here is what he said to himself: "I am above the crowd. Shall I consider myself to be bound to the laws that bind the herd? Will my acquisition of riches be in vain, if I allow others to become rich as well? Shall poor people be allowed to sit in judgement on me? I can only escape from these things if I seize power and put law aside; thus will I be the law to the many, not they to me." Luckily, fortune intervened to keep this man from accomplishing his aims, and he has been brought to justice before you today.

Comparison

A murderer is dreadful but the despot is worse. For the former commits his foul deeds against a single person; the latter changes all the fortunes of the people.

Attack on Motive

Most people distinguish their motives from their actions. However, this person freely admits that he intended to commit his foul crimes. Only a tyrant would feel powerful enough to make an admission of this kind, to claim that his terrible acts were wholly voluntary.

Digression

Ordinarily, people are tried only for a single crime, and, if they have lived otherwise respectable lives, they are often freed. However, this person must be tried for all his crimes, since he has never practiced moderation, and he is presently behaving worse than he ever has. So he must give satisfaction both for his earlier offenses as well as for those committed later.

Rejection of Pity

Do not feel pity for this person's children, who will be bereft if he is punished. It is more just to feel pity toward the laws that have been violated, for the children of this person would have continued his tyranny, had he not been stopped.

Relevent Topics

Legality

If it is lawful to honor those who fight for freedom, it follows that those who reduce the country to slavery must be punished.

Justice

It is just that a penalty should be fixed that is equal to the harm that has been done.

Expediency

The dictator must pay what is due by being removed from his position, for by falling he will cause the laws to prevail.

Practicability

To punish this person will be easy. He needed armed guards to set up his despotism, but we do not need allies to end his rule. All we need to destroy his power is the right vote by the judges.

Sadly, there are still tyrants in the modern world, and their deeds can still inspire compositions against injustice. But commonplaces can concern vices or virtues other than injustice by tyrants; honorable and dishonorable actions, actions that cause evil results, or actions that endanger others can all provide subjects for commonplaces. Was the invention of atomic weapons just? Expedient? Honorable? Is the United States' intervention, military or otherwise, in the affairs of other nations just, expedient, honorable, good? Refer to the lists of common American topics composed by E. D. Hirsch and Howard Zinn (see the chapter on the commonplaces). Compose commonplaces that elaborate on one or two of them.

ENCOMIUM AND INVECTIVE

While commonplace engaged students in composing discourses that examined general vices or virtues, the next two exercises of the *progymnasmata* asked students to compose discourses in which they either praised or denigrated some specific person or thing. Greek rhetors called a discourse of praise "panegyric," but it is still known in English by its Latin name, **encomium.** A discourse that blames or denigrates something or someone, on the other hand, is called **invective.** Both kinds allow students to practice composing **epideictic** rhetoric.

Rhetors have many opportunities both to praise good actions or persons and to heap blame on less honorable persons and activities, and so these exercises provide excellent practice for real rhetorical situations. Quintilian observed that such compositions are often imposed on us, as when we are asked to give eulogies at funerals (a discourse of praise) or when we are asked to serve as character witnesses in court, in which case we may be asked either to praise or to blame an accused person (III vii, 2).

Encomium and invective were commonly practiced by the ancient Greeks and Romans. Encomia were featured in many religious and cultural celebrations in both cultures, and famous rhetors often gave speeches of praise or denunciation to large audiences in order to display their oratorical abilities. Isocrates' *Panegyricus* and *Panathenaicus* are encomia of the city of Athens. Gorgias and Isocrates, among others, composed encomia about Helen, whose abduction by Paris initiated the Trojan war. Popular interpretations of Homer's account of that war suggested that Helen was responsible for starting it. But these famous sophists argued the opposite case in their speeches of praise for her.

Encomia and invective are still being composed today, although we don't call them that. Most Fourth-of-July speeches are encomia to the United States, while speeches and editorials composed for Memorial Day praise those killed in war. Mothers' Day inspires endless essays about the virtues of motherhood, which are examples of encomia to an abstract ideal. Obituaries are encomia to deceased persons, and letters of reference may praise the character of the person being recommended. Invective, which exposes evils or heaps blame on someone who has done wrong, is used in political campaigns when candidates heap blame on one another even more frequently than they praise their own efforts. Invective is also a regular feature of letters written to the editors of newspapers and magazines. Sometimes biographies and histories are extended encomia or invectives. For example, Barbara Tuchman's *March of Folly* (1984) is an invective about war, and unauthorized biographies of famous people are popular precisely because they contain large doses of invective.

Aphthonius defined an encomium as "a composition expository of inherent excellences." He listed its proper subjects as "persons, things, times, places, animals, and also plants: persons like Thucydides or Demosthenes, things like justice or moderation, times like spring or summer, places like harbors or gardens, animals like a horse or an ox, and plants like an olive or a vine." Hermogenes, on the other hand, suggested that students compose encomia about a race (such as the Greeks), a city, or a family.

Ancient teachers defined an elaborate set of directions for composing encomia and invectives: Theon, for example, listed thirty-six possible encomiastic
headings for amplification. The standard list of headings for an encomium of a
person was as follows: a prologue; announcement of the class of person or thing
to be praised or blamed; consideration of the person's origins (nationality, native city, ancestors, parents); education and interests; achievements (virtue,
judgement, beauty, speed or strength, power, wealth, friends); comparison, and
epilogue. The same topics can be used to compose invectives.

Here is Aphthonius' encomium on the ancient historian Thucydides:

To honor the inventors of useful things for their very fine contributions is just, and
just it is that the light coming forth from those men be turned with good reason upon
those who displayed it. Accordingly, I shall laud Thucydides by choosing to honor
him with the history of the man himself. Moreover, it is a good thing that honor be
given to all benefactors, but especially to Thucydides about others, because he invented the finest of all things. For it is neither possible to find anything superior to
history in these circumstances, nor is it possible to find one more skillful in history
than Thucydides.

Accordingly, Thucydides came from a land that gave him both life and a profession. For he was not born from an indifferent quarter but from whence history came,
and by gaining Athens as his mother of life, he had kings for ancestors, and the
stronger part of his good fortune proceeded from his earlier ancestry. By gaining
both force of ancestry and democratic government, the advantage from one supplied a check upon the other, preventing his being rich unjustly through political
equality and concealing public poverty through the affluence of his descent.

Having come upon the scene with such advantages, he was reared under a civil
polity and laws that are by nature better than others. Knowing how to live both under
arms and under law, he determined to be in one and the same person both a philosopher and a general, neither depriving history of military experience nor placing battles in the class of intellectual virtue. Further, by combining things that were naturally
separate, he made a single career in things for which he had no single set of rules.

As he arrived at manhood, he kept seeking an opportunity for the display of those
qualities in which he had been well disciplined. And fortune soon produced the war,
and he made the actions of all the Greeks his personal concern. He became the cus-
todian of the things that the war brought to pass, for he did not allow time to erase
the deeds separately accomplished. Among these, the capture of Plataea is famous,
the ravages of Attica were made known, the Athenian circumnavigation of the Polo-
ponnesus was described, and Naupactus was a witness to sea battles. By collecting
these things in writing, Thucydides did not allow them to escape notice. Lesbos was
won, and the fact is proclaimed to this day; a battle was fought against the Ambra-
ciotes, and time has not obscured the event; the unjust decree of the Lacedaemonians
is not unknown. Sphacteria and Pylos, the great achievement of the Athenians, has
not escaped unseen. Where the Corcyraeans speak in the assembly at Athens, the
Corinthians present answers to them. The Aeginetans go to Lacedaemon with accusations. Archidamus is discreet before the assembly, but Sthenelaides is urging them
on to war. And to these examples, add Pericles, holding a Spartan embassy in no esteem and not allowing the Athenians to make trouble when they were suffering.
Once and for all, these things are preserved for all time by Thucydides' book.

> Does anyone really compare Herodotus with him? But Herodotus narrates for pleasure, whereas this man utters all things for the sake of truth. To the extent that entertainment is less worthy than a regard for the truth, to that degree does Herodotus fall short of the virtues of Thucydides.
>
> There would be many other points to mention about Thucydides, if the great number of his praises did not prevent the enumeration of all of them.

A careful reading of this encomium will show that Aphthonius included a prologue, stated the kind of encomium he has composed (praise of a single person), and commented on his subject's birth and upbringing as well as his studies and achievements. The encomium concludes with a comparison and a summarizing epilogue.

Quintilian suggested that praise of persons include praise of place of birth, parents, and ancestry (III viii, 10). This may be handled in two ways: rhetors may show that someone lived up to the high standards of their places of birth, or that their deeds have made their places of birth even more praiseworthy. Someone's character, physical endowments such as beauty and strength, or deeds and achievements can furnish topics for praise (or abuse). Accidental advantages, such as wealth or power, should not be praised for themselves but only if the person put such advantages to honorable use. The only deeds deserving of praise are those that were done for the sake of others, not on the person's own behalf. Sometimes reputations increase (or decrease) after persons have died; in this case, Quintilian says, it is appropriate to point out that "children reflect glory on their parents, cities on their founders, laws on those who made them, arts on their inventors and institutions on those that first introduced them" (18).

The same topics can be used in denunciations of persons. People who came from privileged backgrounds can be blamed if they squandered those resources or if they used them to engage in vice. While we no longer approve of denouncing persons because of their physical appearance, we can blame someone who demonstrates an immoral character or who engages in reprehensible acts. Quintilian pointed out that the reputations of bad or immoral persons redounds upon their children and their homelands as well (21). Some may not like to admit this, but we think it is still true that we condemn innocent people who are associated by birth or circumstance with individuals who commit immoral acts.

Cities are praised or blamed in the same way. A city's founder can be made responsible for the habits of its citizens in the same way that parents are responsible for their children. Quintilian remarked that great age usually brings fame to a city, as do their settings, public works, and buildings or fortifications. Buildings should be praised for their "magnificence, utility, beauty and the architect of artist must be given due consideration" (27). As an example of an encomium on a place, Quintilian cited Cicero's praises of Sicily in his Verrine orations:

> when Sicily was at the height of its prosperity, and abounded in wealth and resources, there were many fine workshops on the island. For, before Verres' tenure as governor, there was not a home somewhat well off in which there could not be found such things as silver dishes with decorative medallions and figures of the gods, silver bowls used by the women in performing rituals, and a censer, even

though there may not have been much else in the way of silver plate. These things were, moreover, executed in a classic style of exquisite craftsmanship; one would be led to believe that the Sicilians had, at one time, owned many other things of equal value, but, that incurring their loss through changed fortunes, they still retained the objects associated with religious worship. (IV, 21)

Notice how skillfully Cicero managed to praise the Sicilians at the same time as he blamed Verres for their impoverished condition.

In his remarks on the composition of encomia, Aristotle made a subtle point that does not appear in ancient textbooks: discourses of praise or blame must be carefully suited to their audiences (*Rhetoric* I, 9). He quoted Socrates, who is reputed to have said that "it is not difficult to praise Athenians in Athens" (1367b). What is considered honorable in Athens can be an object of blame among Scythians or Laconians. Of course, the same point holds true today. To praise Americans in America is easy enough to do; such a composition would be received quite differently elsewhere in the world. The same holds true for invective; it is easy to blame Americans when writing for other audiences. During the Persian Gulf war, Judith Williamson wrote the following passage for a British publication called *The Guardian:*

> It is the unreality of anywhere outside the US, in the eyes of its citizens, which must frighten any foreigner. Like an infant who has yet to learn there are other centres of self, this culture sees others merely as fodder for its dreams and nightmares . . . The hyped-up concern over US children's fears ("Will Saddam kill me Mommy?") is obscene when you consider that American bombs are right now killing Iraqi children. It isn't that Americans don't care (God knows they care) but that for most of them, other lands and people cannot be imagined as real. (31 January 1991, p. 21)

Americans who accept the accuracy of Williamson's invective may nevertheless be put off by her criticism.

Distinct groups of persons also hold differing sets of values. Quintilian observed that "much depends on the character of the audience and the generally received opinion, if they are to believe that the virtues of which they approve are preeminently characteristic of the person praised and the vices which they hate of the person denounced" (III vii, 23). The boundaries between virtue and vice are also notoriously hard to define; acceptable behavior in one setting may be utterly unacceptable in another (25). Wise rhetors will keep these differences in mind as they compose encomia or invective.

The composition of encomia and invective were popular exercises among educated persons during late antiquity and throughout the Renaissance. Erasmus' *Praise of Folly* (in Latin, *Encomium Moriae,* 1509) is a satiric encomium about foolishness. John Milton composed paired poems called "Joy" and "Thoughtfulness" when he was quite young. The poem about joy contains an invective about melancholy, or sadness, that connects its origins with death:

> Hence loathed Melancholy
> Of Cerberus, and blackest midnight born,

> In Stygian Cave forlorn.
>   'Mongst horrid shapes, and shrieks, and sights unholy,
> Find out some uncouth cell,
>   Where brooding darkness spreads his jealous wings,
>   And the night-Raven sings;
>   There under Ebon shades, and low-brow'd Rocks,
> As ragged as thy Locks,
>   In darks Cimmerian desert ever dwell.

—*John Milton, "L'Allegro"*

The poem about thoughtfulness, on the other hand, contains a lengthy encomium to melancholy. I quote only its opening lines:

> But hail thou Goddess, sage and holy,
> Hail divinest Melancholy,
> Whose Saintly visage is too bright
> To hit the Sense of human sight;
> And therefore to our weaker view,
> Ore laid with black staid Wisdoms hue.

—*John Milton, "Il Penseroso"*

Once again, Milton's performance suggests that arguments can be found to attack or defend anything or anybody, depending on the situation.

Rhetors can adapt Aphthonius' suggestions to any contemporary topic. You can practice writing discourses that praise or blame nations, cities, families, persons, animals, or things. For a relatively simple exercise, choose a favorite relative, a favorite pet, or even a plant, and use Aphthonius' topics to develop a discourse praising it. This exercise does not have to be serious; funny essays can be written in praise or blame of inanimate objects. Isocrates complained about rhetors who composed encomia to salt and bumblebees (Helen, 12). A sophist named Lucian wrote this delightful encomium on a fly:

THE FLY, AN APPRECIATION

The fly is not the smallest of winged things, on a level with gnats, midges, and still tinier creatures; it is as much larger than they as smaller than the bee. It has not feathers of the usual sort, it is not fledged all over like some, nor provided with quill-feathers like other birds, but resembles locusts, grasshoppers, and bees in being gauze-winged, this sort of wing being as much more delicate than the ordinary as Indian fabrics are lighter and softer than Greek. Moreover, close inspection of them when spread out and moving in the sun will show them to be peacock-hued.

Its flight is accompanied neither by the incessant wing-beat of the bat, the jump of the locust, nor the buzz of the wasp, but carries it easily in any direction. It has the further merit of a music neither sullen as with the gnat kind, deep as with the bee, nor grim and threatening as with the wasp; it is as much more tuneful than they as the flute is sweeter than trumpet or cymbals.

As for the rest of its person, the head is very slenderly attached by the neck, easily turned, and not all of one piece with the body as in the locust; the eyes are projecting and horny; the chest strong, with the legs springing freely from it instead of lying close like a wasp's. The belly also is well fortified, and looks like a breastplate, with its broad bands and scales. Its weapons are not in the tail as with wasp and bee, but in its mouth and proboscis; with the latter, in which it is like the elephant, it forages, takes hold of things, and by means of a sucker at its tip attaches itself firmly to them. This proboscis is also supplied with a projecting tooth, with which the fly makes a puncture, and so drinks blood. It does drink milk, but also likes blood, which it gets without hurting its prey much. Of its six legs, four only are for walking, and the front pair serves for hands; you may see it standing on four legs and holding up a morsel in these hands, which it consumes in very human fashion.

It does not come into being in its ultimate shape, but starts as a worm in the dead body of man or animal; then it gradually develops legs, puts forth wings and becomes a flying instead of a creeping thing, which generates in turn and produces a little worm, one day to be a fly. Living with man, sharing his food and his table, it tastes everything except his oil, to drink which is death to it. In any case it soon perishes, having but a short span of life allotted to it, but while it lives it loves the light, and is active only under its influence; at night it rests, neither flying nor buzzing, but retiring and keeping quiet.

I am able to record its considerable wisdom, shown in evading the plots of its enemy the spider. It is always on the look-out for his ambushes, and in the most circumspect way dodges about, that it may not be caught, netted, and entangled in his meshes. Its valour and spirit require no mention of mine; Homer, mightiest-voiced of poets, seeking a compliment for the greatest of heroes, likens his spirit not to a lion's, a panther's, a boar's, but to the courage of the fly, to its unshrinking and persistent assault; mark, it is not mere audacity, but courage, that he attributes to it. Though you drive it off, he says, it will not leave you; it will have its bite. He is so earnest an admirer of the fly that he alludes to it not once nor twice, but constantly; a mention of it is felt to be a poetic ornament. Now it is its multitudinous descent upon the milk that he celebrates; now he is in want of an illustration for Athene as she wards off a spear from the vitals of Menelaus; so he makes her a mother caring for her sleeping child, and in comes the fly again. Moreover he gives them that pretty epithet, 'thick-clust'ring'; and 'nations' is his dignified word for a swarm of them.

The fly's force is shown by the fact that its bite pierces not merely the human skin, but that of cattle and horses; it annoys the elephant by getting into the folds of its hide, and letting it know the efficiency of even a tiny trunk. There is much ease and freedom about their love affairs, which are not disposed of so expeditiously as by the domestic fowl; the act of union is prolonged, and is found quite compatible with flight. A fly will live and breathe for some time after its head is cut off.

The most remarkable point about its natural history is that which I am now to mention. It is the one fact that Plato seems to me to have overlooked in his discourse of the soul and its immortality. If a little ashes be sprinkled on a dead fly, it gets up, experiences a second birth, and starts life afresh, which is recognized as a convincing proof that its soul is immortal, inasmuch as after it has departed it returns, recognizes and reanimates the body, and enables it to fly; so is confirmed the tale about Hermotimus of Clazomenae—how his soul frequently left him and went off on its own account, and afterwards returning occupied the body again and restored the man to life.

It toils not, but lives at its ease, profiting by the labours of others, and finding everywhere a table spread for it. For it the goats are milked, for its behoof and man's the honey is stored, to its palate the *chef* adapts his sauces; it tastes before the king himself, walks upon his table, shares his meal, and has the use of all that is his.

Nest, home, local habitation, it has none; like the Scythians, it elects to lead a wandering life, and where night finds it, there is its hearth and its chamber. But as I said, it works no deeds of darkness; "live openly" is its motto; its principle is to do no villany that, done in the face of day, would dishonour it.

Legend tells how Myia (the fly's ancient name) was once a maiden, exceeding fair, but over-given to talk and chatter and song, Selene's rival for the love of Endymion. When the young man slept, she was for ever waking him with her gossip and tunes and merriment, till he lost patience, and Selene in wrath turned her to what she now is. And therefore it is that she still, in memory of Endymion, grudges all sleepers their rest, and most of all the young and tender. Her very bite and bloodthirst tell not of savagery, but of love and human kindness; she is but enjoying mankind as she may, and sipping beauty.

In ancient times there was a woman of her name, a poetess wise and beautiful, and another a famous Attic courtesan, of whom the comic poet wrote:

As deep as to his heart fair Myia bit him.

The comic Muse, we see, disdained not the name, nor refused it the hospitality of the boards; and parents took no shame to give it to their daughters. Tragedy goes further and speaks of the fly in high terms of praise, as witness the following:

Foul shame the little fly, with might courageous,
Should leap upon men's limbs, athirst for blood,
But men-at-arms shrink from the foeman's steel!

I might add many details about Pythagoras's daughter Myia, were not her story too well known.

A careful reading of this mock encomium will disclose Lucian's use of many of the topics recommended by the rhetoric teachers.

Lighthearted encomia and invective are still popular. Erma Bombeck, the columnist, often composed very funny encomia or invectives about household objects such as vacuum cleaners and garage door openers. Newspaper columnist Mike Royko once wrote an encomium to hamburgers:

"CALIFORNIA BURGER" DRIVES YOU NUTS

I should have become suspicious when I looked in the window and saw all the ferns hanging from the ceiling and walls in the bar section of the restaurant. Bars that have ferns everywhere are not part of the Chicago tradition of interior design.

More suitable Chicago barroom decor includes softball and bowling trophies, hand-printed signs that say: "No Checks Cashed" and somebody taking a nap on the pool table.

But we were looking for a fast lunch and the sign outside said the place served food, so we went in and took a table.

"Hamburger," I said to the waitress.

"With or without pecans?" she said.

"With or without what?" I asked.

"Pecans," she said.

"Uh, maybe you misunderstood me. I asked for a hamburger."

"Yes, I heard you. With or without pecans?"

Well, I didn't know what to say. I had never heard of pecans with a hamburger.

So I asked: "How do you serve the pecans? As a side dish or what?"

"No, they're in the hamburger."

"Ah, of course," I said, trying not to appear unsophisticated. "Of course, I'll have it with the pecans."

"How do you want it done?"

Now she had me. I had stepped right into a trap. I always got hamburgers well-done. As Slats Grobnik once told me: "Real hot grease kills all the germs."

But what about pecans? Should pecans be rare, medium or well?

So I asked: "Could I get the pecans rare and the rest of the hamburger well-done?"

She blinked at me. "The pecans are in the hamburger."

"Ok, well-done for both of them."

Then she asked if I wanted cheese, and I said yes. And she asked: "Swiss, cheddar, blue cheese?"

There is only one cheese for hamburger—plain American cheese. The processed kind. My favorite is Velveeta. That's why I never go to Paris. You can't get real Velveeta from those barbarians.

"Do you have Velveeta?" I asked.

"Velveeta? No, but we have some American cheese."

"God bless America," I said. "I'll have it."

She returned in a while and put a plate in front of me. I gaped at it and asked: "What is this?"

"Your hamburger," she said.

"It is?"

"That's what you ordered."

I had ordered a hamburger. Everybody knows what a hamburger is. And this was not a hamburger.

It was the size and shape of a baseball. And it was wrapped in bacon and covered with melted cheese.

It sat atop half a roll, and the other half was on the side. There was no onion. There was no mustard or ketchup.

I pointed this out and she said: "You didn't order onion. But I'll bring you mustard and ketchup."

The mustard she brought was that brown, French kind. I demanded honest, yellow, American mustard, which is the only mustard you should put on hot dogs or hamburgers.

I doused the burger with the condiments, put the top half of the roll on it and picked it up.

It was impossible. It measured about eight inches from bottom to top. There was no way a person with even a big mouth could take a bite out of it.

"How do you eat this thing?" I asked my companion.

"I don't know. Maybe you should sort of press down on it with your hand to flatten it out."

I tried. Mustard squirted out on my shirt.

I looked around to see what others were doing. They were eating hamburgers, too. With knives and forks. Knives and forks.

There are many gray areas in life. Some things can't be called right or wrong.

But it was wrong to eat certain foods with knives and forks. Ribs, hot dogs, fried chicken, egg rolls and hamburgers should all be eaten with the hands.

To eat a hamburger with a knife and fork is as unnatural as drinking a shot or beer through a straw.

"It's the California influence," my companion said. "That is a California-style burger."

Of course. The ferns should have told me that. And the pecans and foreign mustard.

And the fact that a wan young man at the next table was sipping white wine with his hamburger.

As we were leaving, the waitress said to me: "Was everything all right?"

"Everything was subversive and un-American," I said.

That evening, I stopped at the Billy Goat Tavern, where a hamburger is still a hombooger and a cheeseburger is still a chizbooger: flat circles of meat cooked on a greasy grill, with onions and yellow mustard and slices of pickle.

And I warned Sam Sianis, the owner, that times were changing and he should consider changing with them.

"Ferns, Sam, you had better think about ferns."

"How you cook dem?"

"You don't cook them. They're plants. You hang them from the walls and ceilings."

He shook his head. "No plants een dees place. Plants got bugs. I no like bugs."

"Well, then you should consider pecans in your burgers. It's the coming thing. It's already here."

"Pecans?" he said. "You mean knots?"

"Yeah, nuts."

He thought for a moment. Then he went and got a hamburger and put it in front of me. Next, he turned around and pulled a package of beer nuts from the nut rack on the back bar.

He lifted the top of the bun and put the package of beer nuts on the hamburger. Then he replaced the bun.

"OK, you got nuts in your chizbooger."

Ah, sanity prevails.

Royko's essay nicely illustrates Aristotle's point about suiting the praise to the setting and the audience. What works in California is not always welcome in Chicago.

For a more difficult exercise, develop an encomium or an invective about the city council or other leaders of your town or state. A United States senator has been accused of sexual harassment: write an invective that denounces him for this behavior, or compose an encomium that excuses him from these charges on the basis of his origin, character, or achievements. You can even compose encomia and invective about abstract ideas or issues: how about an encomium to rhetoric? No subject is off limits in this exercise. In fact, its versatility is one of its strengths. Quintilian remarked that compositions of praise or blame were "profitable in more than one respect. The mind is exercised by the variety and multiplicity of the subject matter, while the character is molded by the contemplation of virtue and vice" (IV iv, 20).

COMPARISON

Comparison is an exercise in which the composer implies that someone or something is greater than another. He or she does this by juxtaposing descriptions of both people or things. Comparison is similar to the exercise that precedes it, since a comparison is a double encomia or an encomium paired with an invective. As Aphthonius counseled, "it is necessary for those who make comparisons either to place the good beside the excellent, or the mean beside the base, or the upright beside the wicked, or the small beside the greater." Hermogenes noted that comparison occurs in a number of other exercises, such as commonplace and encomium, as a means of amplification. He counted it as a separate exercise, however, because "some authors of no small reputation" had made comparison "an exercise by itself" (33).

With comparison we arrive at the portion of the rhetorical exercises that were practiced by mature rhetors. Plutarch's *Parallel Lives,* for instance, includes a number of exercises in comparison. Indeed, Plutarch probably learned the techniques used in the *Lives* when he practiced the school exercise called comparison.

Like Plutarch's *Lives,* ancient examples of comparison chiefly concern comparisons of persons. Aphthonius' example compared the Greek warrior Achilles to Hector, the Trojan warrior-prince. Hermogenes recommended comparison between the heroes Odysseus and Hercules. However, he warned that such an exercise required great skill, since the trickster Odysseus was a less heroic figure than the mighty Hercules. The composer's goal in this case would be to praise Odysseus by showing that his virtues were even greater than those of the man who held the world on his shoulders. Hermogenes also suggested that comparisons could fruitfully be made between abstractions, such as justice and wealth.

The composing strategies used in comparison are the same as those used in encomium and invective. However, Aphthonius pointed out that "it is not fitting that those who make comparisons should set one 'whole' beside another, for this is dull and unimpressive, but they should rather set one point beside another for this is indeed impressive." In other words, the comparison should not treat all the details involved in one item and then move to the next; rather, it should compare the two items point-by-point. Here is Aphthonius' point-by-point comparison of Achilles and Hector:

A COMPARISON OF ACHILLES AND HECTOR

Seeking to compare virtue with virtue, I am going to measure the son of Peleus by the standard of Hector, for the virtues are to be honored in themselves. Compared, they become even more worthy of imitation.

Accordingly, both were born of not one land, but each alike sprang from one that is famous. One was of Phthia, whence came the name of Greece itself. The other was of Troy, whose builders were the first of the gods. To the degree that having been born in similar lands is not an inferiority in regard to commendation, by that degree Hector is not excelled by Achilles. And being born, the one as well as the other, of a praiseworthy land, both belonged to families of equal stature. For each was descended from Zeus. Achilles was the son of Peleus, Peleus of Aeacus, and Aeacus of Zeus; Hector, likewise, came from Priam and Laomedon, Laomedon from Dardanus, and Dardanus was a son of Zeus. And having been born with Zeus as a progenitor, they had forefathers nearly alike. For the ancestors of Achilles were Aeacus and Peleus, of whom the former freed the Greeks from want and the latter was allotted marriage with a goddess as a prize for his prowess in overcoming the Lapithes. On Hector's side, Dardanus was a forefather who formerly lived with the gods, and his father, Priam, was in command of a city whose walls were built by gods. To the degree that there was similarity in living with the gods and association with superior beings, by that degree is Hector about equal to Achilles.

And descended from such ancestors, both were brought up for courage. The one was reared by Chiron, while Priam was the tutor of the other by contributing lessons in virtue through his natural relationship. Just as an education in virtue is equal in both instances, so to them both does it bring equal fame.

When both arrived at manhood, they gained similar stature out of a single struggle, for in the first place, Hector led the Trojans and he was the protector of Troy as long as he survived. He remained in alliance with gods during that time, and when he fell, he left Troy lying vulnerable. Achilles, on the other hand, was the leader of Greece in arms; by terrifying all, he was prevailing against the Trojans, and he had the help of Athena in the contest, but when he fell, he deprived the Achaeans of gaining the upper hand. Overcome through Athena, the former [Hector] was destroyed; the latter [Achilles] fell, struck down at the hands of Apollo. And both, having sprung from gods, were taken off by gods; whence they drew their beginning, they also derived the end of their lives. To the degree that there was similarity in life and in death, by that degree is Hector on a par with Achilles.

It would be possible to say many other things on the virtue of both, except that both have nearly equal renown for their deeds. (Matsen, Rollinson, & Sousa, 280)

Persons who are familiar with Homer's *Iliad* are likely to assume that Achilles was Hector's superior, since the Greek hero killed the Trojan prince in battle. However, Aphthonius's exercise demonstrates the persuasive potential of comparison, since his point-by-point consideration of the two heroes shows that Hector is as worthy of imitation as Achilles.

Here is Plutarch's comparison of the two most famous orators in ancient times—Demosthenes and Cicero:

THE COMPARISON OF DEMOSTHENES AND CICERO

These are the most memorable circumstances recorded in history of Demosthenes and Cicero which have come to our knowledge. But omitting an exact comparison of their respective faculties in speaking, yet thus much seems fit to be said; that Demosthenes, to make himself a master in rhetoric, applied all the faculties he had, natural or acquired, wholly that way that he far surpassed in force and strength of eloquence all his contemporaries in political and judicial speaking, in grandeur and majesty all the panegyrical orators, and in accuracy and science all the logicians and rhetoricians of his day; that Cicero was highly educated, and by his diligent study became a most accomplished general scholar in all these branches, having left behind him numerous philosophical treatises of his own on Academic principles; as, indeed, even in his written speeches, both political and judicial, we see him continually trying to show his learning by the way. And one may discover the different temper of each of them in their speeches. For Demosthenes's oratory was without all embellishment and jesting, wholly composed for real effect and seriousness; not smelling of the lamp, as Pytheas scoffingly said, but of the temperance, thoughtfulness, austerity, and grave earnestness of his temper. Whereas Cicero's love of mockery often ran him into scurrility; and in his love of laughing away serious arguments in judicial cases by jests and facetious remarks, with a view to the advantage of his clients, he paid too little regard to what was decent: saying, for example, in his defence of Cælius, that he had done no absurd thing in such plenty and affluence to indulge himself in pleasures, it being a kind of madness not to enjoy the things we possess, especially since the most eminent philosophers have asserted pleasures to be the chiefest good. So also we are told that when Cicero, being consul, undertook the defence of Murena against Cato's prosecution, by way of bantering Cato, he made a long series of jokes upon the absurd *paradoxes,* as they are called, of the Stoic set; so that a loud laughter passing from the crowd to the judges, Cato, with a quiet smile, said to those that sat next to him, "My friends, what an amusing consul we have."

And, indeed, Cicero was by natural temper very much disposed to mirth and pleasantry, and always appeared with a smiling and serene countenance. But Demosthenes had constant care and thoughtfulness in his look, and a serious anxiety, which he seldom, if ever, laid aside; and therefore, was accounted by his enemies, as he himself confessed, morose and ill-mannered.

Also, it is very evident, out of their several writings, that Demosthenes never touched upon his own praises but decently and without offence when there was need of it, and for some weightier end; but upon other occasions modestly and sparingly. But Cicero's immeasurable boasting of himself in his orations argues him guilty of an uncontrollable appetite for distinction, his cry being evermore that arms should give place to the gown, and the soldier's laurel to the tongue. And at last we find him extolling not only his deeds and actions, but his orations also, as well those that were only spoken, as those that were published; as if he were engaged in a boyish trial of skill, who should speak best, with the rhetoricians, Isocrates and Anaximenes, not as one who could claim the task to guide and instruct the Roman nation, the—

"Soldier full-armed, terrific to the foe."

It is necessary, indeed, for a political leader to be an able speaker; but it is an ignoble thing for any man to admire and relish the glory of his own eloquence. And, in this matter, Demosthenes had a more than ordinary gravity and magnificence of mind, accounting his talent in speaking nothing more than a mere accomplishment and matter of practice, the success of which must depend greatly on the good-will and candour of his hearers, and regarding those who pride themselves on such accounts to be men of a low and petty disposition.

The power of persuading and governing the people did, indeed, equally belong to both, so that those who had armies and camps at command stood in need of their assistance; as Charas, Diopithes, and Leosthenes of Demosthenes's, Pompey and young Cæsar of Cicero's, as the latter himself admits in his Memoirs addressed to Agrippa and Mæcenas. But what are thought and commonly said most to demonstrate and try the tempers of men, namely, authority and place, by moving every passion, and discovering every frailty, these are things which Demosthenes never received; nor was he ever in a position to give such proof of himself, having never obtained any eminent office, nor led any of those armies into the field against Philip which he raised by his eloquence. Cicero, on the other hand, was sent quaestor into Sicily, and proconsul into Cilicia and Cappadocia, at a time when avarice was at the height, and the commanders and governors who were employed abroad, as though they thought it a mean thing to steal, set themselves to seize by open force; so that it seemed no heinous matter to take bribes, but he that did it most moderately was in good esteem. And yet he, at this time, gave the most abundant proofs alike of his contempt of riches and of his humanity and good-nature. And at Rome, when he was created consul in name, but indeed received sovereign and dictatorial authority against Catiline and his conspirators, he attested the truth of Plato's prediction, that then the miseries of states would be at an end when, by a happy fortune, supreme power, wisdom, and justice should be united in one.

It is said, to the reproach of Demosthenes, that his eloquence was mercenary; that he privately made orations for Phormion and Apollodorus though adversaries in the same cause; that he was charged with moneys received from the King of Persia, and condemned for bribes from Harpalus. And should we grant that all those (and they are not few) who have made these statements against him have spoken what is untrue, yet that Demosthenes was not the character to look without desire on the presents offered him out of respect and gratitude by royal persons, and that one who lent money on maritime usury was likely to be thus indifferent, is what we cannot assert. But that Cicero refused, from the Sicilians when he was quaestor, from the King of Cappadocia when he was proconsul, and from his friends at Rome when he was in exile, many presents, though urged to receive them, has been said already.

Moreover, Demosthenes's banishment was infamous, upon conviction for bribery; Cicero's very honourable, for ridding his country of a set of villains. Therefore, when Demosthenes fled his country, no man regarded it; for Cicero's sake the senate changed their habit, and put on mourning, and would not be persuaded to make any act before Cicero's return was decreed. Cicero, however, passed his exile idly in Macedonia. But the very exile of Demosthenes made up a great part of the services he did for his country; for he went through the cities of Greece, and everywhere, as we have said, joined in the conflict on behalf of the Grecians, driving out the Macedonian ambassadors, and approving himself a much better citizen than Themistocles and Alcibiades did in the like fortune. And, after his return, he again devoted himself to the same public service, and continued firm to his opposition to Antipater and the Macedonians. Whereas Lælius reproached Cicero in the senate for sitting silent when Cæsar, a beardless youth, asked leave to come forward, contrary to the law, as a candidate for the consulship; and Brutus, in his epistles, charges him with nursing and rearing a greater and more heavy tyranny than that they had removed.

Finally, Cicero's death excites our pity; for an old man to be miserably carried up and down by his servants, flying and hiding himself from that death which was, in the course of nature, so near at hand; and yet at last to be murdered. Demosthenes, though he seemed at first a little to supplicate, yet, by his preparing and keeping the poison by him, demands our admiration; and still more admirable was his using it. When the temple of the god no longer afforded him a sanctuary, he took refuge, as it were, at a mightier altar, freeing himself from arms and soldiers, and laughing to scorn the cruelty of Antipater. (1070–1072)

While Plutarch's comparison supplied a good deal of information about both orators, it is not simply expository. Plutarch used his point-by-point comparison to evaluate the relative personal and professional merits of the two famous orators. In other words, comparison is a way of making judgements, of writing criticism.

Shakespeare's Sonnet 18 is an interesting exercise because it compares a person to a day in summertime:

> Shall I compare thee to a summer's day?
> Thou art more lovely and more temperate.
> Rough do shake the darling buds of May,
> And summer's lease hath all too short a date.
> Sometime too hot the eye of heaven shines.
> And often is his gold complexion dimm'd;
> And every fair from fair sometimes declines,
> By chance, or nature's changing course, untrimm'd;
> But thy eternal summer shall not fade,
> Nor lose possession of that fair thou ow'st,
> Nor shall Death brag thou wander'st in his shade,
> When in eternal lines to time thou grow'st.
>   So long as men can breathe or eyes can see.
> So long lives this, and this gives life to thee.

A day in summer may be fair, but it is short-lived. A loved one is equally fair, but she lives longer, and the loved one immortalized in this sonnet will live as long as people read the poem. Here again, an author used comparison to evaluate relative merits.

We often make comparisons in everyday discourse. Of two manufacturers of video or audio equipment, which produces the better product? Of all the things we might do on weekends, which is the more interesting? The most fun? When we vote, we are often asked to choose between two candidates. Which is the better of the two? Which the lesser? You can use Aphthonius' recommended pattern to compose comparisons that attempt to answer these questions or any questions like them.

Contemporary students are familiar with this exercise in its guise as the "essay of comparison." In fact, comparison may be one of the few ancient exercises that survives in school rhetoric. (Description may be another.) However, modern rhetoric teaches students to compose comparisons as noncontextualized exercises in exposition. Thus it misses an important point about the ancient exercise: comparisons are always persuasive, insofar as they praise someone or something by comparing it to a less praiseworthy person or thing.

CHARACTER

Aphthonius defined this difficult exercise as "an imitation of the character of a proposed person." In other words, students using this exercise were to construct a characterization of some fictional person. In modern schools, this exercise, along with description and narration, is often taught by creative writers—persons who make their living writing poetry and fiction. But the ancients made no sharp distinctions among the composing skills required by rhetors, poets, historians, or novelists. Historians need to know how to depict character just as novelists and poets do. Furthermore, the establishment of a rhetor's character amounts to an important kind of proof in rhetoric.

Aphthonius divided characters into three kinds: *ethopoeia* (to create character), *prosopopoeia* (to create a person) and *eidolopoeia* (to create an image or spirit). In the first kind, students depict the character of some famous historical person by imagining the words that person might say to another. The exercise becomes *prosopopeia* when students imagine a fictional person within a scene, and describe that, too. The dramatic monologs composed by the English poet Robert Browning are skillful examples of this exercise. In the last kind of character, words are put into the mouth of someone who has died. Shakespeare displayed his skill at *eidolopoeia* when he composed the speeches made by the ghost of Hamlet's father.

Hermogenes taught that the compositions called "characters" could be either definite or indefinite. A definite character depicts specific persons, such as Andromache and Hector. The characters in novels—Emma Bovary, Holden Caulfield, Bigger Thomas—are usually definite depictions. But some genres of novels, such as westerns and romances, rely to some extent on stock characters—the retired gunfighter, the ruthless cattle baron, the poor but gutsy heroine, the mad monk. Hermogenes would have classed these as indefinite characters, where the composer attempts to capture typical characteristics of a class of persons. (We have already met with this exercise in the chapter on ethos, where we quoted Theophrastus' characterization of a tactless person.) Hermogenes further classified characters as single or double. A single character depicts someone talking to himself, for example, "what a general might say on returning from a victory"; a double character represents another person or persons as well, as "what a general might say to his army after a victory."

Hermogenes also recommended that characterizations be appropriate to the persons and occasions being depicted: "for the speech of youth is not that of age, nor the speech of joy that of grief" (35). He pointed out that some characters depict a habit of mind, while others depict a passing mood or emotion. In the former kind, the composer should provide details that indicate a person's general habits of mind and action; what, for example, would a farmer say when seeing a ship or the sea for the first time? In the latter sort of character, the composer should portray the effects of powerful emotions on someone: for example, in portraying Achilles' response to the death of Patroclus, the composer should try to depict the hero's rage, pain, and grief.

The chronology of a characterization may be important. Hermogenes suggested that composers "begin with the present because it is hard." (Epic poems conventionally begin in the present, or in medias res—in the middle of things.) Then, Hermogenes said, the composer should "revert to the past because it has had much happiness; then make your transition to the future because what is to happen is much more impressive." Characters need not involve consideration of past, present, or future, of course; they may depict a single moment in time.

One way to indicate character is to create conversation that gives clues about a person's responses to situations. Ancient teachers asked their students to indicate character by imagining what famous people in history or fiction might say on a given occasion: What would Queen Hecuba have said about the fall of her city? What would Medea say as she was about to slaughter her children? Here is a prosopopoeia written by Plutarch, in which he imagined Cleopatra standing over Marc Antony's grave:

> There was a young man of distinction among Cæsar's companions named Cornelius Dolabella. He was not without a certain tenderness for Cleopatra, and sent her word privately, as she had besought him to do, that Cæsar was about to return through Syria, and that she and her children were to be sent on within three days. When she understood this, she made her request to Cæsar that he would be pleased to permit her to make oblations to the departed Antony; which being granted, she ordered herself to be carried to the place where he was buried, and there, accompanied by her women, she embraced his tomb with tears in her eyes, and spoke in this manner: "O, dearest Antony," said she, "it is not long since that with these hands I buried you; then they were free, now I am a captive, and pay these last duties to you with a guard upon me, for fear that my just griefs and sorrows should impair my servile body, and make it less fit to appear in their triumph over you. No further offerings or libations expect from me; these are the last honours that Cleopatra can pay your memory, for she is to be hurried away far from you. Nothing could part us whilst we lived, but death seems to threaten to divide us. You, a Roman born, have found a grave in Egypt; I, an Egyptian, am to seek that favour, and none but that, in your country. But if the gods below, with whom you now are, either can or will do anything (since those above have betrayed us), suffer not your living wife to be abandoned; let me not be led in triumph to your shame, but hide me and bury me here with you, since, amongst all my bitter misfortunes, nothing has afflicted me like this brief time that I have lived away from you." (1151)

Plutarch uses a monologue to convey Cleopatra's character. In this short speech, we learn about the nature of her relationship to Antony.

Probably the most famous example of ethopoeia in all of English literature is Hamlet's "To be or not to be" speech:

> To be, or not to be, that is the question—
> Whether 'tis nobler in the mind to suffer
> The slings and arrows of outrageous fortune,
> Or to take arms against a sea of troubles,
> And by opposing end them. To die, to sleep—
> No more; and by a sleep to say we end
> The heart-ache, and the thousand natural shocks

That flesh is heir to; 'tis a consummation
Devoutly to be wished. To die, to sleep—
To sleep, perchance to dream, ay there's the rub,
For in that sleep of death what dream may come
When we have shuffled off this mortal coil,
Must give us pause; there's the respect
That makes calamity of so long life.
For who would bear the whips and scorns of time,
Th' oppressor's wrong, the proud man's contumely,
The pangs of despised love, the law's delay,
The insolence of office, and the spurns
That patient merit of th' unworthy takes,
When he himself might his quietus make
With a bare bodkin? Who would fardels bear,
To grunt and sweat under a weary life,
But that the dread of something after death,
The undiscovered country, from whose bourn
No traveller returns, puzzle the will,
And makes us rather bear those ills we have,
Than fly to others that we know not of?
Thus conscience does make cowards of us all,
And thus the native hue of resolution
Is sicklied o'er with the pale cast of thought,
And enterprises of great pitch and moment
With this regard their currents turn awry,
And lose the name of action. (*Hamlet* III i, 56–88)

Shakespeare used this speech to tell us a good deal about Hamlet's character. The ghost of Hamlet's father commanded the young prince to kill the person who murdered him, married the queen (who is Hamlet's mother), and usurped his throne. Despite all these provocations, Hamlet is unable to act. In this speech he considers committing suicide, but he can't bring himself to do this either, because of his characteristic inability to make decisions and his preference for philosophy over action.

Here is another well-known example of characterization from English literature—the opening chapter of Jane Austen's *Pride and Prejudice*. Notice how Austen portrays the characters of Mr. and Mrs. Bennet through conversation:

It is a truth universally acknowledged, that a single man in possession of a good fortune, must be in want of a wife.

However little known the feelings or views of such a man may be on his first entering a neighbourhood, this truth is so well fixed in the minds of the surrounding families, that he is considered as the rightful property of some one or other of their daughters.

"My dear Mr. Bennet," said his lady to him one day, "have you heard that Netherfield Park is let at last?"

Mr. Bennet replied that he had not.

"But it is," returned she; "for Mrs. Long has just been here, and she told me all about it."

Mr. Bennet made no answer.

"Do not you want to know who has taken it?" cried his wife impatiently.

"*You* want to tell me, and I have no objection to hearing it."

This was invitation enough.

"Why, my dear, you must know, Mrs. Long says that Netherfield is taken by a young man of large fortune from the north of England; that he came down on Monday in a chaise and four to see the place, and was so much delighted with it that he agreed with Mr. Morris immediately; that he is to take possession before Michaelmas, and some of his servants are to be in the house by the end of next week."

"What is his name?"

"Bingley."

"Is he married or single?"

"Oh! single, my dear, to be sure! A single man of large fortune; four or five thousand a year. What a fine thing for our girls!"

"How so? how can it affect them?"

"My dear Mr. Bennet," replied his wife, "how can you be so tiresome! You must know that I am thinking of his marrying one of them."

"Is that his design in settling here?"

"Design? nonsense, how can you talk so! But it is very likely that he *may* fall in love with one of them, and therefore you must visit him as soon as he comes."

"I see no occasion for that. You and the girls may go, or you may send them by themselves, which perhaps will be still better, for as you are as handsome as any of them, Mr. Bingley might like you the best of the party."

"My dear, you flatter me. I certainly *have* had my share of beauty, but I do not pretend to be any thing extraordinary now. When a woman has five grown up daughters, she ought to give over thinking of her own beauty."

"In such cases, a woman has not often much beauty to think of."

"But, my dear, you must indeed go and see Mr. Bingley when he comes into the neighbourhood."

"It is more than I engage for, I assure you."

"But consider your daughters. Only think what an establishment it would be for one of them. Sir William and Lady Lucas are determined to go, merely on that account, for in general you know they visit no new comers. Indeed you must go, for it will be impossible for *us* to visit him, if you do not."

"You are over scrupulous surely. I dare say Mr. Bingley will be very glad to see you; and I will send a few lines by you to assure him of my hearty consent to his marrying which ever he chuses of the girls; though I must throw in a good word for my little Lizzy."

"I desire you will do no such thing. Lizzy is not a bit better than the others; and I am sure she is not half so handsome as Jane, nor half so good humoured as Lydia. But you are always giving *her* the preference."

"They have none of them much to recommend them," replied he; "they are all silly and ignorant like other girls; but Lizzy has something more of a quickness than her sisters."

"Mr. Bennet, how can you abuse your own children in such a way? You take delight in vexing me. You have no compassion on my poor nerves."

> "You mistake me, my dear. I have a high respect for your nerves. They are my old friends. I have heard you mention them with consideration these twenty years at least."
>
> "Ah! you do not know what I suffer."
>
> "But I hope you will get over it, and live to see many young men of four thousand a year come into the neighbourhood."
>
> "It will be no use to us, if twenty such should come since you will not visit them."
>
> "Depend upon it, my dear, that when there are twenty, I will visit them all."
>
> Mr. Bennet was so odd a mixture of quick parts, sarcastic humour, reserve, and caprice, that the experience of three and twenty years had been insufficient to make his wife understand his character. *Her* mind was less difficult to develope. She was a woman of mean understanding, little information, and uncertain temper. When she was discontented she fancied herself nervous. The business of her life was to get her daughters married; its solace was visiting and news. (1–3)

Austen hardly needs to provide the summary of these two characters that concludes her chapter, for she has beautifully portrayed their characters, as well as their relationship, by means of a short dialogue.

Modern authors, particularly those who write popular fiction, prefer to indicate character by giving details about their characters' habits. For example, Ian Fleming characterized his famous hero, James Bond, by giving details about Bond's habits and tastes. Bond always introduced himself in laconic fashion: "The name is Bond. James Bond." He smoked Players' cigarettes, drove an Astin-Martin, and drank his martinis "shaken, not stirred."

Writers who wish to tackle the very difficult exercise of composing characters might begin by imitating successful characterizations composed by historians, novelists, or poets. You can imitate any of the passages quoted here. It would also be interesting and useful to imitate the characterizations created by writers you admire and enjoy reading. How does your favorite novelist or historian depict habits of mind or action, physical appearance, responses to emotional situations? From imitation, you can graduate to creating original characters. Use Hermogenes' suggestions to depict the characters of friends or relatives, or of famous people. Or try your hand at an indefinite characterization. Theophrastus' characters provide lots of models to imitate. You can also use the depictions of stock characters that appear in novels, or you can try to write a character of any of the many stock characters who appear in films.

DESCRIPTION

According to Aphthonius, a description "is an expository speech, distinctly presenting to view the thing being set forth." Hermogenes wrote that descriptions bring "before one's eyes what is to be shown." Descriptions can be written of people, actions (a battle), times (peace or war), places (harbors, seashores, cities), seasons (spring, summer, a holiday), and many other things. Both teachers chose their examples of descriptions from Homer: "He was round in the shoulders, bronzed, with thick curling hair"; "crooked was he and halt of one foot."

The ancient authorities recommended that composers follow some order when writing descriptions: a description of a person, for example, should move from head to foot; descriptions of places should distinguish between the places themselves and their surroundings. A description of the Vietnam War memorial in Washington, D.C., for example, might begin by describing the memorial itself, then it might move to the immediate surroundings—the people walking slowly past, the gifts left at on the sidewalk in front of the memorial; then it might move outward toward less immediate surroundings—the park, vendors selling war memorabilia, the Lincoln and Washington monuments. Aphthonius recommended Thucydides' description of the harbor at Cheimerium as a good example of description because it locates the port precisely:

> The fleet sailed from Leucas, and, arriving at the mainland opposite Corcyra, came to anchor at Cheimerium in the country of Thesprotia. Cheimerium is a harbor; above it, at some distance from the sea, in that part of Thesprotia called Eleatis, lies the city of Ephyre, near which the Acherusian lake finds a way into the sea; the river Acheron, whence the name is derived, flows through Thesprotia and falls into the lake. Another river, the Thyamis, forms the boundary of Thesprotia and Cestrine, and the promontory of Cheimerium runs out between these two rivers. Here the Corinthians anchored and encamped. (I, 46)

Here is the Roman poet Virgil's description of the wintry land of Scythia:

> Far otherwise is it where dwell the tribes of Scythia by the waters of Maeotis, where the turbid Danube tosses his yellow sands, and where Rhodope bends back, stretching up to the central pole. There they keep herds penned up in stalls, and no blade is seen upon the plain, or leaf upon the tree; but far and wide earth lies shapeless under mounds of snow and piles of ice, rising seven cubits high. 'Tis ever winter; ever North-west blasts, with icy breath. Then, too, never does the Sun scatter the pale mists, either when, borne on his chariot, he climbs high Heaven, or when he laves his headlong car in Ocean's crimson plain. Sudden ice-crusts form on the running stream, and anon the water bears on its surface iron-bound wheels—giving welcome once to ships, but now to broad wains! Everywhere brass splits, clothes freeze on the back, and with axes they cleave the liquid wine; whole lakes turn into a solid mass, and the rough icicle hardens on the unkempt beard. No less, meanwhile, does the snow fill the sky; the cattle perish, the oxen's great frames stand sheathed in frost, the deer in crowded herd are numb under the strange mass and above it scarce rise the tips of their horns. These they hunt not by unloosing hounds, or laying nets, or alarming with the terror of the crimson feather, but as their breasts vainly strain against that mountain rampart men slay them, steel in hand, cut them down bellowing piteously, and bear them home with loud shouts of joy. Themselves, in deep-dug caves, low in the earth, they live careless and at ease, rolling to the hearths heaps of logs, yea, whole elm-trees, and throwing them on the fire. Here they spend the night in play, and with ale and bitter service-juice joyously mimic draughts of wine.

Virgil made these scenes come to life by using plenty of vivid details.

Plutarch included a lush description of Cleopatra's barge in his life of Marc Antony:

> She received several letters, both from Antony and from his friends, to summon her, but she took no account of these orders; and at last, as if in mockery of them, she came sailing up the river Cydnus, in a barge with gilded stern and outspread sails of purple, while oars of silver beat time to the music of flutes and fifes and harps. She herself lay all along under a canopy of cloth of gold, dressed as Venus in a picture, and beautiful young boys, like painted Cupids, stood on each side to fan her. Her maids were dressed like sea nymphs and graces, some steering at the rudder, some working at the ropes. The perfumes diffused themselves from the vessel to the shore, which was covered with multitudes, part following the galley up the river on either bank, part running out of the city to see the sight. The market-place was quite emptied, and Antony at last was left alone sitting upon the tribunal; while the word went through all the multitude, that Venus was come to feast with Bacchus, for the common good of Asia. (1118–1119)

Shakespeare imitated Plutarch's description of Cleopatra's ship in his play *Antony and Cleopatra:*

> The barge she sat in, like a burnished throne,
> Burned on the water; the poop was beaten gold,
> Purple the sails, and so perfumed that
> The winds were love-sick with them; the oars were silver,
> Which to the tune of flutes kept stroke, and made
> The water which they beat to follow faster,
> As amorous of their strokes. For her own person,
> It beggared all description: she did lie
> In her pavilion, cloth-of-gold, of tissue,
> O'er-picturing that Venus where we see
> The fancy outwork nature. On each side her,
> Stood pretty dimpled boys, like smiling Cupids,
> With diverse colored fans, whose wind did seem
> To glow the delicate cheeks which they did cool,
> And what they undid did . . .
> Her gentlewomen, like the Nereides,
> So many mermaids, tended her i' th' eyes,
> And made their bends adornings. At the helm,
> A seeming mermaid steers. The silken tackle
> Swell with the touches of those flower-soft hands,
> That yarely frame the office. From the barge
> A strange invisible perfume hits the sense
> Of the adjacent wharfs. The city cast
> Her people out upon her; and Antony,
> Enthroned i' th' market place, did sit alone,
> Whistling to th' air; which but for vacancy
> Had gone to gaze on Cleopatra too,
> And made a gap in nature. (II ii, 192–233)

Any of these passages is suitable for imitation. Or try rendering the description of Cleopatra's barge into modern prose. (If you need further inspiration, the many films that have been made about Cleopatra usually include the scene of her triumphal entry into Rome on her golden ship.)

The ability to write vivid descriptions is still important, particularly in history and fiction. However, vivid descriptions are also persuasive, and so rhetors should know how to compose them as well (see our comments about enargeia the chapter on pathos). We suggest that you begin by imitating passages of description in novels or essays that you admire. Then try your hand at composing descriptions of people, places, or things that are familiar to you.

THESIS

Aphthonius defined thesis as "a logical examination of any matter under consideration." We have met thesis before, in the chapter on stasis, and the school exercise is probably modeled on mature rhetors' use of the staseis in courtrooms and in legislative forums. In the context of the progymnasmata, however, a thesis is a composition that argues some general point. Ancient authorities distinguished thesis from hypothesis, which argues an issue in connection with a real person caught in real circumstances (such specific arguments are, of course, the province of forensic argument—see the chapter on special topics).

The favorite ancient example of a thesis was "should a person marry?" This question is a thesis because writers who use it must consider the benefits and disadvantages of marriage in general. The question whether Tom, Dick, or Mary ought to marry is a hypothesis.

Aphthonius divided theses into political and theoretical questions. Political questions "admit of an action that holds a city together; for example, whether one should marry, whether one should sail, whether one should build fortifications." Hermogenes added this example: "whether one should study rhetoric." In other words, political theses are questions that concern human activities. Aphthonius distinguished this sort of thesis from theoretical theses, which "are considered by the mind alone; for example, whether heaven is spherical, whether there are many worlds." Cicero's Stoic Paradoxes are theoretical theses that explain and defend Stoic ethical beliefs such as "only what is morally noble is good," and "only the wise person is rich." Theoretical theses concern issues raised by philosophers, pure scientists, and theorists of all kinds.

Hermogenes and Quintilian both noted that an exercise in thesis may have a doubling or relative quality, if in defending one side of an issue the writer must attack another. Quintilian mentioned the famous exercise in which a writer debates whether city life is to be preferred to country life as an example of the double or relative thesis (II iv, 24). Other well-known examples include the ancient debate about whether the active life was to be preferred to the contemplative life, or whether soldiers are more worthy of merit than lawyers. Cicero composed an extended meditation on this thesis in his defense of Murena (9ff). Cicero sometimes slipped into hypothesis in these passages, when he referred specifically to the lawyer Servius and the soldier Murena.

Since thesis is so much like actual argument, Aphthonius advised that theses display the standard arrangement and use of parts recommended for persuasive discourse in general (see the chapter on arrangement). Hermogenes disagreed about this, however. He pointed out that "theses are determined by the so-called final headings: justice, expediency, possibility, propriety." Hermogenes' final headings were drawn from the topics of invention. To use them in the thesis about marriage, a composer would show that marriage is just because married persons "make to life the contribution of life itself"; marriage is expedient because it brings "many consolations"; it is proper because married people must display calm dispositions; and so on.

Here is Aphthonius' example of a fully amplified thesis:

A THESIS: SHOULD ONE MARRY?

Let the one seeking to measure the entire question in a few words hold marriage in high esteem. For it came from heaven or, rather, it filled heaven with the gods and father was set up for them, whence originates the title of father. And having sired gods, marriage produced the natural powers to preserve them. Then, coming down to earth, it endowed all the other things with reproductive power. And bringing under its control those things that did not know how to be lasting, marriage cleverly devised the maintaining of them through their successors. First of all, it stirs men to bravery; it is through these [brave men], since marriage knows how to produce children and wives over whom war is fought, that marriage adds bravery to its gifts. Further, it provides righteous men along with the brave; it is through these [righteous men], since men who are anxious about the things in which posterity takes pride do those things justly, that marriage produces righteous men at the same time as brave men. Nay more, it makes men wise whom it inspires to provide for the dearest ones. And by way of paradox, marriage knows how to supply self-control, and moderation is mingled with the pursuit of pleasures; it is through these [temperate men], since it adds convention to the pleasures, that marriage supplies the pleasures of moderation in support of the convention; and that which by itself is brought as an accusation against itself is admired [when joined] with marriage. If, therefore, marriage produces gods and, after them, each of their descendants in succession, if it provides brave and just men at the same time, and if it furnishes wise and temperate men, how ought one not to esteem marriage as much as possible?

Antithesis. "Yes," he says, "but marriage is a cause of misfortunes."

Solution. You seem to me to be making a charge against fortune, not against marriage. For fortune, not marriage, produces things that men who fare badly encounter, whereas the things that marriage contributes to humankind are not at all those contributed by a desire of gain from fortune. Therefore, it is better to marvel at marriage for the fine things it encompasses, rather than to criticize it for the evil things fortune brings forth. But if we do, indeed, assign the worst of man's misfortunes to marriage, why should one rather refrain from marriage? There are those difficulties that you ascribe to business; these things would not by any means exert an influence toward an escape from business, would they? And let me examine one by one the activities to [each of] which is attributed what you are perhaps charging. Thunderbolts afflict those farming, and hailstorms harass them. Yet a thunderbolt does not spoil the soil for husbandmen, nor do they flee the soil, but they continue tilling it, even if something coming down from the heavens causes damage. On the other hand, seafarers are unfortunate, and attacking storms buffet their ships. Yet they do not thereafter abandon sailing on account of those things that they have suffered in turn, but they attribute the misfortune to chance and they wait for the passage provided by the sea. Furthermore, struggles and battles destroy the lives of the combatants; still, they do not avoid battles because by fighting they will fall; instead, because those fighting are admired, they have become reconciled to death and they join in concealing the attendant drawback because of the associated benefit. For one should not flee from whatever good things there are because of bad attributes, but because of the good things one should endure the worst. Surely then, it is unreasonable that on one side farmers, sailors, and as many as are serving in the army besides, should endure the difficulties arrayed against them for the sake of the praises associated with these activities, but that on the other side we should look down upon marriage because it brings with it a degree of vexation.

Antithesis. "Yes," he says, "but it introduced widowhood for wives and orphanhood for children."

Solution. These are the evils of death, and nature is cognizant of the misfortune; you seem to me to be critical of marriage on the ground that it does not make men gods and to censure marriage because it has not included mortal things for gods. Tell me, then, why do you criticize marriage for the things that death brings about? Why do you ascribe to weddings things such as those which nature [alone] understands? Grant that he who was born to die will die. Further, if men die because they have lived life's span and in dying bereave one dwelling in the same house and make an orphan of him, why will you say that marriage has finished off those things brought about by nature alone? I, on the contrary, hold that marriage corrects orphanhood and widowhood. To one a father is dead and thus a child is an orphan; but marriage brings in another father for the orphans, and this misfortune does not stem from marriage but is veiled completely by marriage, and marriage becomes the occasion of the disappearance of orphanhood, not the beginning of it. And so nature brought widowhood with death, but marriage effected a change with wedding songs. For marriage, as though standing guard over her gift, presents to a man in wedlock the one for whom death has accomplished a bereavement. For those things that it introduced from the first, it restores again when taken away; thus, marriage knows how to take away widowhood, not how to inflict it. Nay more, a father is deprived of children through death, but through the marriage he has a share of others. And he becomes a father for the second time who does not assent to being one but once. Why, therefore, do you pervert the fine things of marriage into a fault of marriage? Further, you seem to me not to be seeking to dishonor the wedding song but to be commending it. For by the very things you force us to enumerate as pleasures of the wedding songs, you have become an admirer, not an accuser of marriage, and you force us to be amazed at betrayers of marriage, and you make the accusations against marriage a list of good features.

Antithesis. "Yes," he says, "but marriage is wearisome."

Solution. And what is set up to halt drudgery like marriage? Whatever is some, through wedding songs it is taken away. Further, there is pleasure generally in coming together with a wife in intercourse. How pleasant it is for a man to go with a wife to the marriage bed! With how great pleasure is a child anticipated! And expected, does he appear! And having appeared, will he call a father! He is then started along his training with care and [soon] he is working with a father and addressing the people in the Assembly and taking care of a father; he becomes everything that it is necessary to be.

> *Epilogue.* It is impossible to cover in a speech the favors that marriage knows how to bestow. A mighty thing is marriage, both for producing gods and for granting to mortals for whom it devises a means of continuing life, that they seem to be gods. And it guides those needing strict rules, it urges a consideration of self-control, and it seeks after pleasures, as many as are obviously not worthy of blame. Wherefore, it is established among all that marriage should be reckoned of the greatest worth. (Matsen, Rollinson, & Sousa, 284–286)

This thesis begins with an encomium to marriage. Then its author considers three topics: fortune, death, and boredom. Finally, the thesis concludes with another encomium listing other topics that might be considered.

Students have composed theses ever since this exercise was invented sometime during the fifth or fourth century BCE. Exercises in thesis were called "themes" during the European Middle Ages and throughout the Renaissance, when the standard question debated in ancient theses were sometimes turned into poetry: the first seventeen of Shakespeare's sonnets, for example, can be read as meditations on the advisability of marriage.

Papers written for university coursework are still sometimes called "themes," and thesis is a bit like the standard essay that students are asked to write in most American college composition courses. Indeed, one of the standard features of the modern college essay is the "thesis statement," a term that may owe its use to the ancient exercise. However, the ancient exercise differed substantially from the modern college essay because it was an exercise in the composition of persuasive discourse. The ancient exercise that is most like the modern college essay is probably the commonplace, since it is an exercise in exposition rather than persuasion. As Hermogenes pointed out, thesis differs from commonplace because commonplace deals with matters already settled, while thesis "is an inquiry into a matter still in doubt." (The preceding paragraph, by the way, is a small exercise in comparison, complete with ancient testimony.)

INTRODUCTION OF LAW

The last, and most difficult, of the *progymnasmata* was called **introduction of law.** Quintilian wrote that "praise or denunciation of laws requires greater powers; indeed they should almost be equal to the most serious tasks of rhetoric" (II iv, 33).

Students using this exercise defended or attacked existing laws. Aphthonius' example concerned an ancient law that required adulterers to be put to death on the spot. He argued that while the law rightly operated "against the crimes of adulterers," it was inexpedient because its provision for immediate punishment threatened the entire system of law. In other words, it allowed people to take the law into their own hands, as a character in a modern western might say.

Typically, according to Quintilian, this exercise centered on one of three issues: whether a law was clearly written and consistent with itself; whether it was just and expedient, and whether it could be enforced. The second of these two approaches is, clearly, the more interesting one, given that rhetors can use the topics of justice and expediency to elaborate on their positions. Aphthonius' example demonstrated that a law can be just (if it is just to punish adulterers) at the same time as it can be inexpedient, if it threatens an entire system of justice.

This difficult exercise is still practiced in modern schools of law. However, its practice should not be limited to persons who have a professional interest in making and enforcing laws. All persons who live in a community are subject to its laws, and hence they should be interested in arguments for and against them. This is as true for laws that affect individuals, like those recently passed in many states mandating stiffer penalties for conviction of drunken driving, as it is for laws that preserve the central tenets of American ideology, such as the first amendment to the United States Constitution: "Congress shall make no law . . . abridging the freedom of speech." Rhetors' lives are affected every day by the laws of their community and the people who interpret them. That is why the ancient exercise called introduction of law is still interesting and useful.

Aphthonius recommended that an introduction of law include considerations of these four topics: constitutionality, justice, expediency, and practicability. The composition should also include an introduction, and should then state a counterargument as well. We composed an example of an introduction to law according to Aphthonius' instructions, and we imitated his introduction and conclusion where possible:

AN OPPOSITION OF A LAW THAT PERMITS PORNOGRAPHY

Introduction

I support Americans' right to freedom of speech. On this occasion I will not interest myself in the many specific applications of this general law, save one: I do not approve of laws that define pornography as freedom of speech. Laws are only valid insofar as they have been carefully examined. So it is not unreasonable for me to examine the laws that protect pornography as a kind of free speech.

Constitutionality

The right to freedom of speech is enshrined in the laws of our country, indeed in the first and most important of those laws, the United States Constitution. Laws that define pornography as instances of free speech cannot be attacked on grounds of their unconstitutionality or their inconsistency, since they are consistent with the fundamental guarantee of freedom of speech to all Americans, a guarantee granted them by their Constitution.

Justice

However, it is not just to protect pornography on the ground that it falls under the kinds of speech protected by the first amendment. The people who profit from pornography are not the people who are photographed or recorded when pornography is produced. Laws that define pornography as free speech protect the freedom of speech of people who produce and profit from pornography; they do not necessarily protect the freedom of speech of the persons who perform it. Often the people who perform are children or animals, or they are people who have been coerced into performing. Consequently, their freedom of speech is not protected. There is no justice in this unequal application of the law.

Expediency

It is not expedient to define pornography as freedom of speech. To include pornography under this head is to stretch the limits of free speech far past the limits envisioned by those who wrote the Bill of Rights, who were concerned primarily to protect the free expression of dissenting political and religious views. To stretch the definition of free speech to include pornography permits the unfettered dissemination of a kind of speech that is harmful to others. This is inexpedient, because it reduces our capacity to make useful distinctions among restrictions on speech that harm the community and those that serve it.

Practicability

It is not practical to define pornography as freedom of speech. When pornography is so defined, it becomes impossible to enforce many other laws that are associated with its production: laws against forced prostitution, against kidnapping, against abuse of children or animals.

Conclusion

The pornographer attains a wicked and complete extreme of premeditated wrongs against the community for his own profit. It follows that his activities should not be defined as activities protected by the first amendment. He should be prosecuted and convicted, and his fate should be made public, because if the punishment meted out to a pornographer escapes notice, he or she may leave behind many others of his or her ilk. For others will strive to emulate one for whose punishment they do not know the reasons, and the punishment will become, not the end, but the beginning of crime.

You may wish to imitate our sample introduction of law, perhaps defending another side of the issue.

For more difficult practice, you may wish to attack or defend other laws, large or small. Since the Bill of Rights was added to the United States Constitution in 1791, all of its amendments have been interpreted and reinterpreted as a result of court cases. Attorneys and judges have argued that in certain cases, observance of the amendments is neither just nor expedient. Here are the full texts of four amendments to the American constitution.

Article I

Congress shall make no law respecting an establishment of religion, or prohibiting the free exercise thereof; or abridging the freedom of speech or of the press; or the

> right of the people peaceably to assemble, and to petition the Government for a re-
> dress of grievances.

Many questions have been raised by cases appealing to this amendment: Is it just to interpret the use of prayer in public school as an abridgement of religious freedom? Is it expedient to ban prayer from public schools? Is it just to protect hate speech on the grounds that it is free speech? Does freedom of the press extend to the publication of information about the private habits of public figures? Is it expedient to restrict the press from publishing the names of rape victims?

Article II

> A well-regulated militia being necessary to the security of a free State, the right of the
> people to keep and bear arms shall not be infringed.

People who oppose gun control appeal to Article II as their constitutional ground for doing so. Should the protection offered by this amendment include the possession of assault weapons? Can Congress or the states ban the possession of guns or impose limits on their distribution without violating this amendment?

Article IV

> The right of the people to be secure in their persons, houses, papers, and effects,
> against unreasonable searches and seizures, shall not be violated, and no warrants
> shall issue but upon probable cause, supported by oath or affirmation, and particu-
> larly describing the place to be searched, and the persons or things to be seized.

Article IV implies that people cannot be searched without proper procedures. Does this so-called "right to privacy" include persons who carry dangerous weapons in public places, such as airplanes? What about people who break laws in their homes, such as those who keep and sell drugs? Is it just that they be protected from searches by authorities? Is it expedient? Recently, someone videotaped a couple who were making love in their home. They were not aware that they were being watched or taped. Did the person who made the tape violate Article IV? If so, was he justified in doing so? Was his act expedient?

Article VIII

> Excessive bail shall not be required, nor excessive fines imposed, nor cruel and un-
> usual punishments inflicted. People who oppose capital punishment do so on the
> basis of Article VIII, because they define the death penalty as cruel and unusual pun-
> ishment. Is their position just? Is it expedient? Is it practical?

Try your hand at composing introductions to law that expound, defend, or attack some question raised by these amendments.

WORKS CITED

Alderman, Ellen, and Caroline Kennedy. *In Our Defense.* New York: Morrow, 1991.

Austen, Jane. *Pride and Prejudice.* 3rd ed. London: Oxford UP, n.d.

de la Fontaine, Jean. *Fables of La Fontaine.* Trans. Elizur Wright. London, 1896.

Erasmus, Desiderius. *De Copia.* In *Collected Works of Erasmus,* Vol 2. Ed. Craig R. Thompson. Toronto: Toronto UP, 1978.

Lucian of Samasota. *The Works of Lucian.* Trans. H. W. and F. G. Fowler. 3 vols. London: Oxford UP, 1905.

GLOSSARY

accumulation   a figure wherein a rhetor gathers scattered points and lists them together.

active voice   a grammatical construction available in English, in which the grammatical subject is the actor in a sentence.

allegory   (AL a gor ee) an extended metaphor.

ambiguous case   (am BIG you us) case that is partly honorable, partly dishonorable in the eyes of an audience; or a case wherein the audience is not sure of the rhetor's position.

amplification   the ancient art of saying a great deal about very little.

anadiplosis   (a na di PLO sis) a figure wherein the last word of a phrase, clause, or sentence is used to begin the next phrase, clause, or sentence.

analogy   (an AL o gee) a comparison, either of particulars or of relations; also, a proof developed by Aristotle wherein a rhetor compares one hypothetical example to another.

analysis   a kind of definition; analytic definition divides the term to be defined into parts and lists all of these.

anaphora   (a NAF o ra) a figure wherein the same word is repeated at the beginning of several successive phrases, clauses, or sentences.

antanaclasis   (an tan ACK la sis) a figure wherein a word is used in at least two different senses.

anticipation   a general name for figures wherein a rhetor foresees and replies to objections.

antihimera   (an tee HI mer a) a figure wherein one part of speech is used as another.

antimetabole   (an tee ma TAB oh lee) a figure that expresses contrasting ideas in juxtaposed structures; also called *chiasmus.*

antistrophe   (an TIS troe fee) a figure wherein the same or similar words are repeated in successive phrases or clauses.

antithesis   (an TITH a sis) a figure wherein contrary ideas are expressed in grammatically parallel structures.

antonomasia   (an toe no MAS ya) a trope wherein a rhetor substitutes a descriptive phrase for someone's name.

apostrophe   (a PAWS tro fee) a figure wherein a rhetor addresses some absent person; also, a mark of punctuation that signals possession or omission.

appendix   additional material included at the back of a book.

apposition   any phrase that interrupts a period to modify or comment on it.

argument   in this book, a rhetorical situation in which the people who are involved disagree about something; also used here as an equivalent term for *proof.*

arrangement   the second canon of rhetoric; concerns the selection and ordering of parts in a discourse.

art   any set of productive principles or practices.

artificial memory   the ancient term for a memory that has been carefully trained to increase its potential.

asyndeton   (ah SYN da tun) a figure wherein normal connectors between words (usually "and") are eliminated.

atechnoi   (AY tek noy) Greek term meaning without art or skill.

audience   any persons designated by a rhetor as hearers or readers of a discourse.

authorities   any persons or sources called upon by a rhetor to support his or her arguments.

BCE   abbreviation for "Before the Common Era." In the Western calendar, indicates years prior to the year 1. Years BCE are counted backwards, as in "323 BCE, 322 BCE."

bibliography   (bib lee OG ra phee) a list of the works used to compose a discourse, usually appearing at the end of the discourse.

bound periodical   older issues of journals or newspapers bound together into a book, usually according to year of issue.

call number   the number used by libraries to identify books and other materials; printed on the cover and an inside page.

canon   ancient term for a division or part of the art of rhetoric.

card catalogue   drawers containing cards that list all the books and other materials kept in a library; usually found in the library's reference room.

case   a rhetor's proposition and proofs developed for use in a specific rhetorical situation.

catachresis   (kat a KREE sis) a trope wherein a rhetor intentionally substitutes a like or inexact word in place of the correct one.

cause to effect   any argument that reasons from causes to effects or vice versa; an ancient formal topic.

CE   abbreviation for Common Era. In the Western calendar, indicates years since the year 1.

character   a rhetor's habitual way of life or reputation in the relevant community; ethos; also an elementary exercise, or *progymnasmata.*

chreia   (KRAY ya) an elementary exercise, or *progymnasmata,* in which the rhetor elaborates on a famous event or saying.

circumlocution   literally, speaking around; a figure wherein a rhetor avoids naming an unsavory issue or term.

class   Latin *genus;* a group, kind, sort.

classification   a formal topic wherein items are grouped under a single general head.

climax   a figure in which terms or phrases are arranged in order from least to most important.

colon   ancient term for meaningful phrase that was shorter than a sentence but longer than a comma.

comma   ancient term for short phrase; in modern English, punctuation that marks an internal pause in a sentence.

commonplace any statement or bit of knowledge that is commonly shared among a given audience or a community; also, an elementary exercise, or *progymnasmata;* also, in invention another term for a *common topic.*

commonplace book a notebook kept by a rhetor as a storehouse of materials to be remembered or quoted.

common topics means of invention developed by Aristotle that are useful for developing arguments on any issue or in any field of discourse; they are conjecture, value, and possibilities.

community authority any person who is judged as an expert or is qualified to offer testimony based on a good reputation in the relevant community.

comparison in the formal topic called comparison, rhetors place two similar items together and examine their similarities; also, an elementary exercise or *progymnasmata.*

complex sentence a sentence that contains at least one independent colon and one dependent colon.

compound sentence a sentence that contains at least two independent colons.

compound-complex sentence a sentence that contains at least two independent colons and at least one dependent colon.

concession a figure wherein a rhetor concedes a disputed point or leaves a disputed point to the audience to decide.

conclusion modern term for the peroration, or final part of a discourse.

confirmation the part of a discourse that elaborates arguments in support of a rhetor's position.

conjecture in stasis theory or in Aristotle's topical theory of invention, any issue or topic that considers a proposed state of affairs.

context the words and sentences that surround any part of a discourse and help to determine its meaning; also, the rhetorical situation and background of an issue that help to determine the meaning of any text.

contraries a formal topic wherein a rhetor compares unlike items, situations, or events.

contrast a formal topic wherein a rhetor compares opposites.

copia (KO pee ya) abundant and ready supply of language; arguments or figures available for use on any occasion.

copying an ancient exercise used to enhance copia.

correction a figure wherein a rhetor replaces a word or phrase with a more correct one.

correctness rules standards of grammar and usage drawn from traditional grammar.

current periodical any recent issue of a periodical.

data a type of proof based on the evidence of the senses, or empirical proof; also includes statistics.

database a computer program that accesses information.

declamation (deck la MAY shun) an art of debating practiced by Roman rhetors and students.

deduction an ancient means of invention; a method of reasoning wherein a conclusion is derived from comparison of general to particular premises.

definite issue   Greek *hypothesis* (hy POTH a sis); an issue involving specific persons, places, events, or things.

definition   in stasis theory, any issue that considers how something should be defined or classified; also, a formal topic that sets limits to a term.

delivery   the fifth canon of rhetoric; concerns use of voice and gesture in oral discourse or editing, formatting, and presentation in written discourse.

description   one of the elementary exercises, or *progymnasmata;* discusses attributes or appearance of something or someone.

dialectic   a heuristic that proceeds by question and answer.

differences   in the formal topic of definition, a list of ways in which the term to be defined differs from other members of its designated class; also, a formal topic that generates a list of ways in which similar items differ.

difficult case   a case that is not honorable or to which an audience is hostile.

distance   a metaphor for the discursive relation obtaining between rhetor and audience; see *rhetorical distance.*

distribution   a figure wherein a rhetor divides a whole into parts and assigns each part to a different field.

division   a formal topic that separates out and lists the parts of any whole; also, a figure that does the same.

editing   stage of composing wherein the rhetor corrects errors and makes sure discourse conforms to formatting and presentation conventions.

eidolopoeia   (eye doe low PO ee ya) an exercise wherein the character of a spirit or an image is depicted.

empirical proof   proof derived from the senses.

enargeia   (en AR gay uh) figure in which rhetor creates a vivid scene.

encomium   a discourse that praises someone or something.

energia   (en ERG ya) a Greek term meaning to energize or actualize.

entechnoi   (EN tek noy) Greek term meaning within or embodied in an art.

enthymeme   (EN thee meem) a means of proof within which the rhetor places probable premises together in order to establish a probable conclusion.

enumeration   a means of definition that lists relevant attributes or parts of the term to be defined.

epanaphora   (ep an AF o rah) a figure wherein a rhetor repeats words at the beginning of successive colons; the repeated words are used in different senses.

epicheireme   (eh pi CHI reem) an enthymeme with four or five premises.

epideictic   (eh pi DIKE tick) one of Aristotle's major divisions of rhetoric oratory that praises or blames.

epiphora   (eh PYF o rah) a figure wherein a rhetor repeats the last word in successive clauses.

epistemology   (eh pis tem OL o gee) any theory of how people know; any theory of knowledge.

epithet   a figure in which a rhetor calls someone a name.

ethical proof   proof that depends upon the good character or reputation of a rhetor.

ethics   any set of guides or standards for human conduct.

ethopoeia   (ee tho PO ee ya) character portrayal; Greek term for discourse that creates a character; also, an ancient exercise wherein rhetors invented a set of traits to describe a kind of person.

ethos   the character or reputation of a rhetor.

etymological definition   a definition that supplies a history of a term to be defined.

etymology   the history of a word.

example   a specific instance; a particular; one member of a class; also, a rhetorical proof developed by Aristotle.

exordium   (ex OR di yum) Latin term for the first part of a discourse.

expediency   an ancient topic of value; considers whether a course of action is useful, efficient, or suited to the circumstances.

extended example   a fully developed rhetorical example.

extrinsic proof   proof that is available within the circumstances of the case; does not have to be invented.

fable   a fictional story meant to teach a moral lesson.

facts   bits of knowledge derived from sensory perception; also, bits of knowledge agreed to by all concerned parties.

fictional example   a rhetorical example drawn from a tale, fable, short story, or novel.

figure   generic term for artful uses of language.

figure of language   any artful patterning or arrangement of language.

figure of thought   Greek *sententia* (sen TEN shya); any artful presentation of ideas, feelings, concepts; figures of thought that depart from the ordinary patterns of argument (also called *figure of speech*).

foreword   a discourse that introduces another discourse.

formal topics   sources of arguments that depend on regular patterns or arrangements of material.

format   conventional means of presentation; includes spacing, margins, headers, and the like.

general issue   Greek thesis; in stasis theory, an indefinite issue.

general/specific relations   an ancient method of reasoning that treats whatever is under investigation as a class composed of specifics or particulars.

generalization   any statement about a group or class.

genus   (GEE nus) the Latin word for class; a group or kind.

genus/species   an ancient mode of definition.

gesture   a persuasive facial or bodily movement; part of delivery.

glossary   a list of terms used in a discourse; supplies definitions (and sometimes pronunciations) of technical or specialized terms.

goodness   an ancient common topic of value.

grammatical person   a grammatical feature of English that indicates who is speaking or writing, and/or the relation of the user to hearers/readers and/or issues; there are three grammatical persons in English.

greater/lesser   a common topic developed by Aristotle; here called values.

hesitation   (also indecision or *dubatio*) a figure wherein a rhetor pretends to be unable to decide what to say or write.

heuristic   (hyur IS tick) any system of investigation.

homoioteleuton   (home ee o TEL you ton) a figure wherein a rhetor repeats words with similar endings.

homonym   (HOM i nim) words that sound the same but that have different meanings.

honor   an ancient common topic of value.

honorable case   a case that is respected by the audience.

honorific language   language that respects or glorifies.

hyperbaton   (high PER ba tun) a figure in which language takes a sudden turn; usually an interruption; also, a trope that transposes a term to somewhere other than its usual place.

hyperbole   (high PER bo lee) exaggeration.

hypophora   (high POF o rah) a figure wherein a rhetor asks what can be said in favor of the opponents.

hypothesis   (high PAH tha sis) in stasis theory, a specific issue.

identification   an ideal rhetorical situation in which an audience feels close to a rhetor.

ideology   any body of beliefs, doctrines, values held by a single individual or by a group or a culture.

imitation   an ancient rhetorical exercise wherein students copied and elaborated on the work of revered or admired authors.

indefinite issue   Greek *thesis;* in stasis theory, an issue or question that is general or abstract.

index   list of important names or topics in a discourse, with page numbers; appears at end of discourse.

induction   an ancient method of invention; a rhetor collects a number of instances and forms a generalization that is meant to apply to all instances.

insinuation   the introduction to a difficult case.

instance   an example or particular.

intrinsic ethos   proofs from character that are invented by a rhetor or are available by virtue of the rhetor's position on an issue.

intrinsic proof   argument generated through use of the art of rhetoric.

introduction   the first part of a discourse, called *exordium* in ancient rhetorics.

introduction of law   the last and most difficult of the elementary exercises, or *progymnasmata.*

invective   a discourse that casts blame on somebody or something.

invented ethos   proofs from character that are invented by a rhetor or are available by virtue of the rhetor's position on an issue.

invented proof   any proof discovered through use of the principles of rhetoric.

invention   the first of the five canons of rhetoric; the art of finding available things to say or write in any situation.

irony   (EYE ron ee) a trope in which an audience understands the opposite of what is being expressed.

isocolon   Greek term for grammatically balanced phrases or clauses.

issue   matter about which there is dispute; point about which all parties agree to disagree.

justice   an ancient common topic.

kairos   (KY ross) Greek term meaning the right time, opportunity, occasion, or season.

litotes   (LIE toe tees) a figure in which the rhetor understates the situation.
logical proof   an argument found in the issue or the case.
logos   (LO gose) in archaic Greek, speech, voice, breath, or even spirit; in Aristotle's rhetoric, any arguments found in the issue or the case.
loose sentence   a sentence whose word order follows the word order of whatever language it is expressed in; phrases and clauses are tacked on haphazardly.

major premise   the first statement in an enthymeme; a general statement about probable human action.
maxim   a familiar saying; a bit of community wisdom.
member   a phrase or clause; in ancient rhetoric, any part of a sentence.
memory   the fourth canon of rhetoric.
memory places   invented mental categories used to store information and images of an artificial memory.
metabasis   (meh TAB a sis) a summarizing transition.
metaphor   (MET a for) a trope wherein one word is substituted for another.
metonymy   (me TAH na mee) a trope wherein something is named by words frequently associated with it.
microforms   written materials that have been photographed and reduced in size; libraries use microforms to reduce the space taken up by printed documents. There are two kinds of microforms: film, which is stored on a reel like video or movie film; and fiche, which is stored on a flat surface.
minor premise   a statement in an enthymeme that names a particular instance.

narrative   the second part of a discourse; it states the issue and may supply a history of the issue.
neologism   (knee OL o jism) a new or coined word or phrase.
network of interpretation   any interpretive framework used to make sense of an array of data or knowledge; ideology.

obscure case   a case that is unclear to the audience.
onomatopoeia   (on o ma to PO ee ya) a trope that uses words to suggest sounds.
oxymoron   (oks ZIM o ron) a figure wherein unlike or opposite terms are used together.

paradox   (PAIR a docks) a figure wherein a rhetor raises expectations then mentions trivia; also, any seemingly self-contradictory statement.
paralepsis   (pair a LEP sis) a figure wherein a rhetor refuses to mention something, all the while doing so.

parallel case   an argument that treats two or more instances as similar.

parallelism   a figure wherein similar grammatical constructions house different words.

paraphrase   imitation with elaboration; imitating sense of a discourse in words other than those used by original author; an ancient rhetorical exercise.

paratactic style   (pair a TACK tick) a string of loose sentences.

parenthesis   a figure in which the rhetor interrupts the train of thought; in modern English, punctuation that has the same function.

paronomasia   (pare oh no MAZ ee ya) pun; words or phrases sound alike but have different meanings; often the juxtaposition is funny.

parrhesia   (pah REEZ ya) frankness of speech.

particular   a single item or a member of a class.

partition   the third part of a discourse; divides the issue into relevant areas.

passive voice   a grammatical structure available in English wherein the grammatical subject of the sentence is not the actor.

past/future fact   a common topic developed by Aristotle; here called conjecture.

pathetic proof   proof that appeals to the emotions or motives of an audience.

pathos   (PAY those) Greek term for emotions or passions.

pejorative language   language that disparages or downplays.

period   Greek term for the sentence; in modern English, the punctuation that marks the termination of declarative sentences.

periodical   magazines, journals, or even books issued regularly and published under the same name over a period of time.

periodic sentence   sentence with obvious structure; meaning distributed among several members or saved until last.

periphrasis   (pair i FRAA sis) trope wherein the rhetor substitutes other words for the term under discussion.

peroration   the final part of a discourse; may summarize, arouse emotions, or enhance rhetor's ethos.

persona   (per SO nah) Latin term used by Cicero for ethos.

personification   a figure that attributes the qualities of living things to things that are not alive, at least in the conventional sense.

phrase   a short string of words; equivalent to the Greek comma.

polysyndeton   (pol ly SIN dee tun) a figure wherein the rhetor inserts all possible connectors between words, phrases, or sentences.

possibility   a common topic.

possible/impossible   common topic developed by Aristotle; here called possibility.

power relation   the social, economic, or ethical relationship that obtains between a rhetor and an audience.

practical issue   in stasis theory, an issue having to do with human action.

preface   a discourse that may introduce a book, an author's methods and rationale; appears at beginning.

premise   a statement laid down, supposed, or assumed before an argument begins.

presentation   how a manuscript looks; depends on width of margins, use of headers, and the like.

probability   a statement about what people are likely to do.

procedure   in stasis theory, any issue that considers how people ought to proceed.

progymnasmata   (pro ghim NAS ma ta) the elementary rhetorical exercises used in ancient schools of rhetoric.

prooemium   (pro EEM ee yum) Greek term for the *exordium* or first part of any discourse.

proof   any statement or statements used to persuade an audience to accept a proposition; also, the section of a discourse where arguments are assembled; in this book, used interchangeably with argument.

proposition   any arguable statement put forward for discussion by a rhetor.

prosopopoeia   (prose oh POE ee ya) an exercise wherein the character of a fictional person is depicted.

proverb   any well-known saying; a bit of community wisdom.

proximate authority   someone who is in a position to offer testimony because of having been close to the events in question.

pun   artful and sometimes funny synonymy.

punctuation   graphic marks used to represent features of spoken language in writing.

qualifier   word in English that mitigates the force of other words.

quality   in stasis theory, any issue that considers values.

reasoning   Aristotle's term for deduction; here, any method of comparing statements in order to draw conclusions.

reasoning by contraries   a figure wherein a rhetor uses one of two opposing statements to prove the other.

reasoning by question and answer   a figure wherein a rhetor inserts a question between successive affirmative statements.

refutation   the part of a discourse wherein a rhetor anticipates opposing arguments and answers them.

representative theory of language   theory of language that assumes language is transparent—that it allows meaning to shine through it clearly and without distortion.

rhetor   (RAY tor in Greek; REH ter in English) anyone who composes discourse that is intended to affect community thinking or events.

rhetoric   (REH ter ick) the art that helps people compose effective discourse.

rhetorical distance   metaphor for the degree of physical and social distance created between a rhetor and an audience by creation of an ethos.

rhetorical question   a figure wherein rhetors ask questions to which they and the audience already know the answers.

rhetorical situation   the context of a rhetorical act; minimally made up of a rhetor, an issue, and an audience.

rhetorician   (reh to RISH an) someone who studies or teaches the art of rhetoric.

scheme   generic term for artful use of language.

sensus communis   (SEN sus co MUNE is) Latin phrase for common knowledge shared among members of a community.

sentence composition   in ancient rhetorics, the artful construction of sentences.

sign   facts or events that usually or always accompany other facts or events.

similarity   a relation between items that emphasizes their likenesses or resemblances.

simile   (SIM i lee) a figure wherein two unlike items are compared.

simple sentence   a sentence that has one independent clause and no other clauses.

situated ethos   proof from character that depends on a rhetor's reputation in the relevant community.

sophist   (SOF ist) in ancient times, name given to any rhetor who taught by example; when capitalized, refers to any of a group of rhetoric teachers who worked in and around Athens in the fifth and fourth centuries BCE; in modern English, term for a rhetor who may use fallacious or tricky arguments.

sophistry   (SOF ist ree) term applied to the rhetorical theory and practice of the Older Sophists; in modern times names tricky or fallacious rhetorical practices.

special topics   a means of invention developed by Aristotle; arguments drawn from specific arts such as politics or ethics.

species   Greek term for an example, an instance, or a particular.

species/genus   an ancient method of definition.

specific issue   in stasis theory, an issue that deals with a particular or individual.

stacks   shelves in a library where books are stored.

staseis   (STAS ay is) Greek term for issues.

stasis   (STASE is) a stand; place where opponents agree to disagree.

stasis theory   theory of invention developed by Hermagoras of Temnos.

style   the fourth canon of rhetoric; has to do with sentence composition and the use of ornament.

style sheet   list of editing conventions used by a specific professional group.

suspension   a figure wherein a rhetor raises expectations.

syllogism   (SILL o jiz im) name for a deductive argument in logic.

symploke   (SIM plo key) a figure that combines epanaphora and epiphora.

synecdoche   (sin ECK doe key) a trope wherein a part of the whole is referred to as though it were the whole.

synonymy   (sin ON o mee) a figure wherein a rhetor uses similar words as means of repetition.

table of contents   page or pages that list chapter headings or subtitles in a book or journal.

tale   a short narrative; an ancient elementary exercise or *progymnasmata.*

techne   (TEK nay) Greek term for an art; any set of productive principles or practices.

testimony   a person's account of an event or state of affairs.

theoretical issue   in stasis theory, any wide-ranging philosophical issue not involved with specific human actions.

thesis   (THEE sis) in stasis theory, a general or indefinite issue; also, an elementary exercise or *progymnasmata.*

title page   the page of a book that gives its title and author's name.

topic   Greek term for a commonplace; literally, place where arguments are located.

traditional grammar   artificial grammar imposed on English in eighteenth century CE; observes grammatical rules borrowed from Latin; treated as grammatical standard by some.

transition   any word or phrase that connects pieces of discourse.

translation   ancient rhetorical exercise wherein rhetors translated discourse from one language to another.

trivial case   a case wherein an audience is not convinced that the issue is important or the rhetor worth paying attention to.

trope   any artful substitution of one term for another.

understatement   figure in which a rhetor deliberately makes a situation seem less important or serious than it is.

usage   customary ways of using language.

value   anything that is deemed desirable or worthy by a community.

verb tense   grammatical feature of English that identifies time of action, such as present, past, or future.

verb voice   grammatical feature of English that allows user to identify the grammatical subject with an actor in the sentence (active voice) or to substitute some other word in the grammatical subject position (passive voice).

voice   persuasive use of loudness and tone of voice.

volume number   number given to all issues of a periodical published during a given span of time, usually one year.

whole/part relation   an ancient method of reasoning that treats whatever is under investigation as a whole that can be divided into parts.

word size   feature of English that influences rhetorical distance.

zuegma   (ZOOG mah) figure wherein the same word is used in different senses in grammatically similar constructions.

Appendix A

A CALENDAR OF ANCIENT RHETORICS

The Greek calendar began with the year 776 BCE, legendary date of the first Olympic games; the yearly calendar was based on the movements of the sun and the moon, but varied greatly from city to city. The Athenian year began in the day of the first full moon after the Spring solstice of June 21.

3000–1100 BCE	**Greek Bronze Age**
2000	First Greek-speaking tribes enter Greece
1900–1400	Minoan civilization in Crete
1700–1100	Mycenean civilization created on mainland by Achaeans
1250	Citadel centers at Mycenae, Argos, Tiryns, Pylos; war waged on Troy
1200–1100	A second group of tribes—Dorians—enters Greece and destroys Mycenean civilization; many Achaeans emigrate to Asia Minor
1100–800 BCE	**Greek Dark Age**
	Mycenean palace culture broken up; strong kingdoms fragmented; writing is forgotten
800–500 BCE	**Archaic Period**
	Around 800 Renaissance begins, blending of Dorian, Achaean, Cretan, and near Eastern elements; a new alphabet appears
	Greek city states assume new political and cultural dimensions under aristocrats, lawgivers, and tyrants
	Homeric poems written down
776	First Olympic games
500–323 BCE	**Classical Period**
427	Gorgias arrives in Athens
392	Isocrates opens his school
370–360	Plato composes *Phaedrus*
335–323	Aristotle composes the *Rhetoric*
323–37 BCE	**Hellenistic Period**
ca. 84	*ad Herennium* composed
90 BCE–450 CE	**Roman Period**
89–85 BCE	Cicero composes *De Inventione*
54 BCE	Cicero composes *De Oratore*
27 BCE	Empire established
ca. 94 CE	Quintilian publishes the *Institutes*
426–427 CE	Augustine finishes *De Doctrina Christiana*

APPENDIX B

SIGNPOSTS IN ANCIENT RHETORICS

Archaic Rhetoric

ca. 1250 BCE: battle of Troy

ca. 1150–850 BCE: Homer composes the *Iliad* and the *Odyssey*; ancient rhetoricians thought that the speeches in these poems demonstrated the great antiquity of rhetoric

Greek Rhetoric in the Classical Period (500–323 BCE)

494–434: Empedocles, a teacher, scientist and magician, may have been a teacher of the sophist Gorgias. Some authorities say he invented rhetoric.

490–429: Pericles, a great statesman and orator, participates in the formation of direct democracy at Athens; everybody who is anybody is a member of his circle, including the famous woman rhetorician, Aspasia, and wealthy, ambitious young men like Alcibiades.

470–450: Corax/Tisias practice rhetoric in Sicilian capital of Syracuse; both apparently wrote *techne*, or arts of rhetoric, that are now lost. These may have been collections of sample arguments, introductions, and conclusions. Some authorities say that Gorgias studied with Tisias.

460–400: Thucydides writes his great history of the Peloponnesian War, which contains many speeches that demonstrate his knowledge of rhetoric.

The Older Sophists

483–375: Gorgias of Leontini, a teacher and theorist of rhetoric, arrives in Athens in 427 as an ambassador from Sicily and takes the Greek city by storm with his fiery displays of stylistic elegance. Like Protagoras, Gorgias was a philosophical skeptic, more interested in ethics, rhetoric, and politics than in metaphysics. We have two entire speeches ("Helen" and "Palamedes") and several fragments of his work. See also Plato's dialogue *Gorgias*, where the sophist is made to look like an unethical fool.

481–411: Protagoras authors the famous phrase "Man is the measure of all things," which some contemporary scholars take to mean that Protagoras scorned the metaphysical speculations of the preSocratic philosophers and perhaps of Plato, as well. He apparently contributed the notion of *dissoi logoi* to sophistic rhetoric, the notion that competing or contradictory statements can be made about any issue. We have only a few fragments of his work, plus the unflattering portrait of him that appears in Plato's dialogue *Protagoras*.

470–399: Socrates is an itinerant teacher and the famous interlocuter in Plato's *Dialogues*. Although modern philosophers might be shocked to find Socrates in a list of Sophists, some contemporary scholars think that he should be included here as being responsible for an inventional scheme called eristic. Socrates was condemned to death in 399 for corrupting the youth of Athens.

436–338: Isocrates founds a very successful school of rhetoric in Athens that competed for students with Plato's Academy. He apparently wrote no systematic treatise on rhetorical theory, but many of his complete orations have been preserved, indicating that people have thought them worth reading ever since his own time. Since he had weak vocal cords, Isocrates did not practice rhetoric for very long, but he was a capable writer of speeches for others—that is, he was a *logographer,* or ghost-writer.

Other persons sometimes classed as Older Sophists are Antiphon, Hippias of Elis, Prodicus of Ceos, and Thrasymachus.

A Handbook

ca. 341: Anaximines(?) writes a textbook called the *Rhetoric to Alexander* (*Rhetorica ad Alexandrum*). The work was given this title because its author pretended to be Aristotle writing a textbook on rhetoric for his student, Alexander the Great. Its importance is that it probably represents the typical instruction given to students by fourth-century sophistic teachers.

Academic and Peripatetic Rhetorics

420–348: Plato develops an anti-Sophistic theory of rhetoric (chiefly in the dialogue *Phaedrus*), which posits that rhetoricians must know the truth before they speak, must be able to separate true knowledge from opinion, must know the souls of humans, must be able to define and divide topics for discussion, and must be able to develop orderly principles of arrangement. In other words, he turns rhetoric into philosophy.

384–322: Aristotle contributes a very full and systematic theory of invention to the history of rhetoric in his *On Rhetoric.* Aside from this text, Aristotle apparently wrote an early treatise on rhetoric, the *Gryllus* (which is now lost), and collected treatises by other teachers into the *Synagoge Technon,* also now lost but known to Cicero, who consulted it to write the history of rhetoric contained in his *Brutus.*

Famous Greek Rhetors of the Classical Era

384–322: Demosthenes, the exact contemporary of Aristotle, is acknowledged by all classical authorities to be the greatest of the Greek rhetors. He is best known now for his clash with Aeschines, which is preserved for us in the speeches *On the Crown.* During Roman times, scholars developed a canon of famous Greek orators (The Attic Orators) whose works had been preserved and who were thought worthy of imitation. They are: Antiphon, Andocides, Lysias, Isaeus, Isocrates, Demosthenes, Aeschines,

Hyperides, Lycurgus, and Dinarchus. Most of these orators supported themselves by appearing in court on behalf of wealthy clients and by working as logographers.

Greek Rhetoric in the Hellenistic Period (323–37 BCE)

Rhetoric becomes the focus of higher education in Greece and elsewhere. During this period teachers of rhetoric elaborated and sometimes conflated Aristotelian and sophistic theories of rhetoric. We have no Greek manuscripts from Hellenistic teachers, although many later accounts of their teachings exist. Only one major theoretical contribution occurs during this period—stasis theory. However, teachers of rhetoric were interested in refining their study of style, and some developed theories about the levels, or kinds, of style.

ca. 370–285: Theophrastus, a student of Aristotle, advances the study of style and perhaps invents systematic study of delivery. He writes a series of character studies demonstrating the construction and use of *ethopoeia*, which is still extant.

345–283: Demetrius of Phaleron writes "On Style," in which he claims that there are four types of style: the plain, the grand, the stately, and the powerful.

Mid-second century BCE: Hermagoras of Temnos apparently invents stasis theory, which will compete for first place in rhetorical handbooks with Aristotlean and sophistic theories of invention throughout antiquity and into the European Renaissance.

Latin Rhetoric

Roman intellectuals come into contact with Greek rhetoric during the second century BCE, and they adopt Greek rhetorical theory almost intact, only later refining its precepts in order to accommodate the Latin language.

Early first century BCE: Cornificius (?) writes the *Rhetoric for Herennius (Rhetorica ad Herennium)*, a very full discussion of Hellenistic rhetorical theory and pedagogy. This treatise contains a discussion of memory, the most complete and oldest available to us.

106–43 BCE: Cicero, who combines an interest in rhetorical theory with skill in speaking, sets stylistic and persuasive examples that will be emulated at least until the Renaissance. Cicero is well acquainted with Greek rhetoric and philosophy, and he writes several important works of rhetorical history and theory: *On Invention, Brutus, On the Parts of Oratory*, and his masterpiece, *Of Oratory*.

35–ca. 90 CE: Quintilian writes the *Institutes of Oratory*, the most complete treatise on rhetorical education available from antiquity.

First century CE: Longinus writes "On the Sublime," wherein he defines *hypsos*, "elevation" or "sublimity," as the quality of excellence found in Greek orators and poets. The sublime has five qualities that are reminiscent of the five canons of rhetoric.

First century CE: Hermogenes of Tarsus writes *On Ideas of Style,* wherein he catalogues the "ideas" or virtues of style: clarity, grandeur, beauty, vigor, ethos, verity, and gravity. Hermogenes's theory is important in rhetorical instruction throughout later antiquity and into the Renaissance.

Rhetorical Exercises

The *progymnasmata* were a series of school exercises used by teachers to hone students' skill in composition. Students imitated, amplified, and composed proverbs, fables, narratives, and arguments drawn from the works of classical authors.

Declamation was a school exercise as well as a popular form of entertainment among Roman adults. Declamation took at least two forms: *suasoriae,* where the speaker took the role of some historical or mythological person; and *controversiae,* where a real or imaginary law was cited alongside a real or imaginary case, and the speaker adopted the role of one of the persons in the case or became their advocate.

Greek Rhetoric in Later Antiquity

The Second Sophistic

During the first four centuries of the Common Era, Greek rhetors traveled throughout the Roman Empire, teaching and demonstrating their mastery of the art of rhetoric by declaiming, whenever asked, on any subject whatsoever. If they taught, they did so by means of example; their students watched them declaim and then did likewise. Most historians of rhetoric claim that the Sophists of this period were more interested in artistry and stylistic display than in public discussion of important issues—something that was very dangerous, after all, in the last days of the Roman Empire.

BIBLIOGRAPHY

CITATION SOURCES OF ANCIENT TEXTS

Aesop. *The Fables of Aesop, Paraphrased in Verse.* John Ogilby. Los Angeles: Augustan Reprint Society (UCLA), 1965. (Originally printed 1668).

Aesop. *Aesop's Fables Told by Valerius Babrius.* Translated by Denison B. Hull. Chicago: Univ. of Chicago Press, 1960.

Antiphon. *Tetralogies.* Translated by J. S. Morrison. In *The Older Sophists,* 136–163. Edited by Rosamond Kent Sprague. Columbia: South Carolina UP, 1972.

Aphthonius. *Progymnasmata.* Translated by Ray Nadeau in *Speech Monographs* 19:264–285 (Nov. 1952). Reprinted in *Readings from Classical Rhetoric,* 267–288. Edited by Patricia P. Matsen, Philip Rollinson, and Marion Sousa. Carbondale: Southern Illinois UP, 1990.

Aristotle. *On Interpretation.* Translated by E. M. Edghill. In *The Works of Aristotle.* Edited by W. D. Ross. Vol I. London: Oxford UP, 1966.

Aristotle. *Posterior Analytics.* Translated by G. R. G. Mure. In *The Works of Aristotle.* Edited by W. D. Ross. Volume I. London: Oxford UP, 1966.

Aristotle. *Rhetoric.* Translated by John Henry Freese. Loeb Classical Library. Cambridge: Harvard UP, 1926.

Aristotle. *The Rhetoric of Aristotle.* Translated by Lane Cooper. New York: Appleton-Century-Crofts, 1932.

Aristotle. *Aristotle on Rhetoric: A Theory of Civic Discourse.* Translated by George A. Kennedy. New York: Oxford UP, 1991.

Aristotle. *Topics.* Translated by W. A. Pickard-Cambridge. In *The Works of Aristotle.* Edited by W. D. Ross. London: Oxford UP, 1966.

Cicero. *Against Verres.* Translated by Palmer Bovie. New York: New American Library, 1967.

Cicero. *Brutus.* Translated by G. L. Hendrickson. Loeb Classical Library. Cambridge: Harvard UP, 1971.

Cicero. *In Defense of Murena.* Translated by Palmer Bovie. New York: New American Library, 1967.

Cicero. *On Invention.* Translated by H. M. Hubbell. Loeb Classical Library. Cambridge: Harvard UP, 1968.

Cicero. *On Oratory.* Translated by E. W. Sutton and H. Rackham. 2 vols. Loeb Classical Library. Cambridge: Harvard UP, 1976.

Cicero. *On the Parts of Oratory.* Translated by H. Rackham. Loeb Classical Library. Cambridge: Harvard UP, 1982.

Cicero. *Oratore.* Translated by H. M. Hubbell. Loeb Classical Library. Cambridge: Harvard UP, 1971.

Cicero. *Topics.* Translated by H. M. Hubbell. Cambridge: Harvard UP, 1968.

Demetrius. *On Style.* Translated by W. Rhys Roberts. Loeb Classical Library. Cambridge: Harvard UP, 1982.

Demosthenes. *On the Crown.* Translated by John J. Keany. In *Demosthenes' On the Crown: A Critical Case Study of a Masterpiece of Ancient Oratory.* Edited by James J. Murphy. New York: Random House, 1967.

Diogenes Laertius. *Lives of the Eminent Philosophers.* Translated by R. D. Hicks. 2 vols. Loeb Classical Library. Cambridge: Harvard UP, 1972.

Dissoi Logoi. Translated by Rosamond Kent Sprague. *Mind* 78:155–167 (Apr. 1968). Reprinted in *The Older Sophists,* 279–293. Edited by Rosamond Kent Sprague. Columbia: South Carolina UP, 1972.

Gorgias. *Gorgias.* Translated by George Kennedy. In *The Older Sophists.* Edited by Rosamond Kent Sprague. Columbia: South Carolina UP, 1972.

Homer. *Iliad.* Translated by Robert Fitzgerald. Garden City: Anchor Press, 1975.

Hermogenes. *On Types of Style.* Translated by Cecil W. Wooten. Chapel Hill: North Carolina UP, 1987.

Hermogenes. *Progymnasmata.* Translated by Charles Sears Baldwin. In *Medieval Rhetoric and Poetic,* 23–38. New York: Macmillan, 1928.

Isocrates. *Isocrates.* Translated by George Norlin. 3 vols. Loeb Classical Library. Cambridge: Harvard UP, 1980.

Lucian of Samasota. *Works.* Translated by H. W. Fowler and F. G. Fowler. 4 vols. Oxford: Clarendon Press, 1905.

Ovid. *The Metamorphoses.* Translated by Horace Gregory. New York: New American Library, 1960.

Philostratus. *The Lives of the Sophists.* Translated by Wilmer Cave Wright. Loeb Classical Library. Cambridge: Harvard UP, 1922.

Plato. *The Collected Dialogues.* Edited by Edith Hamilton and Huntington Cairns. Princeton: Princeton UP, 1971.

Plutarch. *The Lives of the Noble Grecians and Romans.* Translated by John Dryden. New York: Random House, 1932.

Priscian. *Fundamentals Adapted from Hermogenes.* Translated by Joseph M. Miller. In *Readings from Medieval Rhetoric,* 52–68. Edited by Joseph M. Miller, Michael H. Prosser, and Thomas W. Benson. Bloomington: Indiana UP, 1973.

Quintilian. *The Institutes of Oratory.* Translated by H. E. Butler. 4 vols. Loeb Classical Library. Cambridge: Harvard UP, 1980.

Rhetoric to Alexander. Translated by H. Rackham. Loeb Classical Library. Cambridge: Harvard UP, 1957.

Rhetoric to Herennius. Translated by Harry Caplan. Loeb Classical Library. Cambridge: Harvard UP, 1981.

Seneca the Elder. *Declamations.* Translated by M. Winterbottom. 2 vols. Loeb Classical Library. Cambridge: Harvard UP, 1974.

Theon. *Progymnasmata.* Translated by Patricia P. Matsen. In *Readings from Classical Rhetoric.* Edited by Patricia P. Matsen, Philip Rollinson, and Marion Sousa. Carbondale: Southern Illinois UP, 1990.

Theophrastus. *The Characters.* Translated by J. M. Edmonds. Loeb Classical Library. Cambridge: Harvard UP, 1961.

Thucydides. *The Peloponnesian War.* Translated by Benjamin Jowett. In *The Greek Historians.* Edited by Francis R. B. Godolphin. 2 vols. New York: Random House, 1942.

Virgil. *Georgics.* Translated by H. Rushton Fairclough. Loeb Classical Library. Cambridge: Harvard UP, 1942.

Xenophon. *Memorabilia.* Translated by E. C. Marchant. Loeb Classical Library. Cambridge: Harvard UP, 1979.

SUGGESTIONS FOR FURTHER READING

Atwill, Janet M. *Rhetoric Reclaimed: Aristotle & the Liberal Arts Tradition.* Ithaca: Cornell UP, 1998.

Benson, Thomas W., and Michael Prosser. *Readings in Classical Rhetoric.* Boston: Allyn and Bacon, 1969.

Brody, Miriam. *Manly Writing: Gender, Rhetoric, and the Rise of Composition.* Carbondale, Southern Illinois UP, 1993.

Cole, Thomas. *The Origins of Rhetoric in Ancient Greece.* Baltimore: Johns Hopkins UP, 1991.

Enos, Richard Leo. *Greek Rhetoric Before Aristotle.* Prospect Heights: Waveland Press, 1993.

Enos, Richard Leo. *Roman Rhetoric: Revolution and the Greek Influence.* Prospect Heights: Waveland Press, 1995.

Grube, G. M. A. *The Greek and Roman Critics.* Toronto: Toronto UP, 1968.

Jarratt, Susan C. *Re-Reading the Sophists: Classical Rhetoric Refigured.* Carbondale: Southern Illinois UP, 1991.

Kennedy, George A. *The Art of Persuasion in Greece.* Princeton: Princeton UP, 1963.

Kennedy, George A. *The Art of Rhetoric in the Roman World.* Princeton: Princeton UP, 1972.

Kennedy, George A. *A New History of Classical Rhetoric.* Princeton: Princeton UP, 1994.

Kerford, G. B. *The Sophistic Movement.* Cambridge: Cambridge UP, 1981.

Keuls, Eva C. *The Reign of the Phallus: Sexual Politics in Ancient Athens.* New York: Harper & Row, 1985.

Marrou, H. I. *A History of Education in Antiquity.* New York: Sheed and Ward, 1956.

Matsen, Patricia P., Philip Rollinson, and Marion Sousa. *Readings from Classical Rhetoric.* Carbondale: Southern Illinois UP, 1990.

Poulakos, John. *Sophistical Rhetoric in Classical Greece.* Columbia: University of South Carolina Press, 1995.

INDEX

Credits

P. 106—Letter to the Editor, *Arizona Daily Sun,* p. 6, August 4, 1992; pp. 259, 332—excerpts reprinted by permission of the publishers and the Trustees of Amherst College from THE POEMS OF EMILY DICKINSON, Thomas H. Johnson, ed., Cambridge, Mass.: The Belknap Press of Harvard University Press, Copyright © 1951, 1955, 1979, 1983 by the President and Fellows of Harvard College; pp. 1, 15–16, 25, 44, 162, 175, 176, 277, 309, 330—excerpts from Aristotle's *Rhetoric* I, II and III reprinted by permission of the publishers and the Loeb Classical Library from ARISTOTLE, VOL XVI, translated by H. Rackham, Cambridge, Mass.: Harvard University Press, 1937; pp. 15, 115, 152, 154, 177, 183, 198, 211–212, 233–234, 255, 266, 279—excerpts reprinted by permission of the publishers and the Loeb Classical Library from CICERO: RHETORICAL TREATISES, VOLUME III, translated by E. W. Sutton and H. Rackham, Cambridge, Mass.: Harvard University Press, 1942; pp. 49–59, 53, 115—excerpts reprinted by permission of the publishers and the Loeb Classical Library from CICERO: RHETORICAL TREATISES, VOLUME II, translated by H. M. Hubbell, Cambridge, Mass.: Harvard University Press, 1949; pp. 21, 33, 105, 238, 275, 290, 291–292—excerpts reprinted by permission of the publishers and the Loeb Classical Library from CICERO, VOLUME I-III, translated by George Norlin and La Rue Van Hook, Cambridge, Mass.: Harvard University Press, 1928, 1929, 1945; pp. 13, 30, 44, 73, 105–106, 107–108, 154–155, 164, 214, 223, 229, 252, 253, 257, 278, 292–293, 304, 310, 340–341, 346–347—excerpts reprinted by permission of the publishers and the Loeb Classical Library from QUINTILIAN: CHARACTERS, translated by A. F. Hort, Cambridge, Mass.: Harvard University Press, 1916; pp. 146, 234, 235, 237, 238, 247–248, 249–250, 254, 255, 264, 357—excerpts reprinted by permission of the publishers and the Loeb Classical Library from QUINTILIAN: VOLUME I, translated by Harry Caplan, Cambridge, Mass.: Harvard University Press, 1945; pp. 318–319—excerpts from Robinson, F. N. (Editor). *The Works of Geoffrey Chaucer.* Copyright © 1957 by Houghton Mifflin Company. Used with permission; pp. 313–314—excerpts reprinted with permission of Simon & Schuster from THE POEMS OF SAPPHO, translated by Suzy Q. Groden. Copyright © 1966 by Macmillan Publishing Company; pp. 324–325, 328, 339–340, 347–348, 352, 356, 357, 360–362, 363—excerpts reprinted with permission from *Readings from Classical Rhetoric,* from "Aphtonius," pp. 267–268. Patricia Matsen, Philip Rollinson, Marion Sousa, eds. Carbondale, IL: Southern Illinois University Press, 1990. Copyright © 1990 by the Board of Trustees, Southern Illinois University; p. 253—reprinted with the permission of Simon & Schuster from *Cities on a Hill* by Frances Fitzgerald. Copyright © 1981, 1983, 1986 by Frances Fitzgerald.; pp. 196–197—excerpt reprinted with permission from "What Happened at Harvard," by Jon Weiner, from *The Nation* magazine (September 30, 1991), © 1991 The Nation Company, Inc.; pp. 159–160—excerpt from "Breaking the Codes" (Editorial), *The New Republic* (July 8, 1991). Reprinted by permission of THE NEW REPUBLIC, © 1991, The New Republic, Inc.; pp. 316–325—excerpts from THE METAMORPHOSES by Publius Ovidius Naso, translated by Horace Gregory, Translation copyright © 1958 by the Viking Press, Inc., renewed © 1986 by Patrick Bolton Gregory. Used by permission of Viking Penguin, a division of Penguin Putnam Inc.; pp. 23, 81, 152, 184–185, 200, 223—excerpts from Hamilton, Edith and Cairns, Huntington: *Plato: The Collected Dialogues.* Copyright © 1961 by Princeton University Press. Reprinted by permission of Princeton University Press; pp. 344–346—excerpt reprinted by permission from Tribune Media Services. All Rights Reserved. Reprinted with permission; p. 311—excerpts from Aesop, *Aesop's Fables Told by Valerius Babrius.* Translated by Denison B. Hull. Chicago: University of Chicago Press, © 1960 by University of Chicago Press; pp. 230, 240, 241, 243—excerpts from Gorgias. *Gorgias.* Translated by George Kennedy. In *The Older Sophists.* Edited by Rosamond Kent Sprague. Columbia, S.C.: South Carolina University Press, 1972. Reprinted by permission; pp. 33, 34, 35, 267—excerpts from *Dissoi Logoi.* Translated by Rosamond Kent Sprague. *Mind* 78:155–67 (April 1968). Reprinted in *The Older Sophists,* 279–293. Edited by Rosamond Kent Sprague. Columbia, S.C.: South Carolina University Press, 1972. Reprinted by permission; p. 148— excerpt from THE ILIAD by Homer. Copyright © 1974 by Robert Fitzgerald. Used by permission of Doubleday, a division of Bantam Doubleday Dell Publishing Group, Inc.; pp. 312–313—excerpt from PSALMS I 1–50 (THE ANCHOR BIBLE) by Mitchell Dahood. Copyright Trans., Intro. And Notes by Mitchell Dahood © 1966 by Doubleday, a division of Bantam